Miss Mary's Money

Miss Mary's Money

*Fortune and Misfortune in a
North Carolina Plantation Family,
1760–1924*

H. G. Jones
with David Southern

McFarland & Company, Inc., Publishers
Jefferson, North Carolina

ALSO OF INTEREST

*The Sonarman's War: A Memoir of Submarine Chasing and
Mine Sweeping in World War II*, by H.G. Jones (McFarland, 2010)

Royalties will be donated to the North Caroliniana Society.

LIBRARY OF CONGRESS CATALOGUING-IN-PUBLICATION DATA

Jones, H. G. (Houston Gwynne), 1924–
Miss Mary's money : fortune and misfortune in a North Carolina
plantation family, 1760–1924 / H.G. Jones with David Southern.
p.   cm.
Includes bibliographical references and index.

ISBN 978-0-7864-9662-4 (softcover : acid free paper) ∞
ISBN 978-1-4766-1987-3 (ebook)

1. Jones, Francis, 1760–1844—Family.   2. Smith, Mary Ruffin,
1814–1885—Family.   3. Plantation owners—North Carolina—
Chatham County—Biography.   4. Plantation owners—North Carolina—
Orange County—Biography.   5. Plantations—North Carolina—History.
6. Land grants—North Carolina—History.   7. Beneficiaries—North Carolina—
History.   8. Chatham County (N.C.)—Biography.   9. Orange County
(N.C.)—Biography.   I. Southern, David W.   II. Title.
F262.C4J66 2015   975.6'590340922—dc23   [B]   2014038441

BRITISH LIBRARY CATALOGUING DATA ARE AVAILABLE

On the cover: Oakland, the home of the Smith family from 1847,
as it appeared unoccupied after the death of Mary Ruffin Smith,
the last "legitimate" member of the family (courtesy Ernest A. Dollar, Jr.)

Printed in the United States of America

*McFarland & Company, Inc., Publishers
Box 611, Jefferson, North Carolina 28640
www.mcfarlandpub.com*

Contents

Preface: "The wealthy old lady"

The short piece in the *New York Times*, December 6, 1885, was long enough to contain a multitude of errors and omissions, but it reflected widespread interest in the will.

> Miss Smith, the wealthy old lady who died recently near Chapel Hill, and who bequeathed a large sum of money to the State University, did not fail to remember her old slaves, of whom six are now living. The wife of Gray J. Toole, the barber in this city [Charlotte], was one of Miss Smith's slaves, and she has just received notice through the lawyer in charge of Miss Smith's affairs that she figures in the will. The share bequeathed Gray Toole's wife is 100 acres of land in Orange County and $125 cash. Each of Miss Smith's six slaves received an equal amount of property.

"Miss Smith" was Mary Ruffin Smith. She left land, not money, to the University. Five, not six, former slaves received land. The "lawyer in charge" was Kemp Plummer Battle, former state treasurer but then president of the University of North Carolina. The 100-acre tract devised to Laura Smith Toole was located not in Orange but in Chatham County; and one of the former slaves receiving land (Laura's half-brother Julius) was willed only 25 acres and no money.

The report did not reveal that, although Gray Toole's wife and her two full sisters and one half-sister were former slaves of the Smith family, they were also Mary Smith's nieces, born to her enslaved servant Harriet and sired by the spinster's brothers—Sidney, an attorney and state legislator, and Francis, a physician. Furthermore, Mary Smith's wealth had not been earned by her generation; it descended to her, the last legal heir in the family, after barely escaping the profligacy of her father, a physician and two-term congressman who would have squandered it all except for the care with which Mary's grandfather, Francis Jones, had drafted his will a half century earlier.

The reporter had no way of knowing (1) that nearly a century earlier the land left to the University had been offered as a site for the new institution, and that the income from its sale would provide scholarships for students and help finance the first electric power, water, sewer, and heating systems on the campus; (2) that most of the remainder of Mary Smith's estate, including a more valuable plantation containing one of the finest houses in Orange County, was willed to the Episcopalians of North Carolina, whose inter-diocesanal fight over the bequest was eventually settled by a faulty decision of the Supreme Court of North Carolina; (3) that the dioceses used part of the income from the estate to purchase and save St. Mary's School in Raleigh and to support Chapel Hill's Chapel of the Cross; (4) that in the latter church in 1854, five slave children belonging to Mary Smith were baptized;

and (5) that in the same sanctuary, 123 years later, the granddaughter of the oldest of the four slave sisters, the Rev. Pauli Murray—in the capacity of the first African American woman to be ordained a priest in the Episcopal Church in the United States—celebrated the Holy Eucharist and has since (in 2012) been consecrated a saint in that denomination.

Of the other principals of this story, Francis and Mary Parke Jones (no relation to me!) produced a son, Ruffin, who never married, and a daughter, Delia, who married James Strudwick Smith and produced a daughter (Mary) and two sons (Francis and Sidney), none of whom married. Every "legitimate" member of this Jones-Smith family lies under his or her own tombstone in the Jones Grove Cemetery in Chatham County where, for more than a century, their story has been buried with them. Harriet, the faithful multi-race servant who bore four daughters for the white bachelor brothers before dying from a lightning strike, lies in an unmarked grave somewhere on the Price Creek plantation six miles away in Orange County. Memories of the oldest of Harriet's four "girls"—Sidney Smith's Cornelia—were powerfully told by her granddaughter Pauli Murray in *Proud Shoes: The Story of an American Family*. The hundreds of descendants of Cornelia's half-sisters, Emma, Annette, and Laura, all sired by Francis Smith, have been virtually ignored, as has Julius, Harriet's son by a common law husband. They too have a right to know their heritage. This book is for them.

* * *

Historians speak of finding history in our own backyard. Well, I found it. Or rather my fellow resident at Galloway Ridge, John Row, found it. Returning from a hike one afternoon, John asked me what I knew about the Smith lady who established a trust fund at the University of North Carolina and for whom an impressive granite cross stood "out yonder in the woods." As a historian at the University, I might have thought John was kidding except for the seriousness with which he asked the question.

Well, John, here you are. But you need to be patient, because you sent me off on an eight-year search that culminates in this book.

Jones and Smith, none of them my kin. Those two surnames are enough to send a sane historian to an easier subject. But I needed to know something about this Smith woman and her establishment of scholarships at the University of North Carolina, where I still occupied an office despite formal retirement.

Chatham County deed research quickly traced the Galloway Ridge property back to Francis Jones, a Revolutionary War veteran, who willed it to his grandson and namesake, Francis Jones Smith, upon whose death it passed to the latter's sister, Mary Ruffin Smith. So here was the key: Mary Ruffin Smith, the subject of the granite cross, gave the property to the University with the earnings dedicated to scholarships carrying the name of her deceased brother.

But that was the easy part. Soon I discovered that this land—the land upon which John Row and I now live—was not just *any* plantation. For example, back in 1792 commissioners met on this very spot in search of a site for the new state university. And, if Francis Jones and his neighbors had offered more acreage, the University of North Carolina might today be located right here at Jones Grove, not at Chapel Hill. The resulting sense of lost opportunity nagged the land's respective proprietors for a hundred years before, upon the death of the last "legitimate" member of this Jones-Smith family, the plantation was finally given to the University, which divided it, sold parcels at depressed prices, and applied the income to a scholarship fund in the name of its previous owner.

Interestingly, however, not all of the Jones Grove acreage was given to the University. One-hundred-acre tracts each were cut off for Emma Morphis, Annette Kirby, and Laura Toole, three women "of color," formerly slaves belonging to the Smith family. Those bequests sent me off to reread Pauli Murray's *Proud Shoes: The Story of an American Family*. That fascinating book reminded me that there was a fourth "woman of color" (Cornelia Fitzgerald); it also parted the clouds and revealed that I was wading into a subject so complicated that no historian has dared previously to tackle the improbable story of Dr. James Strudwick Smith and his two bachelor sons and spinster daughter. A dysfunctional family, if there ever was one.

Although the story begins and ends here at Jones Grove, most of its action takes place in Hillsborough and on another plantation, Price Creek, six miles north of Jones Grove in Orange County. But the account *always* comes back to the Jones Grove cemetery where the nine graves yield secrets that will be divulged in the following pages.

This unraveling of the Jones-Smith story has not been done alone. Early on, David Southern, an editor at the Duke University Press and a historian with wide interests—including the study of settlement in the Piedmont—volunteered to locate and copy a wide variety of Orange County records, both in the county offices in Hillsborough and in the State Archives. Unlike those of Chatham County, whose deeds have been digitized and are available on the internet, Orange County land records had to be researched *in situ*. More than that, David's broad knowledge of documentary sources in the region led to the discovery of many useful materials that otherwise would have been overlooked. His keen editorial eye is evident throughout the manuscript. Without David's contributions, there would be no book.

Additionally, I was fortunate that Jean Bradley Anderson, who contributed the biographical sketch of James Strudwick Smith in William Powell's *Dictionary of North Carolina Biography*, agreed to read an early version of the manuscript. Her questions and suggestions were enormously helpful.

Ernest Dollar, whose roots go back to the community, assisted in the selection of illustrations and provided the expertise for reproducing them in this book. Finally, to the caregiving of my fellow resident, Dr. Boyd Webb, and the medical staff of Galloway Ridge, The Arbor, and UNC and Duke Medicine personnel, I give thanks for keeping me—a nonagerian—going when quitting would have been easier.

* * *

Following revelation of Mary Ruffin Smith's bequests to the University of North Carolina and the Episcopal Diocese, William Hyslop Sumner Burgwyn wrote, "What an example to the men of the State this quiet modest secluded woman has set. What a volume is conveyed in the simple monument that 'she gave all she had to church and state....'" He hoped that "some future Historian of the State will perpetuate her noble act in fitting words to be recorded alongside of those of David Caldwell, Swain & Cameron." Until another historian discovers a cache of documents and photographs further elucidating the lives of Mary Ruffin Smith and her dysfunctional family, I submit the following pages in response to the nineteenth-century banking magnate's wishes.—H. G. Jones

Chapter 1

Landed Grandfather:
Francis Jones (1760–1844)

Prior to 1607, the area now encompassed by the North Carolina Piedmont was the home of small tribes of Native Americans, including the Siouan-speaking Sissipahaw, who shared the land and its resources without the concept of private ownership. From that year, the Crown of England claimed ownership of North America (excepting French Canada and Spanish Florida) by virtue of the permanent English occupation of Virginia. In 1663, King Charles II issued the Carolina Charter under which all of his North American territory between 36 and 31 degrees north latitude—extending southward from Virginia to Spanish Florida and westward to the South Sea (Pacific Ocean)—was granted to eight of his favorite noblemen, collectively called the "Lords Proprietors." In return, the King was to be paid annually "twenty marks of lawful money of England" and one-fourth of all gold and silver found. These Lords Proprietors held the vast territory as private property and beckoned migrants from Europe. As white settlers moved up the Cape Fear and Haw rivers into what would become Chatham County, most of the Native Americans, threatened by language difficulties and the strange European propensity to claim private ownership of the land, cultivate the soil, and construct permanent buildings, slowly moved farther into the interior, leaving little evidence of their heritage but stone implements, fish weirs, and local place names such as Altamahaw, Saxapahaw, and Ossippee—and of course, the river Haw.

Finding their Carolina tenants obstreperous and their lands unprofitable, seven of the Lords Proprietors sold their shares of Carolina back to the Crown in 1728. The Carolinas were divided, and the two colonies returned to their royal status. However, there was a fly in the ointment: one proprietor declined to sell his one-eighth share. To settle the claim of "The Right Honorable John Earl Granville, Viscount Carteret, and Baron General of Hawnes in the County of Bedford, in the Kingdom of Great-Britain, Lord Proficient of His Majesty's Most Honourable Privy Councill, and Knight of the Most Noble Order of the Garter," his one-eighth share was surveyed in the 1740s. This "Granville District" consisted of all land from the Virginia border southward sixty miles to 35°34' latitude, extending from the Atlantic to the Pacific Ocean. (Few Southern Californians realize that they live in eighteenth-century North Carolina.)

Until the American Revolution, then, all land in Orange County (from which Chatham was formed in 1771) was claimed by Lord Granville, whose line ran roughly along the southern boundary of present-day Chatham. Even so, in the fifteen years before the Granville District became official in 1744, a few intrepid pioneers received royal grants, especially in the Hawfields area, for choice properties within its bounds. These grants were issued in the name of the king, signed by the royal governor, and registered in older eastern counties such as Craven and Bladen, whose western boundary was indistinct. Sometime after the establishment of Orange County in 1752 and its county seat in Corbinton around 1754, Granville's agents opened a land office in what was called successively Corbinton, Childsburg, and Hillsborough; and although grants were suspended between Lord Granville's death in 1763 and the Revolution, unauthorized settling continued, and titles were eventually confirmed for many of these "squatters."[1]

The documented history of the exact site later called Jones Grove—which will feature importantly in this story—can be traced to 1760 when Richard Parker applied for several land grants from Lord Granville. One of those grants, issued January 13, 1763, was for 700 acres on the waters of Bush and Pokeberry creeks. Bush Creek begins just east of the present-day Galloway Ridge and flows northeasterly into New Hope Creek; Pokeberry Creek flows under present U.S. 15/501 a mile south of Galloway Ridge, then joins Haw River east of the village of Bynum. The condition of the grant was the annual payment of a quitrent of 28 shillings sterling. *Quitrent* is a fifteenth-century term signifying a fixed return payable to a feudal lord in commutation of any other services that had previously been required, such as grooming his horses and milking his cows. Following the American Revolution, Captain Richard Parker, Sr., decided to move to Georgia, and on March 6, 1784, for £500 "hard specie current money," he sold the 700 acres to Tignal Jones, Sr., of Wake County, who already held large acreage in Wake, Orange, and Chatham counties.[2]

The ubiquity of the surname Jones in early American history poses problems in itself; the addition of the name Francis narrows the choices but still leaves specific identifications imprecise. Fortunately, the relationship between "our" Tignal Jones, Sr., and the Francis Jones of this story is documented from the father-and-son's residence on Crabtree Creek in Wake County through deeds to real estate and the son's Revolutionary War service. The appearance of more than one person named Tignal Jones in the same county at approximately the same time adds confusion but does not negate the evidence of identity.

The participation of "our" Tignal Jones, Sr., in establishment of the state of North Carolina is documented, and he was a delegate from Wake County in the second and third provincial congresses in New Bern and Hillsborough in 1775 and, the next year, in the fourth and fifth congresses in Halifax. Thus Jones was a delegate when, on April 12, 1776, the fourth congress adopted the Halifax Resolves by which North Carolina became the first colony to agree to join other colonies in declaring "independency" from Great Britain. After creation of the new state, Tignal Jones represented Wake County in the House of Commons in New Bern in 1777 and 1784–85 and in the State Senate in Raleigh in 1797.[3]

A speculator in land, Tignal Jones, Sr., looked westward across New Hope Creek into recently-established Chatham County, where in 1784 he purchased from Richard Parker, Sr., the previously mentioned 700 acres on Pokeberry Creek, a tributary of Haw River. Nearly twenty years later he would give this tract to his son Francis, a Revolutionary War veteran.[4]

The participation in the American Revolution of Francis Jones might have been lost to history except for an act of Congress in 1832 that liberalized pensions for Revolutionary War veterans by including those who served at least two years in the continental line or state troops, whether volunteers or militia.[5] Uncharacteristically, for two decades the legislation escaped the notice of Captain Francis Jones and his son-in-law, former Congressman James S. Smith. Finally, in 1852, the latter sought payment to Jones's only daughter, Delia Jones Smith, for the period from the pension law's enactment until her father's death in 1844.[6] In addition to testimony of Jones's service, the application supplied new information on Jones and his family. In the sworn supporting affidavits, Dr. Smith's hand is evident, including Delia's assertion that "her husband Doctor Smith has been constantly since the death of her father harassed with debt and very vexatious lawsuits so that he had no time to hunt out persons, nor was his mind in a state to think of anything in the nature of business besides his own interests and it is not until lately that he looked into the matter and became sensible that a pension was due to your declarant in right of her father."[7]

Delia Jones Smith, declaring that her father had served more than two years of military service in the Revolution, recalled hearing him and other war veterans talk about their battle experiences. Although she could not document when and where he fought, she had heard him speak of serving under General Nathanael Greene at the Battle of Guilford Courthouse and being sent "in command of a company to destroy the boats on Dan River." She had heard him say that he served in both North and South Carolina, including New Bern and Camden, and that he spoke of "Colonel Lytle," "Colonel Richerson [Richardson]," and "General Butler."[8] She added, "Captain Francis Jones for many years before his death was a helpless old man that could not walk across the room without aid, and he had not been out of his son-in-law's ... yard for 7 years before his death." Explaining the tardiness of the application, she did not believe that her father had knowledge of "any pension being due to officers of the Militia Service and supposed if there was any pensions for anyone it was for poor destitute soldiers of the war"—a condition, she inferred, her father would not have claimed.

William Jackson, who in younger years lived 3½ miles from Francis Jones on Crabtree Creek in Wake County, recollected that his father served under militia Captain Jones and testified that he had often seen Jones, "a very distinguished officer," in command of militia soldiers while dressed in a captain's uniform with sword in hand. He added that he had often heard his father and Captain Jones speak of their more than two years of service in the militia.

James Dollar, a 98-year-old who lived three miles from Jones, swore that he was well acquainted with "Captain Francis Jones of Chatham County—who was a son of Colonel Tignal Jones of Wake—in which county he was born and raised and from which County he removed a few years after the American Revolution to Chatham, where he resided until the last few years of his life." He added, "Francis Jones served in the war of the Revolution and was present at the Battle of Guilford—in which engagement he served as a Captain of Militia in which action this Deponent first saw him." Dollar concluded, "In his neighborhood he was always reputed a soldier of the Revolution and had the title of Capt. in consideration of the Rank he held in the Revolutionary war.... Capt. Jones was always highly esteemed by his neighbors as a tried Whig of the Revolution and a man of the strictest honesty and integrity."

Dr. Smith, adding his own affidavit, remembered hearing his father-in-law speak of military service at Camden, New Bern, and Guilford Courthouse. He recalled a conversation between William Hopson, another veteran, and Captain Jones, during which Hopson called Jones a "Major." Jones corrected him: "I was late Captain—I never was higher in command." Smith added, "I heard him [Jones] not long before his death in conversation with an old

Richard Parker's 1763 land grant from Lord Granville was later purchased by Tignal Jones, Sr., who gave it to his son Francis who, with additional Chatham County tracts, named the property "Jones Grove" (courtesy State Archives of North Carolina).

Meanwhile, Francis Jones was given a 700-acre tract six miles north in Orange County by his father-in-law, Samuel Parke. The Orange County lands were collectively called "Price Creek" (courtesy Mary Ruffin Smith Papers [#3879], 1750–1904, Southern Historical Collection, Wilson Special Collections Library, University of North Carolina at Chapel Hill; hereinafter cited as Mary Ruffin Smith Papers, Southern Historical Collection, Wilson Library, UNC-CH).

neighbor, Eli Hill, who had been in the service with him. Hill said to him 'the first time I saw you in the Army[,] Captain, you were in command and mounted the finest horse I ever saw.'" Smith believed that his father-in-law served several tours of duty, perhaps for a total of three or four years. By another account, Captain Francis Jones is believed to have led his company of Wake County Regiment of Militia in the Battle of Hobkirk's Hill in Camden, South Carolina, on April 25, 1781.

Author Pauli Murray was incorrect in asserting that her great-great-great-grandfather Francis Jones "served as a lieutenant in Sharpe's Company during the Revolutionary War." Her misinformation was based on a pension application (S36653) of a Wake County man named Francis Jones, who claimed that he served "under Captain Sharp, of the 10th Regiment, in the North Carolina line." Tignal Jones's landholding son would never have claimed (as the applicant did) that he was "in reduced circumstances, & stands in need for the assistance of his country for support."[9]

Following the Revolution, Captain Jones moved from Crabtree Creek in Wake County to lands in Chatham County west of New Hope Creek and just south of the Orange County border. It is not known, however, whether he was present on November 5, 1792, at "Tignal Jones's place, commonly called 'Parker's'"—the plantation known thereafter as Jones Grove. There, where a narrow road from Pittsboro joined the more heavily traveled Hillsborough-Fayetteville Road, the captain's father hosted commissioners charged with selecting a site for the building of a constitutionally-mandated university for the state of North Carolina. Let Kemp P. Battle, an eventual president of the new institution, colorfully describe the setting: "We have the journal of these Commissioners, giving a brief account of their labors among the wooded hills of Chatham and Orange in the early days of November, when the forests were clothed with their changing hues of russet and green, and the deer peered curiously through the thick underwood, and the hospitable farmers welcomed them with hearty greetings, and the good ladies brought out their foamiest cider and sweetest courtesies, which on the sideboard, according to the bad customs of that day, stood decanters of dark-hued rum and ruddy apple brandy and the fiery juice of the Indian corn, which delights to flow in the shining of the moon." The commissioners had already decided that the site should be within fifteen miles of Cypret's Bridge over the New Hope (widened enough this far south to be called a river), and Jones Grove appeared to meet the criteria, provided local citizens would contribute sufficient land and/or money for the new institution. The minutes of the commission told the story: "No proposals were offered by the proprietor [Tignal Jones, Sr.]; but Tignal Jones, junior, and Robert Cobb offered a donation of 500 acres of land adjoining the place." The commissioners, appreciative but disappointed in the meager offer, proceeded nine miles to New Hope Chapel Hill in Orange County. At the crossroads community's Episcopal chapel, a dozen landowners offered an aggregate of more than 1,200 acres of land and donations of nearly £800 in money. That generosity destined Jones Grove to remain a quiet country estate while New Hope Chapel Hill grew into the state's most important university village.[10]

In 1803, "for and in consideration of the love and affection I have for my son Francis Jones," the elder Jones deeded the former Parker plantation to his son.[11] However, even before accepting title to his own father's Chatham County land, the younger Jones had become the beneficiary of another 700-acre tract on Price Creek six miles north in Orange County, this in 1789 from Samuel Parke of Randolph County "for and in consideration of the love and affection he hath for Mary his daughter, the wife of said Francis Jones."[12]

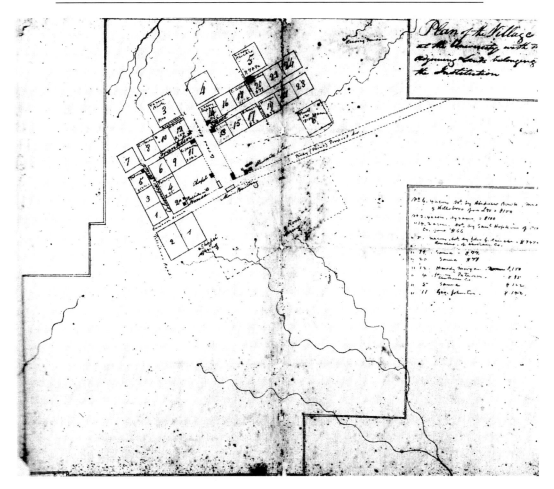

Francis Jones for a few years owned Lot 9 on Franklin Street in the "Village of the University." Currently, much of the lot is occupied by the University United Methodist Church (courtesy University Papers [#40005], University Archives, Wilson Special Collections Library, University of North Carolina at Chapel Hill; hereinafter cited as University Papers, Wilson Library, UNC-CH).

Prior to receiving these beneficences respectively from his father and father-in-law, Francis Jones had put down his own money for vast acreage in Chatham County, as follow: In *1791*, 450 acres on Morgan Creek from John Morgan, and 228 acres on the east side of New Hope Creek from a sheriff's sale of lands of Archibald Cain and Isam Rogers; in *1794*, 225 acres on Ewens Branch and Bush Creek from Robert Cobb, 700 additional acres on Pokeberry Creek from Richard Parker, Sr., 250 acres on Great Bush Creek from Robert Cobb, Sr., and 431 acres on the Orange County line as a grant from the State of North Carolina; in *1795*, 2 acres from his brother Tignal Jones, Jr., on New Hope and Morgan creeks; and in *1797*, 100 acres on Morgan Creek from Charles Blalock. Thus, by 1803 Francis Jones was the owner of almost 3,000 acres near the Chatham-Orange line even after selling 220 acres on the east side of New Hope Creek to Allen Vinson in 1797.[13]

In addition to his rural holdings, Francis Jones dabbled a bit in real estate in the "Village of the University of North Carolina." In 1804 he purchased the western half of the original two-acre Lot 9 (on which in 2014 the Chapel Hill Methodist Church is located); but after a series of complicated transactions, in 1810 he sold the title to Theoderick Love.[14]

During the decade 1805–1815, Francis Jones added further to his land holdings in both counties. Acquisitions included: in *1805*, 315 acres on each side of New Hope Creek in both counties from John Allen; in *1807*, in Orange, 400 acres on New Hope Creek from William Hogan and wife Elizabeth; in *1808*, 210 acres in Orange on the county line from John Morgan, Solomon P. Morgan, and Jacob Flowers (heirs of John Morgan); in *1810*, 13 acres in Chatham on Pokeberry Creek from Tapley Bynum; in *1811*, 257 acres in Chatham adjoining Black, Clement, Hogan, and Nevans, from William Brinkley; and in *1815*, 210 acres in Chatham on the county line from Jacob Flowers and wife Mary.[15]

A complicated transaction, involving one of the state's most prominent statesmen, lasted eight years. Jacob Flowers, Sr., and General Green Flowers were indebted to Francis Jones, so to secure the payment of principal plus interest to Jones, the duo in 1810 transferred to Archibald D. Murphey in trust four tracts totaling about 1,087 acres. In the event the Flowers debt to Jones was not paid on time, Murphey would be required to put the property up for public sale. In 1816, Murphey (by then running for reelection to the state senate against Jones's young son-in-law James S. Smith) was "called upon and required by the said Francis Jones to expose to sale the said lands." At a sale held at the county courthouse, Francis Jones became the purchaser at the price of $4,005.25. The amount of the debt was not disclosed; nevertheless, the acquisition of these rich lands along the branches running into Bush Creek and finally New Hope Creek, was a good deal. The acreage of the separate plantations was estimated at 382, 252, 200, and 253, respectively. Subsequently these lands, collectively known as the "Flowers Place," were willed to Jones's grandson, Sidney Smith.[16]

In the 1820s, Jones sold 314 acres on "Old Seven Island Road" of New Hope Creek to John Wesley Bynum, and 1,017 acres on Morgan and New Hope creeks to William Mason. Another tract of 183 acres on Bush Creek was sold to James Rigsbee in 1831.[17]

Francis Jones appears to have acquired no more real estate, but in 1815 he petitioned the Court of Pleas and Quarter Sessions for permission to build a mill on "the River New Hope," noting that he owned the land on both sides of the stream and that there was not a mill within ten miles of "Park's Old Fish Traps, the place where he purposes to build said mill." Many years later a deed involving this "Park's Neck" land would be the subject of a case decided in the State Supreme Court.[18]

Little is known about the bachelor son Ruffin Jones, born in 1794. In 1817 he received from the state of North Carolina a grant of 50 acres on Bush Creek, and this acreage may eventually have been considered a part of the "Flowers Place." In November 1833 Ruffin Jones entered into an agreement under which J.W. Bynum was allowed to construct a store house "in the Grove at the place where the widow Roper now lives known as the Jones Old Place." The location was further defined as "in the Grove near the road & to have the use of the spring." Bynum could use the "store & store house about the premises" for nine years rent-free, after which the building(s) would revert to Jones.[19] Unknown at the time, most of that land, plus additional Chatham and Orange farms acquired by the family in the nineteenth century—in all, approaching 5,000 acres—would eventually be dedicated to eleemosynary purposes. That story—alternately complex, maddening, and ultimately uplifting—is worthy of being preserved in the popular memory.[20]

Mary Parke Jones died in 1811, leaving the widower Francis Jones with 24-year-old

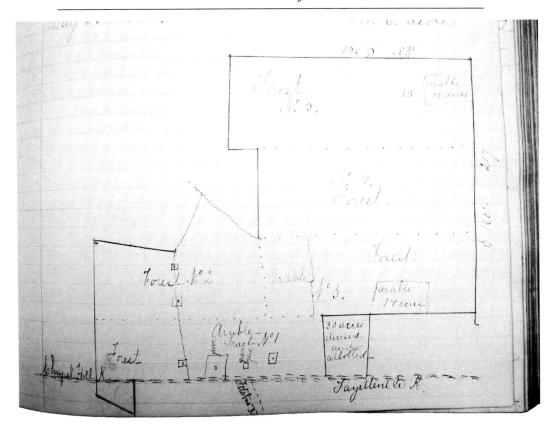

W.C. Cole's rough map, ca. 1890, of the Jones Grove complex at the junction of Pittsboro and Fayetteville roads. Note buildings, graveyard, and 30 (of 100) acres willed by Mary Ruffin Smith to her niece and former slave, Annette Kirby (courtesy University Papers, Wilson Library, UNC-CH).

daughter Delia and 17-year-old son Ruffin. Her body was buried in the garden at Jones Grove. When two years later Delia Jones married James Strudwick Smith and moved to Hillsborough, the Revolutionary War veteran and his bachelor son continued to oversee the extensive plantations, running back and forth across the county line to keep eyes on slaves and tenants working thousands of acres of central North Carolina's finest farm land. Of those farms, Jones Grove was a showplace where, in addition to the complex of buildings, a race track provided a popular destination for periodic sports events in a day when horse racing was a favorite country sport.[21] Although his straight race track indicated participation in the life of Chatham's elite, there is little documentation of those activities. The county court minutes record that he served jury duty and often proved deeds for his neighbors. Occasionally he was involved in court cases, not always on the winning side. For example, in the fall term 1795 of the Court of Pleas and Quarter Sessions, he was assessed damages of twelve pounds and seventeen shillings plus six pence costs after losing a judgment against Jacob Flowers, Jr. Years later Jones would gain ownership of Flowers' land. Jones's "hands," as his slaves and tenants were called, were regularly assigned to work on community roads, and in 1791 neighbors nominated him to oversee the building of a new road crossing New Hope Creek from Moses Parker's Old Place to Gray Barbee's.

A neighbor characterized Jones as a tried and true Whig, and he could hardly have remained silent during the political wars resulting from the rise of parties and the growth of the anti-slavery movement. One wonders about his reaction to the attention being gained by George Moses Horton, a young slave owned by James Horton, who lived just two miles down the Fayetteville Road. The very idea: a black boy, more literate than most Chatham County white men, writing poems for the students and even gaining attention of a white female teacher (Caroline Lee Hentz) at the University of North Carolina—even having some of his "pomes" published by Joseph Gales titled *The Hope of Liberty* (1829), the first book by a black man in the American South. Times were changing.

Shortly after Ruffin Jones died in 1836 at age 42, the elder Jones, in failing health, moved to the Orange County seat of Hillsborough and lived with the Smiths the last seven years of his life. His condition was painfully described in his daughter's affidavit in the pension application in 1852: "Captain Francis Jones for many years before his death was a helpless old man that could not walk across the room without aid, and he had not been out of his son-in-law's ... yard for 7 years before his death." On Saturday morning, February 24, 1844, a neat handwritten notice appeared at the courthouse in Hillsborough: "The Funeral of the late Francis Jones will take place this evening at four o'clock at the residence of Dr. James S. Smith. The citizens of Hillsborough and its vicinity are respectfully invited to attend at the ringing of the bell."[22] Extant records of St. Matthew's Episcopal Church are silent on the subject. His body was taken back to Chatham County and buried near his wife Mary and son Ruffin in the garden at Jones Grove.

A quarter-century earlier, in 1819, six years after Delia's marriage, Jones—"desireth of advancing the said James S. Smith & Delia his wife & in consideration of one dollar to him in hand paid"—deeded the Price Creek plantation to his son-in-law. This included the original Price Creek land given to Jones in 1789 by his own father-in-law Samuel Parke, its total acreage having been increased to over a thousand acres.[23] Then at Francis Jones's death in 1844, all of the extensive estate came under control of the 57-year-old son-in-law whose career had been something less than exemplary in medicine, business, and politics.[24] That control, however, was not absolute. In fact, when Francis Jones signed his will on February 8, 1841, he was emphatic. It was his "will & request" that upon Smith's death "he will give to my grand daughter Mary R. Smith the plantation in Orange County on Prices Creek which I conveyed to him by deed many years past." With the Jones Grove lands, Jones's will was absolute: They were left to Smith "in trust for the sole use & benefit of my only child & daughter Delia Smith ... for & during her natural lifetime free from any rights title or claim of the said James S. Smith or any person from or under him or against any debt claim or demand of the said James S. Smith or any other person whatsoever, and at the death of the Delia Smith then I will & bequeath the said tract of land to my grandson Dr. Francis J. Smith & his lawful heirs." The same requirement was applied to the Flowers Place which, upon Delia's death, was to go to the younger son, James Sidney Smith.[25] Jones also willed all of his slaves "for the sole use & benefit" of Delia Jones Smith, upon whose death they were to be divided equally among his three grandchildren. The servants named were males Yellow[?], James, Simon, Samuel, and Dempsey, and females Tempy, Sally, Betsy, Milly, and Hetty, together with all of their children.

When Francis Jones wrote that will in 1841, he had every reason to believe that his son-in-law would guard his landed legacy for the benefit of Delia Jones Smith and her children. After all, Dr. Smith had served as a physician, local celebrity, state legislator, and United

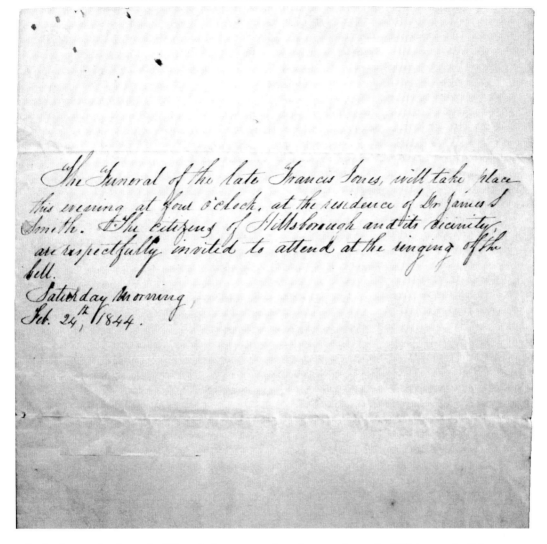

"The Funeral of the late Francis Jones, will take place this evening at four o'clock, at the residence of Dr James S Smith. The citizens of Hillsborough and its vicinity, are respectfully invited to attend at the ringing of the bell.
Saturday Morning,
Feb. 24th, 1844.

Invitation to the funeral of Francis Jones posted at the courthouse in Hillsborough, February 24, 1844. His body was brought back to Jones Grove for burial near his wife Mary and son Ruffin (courtesy Mary Ruffin Smith Papers, Southern Historical Collection, Wilson Library, UNC-CH).

States Congressman. The old soldier was wise enough, however, to wrap his landed wealth in legal protection by requiring that it all be held in trust for the benefit of his daughter, and upon her death, for his grandchildren. His meticulousness would be proven wise; Francis Jones's spirit must have quaked in its grave when, just after his death in 1844, the entire legacy came dangerously close to being squandered by his son-in-law. The fact—the miracle—that the three separate groups of property—Price Creek, Jones Grove, and the Flowers Place—remained in the Smith family was due entirely to the care with which the father-in-law had worded his will.

Chapter 2

Profligate Father:
James Strudwick Smith (1787–1852)

The origin of Francis Jones's son-in-law, James Strudwick Smith, is clouded in mystery, but historian Jean Bradley Anderson's meticulous research led her to believe that he was the illegitimate son of William Francis Strudwick (1770–1810), who served in the state's constitutional convention in 1789, both houses of the legislature, and the United States Congress. That opinion rests largely on the dates of Smith's birth (September 8, 1787) and a bastardy charge laid the following August reading, "James Taylor is deemed sufficient security for Wm. Strudwick to keep the parish indemnifyd [*sic*] by reason of a child begotten on the body of [blank]." The mother's name was omitted, but Anderson noted that the family of Reuben Smith lived conveniently close to Strudwick lands in the area called Hawfields in what became Alamance County.[1]

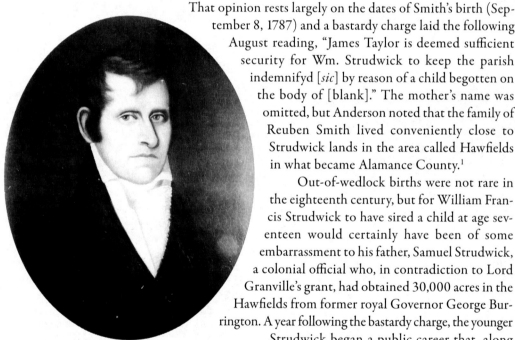

Out-of-wedlock births were not rare in the eighteenth century, but for William Francis Strudwick to have sired a child at age seventeen would certainly have been of some embarrassment to his father, Samuel Strudwick, a colonial official who, in contradiction to Lord Granville's grant, had obtained 30,000 acres in the Hawfields from former royal Governor George Burrington. A year following the bastardy charge, the younger Strudwick began a public career that, along with his farming and business interests, lasted until his death in 1810. Meanwhile, by his own account, young James Strudwick Smith was leading a spartan life. Years later he recalled, "Having been born poor, I have had to be the architect of my own fortune. I procured the means of advancement by hard labor."[2]

Portrait of Dr. James Strudwick Smith (1787–1852), of obscure birth; Hillsborough physician and member of U.S. Congress (1817–1821); son-in-law of Francis Jones; father of Francis, Sidney, and Mary Ruffin Smith, none of whom married. Artist unidentified (courtesy State Archives of North Carolina).

Somehow, by 1810, Dr. James Webb, Hillsborough's leading physician, became interested enough in 23-year-old James Smith to accept him as an understudy in his medical practice. That same year, William Strudwick died at age forty, and Webb assumed the official role as guardian of his deceased friend's nine-year-old son, Edmund Charles Fox Strudwick. Simultaneously, Webb assisted in sending young Smith to the medical school of the University of Pennsylvania; and a decade later he did the same for his official ward, Edmund Strudwick. In those identical humanitarian acts, Dr. Webb may well have been providing assistance to half-brothers. If so, presumably the doctor knew of the blood relationship, but did the boys know it? Interestingly, Jean Anderson found a documentary connection between James Smith and William Francis Strudwick in the sale of the latter's estate in 1811 when the young man purchased a dozen pictures and two pistols with holsters.[3]

Dr. Webb influenced the careers of several other future physicians, and in 1799 he was one of the organizers of a short-lived North Carolina State Medical Society. During his congressional service in 1821, Dr. James Smith, aspiring to head another proposed (but still-born) state medical society, sought and obtained from the University of Pennsylvania an M.D. degree, albeit an honorary one.[4] Twenty years later, in the midst of a distinguished career, Dr. Edmund Strudwick helped organize and served as the first president of a new and permanent North Carolina Medical Society. There, parallels between the careers of Dr. James Webb's two protégées end. The question remains: Was it simply coincidence that Dr. Webb chose both boys as protégées, or was he doing a good deed for a friend who fathered both of them?

Regardless of his background, young James Smith appears to have been accepted by other local leaders, several of whom, including Duncan Cameron, joined Dr. Webb in furthering his education. With their assistance, Smith spent two winters (1810–12) in the University of Pennsylvania's medical department in Philadelphia. His maturity was demonstrated in December 1811 when he explained to benefactor Cameron his decision to return to Hillsborough without a degree: "I feel now under too many obligations to my friends to ask for a further supply [of money]. True it is I have money owing me at home—But that I will want to satisfy what I have already borrowed." Besides, he reasoned, a diploma would be to him gratification but would make him no better a physician. Smith added, "I do not conceive that a diploma would be of much benefit to me as I will be situated in the country of my nativity amongst my friends—on the contrary if I was going to reside in a foreign country I would deem it of the first importance." His gratitude to Cameron was sincere: "I feel much indebted to you and hope to be able at some time to repay you. I have had to depend on my own exertions hitherto in a great degree. But they would have been too feeble had I not had the assistance of my friends among whom you have been the principle [*sic*]."[5]

Father as Physician

Young James S. Smith, without a degree, returned to Hillsborough and began practicing medicine. If in the remaining forty years of his life he had devoted himself unreservedly to medicine, he could have earned a praiseworthy reputation in his native county. Instead, he excelled neither in his profession nor in his search for fame and fortune in politics and business.[6] Still, his extant day and account books reveal a productive career as a doctor of internal medicine through the 1820s and 1830s before he began speculating in real estate.[7]

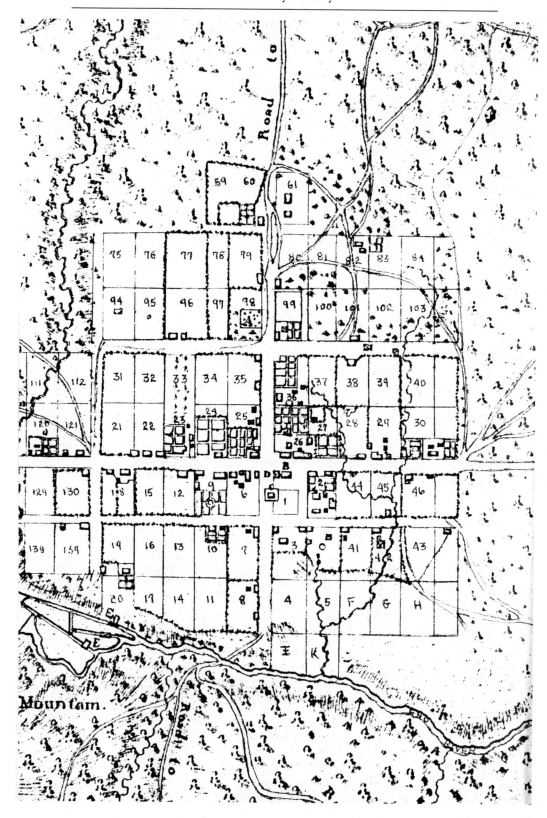

Other physicians—like Thomas Faddis, William Montgomery, Edmund Strudwick, and James Webb—were also practicing in Hillsborough, but Smith's patients included men who subsequently occupied positions such as bishop, university president, chief justice, congressman, senator, governor, and secretary of the Navy.[8] Among the names were a Who's Who of Orange County—names like Christopher Barbee, Jr., John Berry, William A. Graham, Dennis Heartt, Cadwallader Jones, Willie P. Mangum, Archibald D. Murphey, Denison Olmsted, Abraham Rencher, Thomas Ruffin, and Josiah Turner, Sr. One of his unusual patients was John Day "of Colour" who later moved his shop to Milton and emerged as the state's best known antebellum furniture manufacturer. Dr. Smith supplied the young cabinetmaker with a sponge and "Aqua Fortis" in 1824.[9] Years later, Josiah Turner, Jr., left a personal testimonial to Dr. Smith's medical competence: "While tradition informs me of his great success as a Physician, I call to mind a memorable instance in 1846 when Dr. Webb treating myself and brother for measles, Dr. Smith was called in, a week after Dr. Webb, and at first sight pronounced in a moment that his *measles* was *small-pox*." Given appropriate medication, the two boys recovered.[10]

Although Hillsborough was a hotbed *of* politics and Smith was sometime a hothead *in* politics, local animosities appear not to have hindered his medical practice. Episcopalian relations were clearly evident among his regular patients, perhaps because they were associated with the two major academies, one each for boys and girls. Walker Anderson, Francis L. Hawks, and William M. Green gained attention in future years as, respectively, chief justice of the Supreme Court of Florida, historian of the Episcopalian denomination, and bishop of Mississippi. These three men suffered recurring medical problems; and in the cases of Anderson and Hawks, daily visits by the doctor were required at various times. Particularly interesting is the relationship between Smith and Archibald D. Murphey. Less than a decade after Murphey accused Smith (then his opponent for a seat in the State Senate) of preaching "incessantly" against him in a "vilifying style" in a "fungous excrescence," the doctor was riding to Hawfields and tenderly attending his old adversary for days at a time. In February 1826, Dr. Smith spent overnight with the judge, performing venesection (blood letting) and providing a variety of medicines, at a cost of $30—a large amount at the time. Among remedies administered on that and other house calls to Murphey were laudanum, Epsom salts, essence of peppermint, calomel, mercurial ointment, blue pills, asafoetida, paregoric, sulphur, and a variety of prescription medicines. When the rheumatic Murphey settled his bill of $172.40 in 1830, he paid it "by note," meaning that Smith still had to wait for cash. Incidental to this same year, Dr. Smith and Murphey are mentioned by name among the prominent Hillsborough citizens who assembled at a King Street tavern one evening in late February 1830 to pay their respects to Anne Royall, who was visiting and collecting material for her three-volume *Mrs. Royall's Southern Tour* (1830–31).[11]

Somewhat similarly, within three years after Dr. Smith and Francis Lister Hawks clashed bitterly in the House of Commons over the issue of borough representation,[12] Hawks was a

Opposite: C.J. Sauthier's Map of 1768 (as modified with lots numbered by Mary Claire Engstrom) shows Dr. Smith's house in Lot 22, adjoining the lot (23) on which the Masonic Lodge was built. The Hillsborough Female Academy is believed to have been located on or just east of Lot 43, shown on this map near the lower right-hand corner (courtesy North Carolina Collection, Wilson Special Collections Library, University of North Carolina at Chapel Hill; hereinafter cited as North Carolina Collection, Wilson Library, UNC-CH).

frequent patient of his old adversary. For eight consecutive days in October 1824—including one overnight stay—the physician visited Hawks's bedroom. In the next three years, he was given venesections and treated with an assortment of remedies such as laudanum, gum camphor, castor oil, rhubarb, calcium magnesium, arrow root, wormwood oil, ointment, Epsom's salts, and various cathartics; he was even given a vivisection—surgical exploration. Young Hawks, then going through a traumatic decision that led to his abandonment of the law in favor of a career as an Episcopalian minister, was delicate in health, and his medical bill grew to the point that it was eventually paid in 1827 "by order of Wm. M. Green." Meanwhile, the Reverend Green, rector of St. Matthew's and principal of Hillsborough Female Academy, depended upon Dr. Smith for help with his own health problems. So did Walker Anderson, a teacher and cofounder of the new church. Like Hawks, Anderson suffered recurring health problems, sometimes requiring daily visits by the doctor. In 1830 he paid $166.67 as he prepared to leave North Carolina for more fertile fields in Florida, where he eventually served as chief justice.

Of particular interest is the case of Mrs. Maria Spear, the mother of both the better known teacher by that name and the future the Rev. William Wallace Spear. The date of the arrival of mother and children in Hillsborough presumably was 1826, when one or both of the Marias began teaching at the one-year-old Hillsborough Female Academy.[13] The mother's first medical charge was dated September 4, 1826, when Dr. Smith called and gave her a cathartic; his accounts thereafter show extensive service to the family. As examples, there were charges in 1826 for "Visit & medicines Maria $3"; in 1827 for "Extracting tooth (Bill)

Mrs. Maria Spear, mother of the younger teacher of the same name, asked for medical advice in this touching note to Dr. James Smith (courtesy Mary Ruffin Smith Papers, Southern Historical Collection, Wilson Library, UNC-CH).

$1"; and 1830 for "Visit Mary Whitted $1," the latter presumably a white servant. A startling undated note—which illustrates the state of health during that era—was found tipped into one of the daybooks. It reads: "Dr. Smith, Sir, Please to send me a bottle of Croup Syrup, some salts, and a bottle of [illegible]. The little Negro Mary has had a cough and been unwell for some days. I applied cough syrup which always acts as an emetic with her. She threw up thick bile and Saturday she threw up 2 worms about a foot long each. Yesterday she seemed better but coughed badly during the night.... What is best to give her[?]. Please send what you think proper. The weather being so cold I did not like to apply calomel without your order.... M. Spear." Another ledger entry for Mrs. Spear, June 11, 1830, reads, "By settlement with Female Academy. $63.90. This account is credited in full to this date." The entry suggests that the elder Maria Spear taught for a while in the academy with which her daughter's name became indelibly associated.[14]

For Dennis Heartt, Dr. Smith was the source of some of the products used in the printing plant of the *Hillsborough Recorder*: rosin, turpentine, sulphur, lamp black, and Spanish indigo. Occasionally the physician accepted produce in payment, and he apparently exchanged medications with other local physicians from time to time. Accounts seldom show how payments were made, but in the case of Duncan Cameron, a check on the Bank of Newbern settled the bill. Only a few accounts appear to have been taken to court. Doses of medicine were usually 25 or 50 cents, but occasionally the bulk price is given—for example, 15 gallons of castor oil cost $33.75. Smith appears to have limited his practice to internal medicine; almost no injury cases appear in his accounts. In-town visits were charged a dollar in good weather; out-of-town trips were based on distance. For example, a trip to Samuel Kerr in the Hawfields was $6; to Willie P. Mangum's Walnut Hall on Red Mountain (20 miles, in present-day Durham County), $9. One of the largest accounts—William Cain—rose to well over $400, an amount equal to perhaps a hundred acres of Orange County real estate. When consulting with a fellow physician, Smith's charge was $6. Except for venesections and tooth-pullings ($1 each), he seldom performed with an instrument. However, on September 7, 1830, he helped an unnamed physician in "Extirpating Breast For Negro Woman" owned by Mrs. John Ray. His charge—$20—was half the total.

A tattered handwritten note—found tipped in one of Dr. Smith's ledgers—adds a bit of human interest to (and understanding of) both the medical and moral culture of the 1830s. Dated December 9, 1831, it reads: "Dear Sir, Please to send me a vial of those kind of drops that promote labour with directions how they are to be taken. Yours respectfully &c., Hunter McCullock." At the bottom was added, "P.S. Take your pay out of the money I have sent and send back the change."

Dr. James Smith's own health, particularly his sight, became an issue from time to time. A "card" appeared in the *Hillsborough Recorder* on November 26, 1840, reading "Dr. James S. Smith's health is so far restored as to enable him to resume the practice of his profession." However, the notice continued, "He cannot promise to ride in the night, as his eye sight has so far failed him to render night travel dangerous. He has associated his son F.J. Smith with him, in the practice who will be able to attend to night calls and such as offer in inclement weather." By then, Dr. Smith, past age fifty, was deep into politics and on the verge of real estate manipulation which would consume his energy and threaten Francis Jones's legacy.

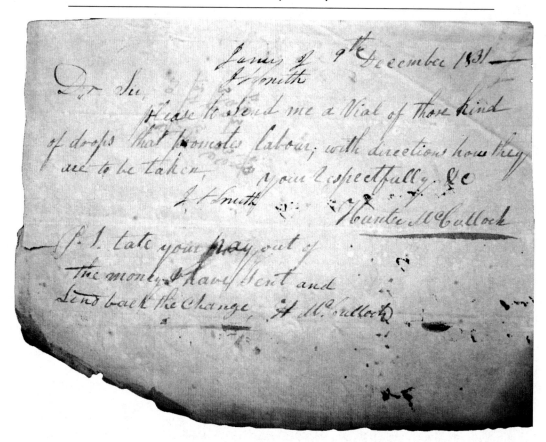

A worried husband sought Dr. Smith's advice about a pill capable of producing labor in his pregnant wife (courtesy Mary Ruffin Smith Papers, Southern Historical Collection, Wilson Library, UNC-CH).

Father as Politician

Twenty-four-year-old James Smith qualified in 1811 for the positions of town trustee and justice of the peace, the first of several local appointments that he was to hold over the years. Obviously, here was a young man on the rise. That became evident when in 1814, exhibiting a brashness that would become his hallmark, Smith challenged Orange County's popular Senator Archibald Debow Murphey, whose progressive views toward education and internal improvements were to bear little fruit until after his premature death in 1832. No newspaper was published west of Raleigh between 1785 and 1820, and except for his medical accounts, Smith left no body of manuscripts. Consequently, his views and activities during the 'teens are obscure, but Murphey, always the historian, left enough evidence to suggest a lively era of politics in and around Hillsborough. Murphey had served his first two years as state senator when he found himself being attacked by "a fungous excrescence"— his description of a political circular put out by the feisty Smith. "Shall I answer Dr. Smith? ... The Dr. preaches incessantly against me in the vilifying style of his letter," Murphey complained to Thomas Ruffin.[15]

Whatever the content of the circular, Murphey published his own searing "Caustic" to the freeholders of Orange.[16] Naming them only as "candidates for public appointments," the senator wrote, "These men find it to be the most convenient mode of gaining their end, to excite the passions of the people, to scatter suspicion and distrust among them, and under the pretense of serving their country, to set one half of the people at war with the other half. How soon would our party quarrels die away, if they were not kept alive by these men! Shall we forever be the dupes of this folly? I trust that we shall not; I trust that the good sense of the people will at length teach them that nothing contributes less to their interest or happiness than disputes about party politics." Directly addressing Smith's "excrescence," Murphey added,

> I cannot therefore but deeply regret to observe the style and sentiments of a publication lately addressed to you, the object of which is to rouse the zeal of party spirit in the next election, and to traduce my reputation. Is the public good expected to be promoted by the exercise of an illiberal, malignant spirit? I apprehend not; and I ask the republicans of Orange County by what authority this writer has put himself at their head? Have they consented to make his opinions the standard of orthodoxy? Have they commissioned him in their name to denounce and traduce whomsoever he pleaseth, and set at naught the rules of decorum and good manners? If they have, I must say that republicanism among us is sadly in the wane.

Murphey continued to criticize the rise of party spirit:

> Why have so many men been lately scouted [*sic*] from the republican ranks? It is because a set of illiberal men have been impudent enough to assume to themselves the name of *honest, orthodox* republicans, and to cry down every one who will not go all lengths with them. They are bringing the cause of republicanism into disrepute: They are prostituting the proud and independent character of freemen to the little purposes of factious malevolence, and waging war against every thing that is exalted and generous in the human character. Mr. Jefferson told the people of the United States, when he first came into the presidency, that we were all federalists, we were all republicans; and that in appointments to office, the only question should be, 'Is the person proposed to be appointed, honest; is he capable?' You are now told that Mr. Jefferson was entirely wrong; that we are not only divided into federalists and republicans; but subdivided into *simple republicans*, and *honest, orthodox* republicans, who will neither *twist* nor *quirk*: and it is intimated that in appointments to office, the question should be, 'is the person proposed to be appointed, one of these *honest, orthodox* republicans?'

If Smith's circular dealt with issues, the young man must have campaigned as a "strict constructionist," opposed to Murphey's positive view of the role of government. And if that is so, Smith's own views would change within the next two decades, by which time he was an avowed Whig, espousing some programs associated with early Federalists.

Perhaps with James Smith in mind, Murphey continued,

> Politics have become a trade, in which bankrupts in fortune and reputation are master-workmen, and the idle, the profligate, the dissipated and the factious, are apprentices. When a man gets out of business he turns politician, undertakes to instruct his neighbors about their rights and the administration of their government: and just at the moment when he loses his prudence in managing his own affairs, he gets wisdom for managing the affairs of the nation.... Party politics have taken the place of everything valuable and praiseworthy.... What inducement has a man who aspires to public employments, to lead a virtuous life, when he finds that the people look upon his notions about party politics to be of more imporantce than all his virtues? ... Party spirit has ruined all the free governments which have heretofore existed: It will ruin ours, unless constant efforts be made to check its influence.

The senator ended his letter with the hope "that the time is not far distant when a difference in opinion about politics shall be accounted as harmless, as a difference in opinion about ploughing our lands and raising our crops."

Murphey was reelected in the heated campaign of 1814, but Smith challenged him again in 1816. That the senator's reelection was warmly contested was reflected in a letter from Willie P. Mangum to Duncan Cameron: "Doct. Smiths prospects are indeed flattering to him and unless Mr. Murphey and his friends make some exertion Smiths election may be expected.—That Mr. Murphey's popularity is in the wane cannot be doubted, and in the southern & south eastern parts of the county Smith will get an overwhelming majority. At the sale of Standfords I have understood that Smith was greatly flattered as yesterday. Those flatteries with his own presumption have confirmed him in the opinion that he will be elected.—That the result will be as he (Smith) could wish I cannot believe, but it would be well that Mr. Murphey & his friends should be aware of the Puffing Doctors strength."[17] Murphey again defeated Smith and remained in the State Senate until 1818, when he was appointed a superior court judge.

Smith, then about thirty, raised his sights in 1817, running for Congress against incumbent Samuel Dickens of Person County. We get a sense of the partisanship from Dr. William Henderson, son of Chief Justice Leonard Henderson, who wrote Thomas Bennehan in August 1817:

> Can't we keep the man [Smith] of many pursuits at home? At least let us endeavor to do so. He is a perfect Proteus, always varying. Here, he is a federalist, an admirer of Washingtons politics, no administration man; in short sir he is every thing, but a federalist. I hope the doctor will pardon me; The pursuit would be a fruitless one too elevated for one of his political persuasion. I enclose the letter of Colonel William Hinton, of this county to you, in obedience to the request of Mr. Dickens; that you may transmit it to Person before the election. Mr. Dickens supposes, if the charges contained in Colonel Hintons letter can be established in his own county, he will command almost, an unanimous vote. It is then important for we are apprehensive, the contest is doubtful there, as well as in Orange. I hope not, I trust we are not so far behind. We can ascribe it to nothing but the supineness of Mr. Dicken's friends. Wake is certainly Federal, when she chuses to rise her strength. Smith's friends have left no stone unturned. It is the intention of Mr. Dickens to make Smith commit himself, by denying the charge, and then to prove it. May God prosper every good word and work (Micklejohn) [sic]. Will you let me know by the messenger, whether you will find it convenient to send to Person, and whether Mr. Dickens called on you, on his return home. I tremble for the fate of the election.[18]

The deteriorating health of Archibald D. Murphey led to a rapprochement with his former political enemy, and Dr. Smith made many trips, some overnight, to minister to the man posthumously called the "Father of Education in North Carolina" (courtesy North Carolina Collection, Wilson Library, UNC-CH).

Apparently the Dickens forces sought to paint Smith as a Federalist, for in August 1817

William Hinton wrote to William Henderson claiming that he had heard Smith at his neighborhood muster utter "sentiments very different from what I calculated on, for they were such as I should have expected from a Federalist and strongly urg'd the necessity of adopting Washingtons principles, and in the Course of his address he made use of sentiments to this effect (if not in the precise words, they had the same meaning) that the administration had been in an error and it was Honorable to retract."[19]

Whatever the issue, Smith refers to it only obliquely in a circular issued during the summer.[20] Claiming to come from "the humble walks of life" without "aid of wealthy and powerful relations to recommend me to your confidence," he boasted of living entirely "by my own exertions; by the labor of my own hand, and the exercise of the little talent that nature was pleased to give me." Consequently, he sought to assure voters of modest means that he was acquainted with their toils and could justly appreciate their work. Because he was one of them, he had yielded to "repeated and numerous solicitations" of friends and now sought their support in his candidacy for the fifteenth Congress of the United States.

Little in the circular clarified Smith's relationship with a particular political party, the lines of which were blurred in the decade following the War of 1812, misleadingly called the "Era of Good Feelings." His views on agriculture, commerce, and manufacturing were hardly controversial. In fact, he wrote, "These are my sentiments; are they not Republican? Are they not Federal? Are they not American?" One statement in the circular, however—"A liberal system of Internal Improvement, is necessary to develope [*sic*] the latest resources of this nation—our rivers, roads, bridges, and ferries, should claim the attention of the National Legislature"—marked him as a future Whig, even as he urged, "Let us forget our party quarrels about politics; let us by our union give strength to our government; let our watch-word be, 'united we stand.'" Notwithstanding this advocacy of federally-funded internal improvements, when in Congress Smith repeatedly voted against federal aid toward projects such as the Cumberland Road.[21] With an oratorical flourish that would become familiar, he ended, "I hope you will not view this as a gasconade of words and sentences artfully combined, to decoy your judgments by the sweetness of their cadence, or the smoothness of their periods. The subject does not require this, nor do these powers belong to me. I cannot adorn any subject with the flowers of oratory, nor dress it in the attire of literary eloquence.—It is plain truth, in a homespun dress, but none the worse for that." In reality, James Smith was denying one of his most enduring strengths.

Smith defeated Dickens and served two terms in the United States House of Representatives. Henry Clay was the speaker, and a dozen years later Smith would become one of the Kentuckian's most ardent supporters for president. Smith developed a warm relationship with William H. Crawford, secretary of the treasury, who furnished him with seeds of a wild olive from his own orchard in Georgia, "a beautiful evergreen" that grew to a height of forty feet and a trunk sometimes two feet in diameter.[22]

Congress convened in those days before the end of the year in which an election was held, so when in December 1817 Smith attended the opening session of the Fifteenth Congress, among his fellow North Carolina representatives were such heavyweights as Weldon N. Edwards, Lemuel Sawyer, and Thomas Settle. The freshman from Orange was not assigned to a standing committee, but he was appointed to a special committee "Respecting Amelia Island," a subject referred to in President James Monroe's address and involving a Spanish island at the mouth of St. Mary's River that was seized by Americans. Unforeseen at the time, Smith's failure to support aggressive military actions of Major General Andrew Jackson in troublesome Florida would figure in his future election campaigns.

In his first speech on the floor in December, Smith objected to a bill proposing an increase in the tariff on bar iron. He began by adverting to another tax, the oppressiveness of which weighed "grievously" on the district he represented—the tax on distillation. That tax was very unequal and, in fact, a tax on agriculture, preventing inland distilleries from competing against imported alcoholic products, he charged. He continued, "Who were the distillers ... particularly of whiskey? Were they the farmers who lived on the seaboard, and obtained great prices for their crops of grain; or were they the farmers of the back country, producing much grain, and at great distance from market, and under the necessity of converting it into spirit, to get it in that shape to a market? It was the latter class ... who paid a considerable portion of that tax, which heavily affected those who converted into spirit the produce of their orchards." He thought that the distiller had the same right to bring his complaint to Congress as the manufacturers of iron, sugar, and any other product.[23]

When the bill came up again in April, Smith delivered a speech that occupied five columns in the *Annals*. Citing Alexander Hamilton's emphasis on developing domestic manufacturing, he exhibited considerable reading about both domestic and foreign commerce, including familiarity with previous congressional debates on the subject. He argued that an increase in the tariff on bar iron would be paid by American consumers rather than by the foreign producers or American importers. The supporters of the bill, he charged,

> appeal to your patriotism—they tell you that you should protect every branch of industry in your country. And, sir, so you should, but you should never sacrifice the interest of the many to the cupidity and mercenary views of the few. But, sir, here—here is the objection: the great agricultural interest must bend before these mercenary few—these fat capitalists. Agriculture must pay the premium; she must be taxed; and the farmer, the most remote from trade, must be taxed most. Yes, sir the man who has the fewest natural advantages, must be taxed most— he is the greatest consumer of iron. To get the surplus produce of his honest labor to the market, he must have wagons, carts, horses, &c. These require much iron to keep them in repair.

Continuing his criticism of "fat capitalists," he added that under the existing tariff,

> iron rose from 50 to 75 per cent cash; no credit now; at the same time the farmer's tobacco was rotting in his barn; it would not bring three dollars per hundred; his wheat spoiling in his garners; flour would not bring four dollars a barrel; his land, his house, his everything, taxed to support the cause of his country, at the same time. Did the capitalist sympathize for the farmer? No, sir; the iron master's patriotism, his sympathy, was suspended; nor never would he have thought of it again, but for his own dear self, who thought it a good pretext to get the advantage of the farmer a little once more. Sir, I look upon agriculture as the first, and the greatest interest of this country; and while I am honored with a seat on this floor, I will always raise my voice in its support, and against these monopolizing principles. If this bill is adopted, it will impose a considerable tax on your agriculture. But, poor old Agriculture? She is, I am fearful, doomed soon to be the packhorse of manufacturers and of commerce. They are always seeking to get some advantage by getting monopolies. Honest old Agriculture has no such feeling; she knows no such principles. All that she asks of you is to keep your hands off her; she is strong; she is athletic; let her alone and she can, she will protect herself.

Asking why no other new country had prospered as quickly as the United States, he answered his own question: "It has been agricultural solely, or nearly so. In less than fifty years this Republic has become a great nation; second in commerce, second as a naval power; most brave in the field; most skilful [*sic*] and most victorious on the water; rich—independent." He concluded, "When you raise your duties beyond the point necessary for raising the revenue necessary for the support of your Government, you encourage smuggling. Your customs are defrauded; your regular merchants are unable to sell their goods; fraud and speculation is the result. The effect that this will have on the morals of your country is too apparent to require comment. And if you commence this system [of high protective tariffs], all classes will have an equal right to your protection."

Oddly, despite earlier advocacy of federal funding for internal improvements, Smith voted against appropriations for the Cumberland Road and several similar projects. This may have simply reflected his conservative views, for he also voted against the purchase of furnishings for the capitol and the "president's house," and he favored the reduction of the daily pay for congressmen from $9 to $8 and travel from $9 to $6 for every twenty miles traveled to and from Washington.

In the second session in November 1818, Smith was appointed to the Committee on Public Expenditures, in which position he voted against appropriation of funds for soldiers to work on the roads and against the Bank of the United States. Not surprisingly, he sided with fellow Southerners on matters relating to slavery. Perhaps anticipating his own acquisition of bounty lands in Illinois from soldiers of the War of 1812, he moved that the Committee on Public Lands be instructed to inquire into the expediency of authorizing someone other than the president to sign patents for bounty lands.[24]

Just before Independence Day in 1819, a four-page circular announced Smith's candidacy for a second term.[25] Virtually all of the text defended two of his votes in the previous congress. Both issues involved Andrew Jackson, the major general who, during the Seminole War in 1818, ordered the seizure of St. Marks and Pensacola in West Florida, executed British subjects named Alexander Arbuthnot and Robert C. Ambrister, and seized the Spanish territory in the name of the United States. After extensive hearings, the Committee on Foreign Relations found no constitutional justification for Jackson's actions and submitted to the House two resolutions of disapproval. On rational as well as constitutional grounds, Smith supported the resolutions. Despite his claim of friendship toward the general and "the administration that put him in office," Smith thus earned the enmity of supporters of the popular "Hero of New Orleans," who was already being mentioned as a potential presidential candidate. The congressman also defended his vote to abolish the rank of major general on grounds that the small size of the army did not merit the additional rank. That, too, was interpreted by many voters as a slap at Jackson, but in a characteristic manner, Smith resorted to ridicule: "To have a host of officers going about the country with their gold buttons and their fine clothes, without any duty to perform, is well calculated to captivate the eyes of young men, and well suited to divert their minds from more necessary and substantial employments." Also characteristically, the candidate ended his circular in a self-deprecating manner: "I have addressed you this Circular, that those who may not see me may know my views and sentiments in their own clothing, not in the attire that my enemies may wish to dress them in— My constituents are mostly plain farmers, and when I address any thing to them I endeavor to do it in a language and style that they can comprehend—I do not fit it up for the palate of the critic or the learned. Permit me, fellow-citizens, to subscribe myself your humble Servant."

Reelected, Smith was appointed to the Committee on Accounts at the first session of the new Congress in December 1819, and in that capacity he recommended, contrary to his vote in the previous session, that the house "doth approve" the expenditure of $24,907.37½ for furnishing the hall and offices of the House of Representatives.[26] Among other expenditures, he supported funds for the fourth decennial census, including proposals to expand it to include enumeration of agriculture, manufacturing, and the professions. Supporting a motion to increase the compensation for marshals for their additional work on the census, Smith contrasted distances within the sections of country. When a New England representative estimated that a marshal could enter three thousand persons on a "market day," Smith said a census-taker in the South might be able to enter only a hundred households a day by riding thirty or forty miles by horse.[27]

At the continued first session in February, debate on the Missouri statehood bill took up much of the time and included many hours-long speeches. While Smith generally voted against amendments to limit slavery, he voted for one inhibiting slavery in territories north of 36° 30" latitude. He voted for a resolution to abolish the Military Academy at West Point but against an appropriation for old soldiers, and he remained opposed to spending federal funds on the Cumberland Road and other internal improvements—that despite his avowed stand on the subject.[28]

An interesting exchange occurred during his first session when Smith objected to a bill to aid "certain sufferers by the late fire at Savannah," which proposed the remission of import duties in the port of Savannah following a disaster there. He argued that Congress had no power to "disburse the public moneys in acts of charity or generosity, or for other purposes than those designated in the Constitution."[29] Representative Thomas W. Cobb of Georgia, remembering an earlier congressional concession to the North Carolina delegation, embarrassed Smith by asking, "Where ... was [sic] the scruples he [Smith] now expressed, when, the other day, a bill passed to remit the duties on a statue of Washington, imported by the State of North Carolina; and what was there in that case to make it stronger than this?" This, of course, was reference to the arrival from Italy of Antonio Canova's statue of President Washington, in classical attire, that was destroyed when the State House in Raleigh burned the following year.

Smith's most substantive legislative efforts related to his cosponsorship of a resolution proposing a constitutional amendment to alter the means of choosing electors for president and vice-president. The Senate had twice passed the resolution, but it was now being considered in the House. At that time, electors were chosen as determined by individual state legislatures. In April 1820, Smith's arguments for the resolution occupied nearly four double-columned pages in the *Annals*. In it, he explained that the proposed amendment would enable each state to be laid out into "as many districts as such a State shall be entitled, under the Constitution and laws of the United States, to elect Representatives to Congress, and that each district shall, as nearly as can, be composed of contiguous territory, and the same district shall elect one Elector to vote for President of the United States and for Vice President. The other two Electors to which each State shall be entitled shall be elected by the States, in such manner as the Legislature thereof shall direct."[30]

His explanation of the inequity of the current law portended his logical thinking on many other political issues: It was possible, he said, "by a species of league, of bargain and sale, to place a person in this high office [of president], who shall only have the votes of three-tenths of the people, contrary to the wishes and the interests of seven-tenths of the people of the United States." Using the states of Massachusetts, New York, Pennsylvania,

Virginia, and North Carolina as examples, he demonstrated that with but a slim majority in each of those five states casting ballots for the same [Federalist] party, they could override all remaining states, regardless of the latter's popular vote. He continued, "The number of Senators in the twenty-two states is 44; the number of Representatives is 186—making, in all, 230; which would be the whole number of votes given for a President: a majority of 230 is 116, which happens to be exactly the number of votes to which the five States above mentioned are entitled. Now suppose that every man in the seventeen States not mentioned, should be [R]epublican, and nearly one half of the five states enumerated [R]epublican also, does it not amount clearly that seven-tenths are defeated by three-tenths of the people?"

He continued, "The census of 1810 gave the population of the United States at 7,500,000. The five large States have one half of that number, say 3,750,000; now, as the federal majority was a bare majority in these States, there will be only in these States 1,870,000 Federalists, who will have elected the President, to the exclusion of a candidate having the united voice of seventeen States, and almost a majority of the other five, and against the votes of 6,630,000 of the people."[31]

Smith concluded by describing North Carolina's sectionalism in which numerous small eastern counties with populations less than those in western counties controlled the state legislature, a situation that the state constitution could not address without the call of a convention—a power not granted in the existing constitution.[32]

In December 1820 the *Annals* noted that Smith "went into a defence, considerably at large, of the expediency of the amendment"—a speech so lengthy that it was not printed. The fate of the resolution was probably sealed in January when John Randolph of Virginia "expressed the grounds of his hostility to this resolution, which he considered as proposing a pernicious innovation on the Constitution, under the influence of fanciful and theoretical notions, under circumstances of the House and of the country not favorable to a correct decision." When the final vote was taken, the count was 92 for, 54 against, a large majority but not quite the two-thirds required to propose a constitutional amendment.[33] Thus, by just a few votes, Smith lost on the issue to which he had given major effort and on which a victory would have put his name in the history books. The matter, however, would be revisited and the proposal would be enacted in the future. Twenty-two years later when the proposed amendment was again being considered by the United States Senate, Smith's fellow townsman, William A. Graham, remembered that at the session of 1820, "the Hon. J.S. Smith, of North Carolina, representing the district in which I reside, offered a similar resolution of amendment to the Constitution, in favor of the district system of choosing representatives and electors; and, on the 25th of January, 1821, the vote of the Representatives of the People on the resolution was, yes 92, nays 54; so the proposition to amend the Constitution failed, for want of a majority of two-thirds in its favor, but the recorded vote is a strong indication of popular opinion of the districts."[34]

While in Congress, Smith became interested in purchasing western lands from veterans who had received, under an act of Congress passed on May 6, 1812, grants for their service in the War of 1812. For example, on November 26, 1818, Robert Sargent, former soldier in Foster's Company of the Fifth Regiment, sold to Congressman Smith for $60 a tract containing 160 acres, "being the Northwest quarter of Section twenty-eight of Township fifteen in Range five east in the tract appropriated by certain acts of Congress, for Military Bounties in the Territory of Illinois...." Smith purchased from various servicemen a total of eighteen

While in Congress, Smith bought from soldiers of the War of 1812 tracts of bounty land granted to them in the unoccupied portions of the state of Illinois (courtesy Mary Ruffin Smith Papers, Southern Historical Collection, Wilson Library, UNC-CH).

such grants with expectation that they would increase in value.[35] In 1820 he sought information on one of the soldiers, Lieutenant Cader Parker, from Nathaniel Cutting, an official in the War Department's Section of Bounty Lands. Cutting could give no information on the man by that name, but the communication gave him the opportunity to seek Smith's assistance in the copying of a record extremely valuable to both state and nation. An inquiry to North Carolina's secretary of state, William Hill, had brought a response to Cutting that there existed in Raleigh a complete and authentic return or muster roll of *the North Carolina Law on Continental Establishment.* However, Hill had added that, "having no assistant in his public Labours, he cannot undertake to send *an authentic Transcript* of the Important Record for the Use of the General Government." Perhaps, Cutting suggested, the congressman might be able to obtain a copy, noting, with understatement, "It might be the means of establishing Claims in behalf of some of your Constituents, which the imperfect state of *Revolutionary Military Records* at the seat of Government, since the Conflagration of the War Office in the year 1800, causes to be rejected."[36]

In February 1820 Dennis Heartt established the *Hillsborough Recorder*, the first newspaper published west of Raleigh in the nineteenth century, and from that time the name of Dr. James S. Smith appeared fairly regularly in its pages, either as news or in paid advertising. For example, in the issue of November 8, 1820, Smith announced that Thomas D. Watts had been appointed his agent to transact business for him during his absence in Washington. The following November 29, Editor Heartt announced that the newspaper had moved to the house "opposite Dr. Smith's office, about one hundred yards west of the market house." The two men were usually on the same side politically, and they shared a distaste for the prevailing practice of electioneering, described this way by the editor: "All public places must be attended by the candidate, and intoxicating liquors profusely dealt out at his expense. And often appointments are made for the sole purpose of receiving the candidate's treat—where a certain class of our citizens are sure to attend."[37]

Congressman Smith was not above using the prestige of his office for personal gain. His training in medicine at the University of Pennsylvania had been cut short without a diploma in 1812, but while in Congress he learned that the formation of a "medical society" was being considered in the General Assembly of North Carolina. What would be a more appropriate position for a congressman than to become the head of such an organization? Without a medical degree, he could hardly qualify, so Smith persuaded Dr. Thomas Sewall, a classmate eight years earlier, to become his advocate. In a letter from Washington, dated December 22, 1820, Sewall wrote Dr. William Gibson, professor of surgery at the university, that it would be "of considerable consequence" for the applicant to have an M.D. degree. Sewall attested that Smith "stood high both with the professors & his class" during his "two full courses at Philadelphia & the Hospital practice," 1810–1812. He added that not more than one or two students ranked higher, but because of unavoidable circumstances, Smith had been "under the necessity of returning home immediately after the close of the last course & thereby was deprived of the opportunity of graduating." He concluded, "I cannot believe that the University of Pennsylvania will in any way suffer by granting Dr. S. an honorary degree."

Indeed, it did not suffer, and at commencement on July 26, 1821, "the honorary degree of Doctor of Medicine was conferred on James S. Smith of Hillsborough in the State of North Carolina."[38] It is surprising that Dr. Sewall's recommendation carried so much weight. A year earlier this graduate of Harvard Medical School had been arrested, charged, and found guilty of robbing eight graves in Ipswich, Massachusetts, two of them his own patients.' Forced to leave New England, the doctor moved to the nation's capital (apparently upon Professor Gibson's suggestion), where in 1821 he was appointed professor of anatomy in the National Medical College. Four years later he was a founding faculty member of the medical department at Columbian College (now George Washington University), where he became known for his graphic and colorful drawings of alcohol-diseased stomachs.[39] Although Smith's ambition to head a statewide medical society was thwarted, in Hillsborough he could exhibit a handsome certificate on calfskin identifying himself as a doctor, albeit an honorary rather than an earned degree. Style was as important as substance in early medical practice.[40]

Style also appeared to be important to the University of Pennsylvania itself, for Dr. James S. Smith was promptly added to its board of trustees. There he sat with prominent Americans such as Nicholas Biddle, president of the Bank of the United States; Joseph Rimer, governor of Pennsylvania; and the Rev. Henry U. Onderdonk, bishop of the Protestant Episcopal Diocese of Pennsylvania.[41]

Urged on by political considerations, the University of Pennsylvania granted "Jacobum S. Smith" an honorary doctorate after only two partial years of study in its medical department (courtesy James Strudwick Smith Papers [2930-Z], Southern Historical Collection, Wilson Library, UNC-CH).

With his prestigious medical certificate in hand, Dr. Smith promptly was elected also to the board of trustees of the University of North Carolina. There he served with—in addition to his sometime political adversaries Archibald D. Murphey, Francis Lister Hawks, and Romulus M. Saunders—other prominent citizens including future cabinet members George E. Badger and John Branch, governors Richard Dobbs Spaight, Jr., and Benjamin Smith, senators Montford Stokes and Bartlett Yancey, and chief justices William Gaston and Thomas Ruffin. He remained a trustee the remainder of his life and was adjudged by Kemp Battle as a good one. However, Dr. Smith's interest in the University may not have been entirely altruistic, for in 1824 he proposed the imposition of a student fee for the employment of an official university physician. He offered to take the position if established and, at no additional charge, to conduct an "Eye Infirmary." The proposal was politely rejected, but Smith tried again when, following the death of three students from diseases suspected to have been brought from home, he supported Elisha Mitchell's unsuccessful advocacy of a resident physician. At about the same time, Mitchell, then acting president, and two other faculty members were assaulted by students Augustus Alston and Leonidas King, and the task of trying and expelling the students fell to a committee consisting of Smith, Thomas

D. Bennehan, Duncan Cameron, Francis L. Hawks, Thomas Ruffin, and James Webb—all from Orange County.[42]

It is not clear whether Smith stood for reelection to the Seventeenth Congress in 1821. A letter from "A Citizen" published in the *Hillsborough Recorder* commented that "I believe it is generally understood that our late worthy representative in Congress declines becoming a candidate at the next election.... Should he not again offer his services, the tribute of praise is due to him from his constituents, for his faithful and independent discharge of duty."[43] If he ran, he lost, for he was succeeded by Josiah Crudup, a Baptist preacher from Wake County, who the previous year had been expelled from the state Senate because North Carolina's constitution prohibited ordained ministers from holding public office. Also elected to the Congress that year was Romulus M. Saunders, a sharp-tongued Caswell County Jacksonian and a Smith antagonist, who wrote Thomas Ruffin, "I have learnt here to my surprize that yr. representative [James S. Smith] is unfriendly to [William H.] Crawford. If this be a fact he ought to be put down in Hillsb. I hope you will see to it, for if North Carolina equivocates, he [Crawford] is gone."[44] Saunders may have been mistaken, because Smith remained friendly to Crawford, although he preferred John Quincy Adams. Party politics, fairly dormant during the "Era of Good Feelings," was again raising its ugly head.

Modern view of the Masonic Lodge, Hillsborough, on whose building committee Dr. Smith served. Upon his return from congressional service, Smith was swiftly elevated to Grand Master without going through the usual ranks. He owned portions of the lots west and north of the lodge (H.G. Jones collection).

While still in Congress, September 8, 1819, Smith was accepted as "Entered Apprentice" in Hillsborough's Eagle Lodge No. 71, A.F. and A.M., and quickly was raised to the degree of Master Mason. Within three years, he was elected Grand Marshal of the Grand Lodge of North Carolina for 1822–23 with James Iredell, Joseph H. Bryan, Richard Dobbs Spaight, William Boylan, and Benjamin A. Barham his assisting officers. The following year Robert Strange was Grand Master and Francis Lister Hawks the Deputy Grand Master. Dr. Smith was moving in high circles. His biographer, understating the obvious, considered it "remarkable" that one who had never been elected to a regular office in his own lodge should become the leader of all Masons in North Carolina in so short a time. The author added, "His Masonic career must have been meteoric, to say the least." Back in Hillsborough, Smith was elected to a committee charged with the construction of a new brick Masonic Hall on property bought from William Norwood and located "next door" to Smith's own home. And on November 22, 1823, he was in charge of laying the new building's cornerstone "in Masonic Order." In the following decade, Smith was elected a commissioner of police and, with Cadwallader Jones and James Webb, served on a committee to build a stone jail.[45]

Sectional conflict in North Carolina was not new, but as settlers took up lands in the piedmont and mountain regions, tensions between east and west grew to a breaking point. Dr. Smith, echoing his opposition to the unfair system of electing presidents, joined the fray. The problem lay in the Constitution of 1776 under which each county, without regard to population, was allotted one state senator and two representatives in the House of Commons. Additionally, the towns of Edenton, Halifax, Hillsborough, New Bern, Salisbury, and Wilmington sent a representative each to the House of Commons (Fayetteville was added in 1789). As newcomers substantially increased the population of western counties covering large areas, the controlling easterners were reluctant to create new counties that would reduce their control of the two houses. The unfairness was magnified with each passing decade, and the growth of sectionalism threatened the unity of the state. The problem was exaggerated by the fact that the Constitution provided no specific means of amendment. While in Congress, James S. Smith had criticized unequal representation, and back home he worked tirelessly to correct the problem at the state level. Public meetings sprang up, demanding amendments to the state constitution to correct its most objectionable provisions—unequal representation being the first one. The problem was addressed particularly at Fourth of July celebrations. In 1822, among 24 toasts, one refers to the state constitution as "It wants mending"; in 1823, of 13 toasts, one of them characterized the constitution this way: "We think it *is* defective and *ought* to be amended." And at a public muster Thomas Ruffin, Willie P. Mangum, and James S. Smith were recommended as "proper persons" to represent Orange at a forthcoming statewide meeting to propose constitutional amendments.[46]

Years before—in 1816—a group of western legislators had formed themselves into a "Convention Committee" and published a report, edited by Orange County's Senator Archibald D. Murphey.[47] The committee found several defects in the original constitution, the most glaring of which was inequality of representation in the General Assembly. There were at the time sixty-two counties with a statewide total white population of 386,676. Of the counties, thirty-seven with a population of only 152,586 whites sent 111 members to the legislature, while twenty-five counties with a white population of 234,090 were represented by only 75 members. If the ratio of legislators to population were equally apportioned, the first-mentioned thirty-seven counties would be entitled to only 74 members and the other twenty-five counties would be entitled to 112 members. Based on equality, legislative representation would range from one delegate each in fifteen counties (all but one in the east) to five each for Mecklenburg and Wake, six for Lincoln, seven for Orange, and eight for Rowan—all in the west. Without reapportionment, Murphey warned, the "time is not distant, when, without some change in the Constitution, three fourths of the people will be under the domination of one fourth."

The committee found other defects in the Constitution—examples being annual elections, short terms, and an excessive number of delegates in each house. Surprisingly, in view of Murphey's other progressive views, the report was critical of the early age for voting qualification. One wonders if he might have had in mind young James Smith when he wrote, "The ardour and inexperience of youth are not suited to the sober and complicated purposes of legislation." The committee proposed that voters casting ballots for legislators at the next election write on the ballots the words "Convention" or "No Convention," that sheriffs count those votes, and that the results be reported to the governor and General Assembly. The committee's report bore no fruit in the following General Assembly.

Smith's taste for politics had not been satiated by his congressional service, and he was hardly back in Hillsborough before he ran for and won election in 1821 as representative to the House of Commons from Hillsborough, one of seven towns granted a seat in the General Assembly on the basis of the English borough system.[48] That session featured a resolution by Salisbury's Charles Fisher calling for a more formal referendum in which the people would vote for or against a convention to address the reapportionment issue and other weaknesses of the Constitution of 1776. Fisher revised the figures published by Murphey in 1816 by showing that the representational imbalance had become even more pronounced. The debate in the House of Commons featured arguments from some of the most eloquent speakers representing both the east and west. Among the most vociferous advocates for convention was Hillsborough's Smith, who, in supporting his case, repeatedly quoted Emerich de Vattel, an eighteenth century Swiss philosopher and jurist whose legal writings advocated liberal revolution on the basis of natural laws. Among the representatives who most strongly opposed the convention bill, also quoting Vattel, was the borough delegate representing New Bern, 24-year-old Francis Lister Hawks.[49] The debate, which occupied two days in December 1821, was important enough for Joseph Gales to take down in shorthand the lengthy speeches and subsequently to publish them in book form.[50] Predictably, the easterners prevailed, and the report of the committee of the whole, recommending rejection of the convention resolution, was passed 81 to 47. Similar resolutions in the Senate fared no better; the journal curtly reported, "owing to the pressure of business, and the Session being near its close, they underwent no discussion" and were postponed indefinitely by a vote of 36 to 23.

Thomas Clancy was elected as the Hillsborough delegate the following year, so he probably was a member of the "Friends of Convention," a caucus that met during the 1822 legislative session and, noting the absence of a means of amending the constitution, recommended again that in the next year's election voters in each county be given a choice to vote for or against a convention. Under the proposal, voters would also choose delegates (one for every 5,000 population) to attend such convention if approved by a majority in the respective counties.[51] Enough counties voted for convention, and Orange, whose vote was 1,158 to 4 in the affirmative, sent Smith—along with Willie P. Mangum, Michael Holt, and Thomas Ruffin—as a delegate to the resulting convention that met in Raleigh November

10–15, 1823.[52] Interestingly, the only eastern county represented was Cumberland, some of whose voters might have envisioned a deal with the western delegates in which—in return for their support for reapportionment—Fayetteville might be favored for the relocation of the state capital, still too far west for many easterners. The extralegal convention included among its delegates men whose names were, or soon would be, familiar throughout the state, including a former governor, a future senator, and future congressmen and judges. Except for his appointment to a seven-member committee to "enquire into the most advisable plan for submitting the amendments to the Constitution agreed upon by this Convention, to the people, for their ratification," James Smith's contributions are not identified. Delegates were requested to contribute four dollars each to cover all costs of the convention, including the printing of one hundred copies of the convention proceedings and five hundred copies each of the existing constitution and the constitution as proposed to be amended.

For another decade, even so powerful a combination of respected leaders of the state failed to overcome the firmness with which the eastern counties held legislative reins. Not until 1834, by which time secessionist sentiments were growing in the west, did the General Assembly finally agree to a referendum on a convention. In the intervening years, James Smith practiced medicine, dabbled in real estate, and worked against Andrew Jackson in the race to succeed President Monroe. Smith wanted to vote for John Quincy Adams for president in 1824, but the New Englander's name was not allowed on the ballot in Orange County. The hero of New Orleans carried Orange by fewer than 40 votes over William H. Crawford. The vote nationally was so close that the decision was finally settled in the United States House of Representatives, where Adams was elected.[53]

Smith continued to reveal his Whig leanings. Although he still supported John Quincy Adams, in 1825 he predicted to Congressman Willie P. Mangum that Jackson would be the next president, his "want of good Moral character notwithstanding." He worried, moreover, that the slavery issue was becoming "a bone of contention between the north & the south & it has been a matter of doubt with me whether Mr Adams has not been one of the prime movers of the Missouri question." Although normally stingy on the expenditure of federal funds, Smith complimented Mangum for voting for a congressional gift of $200,000 to the Marquis de Lafayette, adding with reference to the aging Nathaniel Macon's vote in the negative, "Some have ventured to anathematize *Uncle Natt* for his vote. But be assured that although the good feelings of the house & of the nation gave the money & the land & I rejoiced that they did so—yet I think that Mr Macons ground is a Just & tenable one & with me his vote is but an other proof of the Stability of that miserable old Mans principles[.]" He added, "I believe that I can say to you from a very respectable authority that you will not have Mr Crudup [who had served between Smith's and Mangum's terms] on the turf next August.... I hope that you will [have] no opposition."[54]

Within two weeks (February 9), Smith reversed his prediction and wrote, "It is thought here, that Adams will be president, from the last accounts; & the Jackson people are in an ill humor, as might be supposed—for myself, I shall be content altho not pleased." He made a personal request of Mangum to pay his unspecified debt to Secretary of War John C. Calhoun, noting that it would save him from the risk of transmitting currency by mail. Furthermore, he did not know the amount of discount "on our money," not expecting Calhoun to require a discount but feeling "bound to reimburse him fully with interest for his kindness."[55]

One of Dr. James Strudwick Smith's most noteworthy achievements was the establishment of the Hillsborough Female Academy, chartered by Chapter 69 in *Private Laws of North Carolina, 1824.* Several schools had operated previously in the town, including an original Hillsborough Academy, which in 1801 was "opened upon a more extensive Plan [than formerly] for the Reception of Youth of both Sexes, under the Management of the Rev. Mr. Andrew Flinn." Eleven years later the Rev. William Bingham, formerly head of Pittsborough Academy, took over the school and engaged Elizabeth Russell to superintend the female department. In 1818, Bingham moved to the Hawfields and conducted Mt. Repose Academy, only to return to Hillsborough Academy in 1826. John Witherspoon and John Rogers served as principal during the interregnum. In 1825, Hillsborough Academy was converted into an all-male classical school designed to prepare boys for entrance to the University of North Carolina. Its trustees were William Norwood, Francis Nash, David Yarborough, William Kirkland, Francis L. Hawks, James Webb, John Taylor, A.B. Bruce, and James Phillips.[56]

Dr. Smith was joined in chartering the Hillsborough Female Academy in 1824 by Walker Anderson, William Cain, Jr., Thomas Faddis, Frederick Nash, John Scott, and Jonathan Sneed. The seven were declared a "body politic and corporate, known and distinguished by the name of 'The Trustees of Hillsborough Female Academy,' and by that name and style shall have perpetual succession and ... shall be able and capable in law, to take, demand, receive and possess, money, goods and chattels, lands and tenements, for the use of the said Academy, and apply the same according to the will of the donor."[57]

The new female school was located in the southeast quadrant of the town on what was designated as Lot 43, facing north on Margaret Lane. Jean Anderson's research, based on court records, indicates that the property, once owned by the Brooks family, was reclaimed by the town commissioners some time before 1824, in which year a "brick school house" was erected and allowed to be used by the trustees of the new Hillsborough Female Academy.[58] For many years, under the superintendence of the Rev. William Mercer Green and with teachers such as Maria Louisa Spear and Elizabeth Smith, the academy held a reputation as one of the best schools for girls in North Carolina. Conveniently located near both the superintendent's residence and St. Matthew's Church, the academy was virtually an adjunct of the church. To reach the school from her father's home on Lot 22, Mary Ruffin Smith had only to walk along King Street less than a block to Churton Street, southward around the county courthouse, and eastward five blocks on Margaret Lane. Nearby lived Susan Baker, who provided a home for her sister, the elder Maria Spear and the latter's children, as well as some students.

Mary Ruffin Smith, eleven years old in 1825 and, unlike her brothers, ineligible to attend the original academy, may have inspired her father's activism in establishing the separate school for girls. On behalf of the other trustees, Dr. Smith called upon Congressman Willie P. Mangum to "inquire of your acquaintances from New England, whether a Suitable Lady could not be procured from there, to take charge of the school in this place." A good building had been completed, but there was no endowment sufficient to offer a specific salary; yet the success of the older academy under John Rogers suggested that "if a suitable Lady & Gentleman, possessing the requisite character & qualifications were to take the School, that they could make in a year or two a handsome business of it." Smith inferred that the male trustees would find it delicate to deal solely with a female as head of the school, and he exhibited a sexist attitude by opining that some subjects, such as English grammar and geography, were "never so well taught by a female as by a male teacher." However, if a male-female couple could not be found, he groaned, "we must do the best we can, & will have to take a lady alone."[59]

No record has been found of a response by Mangum, but Smith's quest to attract teachers to Hillsborough encouraged at least two families to become associated with female education in North Carolina. The first is mentioned in the announcement of the new Hillsborough Female Academy in 1825: "The Exercises of this Institution will commence on the first day of August, under the immediate care of Miss Lavinia Brainerd, and under the inspection and superintendence of Rev. William M. Green." Studies were to be divided into four classes; in addition, special instruction would be available in music, drawing, painting, needlework, and "in making Fruit and Flowers in Wax." Tuition for a session was from $10 to $15 per class. Pupils could board with the "most respectable families" at $10 per month; instruction for more advanced pupils was to be provided in "house-wifery and in all the various branches of domestic economy." While attention would be paid to the "ordinary and the ornamental branches of education," the instructors would deem it their "imperious duty to pay especial regard to the morals & manners of the young ladies committed to their care." In the announcement for the second year, the superintendent wrote: "Deeply impressed with the importance of rightly training those who are now the daughters, but are shortly to be the wives and mothers of the community, [he] pledges himself, as before, to exercise parental watchfulness over his pupils, and to give such direction to the instruction of the Seminary, as shall adapt them to the eternal as well as temporal interests of those committed to his care." Thus, while the old academy would prepare boys for the University of North Carolina, the new school would train girls to be good wives and homemakers.[60]

The school's superintendent, William Mercer Green, was an 1818 graduate of the University of North Carolina, where he earned second honors behind James Knox Polk of Mecklenburg County. A native of Wilmington, Green came to Hillsborough's St. Matthew's Episcopal congregation from St. John's in Williamsborough at the behest of precocious Francis Lister Hawks, who himself had moved from New Bern to Hillsborough to study law a couple of years earlier. It was to Green that Hawks first divulged—and received encouragement for—his desire to switch from law to the ministry. In 1825, while Hawks served as a trustee for the boys' academy, Green superintended the new female school. After leaving Hillsborough, both rose to prominence in the Episcopal hierarchy, Green as founder of Chapel Hill's Church of the Cross and eventually bishop of Mississippi, Hawks as the denomination's historiographer and first president of the University of Louisiana. Green contributed significantly to an understanding of early nineteenth-century education by publishing and mailing to many prominent North Carolinians in 1826 a three-page "Tabular View of the Order and Distribution of Studies Observed in the Respective Classes of the Hillsborough Female Seminary." Each department (e.g., orthography, grammar, geography, etc.) identified textbooks and method pursued, then explained the teaching approach.[61]

Lavinia Brainerd—a Vermonter described as "small, with a delicate, refined face, fine teeth and an abundance of auburn hair"—came to Hillsborough after having taught among the Oneida Indians. Simultaneously with her arrival in Hillsborough, her family went to Warrenton, where her father and brother, the Reverends Elijah Brainerd and Carolus Columbus Brainerd, took over the Warrenton Female Academy from Jacob Mordecai and J.D. Plunkett.

The teachers included the elder Brainerd's wife Parthenia and their daughters Ann C. and Susan L. Brainerd. After just one year in Orange County, Lavinia—described in the press as "the recent Directress of the Hillsborough Female Academy"—joined her family in Warrenton. Death stalked the Brainerd family, however; the wife and son died in 1826 and the father succumbed two years later. The result was the return of the Warrenton Female Academy to Mrs. Plunkett, who advertised the buildings for sale. By 1831, Lavinia Brainerd was running South Carolina's prestigious Charleston Female Seminary. There she met and married another New Englander, portrait artist John Goff Rand (1801–1873), who in 1841 patented the screw-cap collapsible paint tube that revolutionized the art of painting. The couple lived in England for many years but eventually settled in New York City.[62]

Whatever eleven-year-old Mary Ruffin Smith thought of Lavinia Brainerd, she fell in love with one of the Vermont teacher's successors, with whom she shared a storied friendship and with whom she shared her home in the fading years of their lives. Maria Louisa Spear, a native of England, arrived in Hillsborough in 1826 with her mother, also named Maria Spear; a brother, William Wallace Spear; a sister, Elizabeth Spear; and an aunt, Susan Esther Baker. The elder Maria died in 1835 and was buried in the cemetery of St. Matthew's Church in Hillsborough. She and both of her daughters taught at the academy, and her son was graduated from the University of North Carolina and became a prominent Episcopalian clergyman.[63]

Except for Mary Ruffin Smith's relationship with the new Chapel of the Cross following the family's move in 1847 to "Oakland," the newly constructed country home near Chapel Hill, little is known about the Smith family's role in organized religion. The eighteenth-century Anglican congregation in Hillsborough was little more than a memory after the Revolution, but at the annual convention of the Diocese of North Carolina in 1825, Bishop John Stark Ravenscroft happily reported, "At Hillsborough a congregation has been formed, and a neat and commodious house of worship commenced, which will be completed during the ensuing summer."[64] In fact, the handsome building was finished in time to play host to the diocesan convention in 1826. The Rev. William M. Green's certificate of organization was accepted, and St. Matthew's, then with just 17 communicants, was admitted into union with the convention. James S. Smith was added to the St. Matthew's vestry in May 1826 (the same year in which the two Maria Spears joined the church), and he was one of the parish's four lay delegates—the other three were Francis L. Hawks, William Norwood, and Thomas Ruffin—to the diocesan convention that year. Mary Ruffin Smith was first listed as a communicant in 1832.[65] Strangely, though, James Smith's name does not appear in future minutes of the conventions or extant records of the church. Despite that silence, Joseph Blount Cheshire, later bishop, wrote, "Associated with these [wardens and vestrymen] in the history of the parish have been others.... There was Dr. James S. Smith, member of Congress from this District, father of my old friend and parishioner, Mary Ruffin Smith ... and others no less worthy."[66] Mary Smith and both of her parents were buried with Episcopalian rites, but no record has been found relating to church relations or funeral services—if any—for Francis and Sidney Smith, who heaped shame upon the family.[67]

Meanwhile, Rector Green, until his departure from Hillsborough in 1838, was a particularly strong spiritual leader in Orange County, attending not only to the chapels of St. Jude's in the western part of the county and St. Mary's east of the county seat, but also to the small private Salem Chapel on Duncan Cameron's plantation. As superintendent of the

Dr. Smith's role in religion is shadowy, but in 1826 he was one of four delegates to the diocesan convention held at the newly consecrated St. Matthew's Episcopal Church in Hillsborough (courtesy J. Boyd Webb).

Hillsborough Female Academy, of which Smith was trustee chairman, Green also utilized its teachers, including both of the Maria Spears, as adjuncts of the church. In 1831, he wrote, "The Sunday School of this Congregation continues to prosper under the judicious care and pious attention of its Directress and Teachers. The Ladies Working Society, also still merits the approbation of the Diocese for its zealous and untiring labour on behalf of this portion of the Church."[68] It is interesting that Smith's name does not appear among the several temperance groups active during his lifetime, although he was publicly critical of other candidates' generosity in providing liquid spirits at poling places.

Dr. Smith considered running for Congress again in 1826. Priestley Mangum wrote his brother Willie P. Mangum, "If [Josiah] Crudup runs, I think Doc. Smith will come out— & *I* think Crudup would beat him *easily* tho' the Doctor thinks that he could beat Crudup easily, which I set down to the Doctor's vanity. These things however have not yet made much stir."[69]

In 1828, Smith was an elector for the "Administration" (Adams) ticket, and Willie P. Mangum was an elector for the Jackson ticket, thus marking their temporary divergence in party association. (Mangum would soon break with the Jacksonians and join the Whigs over the national bank issue.)[70]

Whether or not his recommendation was of value, Smith in 1829 supported his fellow townsman Thomas Ruffin for a judgeship on the State Supreme Court. He discussed the suggestion during a visit from General Alexander Gray of Randolph County, a member of the Council of State, and reported that he had written to Governor Owen. To Ruffin he wrote, "I feel much interest in this matter, first from my own good wishes to you individually, and secondly from a desire to see the Bench of the Supreme Court, such as will confer credit on the State, and insure Justice in the last resort to its citizens." Ruffin joined the court later that year.[71]

Smith announced his candidacy for the state legislature in 1829, now running on a platform advocating internal improvements.[72] His circular letter continued to depend more on appeals to voters' empathy than on clear political issues. Take this for example:

> I think it is apparent to all persons who will take the pains to reflect, that my case is essentially different from the other candidates. With the farmer, harvest is over, and he can entrust to his sons, or overseer, the care of his farm, whilst he is absent. The merchant can have his clerk, who can vend his goods at the prices marked, receive his cash, and post bill books, as well as if the principal were present. The lawyer has no courts to call his attention, so that he is at liberty to absent himself without prejudice to his client. Not so with the physician. Is his harvest at hand? If so, no one can reap but himself; no clerk, deputy, or overseer will do, no one but the physician himself. With these explanatory remarks, I will venture to submit my election to a generous and intelligent people, whose kind and liberal support on former occasions claims of me the humble tribute of my most profound respect, and has imprinted in my memory a sense of gratitude which death alone can efface.

With that introduction, Smith launched two attacks—on the "banking system of North Carolina, from the great errors and oversights in its original charter, with the bad management of those who have been charged with its concerns, has greatly disappointed the hopes and expectations of the public"; the other, mismanagement of internal improvements, whose failures he blamed on "wild schemes of visionary theorists, unskilled pretenders in the character of engineers, and dishonest contractors." His facile solution: "Let North-Carolina procure competent persons skilled in these matters. Let the most important points be first examined; the practicality of their improvement ascertained; the expenses of effecting them estimated." He added simply, "I cannot say what other subjects may be brought before the legislature, and therefore I can only say, that I will exercise my best judgment on all matters that may be presented to me to act upon." Of course, he added that he had no predisposition to disparage the pretensions of his opponents: "It is to you I confide the issue. Should it be in my favor, I shall be gratified; if against me, it is also my duty to acquiesce." He was not elected.

Smith appears to have been an unsuccessful candidate for state Senate in 1832. William Montgomery wrote Willie P. Mangum[73]: "[T]here is warm work pending between doctor Smith and me. He has made the attempt, as I expected to rally the Clay men against me, in private, but with the exception of Joshua Johnson, he has failed."

Archibald Murphey died penniless in 1832, but his zeal for internal improvements became infectious—even to Dr. Smith—particularly with the extension of the Petersburg railroad southward to Blakely in Northampton County the following year. James J. Jeffries of Red House in Caswell County opened a "Four Horse Post Coach" on which, for a fare of $7, travelers from Hillsborough could reach Blakely in 25 hours, arriving just in time to catch the "car" to Petersburg and places north. Excitement swept the state, and "conventions" were held in the Piedmont to rally support. At a mass meeting of Orange County citizens on September 3, 1833, fifteen men, including James S. Smith, Thomas Ruffin, John Webb, and Willie P. Mangum, were elected to represent the county at a district convention, at which, when it met the following week, the delegates conducted a contested election for the chairmanship. Judge Thomas Ruffin was elected for the honor over Governor David L. Swain by a vote of 26 to 16; the governor, a mountaineer, may have had less enthusiasm toward the railroad as a new mode of transportation. Leading proponents called for an extension of the line from Blakely westward through Hillsborough. On this issue, Dr. Smith and his frequent opponent for political office, Dr. Montgomery, worked together. During the convention, Christopher Barbee, Sr., ran a "Lost or Mislaid" advertisement in *The Harbinger*: "Two Notes of Hand, executed by Dr. James S. Smith to Christopher Barbee, senr. One for about ninety five dollars, given about year 1825 or '26, date not recollected, and has a credit in it of about twenty-four dollars—The other Note for about twenty dollars, given either in the year 1829 or '30. I forewarn all persons from trading for either of the above Notes, or the maker from paying to anyone but myself."[74]

James Graham of Rutherfordton in 1833 wrote his brother William A. Graham, "I am informed you are a Candidate for the Town of Hillsboro and I feel a deep solicitude for your election but as your competitor Smith is *great in small things* I am fearful the result is doubt-ful. Let me know as early as possible what is the event."[75]

Smith wrote Senator Willie Mangum in 1834, "It may be gratifying to you to lear[n] that all the intelligent part of the people approve the course you are persuing [*sic*] so far as it has been yet developed on the Bank Question—I think as far as I am able to fathom public sentiment[,] a counter current is beginning to tell against the Hero & Co—O! How the folks are repenting of their political sins here, Nash—Waddell—Scott—Jones—Moore &c. &c.—I do believe that if Hillsboro was poled tomorrow that Jackson would get but one vote in it—and that would be Child." Curiously he added, "Go ahead Judge (as Davy Crockett says) you will find N.C. with you in due time in my opinion—Say to Mr. Calhoun that his speech has almost made nullifiers of us here, even Dr. Webb says that nullification is not half so bad as he thought it was at first."[76] At Independence Day festivities, Smith gave a strange toast on "nullification and the American system, the two political extremes, and when they meet we may hope for political purity and security." He was again elected one of the commissioners of police in Hillsborough.[77]

Aggrieved advocates of legislative reapportionment continued to lose their battle— even after an extralegal plebiscite in 1833 overwhelmingly favored convention. There was outright talk of secession, but, fortunately, additional issues and changing political views— solvable only by amending the Constitution of 1776—gradually produced allies. Among them were the religious test for officeholding, free Negro suffrage, qualifications for judges, and annual gubernatorial elections. Finally, in early 1835, both houses of the legislature yielded to a plebiscite, some easterners assuming that they could defeat the convention effort. The results revealed the depths of sectionalism: pro-convention forces won 27,550 to 21,694 statewide, but only 3,611 easterners favored the convention and just 2,701 westerners opposed it. Orange's vote for convention was 1,648 to 111.[78] Smith, who had recently been elected one of the town's police commissioners, promptly announced his candidacy for delegate and issued a long statement in the local paper promising to work for the abolition of borough representation, reduction of the size of the General Assembly, limitation of General Assembly sessions to 50 days biennially, popular election of the governor, abolition of double-officeholding for judges, and a provision for future amendments to the constitution.[79] In the election for two delegates from Orange, Dr. William Montgomery led the ticket with 785 votes, followed by Smith with only 331, just 11 votes more than the third-placer, Joseph Allison. The fact that more than 1,500 additional votes were split between eight other candidates revealed Smith's relative weakness among the voting population in this particular election.

Despite Smith's narrow election margin, in the convention that opened in Raleigh on June 4, 1835, he showed no humility, becoming involved in controversies from the beginning.[80] When two secretarial positions were proposed, Smith, sensing that the two nominees represented different political factions, moved unsuccessfully for a differentiation between recording and reading secretaries so that neither would consider himself subordinate. He wanted to avoid anything like "party spirit," wishing all would "consider only what would best promote the public good." He also became embroiled in the selection of a printer, suggesting a committee of three to have the printing done on the best terms and afterward to audit the account. When it became clear that politics rather than economy would dictate the selection, 48-year-old Smith described himself as an humble man who "had not the advantage of all the new lights which other gentlemen possessed, and it was because he was old fashioned, that he deprecated the whole system of electioneering, caucusing, &c."

That Smith was still held in considerable respect, however, was indicated by his appointment to a committee, chaired by William Gaston, to recommend procedures for the convention. When a proposal was made to add seats in the hot and sultry meeting room to accommodate the public, the doctor objected. A throng of visitors on the floor, he said, would "add greatly to the heat of the room: diseases had been generated by crowding people too closely together in hot weather." Smith's point was supported; and on a motion to invite only ladies and ministers of the Gospel to witness the proceedings, Judge Gaston joined him in opposition, observing that "Ladies would feel a delicacy in coming here unattended by their *beaux*; and we have already voted to exclude the latter." On the question of committees, Smith—whether in good humor or sarcasm—favored select committees to afford members an opportunity for "letting off some of the surplus gas, which evidently seeks vent here, and the sooner it escaped the better."

Perhaps surprisingly, Smith was appointed to represent his congressional district on the Select Committee composed of several of the leading statesmen of the day, including Daniel Barringer, John Branch, Charles Fisher, William Gaston, William B. Meares, John Motley Morehead, and Governor David L. Swain. Thus, he was among the major players on virtually all of the issues facing the convention. His influence was tested early when he moved to abolish borough representation in the House of Commons. Calling attention to the fact that he had represented Hillsborough as a borough representative fourteen years earlier, he recognized the "evils" arising from their annual elections which, he said, were "productive of feuds, quarrels and bloodshed! Mechanics and others are excited by the parties interested in such elections, business is neglected, and the morals of the people are corrupted." If towns were deprived of members, the same men could be elected as county representatives, and no talent would be lost. The strongest opposing view came from William Gaston, who pointed out that voters in the boroughs had provided many of the votes by which the convention was authorized, thus implying considerable sympathy with western views. Governor David L. Swain (also sitting as a delegate from Buncombe), while supporting representation from the larger towns, suggested a possible compromise by "withdrawing from the estimate, in the apportionment of representatives to the counties, the population and revenue of these boroughs."[81]

Smith strongly supported an amendment for biennial sessions of the General Assembly. He said that of the annual expenditure of $70,000 for the operation of the state government, $45,000 was consumed by the legislature; what, he asked, were the benefits accruing to the country from this expenditure? His proposed limit of fifty days per biennium failed. He preferred voting by ballot; instead, an amendment was adopted requiring voting *viva voce*.[82]

On the subject of voting rights, Smith argued that free Negroes were citizens under the constitution. Still, he was averse to having the convention express itself on so "abstract" an opinion as their access to the ballot box. He believed that "this class of persons ought not to be deprived entirely of the right of suffrage; he would give those possessing $100 value of real estate, a right to vote." Accordingly, he voted against the amendment (passed 66 to 61) to abrogate the right of free Negroes to vote.[83]

Dr. Smith was less tolerant on the proposal to change the religious test allowing only Protestants to hold office, arguing that when man enters into society, he has to surrender a portion of his natural rights. He noted that the 31st constitutional article prohibited any minister of the Gospel—a class of men "perhaps better qualified than any other to perform the duties of office"—from holding a seat in the legislature. The implication was that *natural* rights did not extend to religious beliefs; furthermore, no doubt alluding to William Gaston, he pointed out that Catholics had not been "excluded" because "they had held seats in the Legislative Hall, and occupied the highest seats on the Judicial Branch." The constitutional restriction, therefore, was a dead letter. But instead of deleting the provision, he urged that it be laid aside as "Sleeping Thunder, to be called up only when necessary to defeat some deep laid scheme of ambition." Governor Swain disliked retention of "the Sleeping Thunder" to be used in some emergency, fearing that men in power might abuse it by "Dealing damnation round the land / On all they deem'd their foe." During the lengthy debate, William Gaston pointed out that Smith had supported repeal of the article when resolutions were adopted by the "Western Convention" in 1823. The Craven delegate also took note of the narrow margin by which Smith had been elected a delegate to the current convention, thus questioning how accurately he was representing the views of his fellow citizens of Orange County. Smith no doubt bristled as he explained that there had been ten candidates, and despite his narrow margin of victory, he considered himself as representing the whole county. He snapped that he was born and raised there, and "ought to be presumed to know the feelings and wishes of the people." Noting that he had been called a bigot, he imagined himself "about as free from the influence of Priestcraft as any gentleman on that floor." Still, he was "not willing, by expunging this Article, to let in Turks, Hindoos and Jews." When the issue was finally put to a vote, Smith was joined by Orange's other delegate, William Montgomery, in voting with the minority against the amendment that substituted the word "Christian" for "Protestant." The tally was 74 to 51.[84]

The amendments proposed by the Convention of 1835 still faced a referendum, the results of which were about as sectional in nature as had been the call for the convention. Pro-ratification forces won by a few more than 5,000 votes, but the sectional split remained unhealed—26,771 for and 21,606 against. Only 2,327 easterners voted for the amendments and just 3,280 westerners opposed. Orange County favored adoption 1,031 to 246.[85] Under the newly amended constitution, the easterners remained in control of the state Senate, but western counties were apportioned more seats in the House. Combined, the amendments presaged fifteen years of progressive government, much of it envisioned years earlier by Archibald D. Murphey, by then dead for three years. At a Fourth of July celebration at Gravely Hall in the Hawfields community, John Hart, predicting Dr. Smith's election to the legislature, offered a toast to Dr. Smith, "at home now, in Raleigh next winter—two guns and three cheers." He was wrong; Dr. Smith would spend all of his remaining winters in Orange County.

In December 1835 Smith wrote William A. Graham, recently the borough representative for Hillsborough: "I see that you have stormy times & that party promises to run high before the termination of the session. I am unable from any thing that I can learn to know whether the friends of Mr. Van Buren will attempt a legislative nomination for the next presidency. But it is certain I presume that an Electoral ticket will be made out before the end of the session."

The exceedingly long letter continued,

> Now if the opposition do not use great prudence in forming their ticket[,] defeat is certain. We have original Anti-Jackson men, the seceders from the Jackson party, and the Nullifiers. We have White men, Harrison men, & Webster men, and Clay men, & Calhoun men. Now if some plan is not fixed upon to unite all these interests defeat is certain. Would it not be well to form a ticket on the plan of the old *Murphy* ticket which gave the vote of the State to Jackson against the caucus nomination of Crawford? That ticket united all the discordant materials that then existed. I would say that the matter should be seriously considered before a final nomination should be had. I congratulate you and all our western friends on the ratification of the amendments to the Constitution. I hope that a new era will be formed in the legislative history of the State.

Smith then turned to a subject that no doubt had been preying upon his mind; it reveals the seriousness with which he treated some subjects to which most politicians paid little attention:

I presume that before you rise you will designate a suitable candidate to fill the executive office under the new Constitution. What direction the public mind may take on this subject I do not pretend to know nor who may be a favourite of the legislature. But as I entertain an opinion on this subject, which may not be common but which will influence me in my vote and in the exercise of any little influence I may possess I presume I may without any offense suggest it to you. I have then determined that I will not vote for any man under the new order of things for Governor who is a Lawyer. Do not suppose that I am going to proclaim war against you and your talented and respectable fraternity[,] very far from it. No one who is not of the profession entertains more respect for the talents and usefulness of that body than I do. But my reasons are these: The gentlemen of the law have the exclusive monopoly of fifteen of the important offices of the State—3 Superior Court Judges, 6 Circuit Judges, the Attorney General, the Solicitor General, and 4 Solicitors—engrossing exclusively upwards of 26,000 dollars of the public revenue with one third of the members of the legislature making 15,000 thousand dollars more. Here then is 40,000 dollars[,] more than one half of the whole revenue of the State with all the places of Honour and profit going to one class to the exclusion of the great mass of the people.

The letter—almost a treatise—continued:

Now I do humbly concur that there should be at least one high office in the State reserved as a reward for long services and experience in political life which should be conferred on some citizen who does not belong to the profession of the law. Is not there sufficient liberty, integrity, and political experience to be found out of the legal profession to fill the executive office? I do concur that there is. Would not an executive recommendation to improve the system of the Judiciary carry home force with it and seem more disinterested if it come from a man not of the profession?

I think then that the profession should act in this matter with a spirit of liberality in this particular. Would not such a course arrest that spirit of Jealousy that pervades the community against lawyers holding offices in the legislature—at least in some degree? Even will [sic] informed and liberal minded men will find this Jealousy for they know the great advantages that the lawyers have—their constant intercourse together—their riding extensive Circuits— and the well known Esprit du chouer [sic] of the profession, etc.

These are some of the reasons that influence my mind; they may be selfish or illiteral [sic] in the eyes of some but for my own part I think them reasonable and capable of being sustained on the soundest and most liberal principles.

Finally, having relieved himself of a profound concern, the doctor concluded, "I presume your session will close before the first of the new year as your term according to my construction of the ordinance of the Convention, is out then. I should think that no very important matters should be taken up during this session."[86]

Perhaps stung by Gaston's sarcasm during debates in the constitutional convention earlier in the year, Smith may have left early, because his name does not appear again in the journal. The doctor was not yet ready to retire from politics, however, and in 1836 he was an elector for the Whig ticket of Hugh L. White for president and John Tyler for vicepresident. Although Van Buren carried Orange County 1,162 to 905, White led in Hillsborough 202–107.[87] Smith was spoken of as a senate candidate against Joseph Allison and Hugh Waddell, but he may not have run. However, the Anti-Jackson ticket received eleven electoral votes in 1836.[88]

Francis and Sidney Smith Enter the Fray

Meanwhile, trouble was brewing in Smith's own household. The doctor's two sons appeared on the political scene—Francis Jones Smith and James Sidney Smith—both fresh from attending (but not graduating from) the University of North Carolina, of which their father was a trustee. Both burst upon the public scene at Hillsborough's Independence Day ceremonies in 1839, when they volunteered toasts. Frank drank to a "speedy union to every lad and lass—days of ease, and weeks of pleasure—may the wing of love never lose a feather." Sidney's was more patriotic—to Orange County, "the land of our birth and the home of our affection—may attachment to every foot of her soil, and to all the great interests of her citizens, be our ruling passion through life." Frank was already being addressed as doctor, but 21-year-old Sidney's predilection toward politics displayed itself in 1840 when he emerged as chairman of the resolution committee for the Democratic-Republican Party (forerunner of the antebellum Democratic Party). In opposition to his father's Whigs, Sidney and fellow Jacksonians advocated strict construction of the constitution and a metallic medium of currency but opposed a national bank. The young Democrat made quite an impression on a newspaper reporter: "His speech both in the sentiments expressed and manner of delivery could have done credit to a much older head." Meanwhile, his father boasted to his neighbors that he had served in Congress with both William Henry Harrison and John Tyler, the Whig nominees for president and vice-president in 1840.[89]

The campaign between Whig Harrison and Democrat Van Buren was a bruising one in Orange, and relations between father and son must have been strained to the breaking point. The Whig-leaning *Hillsborough Recorder*, while extending coverage to both camps, no doubt went to more effort in reporting on the Whig campaign. Log cabin meetings and the speeches of Dr. Smith, chairman of the "Central Committee of Orange," were frequently mentioned. One mass meeting at the Masonic Hall in September was attended by United States Senator Bedford Brown, a Democrat from Caswell County. The editor reported, "The speaking was commenced by Dr. James S. Smith; he entertained the company in quite an animated strain for nearly two hours, giving much valuable information in relation to the political history of the country, and occasionally illustrating his points with amusing and appropriate anecdotes. His speech was plain and comprehensive, and well calculated to powerful effects upon the minds of his hearers." Smith then yielded to Senator Brown, who spoke for two hours but "threw few new lights upon the question in debate." Whig Senator Willie P. Mangum, who had broken with President Jackson over the national bank, responding and "utterly demolishing all that Mr. Brown had said," spoke until dark. The meeting was resumed the next day, and the debate continued "until a little before sundown." A week or so later Dr. Smith spoke at a Chapel Hill Festival "with his usual ability for nearly two hours." A "Log Cabin and Hard Cider Festival" was held at Yanceyvlle, and excitement swept the area.[90]

The elder Smith really blossomed in 1840, serving as chairman of the Whig "Central Committee of Orange," and he spoke at rallies throughout the district as an elector for Harrison and Tyler. He must have really enjoyed himself at a great Whig rally in Raleigh, where a Revolutionary War veteran carried an American flag perforated by a British bullet in the Battle for Guilford Courthouse, and in Chapel Hill where the Tippecanoe Club carried an Orange County banner reading "Regulators 1770—Rebellion 1776—Reformers 1840." The *Hillsborough Recorder* on November 12 bore the headline "Glorious News. The People Triumphant." The Whig vote in Orange County was 1,835 to the Democrats' 1,445; in Hillsborough, 404 to 180; and in the university town of Chapel Hill, 173 to 65. Harrison and Tyler carried North Carolina over the Van Buren ticket by a significant margin.[91]

By 1840, Orange County's prominence in the state's political leadership was evident as the home of both United States senators (Graham and Mangum), the congressman from the district (William Montgomery), the chief justice of the state supreme court (Thomas Ruffin), and the speaker of the House of Commons (Graham, before his election to the Senate). Of the quintet, only Montgomery was an outspoken political enemy of Dr. Smith. A history of Orange County described the pair this way: "Two of Orange's doctor-politicians had strangely parallel careers. Dr. James S. Smith and Dr. William Montgomery were both practicing physicians and seekers of public office. Smith was perhaps the better doctor and Montgomery the better politician." Montgomery, who remained a Democrat all his life and lost only one election, polled more than twice Smith's votes when both were elected to the Convention of 1835.[92]

Dr. Smith, whose failure in the business world would become evident within five years, must have felt vindicated by the election results. Now fellow citizens could boast that one of their own was a friend of both the new president and vice-president. No wonder that a cheery "card" appeared in the November 26, 1840, issue of the *Hillsborough Recorder*: "Dr. James S. Smith's health is so far restored as to enable him to resume the practice of his profession." However, the notice continued, "He cannot promise to ride in the night, as his eye sight has so far failed him to render night travel dangerous. He has associated his son F. J. Smith with him, in the practice who will be able to attend to night calls and such as offer in inclement weather." If he needed more cheer, it came when the same paper quoted a sentence from the *Norfolk Herald*: "Rip Van Winkle—we have it from the best authority that this venerable so innocent personage has resolved to quit his bed [in] North Carolina and seek some more congenial atmosphere, where he may enjoy his nap without interruption."[93]

A few months later, the elder Smith announced another run for Congress, reminding voters of his previous service from which he claimed to have retired "to earn my bread by the sweat of my brow, in the private and peaceful walks of life." He was anxious to go back to Washington and help his old friends, President Harrison and Vice-President Tyler, the latter a turncoat. Simultaneously, a letter signed "Cato" characterized the doctor as combining sound practical sense with a diversity of learning—"plain and unostentatious in his manners and habits that political distinctions can never make him forget that courtesy, good will and respect due to those in the humble walks of life, as becomes a servant of the people."[94] Smith's single-page circular reminded his readers of his sympathy with the working man: "Having been born poor, I have had to be the architect of my own fortune. I procured the means of advancement by hard labor. The laboring man I have always looked upon as my brother; and it has always been my pride and pleasure to sustain such true principles of equality and liberty as shall award to the honest laborer that reward for his toils which true republicanism demands." After referring to "Those who have administered the government for the last twelve years," he catalogued some of their sins—"They promised economy, and spent thirty-eight millions of your money annually. They spoke of equality, and offered [N]egro testimony against white men. They spoke of the poor, and proposed a bankrupt law for the rich.... They called the Whigs bank federalists, and they have issued tens of millions of rags in the form of treasury notes.... They spoke of decency and good manners, and vilified and traduced Gen. Harrison."

Having called out the sins of the Democrats, he appealed to them for unity and a fair trial for the new Whig administration in Washington. Such was the heat of partisanship as the country neared mid-century. As for his own views, he advocated a single term for a president without the power of veto except "to save the constitution from infraction, or to arrest hasty and rash legislation under high party excitement"; and he was now opposed to the doctrine of nullification, "a most dangerous political heresy." A half century before the subject rose to the top of the national agenda, Smith proposed a national currency based on metallic specie with equal value throughout the nation. As for political philosophy, he wrote, "I believe the old republican track of 1816, which was opened by Mr. Madison and his party, the true one. It led to union, peace and prosperity."[95]

Smith's congressional campaign against Romulus M. Saunders, the Democratic nominee who was by then living in Raleigh, was briefly interrupted by the death of President Harrison a month after his inauguration. When at an Orange County meeting a committee was proposed to memorialize the late president, Smith diplomatically moved to amend the resolution to require the committee to be composed of six individuals, to be selected from both political parties, "it being an event to be deplored by the whole country, and not by one party alone." At a procession memorializing the deceased president, Senator William A. Graham gave an oration, and an ode was read by John Cameron. Bipartisanship was brief, however, for soon Smith and Saunders were canvassing the district with bruising attacks carried over from the previous year's presidential campaign. Appointments in Wake and Person prevented Smith from joining his opponent for a joint appearance in his own Orange County, but he issued a statement trusting his neighbors: "I cannot believe that any man can interest themselves against me, unless they belong to that violent class of politicians who always delight to have the public mind in a ferment, and who can only make themselves conspicuous by their party [illegible]." Smith had the satisfaction of carrying his home town 306 to 121, the university community of Chapel Hill 139 to 66, and his county 1,216 to 1,180, but Saunders won the seat with larger margins in Person and Wake.[96]

Shortly after Vice-President John Tyler succeeded to the presidency, he provoked strong disagreements with old-line Whigs in Congress. The preceding campaign had been long on showmanship and short on issues—"Tippecanoe and Tyler Too," the "Log Cabin Campaign"—and Henry Clay remained the most popular leader among the Whigs. In November, Dr. Smith called and presided over a Whig meeting that, looking forward to the election three years in the future, repudiated Tyler and issued a ringing challenge: "Grievously disappointed by our present Chief Magistrate ... we cannot and ought not to recognize him as a Whig President." The caucus instead proposed the nomination of Clay, who had been speaker of the House of Representatives during Smith's congressional terms more than two decades earlier.[97]

In 1842, *two* Doctor Smiths—James and his son Francis—were chosen delegates to the county Whig convention. Thus developed an interesting family schism, for the previous year the younger son, 22-year-old Sidney Smith, had accepted the chairmanship of the Democratic-Republican Party's resolution committee, and his report was highly lauded by a participant.[98] Tongues must have wagged throughout Orange County—a father and his eldest son embedded with the Whigs while the younger son strayed to the opposition Democratic-Republican party (which would soon drop the second half of its original hyphenated name.)

Meanwhile, the residents of the rural western part of the county, complaining of the distance from the courthouse and feeling marginalized by the heavy population in the earlier settled areas, presented a challenge by demanding that a new county be carved out of old Orange. On this one issue, Whigs and Democrats in Hillsborough united in opposition. In a rare example of solidarity, a committee was formed consisting of seven Whigs, of whom James S. Smith and his son Francis were members, and six Democrats, of whom the other son Sidney was a member. In an 1842 county-wide referendum on the issue, the proposal for division was defeated 1,697 to 1,155 county-wide; in Hillsborough the vote was 495 against, only 32 for. Even if one family was solidified against the proposal, the votes in Geringer's precinct (184 to 1 for division) and Turner's Mill (101 to 5 for division) portended a perennial tug of war between the western citizens and those in the earlier settled portions of the county until the case was settled. John M. Morehead, a Whig, carried Orange 1,576 to 1,472 for governor, but Democrats took all but one of Orange's seats in the House of Commons.[99]

It is not known whether the partisan schism extended to a serious personal rift between father and son, but if the elder Smith could forgive the politically errant Sidney, he could take pride in his son's rapid ascent in the Democratic Party. The following year a letter from "E.G." of Person County recommended Sidney Smith for the congressional seat representing Orange, Granville, Person, Franklin, Warren, and Halifax: "I cordially second the nomination, and hope he will give his consent to run.... Mr. Smith is my choice.... I know him to be a fine young gentleman of talents, handsome speaker, and a Democrat of first water. Though young, he has none of the ostentatious pride that renders [illegible] most of the young men of that age and enviable talents, odious. Mr. Smith's principles on the one hand, and his connections (who I am told are numerous and most of them Whigs, including his father, who was formerly a member of Congress) on the other, he would combine more strength than any other candidate...."[100]

Between his sporadic practice of medicine and constant dabbling in politics, Dr. James Smith was also involved in local cultural programs. For example, in 1841 a Hillsborough Lyceum, a literary organization with Smith as a vice-president, was formed, but it was eclipsed the next year by the Hillsborough Literary Society, of which Frederick Nash, a future chief justice, was president, and Smith, Cadwallader Jones, and Rev. Robert Burwell were vice-presidents. With Dennis Heartt as secretary, the newest organization appeared to have a bright future in promoting "social intercourse and mutual improvements" by sponsoring lectures and debates in the Masonic Hall. Unfortunately, politics—the fierce partisan battles between the divergent Democratic and Whig parties—encroached on cooperative efforts toward enlightenment, and the Literary Society, formed "with the flourish of trumpets," faded. A letter-writer to the *Hillsborough Recorder* observed, "Another society was previously formed, bearing the imposing name of the 'Hillsborough Lyceum'—This, too, I understand after many desperate struggles, has departed this life. In short, the place seems totally void of anything like public spirit."[101]

The elder Smith performed a familiar duty by serving as presiding officer of Fourth of July ceremonies in Hillsborough in 1843, at which thirteen toasts were made, and the next year he eagerly supported the decision to build a new courthouse to replace the one that Dennis Heartt called "a reproach" to the county.[102] Not surprisingly, Dr. Smith was on the building committee. That decision, however, became more controversial as the movement for a division of the county gained momentum.

During those same months, at a Democratic meeting in September 1843, Sidney Smith submitted a resolution and was elected a delegate to the state convention. The younger son's name appeared on Democratic promotional materials; he served on a committee to draft a resolution opposing a tariff and a national bank, was appointed to a committee to build a new courthouse, and was nominated—along with John Berry, William Patterson, and John Tapscott—as a candidate for the House of Commons. Sidney's stand against division of the county and a controversy over the need for a new courthouse, however, stirred up enough opposition to lead him in June to temporarily withdraw as a candidate. He wrote, "I withdrew from the canvas under the belief that such was the excitement at that time of questions of a local nature, that the candidates would find much trouble and difficulty in defining what course was best to be adopted on the subject." Once the county officials agreed to recommend a referendum on the question of division, he reconsidered and pledged to follow the voice of the people on the subject. One citizen wrote that Sidney Smith "makes an able defense of our cause and charges boldly upon his enemy while one of his opponents, known here as the *pad-lock* candidate, endeavors to amuse himself and his hearers by telling Col. Hoke's jokes." When the votes were counted in 1844, Whigs had swept all four seats; Sidney Smith lost by a few votes, but his name now was indelibly associated with the political party held in contempt by his father. His loss was largely due to a controversy in which Whigs accused John Berry, the builder of the new courthouse and a leading Democrat, of having been paid too much for his services. Michael Hoke, from Lincoln County, was the unsuccessful Democratic nominee for governor in 1844 against the victor, Whig William A. Graham, Sidney Smith's former law teacher.[103]

Throughout the year, Dr. Smith had been busy promoting the Whig cause; only he probably knew if he held his nose and crossed party lines to support his son. Regardless, the doctor was properly circumspect on September 7, 1844, when he served as grand master of the Brethren of the Eagle Lodge and led the ceremonies in which the cornerstone was laid for a the new courthouse with its historic clock. The main speaker was the Rev. William Mercer Green, former teacher of Mary Ruffin Smith at the Hillsborough Female Academy. Ladies filled the hall, so most of the men had to listen from the grounds.[104]

Dr. Smith was in full Whig dress when on October 9 and 10 nearly 5,000 campers and bands from surrounding counties gathered at the "Regulation Battle Ground" to commemorate the 1771 Battle of Alamance. Five or six acres had been cleared, and water was provided in hogsheads. In the crowd were about 200 "fair daughters," and planners regretted not having advertised for more ladies. On their way back, the Wake County delegation paraded through Hillsborough to the Masonic Hall, where Dr. Smith addressed them. The local editor reported, "Dr. Smith was particularly happy in his remarks, having had an intimate personal acquaintance with Mr. [Henry] Clay. He spoke of him with feeling and animation, which brought forth loud shouts of approval." The following month must have been bittersweet for Dr. Smith because, although his friend Clay carried Hillsborough 412 to 172 and Orange County by just 97 votes, the Whigs lost the national election to a North Carolina native. Interestingly, in the university town of Chapel Hill, where 26 years earlier student James K. Polk had edged out the future Bishop Green for first honors, he trailed Clay 210 to 118. Statewide, North Carolinians went for Clay over their native son by about 5,000 votes.[105]

No matter how hard the party of Jackson sought to popularize the name "Democrats," Whigs like Dennis Heartt habitually referred to them as "Loco-Focos"; so when John

Dr. Smith presided over the cornerstone-laying ceremonies for the new Orange County Courthouse in 1844. The main speaker was William Mercer Green, head of the Hillsborough Female Academy of which Smith was board chairman (courtesy J. Boyd Webb).

R.J. Daniel defeated his Whig opponent Nash for Congress in 1843, it was a "Loco-Foco" victory. Orange County voted Whig in 1843, Democratic in 1845, and Whig again two years later.[106]

On August 19, 1845, a "card" in the *Hillsborough Recorder* may have indicated that the doctor's health had improved and it certainly indicated his need for money: "Dr. James S. Smith, intending to devote himself exclusively to the duties of his profession, offers his services to the public, and will cheerfully accept any call." Now approaching sixty, Smith's financial fortunes were collapsing, and he was in dire need of income. His plight was even more serious when in the December 17, 1846, issue of the same newspaper he and his son announced: "We, the undersigned, having become satisfied that the professional charges heretofore made in this portion of the country have been in many instances beyond the means of the ordinary [illegible] of the citizens, and that many suffer from want of medical aid on that account: From the foregoing considerations, we have reached [a decision] to reduce our charges to such a standard as will enable all to avail themselves to medical aid who desire it. Mileage, after one mile, reduced from fifty cents to thirty cents, and all other charges reduced in proportion. Night and inclement weather additional."[107]

This desperate effort to attract paying patients came too late. Dr. James Smith's political career was over. Thereafter his name appeared less often in the newspaper than in Orange County land and court documents.

Father as Businessman

Dr. James Smith was satisfied with neither practicing medicine nor holding political office. His poor decisions and indiscretions in seeking wealth through the manipulation of real estate transactions eventually tarnished his reputation, embarrassed his family, and came close to alienating the landed estate left by Francis Jones for Delia Smith and her children.

Prior to his association with Dr. James Webb, young James Smith became a landowner when in 1807 he paid his putative father, William Francis Strudwick, $500 for 490 acres on Wynn and Meadow creeks in the western portion of Orange (later Alamance) County. Even if the modest price reflected filial love and thus an affirmation of kinship, that still was a substantial amount for a 20-year-old. Then after returning from the University of Pennsylvania in 1812, Smith paid $3,500 to Archibald D. Murphey for tracts of 228 and 255 acres located west of the Island Ford-Hillsborough roads, not far from the present town of Swepsonville.[108] The transaction was noteworthy for four reasons: the $3,500 price was an exceptionally large sum for a 25-year-old medical apprentice already heavily in debt; the seller and buyer would soon be pitted against each other for political office; the seller would become one of the best known progressive leaders ever produced in the state; and Dr. Smith would serve as Murphey's physician in the last tragic years of the statesman's life. Both men exhibited inexplicable naiveté in business dealings.[109]

The following month Smith paid David Yarbrough $750 for 7,000 square feet of Hillsborough Town Lot 25 adjacent to Josiah Turner, Churton Street, John Taylor, and the "southeast corner of the house at present occupied by James S. Smith." More importantly, in 1817 Smith purchased from David Ray the one-acre Lot 22, bounded on the south by King Street, east by Lot 23, north by Lot 32, and west by Lot 21. This lot became the Smith residence that would later provide the birthplace of at least one mixed-race girl—a subject requiring an entirely different narrative.[110]

Even by eliminating additional James Smiths whose deeds failed to include a middle initial, Jones's son-in-law can be documented as acquiring and losing a substantial amount of property beginning in 1820, when he purchased from William Oldham 250 acres on Obed's Creek not far from the Price Creek plantation; the price was $750. The following year he acquired from David Strayhorn, Sr., 218 acres southeast of Hillsborough on Eno River for $1,000, and in 1821 from Abner B. Bruce the one-acre Hillsborough Lot 119 for $50. In 1822 he purchased for $400 from Strayhorn 100 acres on the Eno. A deed to Smith from his father-in-law dated January 19, 1825, transferring to him 1,810 acres on Crooked Creek of New Hope in Chatham and Orange in return for $7,000, was not entered into the land registry until 1853–28 years later.[111]

For a doctor of medicine to deal in real estate was not unusual, but Dr. James Smith also dabbled in a variety of other short-term business interests. Biographer Jean Anderson wrote, "Throughout his life he engaged in a variety of business partnerships, starting in 1815 with a relation of his wife when he established the firm of James S. Smith and Company, probably a short-lived merchandising business. His next venture was with Dr. Thomas Jefferson Faddis. They started another general store in Hillsborough in 1819, but their account books show that in 1824 the partnership became entirely medical; their later accounts were only for medical services and drugs." Anderson continued, "During the same period of the early 1820s, Smith was a partner of Josiah Turner in a copper shop, though he sold his share of the business. His largest venture was with Thomas D. Crain in the operation of mills, distilleries, and tanyard of which Smith became sole owner in the 1830s."[112]

More specifically, in 1820 Smith and Turner advertised the stock and work of James Jeffers & Company, including steel, copper, and pewter. They added, "The still-making business will be carried on hereafter by Josiah Turner and James S. Smith. They have in hand a quantity of good stills, and will be ready at any time to have stills made to suit purchasers after any patern [sic] they may request." At about the same time, Smith issued an urgent notice, "All persons indebted to James S. Smith & Co., or to James S. Smith, are requested to settle their accounts, as he can give no further indulgence." To handle his business while he was a member of Congress, he appointed Thomas D. Watt. The site of Smith's medical office was identified when Dennis Heartt announced that his newspaper office had moved "to the house opposite Dr. Smith's office, about one hundred yards west of the market house."[113] The following year Smith advertised for sale two young milk cows with calves and was named one of five "managers" of the Hillsborough Masonic Lottery, the result of which was postponed from time to time but was eventually successful.[114]

The doctor's early prudent investments eventually gave way to wild schemes that ruined his reputation and came close to squandering the vast estate left to him in trust by Francis Jones for Delia Jones Smith and her children. In 1824, Smith advertised for sale 336 acres on the "great road to Raleigh," three miles from Hillsborough,[115] and that the doctor had become a land speculator was suggested the next year when he sold three properties: 142.6 acres on both sides of New Hope Creek in both counties to Franklin O'Kelly for $713; 345 acres nearby to Josiah Atkins for $729; and 757.4 acres in the same vicinity to James H. Gant for $3,030. These three tracts together brought him about $4,500.[116]

At a sheriff's sale of property owned by Thomas N.S. Hargis, Smith in 1825 purchased for $13 lot numbers 434 and 418, and for $10 lot numbers 86, 134, and 425 in the town of Haywood near the junction of Deep and Haw rivers in southeastern Chatham. With luck, these might have been shrewd transactions, because Haywood had been considered as a site for the state capital before Raleigh was chosen; then, following a fire that burned the State House in 1831, the idea of relocating the capital again came to the fore. In actuality, the lots were probably worth about what Smith paid for them as the once-ambitious village of Haywood was gradually overtaken by weeds and woods.[117]

The price of land apparently plummeted in the 1830s, for Dr. Smith went on a buying spree and, if the prices paid are correctly recorded in the deeds, he took advantage of bargains. For example, he paid only $250 to Joel Parrish for four tracts totaling about 480 acres near the county line; $150 to Samuel Child (through his agent J.W. Norwood) for 300 acres on the Eno four miles from Hillsborough; and $216 to John A. Faucett for 78 acres on the same waterway. During the decade he also acquired additional property in Hillsborough, including from Thomas J. Faddis a one-acre tract adjoining Lot 4, containing a "blacksmith shop" and bordering on the south "by that portion of Ground on the North bank of Eno River surveyed

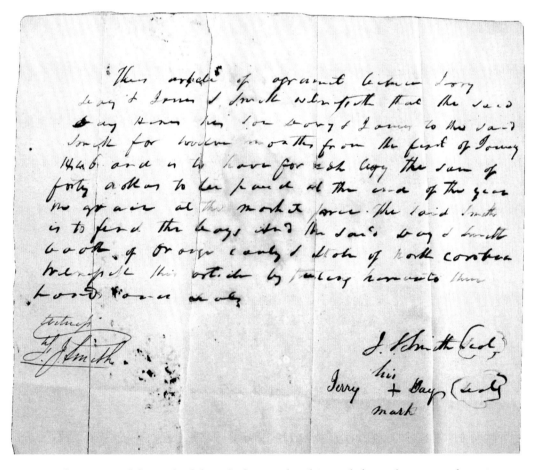

Dr. Smith augmented the work of slaves by hiring white boys to help on the various plantations that he held in trust for his wife and their three children (courtesy Mary Ruffin Smith Papers, Southern Historical Collection, Wilson Library, UNC-CH).

by Thos. N.S. Hargis to Samuel Hancock for a pass-way from the brickyard to Churton Street." The price was $200.[118]

In 1835, when a fire destroyed Dr. Smith's stable, his dwelling house escaped burning only because the wind was blowing in the opposite direction. The newspaper editor commented, "The proprietors having always been careful that no light should be carried to the building, there appears little doubt that the fire was the work of an incendiary." No mention was made of whether there had been a danger to Smith's race horse, "fine stout young Jack of Spanish stock," six years old, whose service was available the next spring at Crain and Smith's Mill a mile and a half west of town. The charge was $5.25 for the season if paid early, $7 "to ensure."[119]

The next year, Smith joined James Webb and Cadwallader Jones in seeking proposals for the construction of a two-story stone jail, 48 by 24 feet, to cost no more than $4,000; builder John Berry won the contract. Later that year Smith announced a "New Establishment of Leather Shop in the house lot many years occupied by Mrs. Wilfong, nearly opposite to Mr. Stephen Moore's Store." The leather came from the "new Tan Yard at his mill"—that is, the operation on Eno River purchased that year from Thomas D. Crain. He also advertised wheat, corn, rye, flax seed, tallow, mutton suet, tan bark, whiskey, and brandy, boasting of being the first local merchant to deal only in cash or barter—no more credit.[120] Smith continued to advertise for 500 barrels of corn for his liquor manufacturing, and he was selling pine shingles from his mill.[121]

Deeds often reference adjoining properties and other information valuable to researchers tracing historic development of an area. For example, in 1837 Smith acquired from William McCauley, "son of John who was the son of Col. Wm. McCauley," a certain property "which house & lot was owned by Col. Wm. McCauley in his life time and was given by him in his will to his son John McCauley for & during life and at his death to his grandson Wm McCauley ... which house & lot as aforesaid was for a long series of years used as a tavern or house for retail of Spiritous Liquors." It was bounded by "Wm. Andersons corner Store house on the North, by John U. Kirkland Allison house [sic] on the North, and by Josiah Turners house on North, and on the West by the lot formerly owned by John Casey in his life time, on the west, & by the house owned by Samuel Thompson on the South, by the said street on the East." When that lot was resold in 1838 to Catlett Campbell and Cadwallader Jones, Jr., for a profit of $100, changes in ownership of surrounding property provided additional information for title searchers.[122]

In 1837 Smith also purchased at least one tract across the county line in Chatham (the deed was registered in 1841), paying $706.60 to William H. Merritt for 353.3 acres in the fork between Morgan and New Hope creeks, adjoining Merritt's own and the lands of James Gant and William Williams. Part of the land purchased by Smith from Joel Parrish in 1833, adjoining the Price Creek plantation, also lay in Chatham.[123]

Perhaps the most significant acquisitions made by Smith in the 1830s were three tracts from Thomas D. Crain [Crane] on Eno River—totaling about 160 acres—together with all mills, distilleries, tan yard, and stock of every kind located on the premises. The previous year Smith and Crain had jointly purchased from Elizabeth Minor 18.25 acres on the east side of the river near the mills. These tracts were purchased in October 1836 for $2,850 and formed a complex later known as Dimmock's Mill, started in 1817 by John Taylor, Jr., at the confluence of Seven Mile Creek and Eno River, just west of Hillsborough. Its history was traced when in 1845 James Smith sold it for $3,000 to his son, Dr. Francis J. Smith: "It being the tract of land on which John Taylor erected a merchant, corn & saw mill, and which he purchased from Thomas Crabtree & John Thompson, and which was conveyed by said John Taylor & James Webb to Alfred Moore and Thomas D. Crain one the undivided moiety of said Moore to Thomas D. Crain and by the same Thomas D. Crain ... to James S. Smith."[124]

The transfer of the mill and site to his son signaled trouble in the father's affairs. He had overdrawn his credit line, and repeated advertising in the local newspaper revealed his urgent need for cash. Under the heading "Bacon and Leather," Smith offered the "best corn fed bacon for sale, which he will sell very low for cash alone." In addition, he offered his entire stock of leather "at very reduced prices for cash, or on credit for ninety days to those he knows to be punctual." His health had been affected further, but, in dire need of money, another "Card" announced that "Dr. James S. Smith, intending to devote himself exclusively to the duties of his profession, offers his services to the public, and will cheerfully accept any call."[125]

Puzzling, indeed, are Smith's whirlwind purchases and sales during the mid-forties, and the transactions are listed with the hope that a later researcher may find some of them of interest. Among his purchases: From a sheriff's sale (against Nathaniel J. King, Jones Watson, and John W. Carr), $631.30 for tracts of 230 and 150 acres on Morgan Creek; from James Webb (clerk of court) for $112.50, part interest in real estate of the late John Fann, also on Morgan Creek; from Ilai W. Nunn for $100, additional interest in the Fann land, also on Morgan Creek; from Tabitha Pendergrass of Tennessee, for $22, another interest in Fann land; and from James Webb (clerk of court), $500 for 500 acres on Morgan Creek (Fann land). Sales by Smith during the decade included $1,000 from Archibald D. Borland for a portion of Town Lot 6 purchased previously by Smith from William McCauley; $300 from James C. Turrentine for 59 acres on Eno River "a short distance northwest from Hillsborough" and a one-acre Town Lot 119; $1,775 from Turrentine for Town Lot 22 and a part of Lot 23; and, from William H. Merritt, $81 for 27.3 acres on Fann's Creek. Smith acted as good neighbor when he deeded to Manly Pendergrass, without charge, a bit of the Fann land to straighten a boundary.[126]

A web of deception was becoming visible at mid-decade. In a deed dated December 10, 1841, but not registered until four years later, "for & in consideration of the love & affection which he has for his said Daughter Mary R. Smith and with the motive of advancing her in life and providing for her a home after his death as well as in conformity with an injunction imposed on said Smith by his father-in-law Francis Jones, who granted & gave the said tract to the said Smith with a promise that he should at his death give it to his daughter Mary Smith, and for the further consideration of one dollar to him in hand paid," James S. Smith deeded to his daughter—subject to lifetime estate for himself and Delia Smith—six parcels totaling about 1,700 acres in Orange County (Price Creek, Massey, Pendergrass, Wood, and two unnamed tracts) and 200 acres in Chatham, plus his interest in the 400-acre Fann land in Orange. The deed was witnessed by Francis and Sidney Smith. One may wonder why the father made the decision at this particular time when the head of the family's own financial condition was collapsing, and why the deed was not registered until four years later.[127] The question was answered by another deed dated November 21, 1845 (and registered simultaneously): James S. Smith was on the verge of bankruptcy, and he was trying to shield the plantations from his creditors. Francis Jones's will written in 1841 provided for a life estate in the property for both Delia and her husband. Now, in 1845, it had become necessary for Smith to "dispose of his remaining interest in said lands for the payment of his debts," and for $1,000 plus $1, he signed away his interest (but not Delia's) in the seven tracts plus all movable property—"stills, hogsheads, & apparatus appertaining to the Distillery on said premises, also the thrashing machine, fan & fixtures of every kind about the barn on said premises, also the blacksmith tools, also the paints, oils, lime & bricks intended for the completion of the house on the Price's Creek tract of land."[128]

In a supplemental document designed to shield his personal property from creditors, Smith signed it over to Delia. Among the values assigned were carriage and harness $250, omnibus $50, wagon and gear $75, old wagon and gear $20, carry-log $15, 4 horses ("mostly old") $75, 4 mules $75, 8 cows and calves $40, 2 steers $12, 60 head of hogs $60, 19 sheep $10, 16 geese $3, 4 yearling calves $6; varying quantities of farm produce, including 1,000 pounds of seed cotton at $10; and farm tools at various prices. Exceedingly modest home furnishings included a sideboard $25, 12 chairs $12, bed and bedstead $10, 2 tables and stands $6, 2 looms $10, wheel and reel $5, and clock $10. The doctor's library was valued at $50. With "one old Negro named Joe" at $50, the value of all the personal property was estimated at about $1,300—a remarkably modest estate for so eminent a citizen of Hillsborough who counted leading national figures among his friends.[129]

Smith's financial woes accelerated. In March 1846 he advertised 500 sides of "best oak tanned leather and a quantity of Russet and Waxed uppers, harness, and Kip-skins." Then in August came the announcement that he would offer to sell, at his leather shop on Sunday preceding September court week, a "valuable estate consisting of land, mills, & tan yards," along with his store house and lots in Hillsborough, 60 acres on the Stage Road, and "all the right, title and interest which I have in the Price's Creek Plantation"—all this despite his prior sale of the same mill and tan yards to his son Francis and his relinquishment of his lifetime interest in the Price Creek lands. He also offered to sell his slaves and quarter sections of bounty lands in Illinois. Uncharacteristically, in this announcement Dr. Smith appeared humble, as if pleading with the public: "I here offer an estate and means the ordinary value and assessment of which is not less than 35,000 dollars, to pay an amount of debt of some 15,000 or 16,000 [dollars]. I would be much grateful if my creditors were present at said sale, and if they would appoint a faithful and competent agent to be also present and record every sale I make and the disposition of the proceeds of such sale. In this I have done what is good and lawful to protect myself and all of my creditors." Apparently nothing sold, for on October 1, he announced, "Mills and Tan Yards Still for Sale," adding, "a Negro man about 36 years of age, a good distiller, sound and healthy, honest, and of industrious and temperate habits," plus a milk cow, a number of beef cattle, a cast iron bark mill, two copper boilers for boiling tan bark, and a three-horse [sic] wagon.[130]

The crisis was further illustrated by the publication of another "Card" reading, "We, the undersigned [Doctors James and Francis Smith] having become satisfied that the professional charges heretofore made in this portion of the country have been in many instances beyond the means of the ordinary [illegible] of the citizens, and that many suffer from want to medical aid on that account. From the foregoing considerations, we have reached [a decision] to reduce our charges to such a standard as will enable all to avail themselves to medical aid who desire it. Mileage, after one mile, reduced from fifty cents to thirty cents, and all other charges reduced in proportion." There was, however, a higher charge at night and inclement weather.[131]

Earlier, in July, Smith had commissioned John W. Norwood to collect debts owed him by patients and to use the funds to satisfy his debt to Mary Clancy ($500 plus interest less $209.45 already paid). Any amount collected above the debt was to be paid back to Smith.[132] By that time, the doctor was over his head in debt—at least $8,130, a fortune at the time— including $1,500 owed to the State Board of Internal Improvements, $550 to William Carrington and son Duncan Carrington, $2,500 to Thomas D. Bennehan, $1,200 to John Parker of Person County, $500 to Rex trustees in Raleigh, $340 to Mrs. Robina Norwood, $500 to Mary Clancy, $150 to Joseph Woods, $240 to Alexander Woods, and $650 to Bank of Cape Fear at Hillsborough. His chief security was the former sheriff, Josiah Turner, Sr., but creditors included also Cadwallader Jones, Richard Tapp, William Paul, James Jackson, and John A. Faucett. Faced with foreclosure on everything he owned, Smith earlier (January 27, 1846) entered into a deed of trust with James C. Turrentine, who conditionally accepted as trustee from Smith the quarter-sections of 160 acres each in the state of Illinois—tracts that Dr. Smith had purchased from soldiers to whom they had been granted for service in the War of 1812. The condition was that Turrentine would advertise the Illinois lands in the *Hillsborough Recorder, Greensboro Patriot,* and otherwise offer them for sale at the courthouse in Hillsborough, then use the revenue to satisfy Josiah Turner and the other creditors (in descending order). Turrentine, of course, was to receive a handsome commission.[133]

Other Orange County citizens, some debtors, some creditors, were drawn into the web of Dr. James Smith's real estate and slave-trading gambits, and soon he was charged with illegally transferring as much as $17,000 worth of property to his children with the intent of shielding it from his debtors. In a case brought in 1847 by Joseph Wood and others, even Smith's gift to Mary of the favorite household slave Harriet and her children, Julius and Cornelia, was challenged. The Smiths' answer speaks volumes concerning the inhumanity of the slave trade in the 1840s: "Mr. F. Jones by deed of gift registered in Orange gave to Miss Mary Smith a girl called Patsy. When grown not suiting the family she [Patsy] was sold to Zack Trice for $800 & with this money a woman called Love & her children were bought at Clancy's sale. When one of her [Love's] children called Tipp or Jim was well grown & of value Dr. S[mith] proposed (instead of selling the girl Harriet & her two children which he was about to do) to exchange them with Miss M[ary] for Tipp or Jim. In this Miss M[ary] agreed to. G[eorge] Laws was called in to determine their relative value & gave as his opinion that Tipp was worth as much as Harriet & children [together]. Accordingly the exchange was made & Tipp was sold in place of Harriet & children." This is a telling statement—the only documentary evidence found revealing that Dr. Smith actually contemplated selling his own granddaughter (Harriet's daughter Cornelia) through the slave trade.[134]

Faced with the possibility of losing the entire Francis Jones legacy to the creditors, the Smith family coalesced and proposed to submit all disputed matters to arbitration through Cadwallader Jones, Duncan Cameron, George E. Badger, and John W. Brown. When Turner declined both Smith's plea that he continue as his security and the offer to arbitrate, the Smiths boldly sought to take the initiative by bringing suit against the former sheriff. Asked "To whom do you attribute the great sacrifice you had to make of your property to pay your debt to Josiah Turner" if he had continued his endorsements and aided in the sale of the property, Dr. Smith responded, "I should have paid and had thousands of dollars left. It seems to me to have been the purpose of Josiah Turner to hunt me down and ruin me. But

Following his father-in-law's death in 1844, Dr. Smith went on a spending and trading spree that came close to squandering the large holdings that he held only in trust for the benefit of Francis Jones's daughter and three grandchildren. Smith's slave-trading activities even included his grand-daughter, Cornelia, the blood daughter of his son Sidney and the slave woman Harriet (fragment of papers awaiting cataloging for the Mary Ruffin Smith Papers, Southern Historical Collection, Wilson Library, UNC-CH).

he has since then endeavored to ruin me by propagating false rumors as to my charges and to prevent me from getting business in the line of my profession."

If it accomplished nothing else, Dr. Smith's airing of his dirty legal laundry brought the dysfunctional family together temporarily. Even Sidney appeared in his father's defense: "Save witnessing a deed in 1841..., I have had nothing to do with his sales and transfers of property to others.... I can say with truth that I believe all his transfers of property were bone fide made and with the fairest and honest intent for the payment of his debts—that every dollar he had and the proceeds of every sale went to the honest and faithful payment of creditors. He has been an injured and persecuted man." Of course, Sidney could not resist accusing the accusers of trying to sully his character as well as that of his family.

Meanwhile, a scenario involving the "perpetuation of memory" was being played out all the way to the North Carolina Supreme Court. When in 1846 James Smith's debtors brought suit against him and his surety Josiah Turner, Sr. (the former county sheriff),[135] all three plantations were ordered sold to pay Dr. Smith's debts; and at a sheriff's sale Turner was the highest bidder. Suddenly, partner became adversary, and perhaps for the first time Mary Smith and her brothers became fully aware of their father's reckless, sometime fraudulent, real estate transactions. Searching her memory of earlier dealings between her father and grandfather, Mary clearly recalled that in addition to his gift of Price Creek lands to James S. Smith in 1819, Francis Jones had on January 19, 1825, conveyed to Smith "other lands, called the Park's Neck lands, for the sum of $7,000, and also, upon an express agreement between the said parties, that the said Smith should reconvey to the said Francis Jones the lands on Price's creek." In other words, Jones had reclaimed title to the Price Creek plantation in exchange for the Park's Neck lands. The deed, if it could be found, would prove that the Price Creek property was still held in trust for Delia Jones Smith and her children, incapable of being claimed as a part of Dr. Smith's personal holdings.

Mary Smith testified that the deed for the latter transaction was delivered to Francis Jones, was seen by sundry persons, "some of whom are advanced in years, others have left the State, and recently departed this life," and that the "said deed remained in possession of Francis Jones many years, but ... was taken from his possession by Ruffin Jones, his only son, and was by him destroyed; and that the said Ruffin Jones died many years since." She asked the court to help her "perpetuate memory" by authorizing her to seek the sworn corroboration of witnesses who were familiar with the deed. The Court of Equity of Orange County, Judge William H. Battle presiding, ruled that depositions might be taken on three days' notice from two persons—"M.S. and C.Y."—one of whom was ill and the other about to leave the state. Turner, arguing that such a deed never existed—and by implication that the Price Creek plantation was subject to sequestration—appealed the ruling, *Mary R. Smith vs. Josiah Turner & Al*, to the State Supreme Court.[136]

The Supreme Court's decision was issued at the June 1847 session by Chief Justice Thomas Ruffin, a Hillsborough neighbor, who knew a great deal about both the Smith and Turner families. In its verdict favoring Turner, the court criticized the weakness of the appeal and made clear that a Court of Equity "does not like to entertain bills to perpetuate testimony." In other words, unless the deed could be produced, the Price Creek plantation could be subject to sale to pay off Dr. Smith's debts. As will be indicated below, Turner eventually agreed to a compromise that skirted the issue, but Mary Smith's memory was in fact proven correct when, after the death of her father in 1852, she found among the clutter of his office the unrecorded deed of January 19, 1825. By it, Francis Jones deeded his son-in-law the Park's Neck/Crooked Creek lands, half of the bargain by which he took back the Price Creek property originally given to Smith in 1819. The deed was finally registered in 1853—a year after Dr. Smith's death and twenty-eight years after it was written. Signatures of Francis and Ruffin Jones, both long dead, were proved by Austin Kirby before Judge Battle.[137] Francis Jones, having witnessed his son-in-law's profligacy as his own health failed, prepared his will in 1841 to protect the three large plantations—Jones Grove, Flowers Place, and Price Creek— for his daughter and, upon her death, for his grandchildren.

Perhaps convinced of the accuracy of Mary's memory, the adversaries did not wait for the court's ruling in the case of *Mary R. Smith vs. Josiah Turner & al.* A complex agreement was signed on March 12, 1847, certifying that James, Mary, Francis, and Sidney Smith "promised to perform certain acts in favour of the said Josiah Turner" and that the quartet had "faithfully done & performed all that they have bound to do & perform all the terms" of the agreement. Among terms of the agreement, Turner assigned to Francis J. Smith (with Sidney's consent) "all claims, liens, or titles to property or effects of James S. Smith belonging to the said Josiah Turner as creditor or security of the said James S. Smith," as well as any claims that he (Turner) might have in the administration of the estate of Thomas J. Faddis. One suspects that Dr. Frank Smith had saved the day out of his own pocket.[138] Referring to an agreement reached on March 12, 1847, Turner provided a somewhat similar indenture to both Francis and Sidney Smith, conveying back to them the Grove and Flowers tracts, respectively.[139]

While the suits involving debts among Smith, Turner, James C. Turrentine, and others were being played out in Hillsborough, another was instituted in Chatham County. To recover $1,200 from the three mentioned men, John Y. Parker brought suit and forced the Chatham County sheriff to put up for public sale three properties owned outright by Smith—of 197 and 86 acres, plus a portion of the Price Creek tract lying in Chatham. At a sale in Pittsboro on August 10, 1846, Turner himself bought all three pieces for just five dollars.[140] Obviously, serious behind-the-scenes agreements had been reached, the details of which remain hidden.

Another indenture, dated August 26, 1847, from Turner to Mary, Francis, and Sidney Smith, referring to their father's indenture of January 1846 conveying to James C. Turrentine quarter-sections of bounty lands in Illinois, read, "Whereas the said Mary R. Smith, Francis S. Smith & Sidney Smith, together with the said James S. Smith, entered into certain articles of agreement bearing date of 12th day of March 1847 with the said Josiah Turner whereby they stipulated & promised to do & perform certain acts & things to & in behalf of the said Turner, as will more fully & at large appear reference being had to the said articles or memorandum of agreement," Turner released "all his right title & interest in & to the eighteen quarter sections of land in the state of Illinois before mentioned, which were conveyed by said James S. Smith to said James C. Turrentine, in trust as aforesaid."[141]

Dated two years later, June 1849, Turrentine issued an indenture to Mary Smith, Francis J. Smith, and Sidney Smith referencing conveyance in Book D [33], pages 441–448 of the quarter-sections of bounty lands in Illinois. As trustee, Turrentine asserted that he did advertise the lands sixty days in the *Hillsborough Recorder* and *Greensboro Patriot* and sold them at the court house door on April 21 "when and where the said Mary Smith and Francis J. Smith and Sidney Smith became the purchasers and have duly complied with the terms of the sale by giving bonds and security for the purchase money," and for one dollar transferred the title.[142]

An additional indenture from Turrentine to Mary, Francis, and Sidney Smith, November 29, 1849, appears to be the same as the document registered in August, except that it carries a report that at the Court of Pleas and Quarter Sessions on November 4, 1849, it was duly acknowledged by Turrentine in open court and was ordered to be registered. Clerk of Court Joseph Allison authenticated the document November 29, 1849, and ordered it registered.[143]

New Home at Price Creek

Remarkably, throughout the tumultuous years of suits and countersuits in the county seat, a new residence—one of the largest in Chapel Hill Township—was being constructed on the Hillsborough-Fayetteville Road (later called Smith Level Road). Construction may have begun as early in 1845, for in a case of *Wood vs. Smith & Turner* it was charged that "to 21st Nov. 1845 the said James Smith has not procured materials and carpenters to be used [for] a large and [illegible] dwelling house in the Price Creek tract and [illegible] for the work and materials for said building & other buildings." That it was to be Mary's house, not her family's, was emphasized when she answered another suit brought by Josiah Turner: "Your orator lived with her father until she left Hillsboro in 1847. But it is false that from that time to this that she has lived with her father. In Nov. 1847 she removed to her own plantation on Price's Creek where she has resided ever since & that her father & mother live with her." Being unmarried, she needed her father's aid to manage her farm and other business; besides, she wanted her mother to live with her. To emphasize that the arrangement was her choice, Mary snapped that her parents "could if they desired live in Chatham on the valuable estate [Jones Grove] that her grandfather gave in trust to her father for the use of her mother during her life."[144]

Little information has been found concerning the original design and construction of the house documented as "Oakland" in Frank Smith's accounts and Maria Spear's correspondence. However, involvement is suspected of Hillsborough builder John Berry, with whom Dr. Smith was associated during the construction of the 1825 Masonic Lodge on the lot adjoining his own on King Street in the county seat. In addition, Smith served as master of ceremonies at the dedication of the 1845 Berry-built Orange County Courthouse. John A. Faucett, a skilled carpenter often associated with Berry's projects, also may have been involved, for in 1847 he brought suit, charging Smith with malice, fraud, and collusion when real estate was transferred to Francis and Mary Smith in an effort to avoid payment of the father's debts.[145]

John G. Zehmer, Jr., architectural historian in the North Carolina Department of Archives and History, provided a preliminary description following an inspection in 1970. He described the house as "one of the most interesting buildings in the Chapel Hill area as it shows very clearly the transition from traditional vernacular building forms to the Greek Revival. It is essentially a five-bay, two-story structure, two rooms deep with a center hall. Considering its overall design, one might well think it was built during the first quarter of the nineteenth century rather than in the 1840s."

Zehmer continued,

> It is built of plain weatherboards with flush siding beneath the full-length shed porch on the front. This porch originally had chamfered posts which have been replaced by primitive columns taken from a demolished building in Chapel Hill. The original posts have been revised in a later porch on the rear. The windows have nine-over-six sash on the second floor and nine over nine on the first. Many of the original blinds with stationary louvres remain. The center door is framed by two-over-two sash rather than the usual fixed lights. On either side are pairs of tall straight-sided chimneys laid in five-to-one American bond. At the rear an early shed porch has been enclosed and a small one-story ell added.
>
> On the interior the mixture of traditional elements with those of the coming mode is more apparent. The chair rails and well-executed curvilinear stair brackets are of traditional design,

but the mantels are of the purest Greek Revival with no trim whatever. In the two rooms to the right of the hall all of the woodwork was replaced in the late nineteenth or early twentieth century. It consists of a high wainscot with double ranges of panels and mantels with colonettes and elaborate overmantels. It is the unusual doors of the Cole house which are most interesting. They have the traditional six panel scheme with two small panels at the top over four larger ones. On the rear, the panels are slightly beveled; on the front, they are flat and are outlined by shallow Greek Revival mouldings. In short, the backs of the doors would be normal at any period during the eighteenth or early nineteenth centuries, while the mouldings on the front could only appear long after that time. This same statement could be made to compare the mantels and the original wainscot, and, to a lesser degree, the late chimney design with early exterior features like the chamfered posts and flush siding. The designer of the Cole house was certainly using remembered forms, but tempered them with elements of the fashionable Greek Revival mode.[146]

During those years of speculation in real estate and construction of a dwelling house, the Smiths also dealt in a large amount of human flesh. Notoriously difficult-to-read federal census records appear to show father-in-law Francis Jones with 13 slaves in 1790 and 1800, 15 in 1820, and 17 in 1830; all those living in 1844 were inherited by James Smith in trust for Delia and their children. Smith himself appears already to have owned nine slaves in 1820, 17 in 1830, and 30 in 1850. Among dealings documented in the county registry is one in 1836 in which Smith sold to his 22-year-old daughter Mary, for $800, a Negro woman named Love, about 44 years old, along with her daughter Amy, about 8 years; son Jim, about 5; and, daughter Virginia, about eleven months. The bill of sale was dated December 10, 1836, but it was not recorded until November 1845.[147] In another bill of sale, dated September 30, 1834, but not recorded until November 1845, William Kell sold to James S. Smith for $450 "a Negro girl named Herritt [sic] aged fifteen years past, a slave," warranting the girl to be "sound & healthy & clear of any defect whatsoever as to her health."[148]

In the same year, James Smith sold to his wife and three children for $700 "a Negro man named Willis, aged about 24 years, a tanner and currier by trade," who had been willed by Francis Jones to James Smith in trust for Delia during her life (and at her death to her children). The bill of sale explained that Willis was in exchange for another slave named Dempsey, who also was willed by Jones to Smith in trust for the latter's wife during her life and at her death to the three children; consequently the transaction did not violate Jones's conditions.[149]

Then, as previously noted, on August 25, 1845, of enormous importance to this story, James Smith sold to his 31-year-old daughter Mary, for $550, "a [N]egro woman Harriet aged about twenty-six years, and her boy child Julius aged about three years, and her daughter Cornelia." James Smith was not averse to making a hundred-dollar profit at the expense of his blood daughter, and life would never be the same for the dysfunctional Smith family.[150]

The Census of 1850 was the first to require the names of all free persons—but, unfortunately, not of slaves. It did, however, include an enormously valuable special census of agriculture and manufacturing, a broadening that Smith had supported when he was in Congress.[151] The James S. Smith homestead at Price Creek owned 30 slaves. Three separately listed mulatto females appear to be identifiable: a 30-year-old (Harriet), an 8-year-old (Cornelia, actually only 6 years old), and a 3-year-old (Emma). Census-listers were known for guessing the spelling of names and for loosely estimating ages, so discrepancies within and between decennial schedules were not unusual. In Orange County alone, the Smith family was credited with 500 acres of improved and 1,300 acres unimproved land with a combined value of $8,000. Implements and equipment were valued at $1,000, and livestock (including 6 horses, 3 mules, 10 cows, 4 work oxen, 40 other cattle, 60 sheep, and 100 swine) at $870. During the preceding year the property produced 350 bushels of wheat, 150 bushels of rye, 2,000 bushels of Indian corn, 150 bushels of oats, 30 bushels of peas and beans, 100 pounds of butter, 40 pounds of wool, 50 pounds of flax, and 4 bushels of flaxseed. It was obvious that once the bankruptcy issue had been settled, the Price Creek plantation remained a large and productive operation.

Saving Francis Jones's Legacy

Dr. James Strudwick Smith's health, both mental and physical, succumbed to trying bankruptcy proceedings, and he was a virtual physical and mental cripple from 1846 until his death on December 7, 1852. The *Hillsborough Recorder*, in which his name had appeared many times previously, announced simply, "James S. Smith, M.D., 66, at his residence in Orange, 7th inst. Doctor, politician, Episcopalian." The *Fayetteville Observer* provided additional succinct information: "Died in Orange County, Dr. James S. Smith, formerly a member of Congress, of the State Legislature, and of the convention which amended the State Constitution."[152] Instead of burying the doctor at Jones Grove, Delia and her children selected

His widow chose to bury Dr. Smith on a knoll within sight of "Oakland," the new home occupied at Price Creek five years earlier. Later, Delia and their son Sidney also were buried there, but Kemp Battle had all three bodies exhumed and moved to Jones Grove in 1897. The stone walls, without their former occupants, remain visible on the property of the Long family (photograph by Bill Barber, courtesy Allen Dew).

a prominent site on the Price Creek plantation, less than a mile northwest and in plain view of the new residence.[153]

At last, Delia Jones Smith—born to Francis and Mary Parke Jones in 1787, married to James Smith in 1813, mother of two sons who mortified her and a daughter who sought to ameliorate the sins of her brothers—was the head of a strange family living in a big new house on the road from Hillsborough to Fayetteville. Like many nineteenth-century women, Delia Smith had lived in the shadow of her husband as he sought public approbation of his career and searched for fortune at the expense of his family's moral and financial health. She and her daughter Mary shared the burden of the two boys' production of mixed-race girls and the consequent complexity of treating as blood-kin children governed by an entirely different statute law. The two women were little more than white servants to the male trio, and when bankruptcy in the mid-'40s broke the elder Smith's health and spirit, they were largely charged with moving the family's furnishings from Hillsborough to the still incomplete mansion—and it was considered a mansion by neighbors—three miles southwest of Chapel Hill.[154] Delia's health was additionally taxed by the size of the house, far too large for her needs, and the deprivation of essentials for the life-style expected by her haughty husband and sons. That the mother and daughter had been shamefully treated was proven by the testimony in 1847 of Mary's best friend and confidante, Maria Louisa Spear. When in a deposition Maria Spear was asked whether Dr. Smith had "within the last 4 or 5 years paid his wife any amount of money above what was necessary for her clothing," the teacher

Dr. Smith's tombstone, exhibiting his Masonic emblem, was moved by Kemp Battle from Price Creek to Jones Grove in 1897 (H.G. Jones collection).

replied, "If he has I never heard of it. I have heard her [Delia Smith] complain that he has not & Dr. Smith has never been in the habit of advancing money to any member of his family." When further questioned, "Do you not know that Mrs. Smith & her daughter Mary are very economical & that they have received very little money from Dr. Smith," Maria's answer was, "They live very economically & have received less money from Dr. Smith than I have ever known ladies in the same circumstances to receive from the head of the family."[155]

The dysfunctional household was further torn by the bitter jealousy between sons Francis and Sidney over Harriet, the favorite slave woman. Consequently, the widow depended during the last year of her life on Mary and Harriet, the latter encumbered with four multi-race daughters sired by the brothers, one a liquor-drinking politician-lawyer, the other a lecherous part-time physician. Within that milieu—a widow, a spinster daughter, two depraved sons, a bound woman with four enslaved children ranging in age from 10 to 3, and more than twenty other slaves—the *Hills-*

borough Recorder on November 22, 1854, poignantly announced, "Died, on the 8th inst., at the family residence in the county, Mrs. Delia Smith, widow of Dr. James S. Smith, in the 69th year of her age. During her last illness, Mrs. Smith made a profession of her faith in God—the Father, Son, and Holy Ghost and was received in the communion of the church, and partook of the Holy Sacrament of the Lord's Supper, administered by the Rector of Episcopal Church in Chapel Hill." Her body was buried beside that of her late husband at Price Creek.

In accordance with Francis Jones's will, upon the death of Delia Jones Smith, the Price Creek lands went to Mary Ruffin Smith, the Jones Grove lands to physician Francis Jones Smith, and the Flowers Place to lawyer James Sidney Smith. Each plantation contained more than 1,500 acres of some of the finest agricultural land in two counties. Mary was then 40 years old, Francis 38, and Sidney 35. When measured against most of their neighbors, and considering the relative value of the dollar, the siblings were wealthy; and in subsequent years many of those neighbors became debtors to one or the other of the Smith trio. In the absence of modern-day banking and investment opportunities, most loans were made either as mortgages on real estate or simply in return for a signed note—essentially a promise to pay the debt by a certain date. However, creditors were seldom in a hurry for redemption of the notes so long as the interest (sometime eight percent per annum) was paid. Thus, despite the reckless transactions of the late James S. Smith, Francis Jones's grandchildren in 1854 were citizens of substance in Orange and Chatham counties.

Francis Jones's will also decreed that the personal property, including the slaves, be equally apportioned among his grandchildren. Consequently, Mary, Francis, and Sidney petitioned the Court of Pleas and Quarter Sessions for a division. James C. Turrentine, John Carr, and George Laws were appointed for the purpose, and their report, dated February 9, 1857, made the following awards (with the value of each slave): *For Mary*: Sam $950, William $900, Julia $750, Adeline $550, Sally $500, Lucy $275, total value $3,925. *For Francis*: Tom $1,150, John $900, Fanny $800, Duncan $500, Edward $350, Simon $75, Hetty $75, and pay his sister Mary $16, total $3,866. *For Sidney*: Ben $1,100, Amy $800, Mary Ann and child Barney $1,000, Joan $750, Tempy $175, Old Amy $0, total $3,825. (Old Amy was noted as "tax free.") Small amounts of cash were to be exchanged among the trio to make the division even. In all, the twenty slaves (including the child) were valued at more than $11,500.[156]

There was additional personal property to be sold at auction. Jones Watson, a Chapel Hill hotelier and administrator of Delia's estate, listed $2,924.28 in notes due her, including several small obligations from familiar names like Oldham, McCauley, and Purefoy, each marked "Doubtful." Two exceptions were marked "Good"—a note from Ed Mallett for $2,252 and another from Elbert Cole for $300. Other personal property was sold at auction for $2,242.66, much of the total from farm produce or animals—for example, 121 bushels of corn for $557, 2,000 pounds of pork for $200, three mules for $315, and a work steer for $14, all bought by Dr. Frank Smith. Sidney Smith bought a carriage for $50.

Beyond producing a considerable amount of additional money for the siblings, the public sale delivered a profound message of respect and understanding toward the long-suffering daughter, Mary Ruffin Smith. Not a single bid was made against her for the house-hold furnishings; each of her bids was met by silence from her friends and neighbors: a bed and stead for one cent, a dozen chairs for one cent each, a side board for five cents, two tables for five cents each, a clock for five cents, a carpet for five cents, and a lot of kitchen furniture for one dollar.[157] Burdened by her brothers' four mixed-race children ranging in age from ten to three—all bastards according to law—Mary Smith must have felt the warm sympathy implied by the silence of her neighbors. At the age of 40, her destiny as a spinster already determined by the sins of her brothers, she would remember the kindness of those neighbors during her remaining 31 years.

The federal census of 1860—the first following the death of the Smith parents and the last and most helpful in quantifying slavery—revealed the siblings' wealth: Francis Smith owned twelve slaves and two slave houses; Sidney Smith, six slaves and one slave house; and Mary Smith, eleven slaves and one slave house. That made a total of 29 men, women, and children held in bondage by the siblings. Although they were not listed by name, the enslaved were categorized by sex, age, and whether black or mulatto. Only Mary owned mulattos: an eighteen-year-old male and five females. Neither Frank nor Sidney reported a female of an age comparable to that of the woman who had borne them daughters, so of special interest are Mary's five separately listed mulatto females who, though not named, may have been (by age): Harriet (40) and her daughters Cornelia (15), Emma (14), Annette (12), and Laura (9). The fact that slaves were property on which taxes were levied supports the assumption that the five mulatto females credited to Mary were indeed Harriet and her four daughters. Only a twenty-four-year-old white carpenter named Van Sparrow lived in the big house near Chapel Hill with the siblings. Mary was listed as owning $31,800 in real estate and personal property, compared to Frank's $15,000 and Sidney's $21,000. In the separate 1860 agriculture and manufacturing schedule for Orange County, "F.J." Smith, rather than Mary, was listed as the head of the household on Price Creek with 400 acres of improved and 1,600 acres of unimproved lands with a value of $20,000, supplemented by $800 in farm implements and $2,100 in livestock. Farm productivity appeared roughly comparable to that of the 1850 census, but with the addition of 1,000 pounds of tobacco. The agriculture schedule for Chatham County listed Frank Smith's Jones Grove plantation with 200 acres of improved and 1,800 acres of unimproved land valued at $15,000. Blanks on the remainder of the Chatham return may have indicated that the Jones Grove lands were not producing income at that time.[158]

As clouds of civil war began forming, much of Francis Jones's legacy was intact, and the Smith siblings, even with their moral baggage, were citizens of substance in Orange and Chatham counties.

Chapter 3

Boozing Politician Son:
James Sidney Smith (1819–1867)

The Smith sons died in reverse order of their birth. Sidney Smith lived only 48 years, Francis 61. Neither would merit more than a footnote in history but for dastardly acts perpetrated against Harriet, the slave mother of their out-of-wedlock daughters.

Little is known of Sidney's early years, but presumably he attended one of the several male academies in Hillsborough.[1] His name entered the public records in 1833 when he enrolled at age 14 in the University of North Carolina. He lived with his brother Francis in West Building (Room 15 in 1833, Room 14 the next two years) and was elected to the Dialectic Society. He did not remain for graduation from the institution on whose board of trustees his father had been a member since his congressional service. From Chapel Hill, the brothers' paths diverged, Francis becoming a half-trained physician, Sidney a poorly-trained lawyer. Both died, in 1867 and 1877, respectively, as disgraces to their sister, the sole surviving heir to Francis Jones's legacy.

One of 28 freshmen in a student body of 109 at Chapel Hill, Sidney was among the sons of the state's elite. He joined the Dialectic Society and presumably attended classes taught by Joseph Caldwell, Elisha Mitchell, William Hooper, James Phillips, and Walker Anderson. The curriculum, aside from language, arithmetic, and geography, was largely classical. Tuition was then $15 per session plus $8 for washing, mending, and bed; $1 for room rent; $2 for servant hire; and from $6 to $8 per month for meals. Sidney was classified as a sophomore the following year, but the catalogue of 1836–1837, the last in which his name appeared, listed him as a "non-graduate."[2]

Leaving the University in 1837 without a degree, Sidney Smith returned to Hillsborough and began his study of law under a young attorney, William A. Graham, just then establishing himself in the Orange County seat. The two were not cut from the same political cloth, however, for Graham emerged as one of the nation's Whig leaders while young Sidney became a Jacksonian Democrat, an apostate in the eyes of both his father and his teacher. Despite their disparate political views, the teacher and student remained friends, and Graham, who narrowly missed becoming vice-president of the United States, would die financially indebted to his former student.[3]

From an early age Sidney Smith was recognized for his oratorical talent. At age 17 he was identified as one of the "declaimers" at university commencement exercises in 1836 and as a future lawyer and assemblyman "with reputation as a speaker." Three years later he was complimented by the local newspaper editor for his Independence Day oration: "His speech both in the sentiments expressed and manner of delivery could have done credit to a much older head." When 21 years later he was accused of being a party to his father's questionable land deals, he emotionally defended himself: "I appear your honor in the character of an injured, abused and persecuted young man. No act has been left unpayed [sic], no experiment left untried to injure me in my profession, to wound my feelings and my honor, and dispossess me of my right claims to property." He turned his sharp tongue toward his adversary, Josiah Turner, the former sheriff of the county, whose "known mode of legal warfare is an indiscriminate abuse and slander of all ages sexes and conditions in life with whom it has been his lot to have legal controversy, who has as little regard for the calumnies he heaps upon unfortunate characters as his prey [remainder torn]." He denied having been his father's legal advisor in the sale and transfer of property, admitting only to having been a witness to a deed in 1841 when his father "was a man of handsome estate and his credit was sound and as good as any man in the community.... He has been an injured and persecuted man...."[4]

Attorney Sidney Smith's boarding bill for himself and his horse in 1850 was paid by his sister seven years after his death (courtesy Mary Ruffin Smith Papers, Southern Historical Collection, Wilson Library, UNC-CH).

In 1862 Sidney Smith boarded at Hugh Guthrie's hotel in Chapel Hill, paying his bill with $40 in cash plus the year's rental of Smith's slave Ben, figured at $120 (courtesy Mary Ruffin Smith Papers, Southern Historical Collection, Wilson Library, UNC-CH).

On the eve of the Civil War, Sidney Smith joined "noted gentlemen," including former governor (and then UNC president) David L. Swain, in delivering inspirational addresses to the Orange Guards as they prepared to depart for the defense of the South.[5] Finally, Pauli Murray, basing her impression on the memory of Sidney's daughter Cornelia, wrote, "He was a fiery orator and developed into one of the county's most effective stumpers."[6]

No substantial body of manuscripts has been found to illuminate Sidney Smith's law practice. It is not even clear where he regularly resided in his adult life, for his postal address varied from Chapel Hill to Pittsboro; and only the Census of 1860 places him with his sister and brother at Price Creek. His daughter Cornelia referred to his book-filled study, which presumably would have been in the big house near Chapel Hill, but did he also have an office near the courthouse of either Chatham or Orange county, as was customary for many attorneys? Both county seats were several hours' horseback ride from Oakland, and his alma mater, which he probably visited frequently, was within a half-hour gallop from the Price Creek plantation.[7]

A few manuscripts among his sister Mary's papers give only occasional glimpses into Sidney Smith's life as a country lawyer. An overdue bill for $9.75 owed to E.R. Goldston for Sidney's and his horse's board for various dates in 1850–51 was paid by Mary Smith to Goldston's executor in 1874, seven years after her brother's death. On January 31, 1862, Hugh Guthrie agreed "to board him [Smith] at his Hotel for the year 1862," for which Smith was to pay $120 in value, defined as "the hire of his slave Ben for the year 1862 and forty dollars in money." Guthrie had purchased the Eagle Hotel from Nancy Hilliard, so Sidney Smith apparently lived there at least in 1862. Thomas J. Hogan and J.T. Hogan agreed to pay Smith $40 for the hire of "one Negro woman for the year 1862" and promised to furnish all food & good clothing for the woman and her child. There is documentation that Sidney Smith hired out other slaves. In 1863 he leased out several females, and three men paid him a hundred dollars for the hire of his boy Ben. Abner Brown signed an agreement in 1864 reading, "On or before the 1st day of January 1868 I promise to pay Sidney Smith nine hundred dollars for the hire of his boy Anderson for the year 1865. I also agree to furnish said Negro with 1 winter and 2 summer suits of clothes, 2 pr. of good shoes, 1 pr. of socks, 1 hat, 1 blanket or quilt & to deliver said boy to Dr. Fr[ancis] Smith on 25 day of December 1865." Jones Watson, a prominent Chapel Hill merchant, paid Smith $200 for the hire of an unnamed Negro girl for the year 1865. Dated January 9 when the fate of the Confederate dollar was questionable, the agreement required that the rent was to be paid "in common currency."[8] With the income from the sale of the Flowers Place invested at six percent interest, and with rent from his slaves, Sidney Smith had no need for a lucrative law practice.

After his sale of the Flowers Place in 1855, heavy-drinking Sidney Smith received much of his income from the rental of his slaves, for whom he required adequate clothing (courtesy Mary Ruffin Smith Papers, Southern Historical Collection, Wilson Library, UNC-CH).

It is known neither what the storied orator looked like nor how he sounded. Even Cornelia's published memories provide only a few peeks into her father's appearance and character. She described him as a "ruddy-faced, sharp-eyed, wiry little man with a long bullet-shaped head and quick catlike movements." He also "walked like he was strung on electric wires and he had a voice that could hold you spellbound for hours," and he was "a hot-blooded, impetuous little fellow who hurled himself with single-minded fury into whatever caught his interest."[9]

The Young Rapist

The memories of an aging woman—as heard by a young grandchild who reinterpreted and recorded them decades later—provide weak evidence for historians seeking to reconstruct the truth, but there is little reason to doubt that Pauli Murray's account of the initial rape of the light-skinned slave Harriet by Sidney Smith could have occurred essentially as is told in *Proud Shoes*. That account describes the brutal banishment of Harriet's common-law husband, Reuben Day, freedman, by the Smith brothers, and their subsequent and repeated sexual attacks on the woman, first by Sidney in the early summer of 1843: "The other slaves heard Marse Sid break open Harriet's door. Ear-splitting shrieks tore the night, although he stuffed rags in the door and window cracks to muffle Harriet's cries. They heard little Julius screaming." Similar attacks continued until Francis waylaid his brother and left him "lying unconscious in the yard, his clothes soaked with blood and an ugly hole in his head." Following the fight, Cornelia's story continued, Sidney "took to drinking and brooded his life away. He went down to Raleigh for one term in the legislature and there were flashes of brilliant success here and there when he was sober but in the end he turned out to be one of the worst drunkards in the county."[10]

The damage had been done, and in February 1844 Harriet gave her newborn the name Cornelia. Although biracial births were not particularly rare in the antebellum South, this one caused tongues to wag in Hillsborough, particularly when Delia and Mary Smith chose to keep Harriet and her baby in their home next door to the recently finished Masonic Lodge on King Street. Unrepentant, Sidney went around bragging about his fatherhood.

We have only Murray's opinion that, beneath Sidney Smith's virulent public defense of slavery as an antebellum Democrat, he privately harbored antislavery sentiments: "He was a creature of paradoxes: a man of unrestrained passions and deadly pride, yet tormented by idealism. He had come under the anti-slavery influence of liberal professors at the University when a student there. He was fully aware of the degraded position of the slave in the society. Grandmother [Cornelia] said that when he was full of liquor he would tell anybody how he hated slavery and that he was a 'Union man' even though a Democrat. Yet he had perpetuated the very evil he secretly deplored."[11]

Still, according to Murray,

> this contradictory little man had had [*sic*] a compassionate streak in him. While he made most of his money defending the property rights of slaveowners, he often represented without charge free Negroes accused of crime. It was unpopular to defend them in the courts but he never turned them down and won many an acquittal for them. Grandmother [Cornelia] told me how once her father came home from court after having saved from the gallows an old

Negro man accused of stealing a mule. The slaves met 'Marse Sid' at the gate, picked him up and danced about the yard with him on their shoulders. She said his idea of celebrating a legal victory was to come home, turn his coat inside out, knock the top out of a jug of apple cider and go on a big drunk. In spite of his faults, I couldn't hate Sidney Smith when Grandmother talked about him.

Elsewhere, Cornelia claimed that "before the Civil War, he [Sidney] saved fourteen poor Negroes from the gallows free of charge. He got many colored folks out of trouble and kept 'em from rotting in jail."[12]

It is not surprising for a father of an out-of-wedlock, mixed-race child to have conflicting emotions regardless of his abstract political theories. The most touching and memorable passages of *Proud Shoes* are those describing the love between father and daughter, each acknowledging a societal gap impossible to be completely closed in the prewar South. Especially revealing and touching is this from the author, Sidney's great-granddaughter: "He instilled in her [Cornelia] that she was inferior to nobody. He gave her pride in her Smith-Jones ancestry. She said he told her that she was an octoroon and could therefore marry into either race if she chose. He tried to protect her from the wounds of slavery by making her believe the one-eighth nonwhite ancestry was Indian instead of Negro. He made it impossible for her to adjust to her later Negro status and yet he could not offer the recognition to support the notions he planted in her fertile mind."[13]

Sidney Smith as Politician

Astonishing, as viewed a century and a half later, is the fact that within two years after he raped his sister's favorite slave and fathered the child Cornelia—a deed for which he boasted rather than denied—Sidney Smith was elected by the voters of Orange County to the North Carolina legislature, where he moved socially and politically among the state's elite, two of whom—William A. Graham and Kenneth Rayner—came close to attaining the presidency of the United States. Even later, as slavery drove the nation toward civil war, Smith remained a potential candidate for the United States Congress. In the nineteenth-century South, the charge of bastardy was seldom laid when the perpetrator was white and the female was nonwhite. But history tends to deliver its judgments indiscriminately. Perhaps its judgment for Sidney Smith is that he is remembered only for one dastardly act; nowhere does his name appear among those honored for their meritorious or patriotic lives.[14]

The Democrats of Orange County nominated Sidney Smith for the House of Commons in 1846, along with running mates William N. Pratt, Patterson H. McDade, and Wilson Patterson. John Berry was that party's nominee for the State Senate. Of this quintet, only Sidney Smith was elected—and by just five votes. His victory might have been due to his conciliatory gesture during the debate over the division of the county. His fellow commoners were Whigs Giles Mebane, Chesley F. Faucett, and John B. Leathers. Whig Hugh Waddell beat Berry for the Senate.[15]

When the General Assembly convened in December 1846, Representative Sidney Smith—dropping his first name (James) perhaps to avoid confusion with his father—was appointed to the Internal Improvements Committee; Joint Committee on an Agricultural, Geological and Mineralogical Survey of the State; and Committee on Enrolled Bills.[16] Both chambers were controlled by Whigs, but the margins were not so great as to make the Democrats impotent except on near-party-line votes. Even so, among the few questions upon which both Democrats and Whigs agreed was an amendment to the rules of order requiring that "The members of this House shall uncover their heads upon entering the Hall, whilst the House is in session, and shall continue so uncovered during their continuance in the Hall."

Not surprisingly, Sidney Smith voted for losing candidates for officers in the House of Commons and members of the Council of State. The depth of his partisanship was exhibited when he even voted against his fellow Orange County citizen, Willie P. Mangum (a convert from Democrat in 1828 to Whig by 1834), for United States Senator. As the session dragged on, Smith's voting record revealed that he was against publicly-funded internal improvements, taxation of billiard tables, altering the mode of electing United States Senators, appointing a common schools commissioner, enclosing the governor's mansion with a fence, and creating new counties in which Whigs would be more numerous. In the face of the Whig majority, most of his votes were in the negative.

The sitting governor was a Whig neighbor of the Smith family, William A. Graham, a former United States Senator and future vice-presidential nominee, who had once taught law to freshman Representative Sidney Smith. So Smith, only 27 years old, found himself a political opponent of his former teacher and among legislative heavyweights in both parties, such as John W. Ellis, William W. Holden, and Edward Stanly. Also among the heavyweights was Kenneth Rayner, a Whig already known for his feistiness during three terms in the United States House of Representatives. There Rayner clashed both verbally and physically with other congressmen, and three years later he barely missed becoming a future President of the United States when he lost the Whig nomination for vice-president by a single vote to Millard Fillmore. In 1850 upon the death of the new president, Zachary Taylor, Fillmore moved into the White House.[17]

One of the bitterest fights of the 1846–47 session was over a Whig bill to replace a congressional redistricting law adopted four years earlier that, as provided in the federal constitution, had been intended to remain in effect until after the next decennial census in 1850. With the Whigs in control of state government, however, a bill drawn by Rayner was introduced to redistrict the state into nine districts, the lines drawn to virtually assure a Whig congressional majority. Orange County would be in the Fifth District with Caswell, Chatham, Granville, and Person. Rayner's initial speech supporting the bill was printed on the front page of Dennis Heartt's *Hillsborough Recorder*. Despite his personal allegiance to the Whig Party, Editor Heartt the following week devoted virtually all of the front page and a part of the second page to Sidney Smith's bitter response. In it, the youthful representative exhibited no intimidation from the powerful Rayner. The plan, he charged, was a violation of the federal constitution, "cunningly" and "ingeniously devised with the sole purpose of assuring the ambitious desires of the Whig party." By his count, the bill was designed for the election of six "Federalists" and only three Democrats. Replying to Rayner's taunts against the Democratic Party, he lampooned the Harrison-Tyler campaign of 1840, referring to "those degradations which have been submitted to with disgust and shame—those midnight orgies in 'log cabins'—that immense expenditure of money from some hidden source." Smith also took a shot at the character of General Winfield Scott, a known Whig, whom he characterized as having "more taste for a plate of soup than for the burning sands of Mexico." Rayner's sizzling response filled much of the first two pages of Heartt's paper the next week.

He took great offense to Smith's characterization of Whigs as "Federalists." He added, "I could admire the bold and spirited manner with which the gentleman from Orange stood up for his party, and in the advocacy of a desperate cause," but berated him for questioning the military leadership of General Scott. Stingingly, he added, "There will always be some one to do the low and dirty work of party, and who is fit for nothing else ... to say nothing of the bad taste of so young a man." Ouch![18]

A second bruising battle occurred over a Senate-passed resolution appropriating $10,000 to equip and pay expenses to Wilmington and Charlotte of a regiment of volunteers requisitioned from North Carolina by President Polk. The Democrats bristled over the preamble, which began, "Whereas, by the action of the Executive and the subsequent sanction of Congress, this republic is involved in a Foreign War and our State is called upon for Volunteers." This wording blamed the Mexican War on President Polk, thus supporting Whigs' characterization of the conflict as "Mr. Polk's War." Democrats of course supported the appropriation—they even tried to increase the sum to $15,000—but they could not accept the imputation that the conflict was caused by presidential policies. Democrat after Democrat tried unsuccessfully to amend or delete the words immediately following the opening "Whereas"; each effort was defeated by from one to a few votes. Among those efforts was a motion by Sidney Smith to insert, at the close of the preamble, a rambling statement:

> The course of Mexico towards the United States, has presented a catalogue of aggressions and insults, of outrages on our National Flag, and on the persons and property of our citizens, of the violation of treaty stipulations, and the murder, robbery, and imprisonment of our countrymen; and whereas, War exists by the act of Mexico between that republic and the United States; and whereas, the United States is in the right and Mexico in the wrong, this country, in the just, righteous and necessary prosecution of this war, is but protecting the national honor, according to the settled and established usages of all civilized nations; and whereas, the President of the United States has made a requisition upon North Carolina for one Regiment of Volunteers, to serve during the continuance of the War.

Smith's motion, worded as if it might have been written under the influence of alcohol, was promptly rejected.

The Democrats next sought to separate the preamble from the resolution, but the Whig speaker, Edward Stanly, ruled that the question was not divisible; his ruling was upheld 63 to 52. Even the minority leader's innocuous motion to add the sentence, "Resolved therefore, That it becomes the State of North Carolina to contribute her aid for the support of this War," was rejected by four votes. The Democratic leader moved that an explanatory statement be added that "on its second reading, when the names of the following members of the House of Commons were called, they voted in the affirmative, protesting against the preamble [the names, including that of Sidney Smith, followed]"; that too was rejected 59 to 53. Wiatt Moye's statement on behalf of himself, Richard Jones, and Elias Barnes complaining that "we protested against the preamble as being untrue, and voted for the resolution; and our vote is recorded in the negative," was rejected 60 to 51. John W. Ellis (a future governor) then offered a "paper as a protest," but the chair ruled that he had no right to protest since he had first voted for the resolution. The engrossed resolution was read a third time, passed, and ordered to be enrolled. Only then did the Whigs relent enough "by general consent" to adopt a Democrat-introduced resolution for an appropriation to purchase a regimental flag for the volunteers. Despite their repeated defeats, the patriotic Democrats did manage to leave behind journal entries that for several years tarred the Whigs as being unpatriotic in the war with Mexico.[19] A similar picture was painted in the Senate, where Orange County's Senator Waddell voted with the Whigs.

The political divide in regard to the war reached into the troops. G.W. Caldwell's company in Mecklenburg County refused to be mustered because of the partisan preamble as well as the transfer of authority to choose company officers to the governor. One of the cool heads during the controversy was Congressman James Graham, a Whig who, feeling that "every vestige of patriotism is lost in blind devotion and bigotry to Party," urged his brother, Governor William Graham, not to punish the soldiers for their "gross mutiny" but to leave the matter to public censure. "The Question ... is not how we came into the War, he wrote, but *"how we are to get out of it?* It requires *two* to make a peace."[20]

The war did not divide all North Carolinians. The Caswell County Volunteer Company, on the way to the war front, was patriotically welcomed in Hillsborough, where the hotels and residents joined in providing meals, entertainment, and beds for the night. Under Captain Williamson, the Caswell men carried a flag described as showing "a spread-eagle, amid a cluster of stars, neatly painted on white satin" and bearing the motto "Conquer or Die."[21]

Perhaps the only bill introduced by Representative Sidney Smith—concerning "the expediency of providing by law, that the Judges of the Supreme Court of the State shall publish such of their decisions only as shall determine unsettled questions of law"—was repeatedly postponed and finally tabled. Smith thus left little to dignify his legislative service during those years of intemperate partisan politics.[22]

Sidney Smith's Samsonian defense of President Polk's role in the Mexican War was only three months past when his hero arrived in the flesh and spent three days celebrating his acceptance of the honorary degree granted him by the faculty of the University of North Carolina two years previously. It was Polk's first return to Chapel Hill since 1818, when he graduated with first honors ahead of the Rev. William Mercer Green, who was the Smith family's minister in Hillsborough and was now a professor at the University, busily organizing Chapel Hill's Episcopal Church of the Atonement (later named the Chapel of the Cross). Accompanying the president were the current Secretary of the Navy, James Y. Mason (Class of 1816), and a previous holder of that cabinet post, John Branch (Class of 1801), then the governor of Florida. For the first time, commencement was covered by a unnamed northern reporter, representing the *New York Herald*.[23] All the king's horses could not have kept the 29-year-old Democratic commoner from joining the frenzy of activities surrounding the presidential visit, and it is a good bet that Representative Smith's defense of the Democratic Party in the General Assembly earned him an audience, perhaps even in the new rooms that hotelier Nancy Hilliard built especially for the accommodation of the president. Certainly, tongues wagged about Sidney and the president whom he so vociferously defended against the criticism of North Carolina's legislative Whigs.

The president's personal appearance in Orange County probably had little effect on the local electorate; Representative Smith lost his bid for reelection to the House of Commons in 1848. Consequently, he was not in the legislature to vote on a divisive bill authorizing a referendum on dividing Orange County. The vote for division carried 1,257 to 1,007, the western region almost solidly in favor, the eastern portion firmly opposed. The new county of Alamance, the name of Indian origin, thus began its existence in 1849.

Sidney Smith's failure to be reelected may have been due partially to several court cases in which his father was accused of colluding to defraud his creditors through a morass of questionable land transfers among the family. Noting that ten years previously he had appeared before the court to obtain his law license, he began, "Little did I then expect that my next appearance before you I would be involved in a suit implicating my character as a man of moral character, integrity and in plain parlance common honesty.... I appear your honor in the character of an injured, abused and persecuted young man. No act has been left unpayed [sic], no experiment left untried to injury me in my profession, to wound my feelings and my honor, and dispossess me of my rightful claims to property." He turned his biting oratory on Josiah Turner, the former sheriff, whose "mode of legal warfare," he charged, was "an indiscriminate abuse and slander of all ages, sexes and conditions in life with whom it has been his lot to have legal controversy, who has as little regard for the calumnies he heaps upon unfortunate characters as his prey."[24]

In light of the fierce political division between Whigs and Democrats during this period, an interesting situation arose in 1848 when in Orange the election returns showed a tie vote for state senator between Hugh Waddell and John Berry. The county sheriff certified Whig Waddell the winner, but the Democrats, charging that the records had been corrupted, took the fight to the Senate. A committee first ruled that Berry had won 754 to 747, but then, after reviewing a Supreme Court opinion on the qualifications for voting, threw out all contested votes, leaving Democrat Berry still the winner by a vote of 736 to 731.[25] Politics remained at fever pitch in Orange County.

The commoner's father, Dr. James S. Smith, who was seldom reluctant to give his own advice and share his wisdom, made a brief reappearance on the political scene when, in September 1851, he wrote from Oakland, the new Price Creek home, to William A. Graham expressing his opinion on the "Cuban affair": "[T]he Government will have trouble with this matter, for it is my belief that the Southern people will never desist until they have charge of that Island." He added, "If it were possible to purchase it [Cuba] from the queen of Spain at a reasonable price, & it could be done without giving offence to England, and other European states, it might be wise to arrest the difficulty in that way. It is my deliberate opinion now, that our people never will rest long in a state of quiet until they have driven all races from the North American continent except our own Anglo Saxon race, & such others as have come to live with us under our own form of Government."[26] Interesting speculation: Two days after Smith's letter was written, Graham was in Washington and sent a message to President Fillmore: "Important despatches from Cuba. If you desire I will bring them over at any hour you may appoint." Fillmore made a notation, "Bring despatches at 12. Will meet Cabinet at that hour." Had Smith's letter reached Graham, and if so, was it among those "despatches" given to the president?

Soon afterward, an intriguing affair was reported by James W. Bryan to William A. Graham on January 25, 1852. After discussing Whig politics, Bryan wrote, "Gov'r [David] Reid has given a levee! (I send Cousin Susan's 'sample invitation' inclosed.) Before the most interesting part of the ceremonies began, Mr. Sidney Smith of Orange attempted to pull the Hon. Wm. H. Haywood's nose—they created quite a democratic uproar in the levee or melee. Mr. Haywood & son met Mr. Smith next day, & Mr. H. struck Smith on the head with a stick, and his son jumped on him and choked him—they were seperated [sic] & thus ended for the present the affray, although Smith swears vengeance, etc."[27]

Except for that broil, there had been little news of political action by the Smiths since Sidney's single term in the House of Commons, but on June 9, 1852, the *Hillsborough Recorder* carried a surprising report: At a convention of the Democratic Party of Alamance and Orange counties held at Hillsborough during May Court, "Dr. James S. Smith was called to the chair." The report announced the nomination of John Berry and Bartlett Durham for the state Senate, both of whom declined; instead, John F. Lyon was nominated. The report was signed by "Jas. S. Smith, Ch'n." Changing times, changing issues, changing views had finally led the devout Whig, Dr. James Strudwick Smith, to cross party lines to join his son in the party of Democrats, then seeking to shed their Loco-Foco image.[28] However, Dr. Smith did not live long to contemplate his new political allegiance; he died six months later. His death was recorded in the *Hillsborough Recorder* on December 15, 1852: "Died. James S. Smith, M.D., 66, at his residence in Orange, 7th inst. Doctor, politician, Episcopalian."[29] The loquacious physician/politician/land speculator would have been disappointed with such a short notice of his half-century of stirring the political pot.

Orange County had not heard the last from the younger Smiths in politics. In 1855 "Sidney A. Smith" attended a convention of the new American ("Know-Nothing") Party at Louisburg and urged James B. Shepard to accept nomination for Congress. It would be easy to believe that this was not Hillsborough's James Sidney Smith, but Frederick Nash Strudwick of Hillsborough also was present, and the editor of the *Hillsborough Recorder* played up the story. More persuasive was an odd report of a meeting at which Henry W. Miller, speaking to the anti–Catholic Know-Nothings, raised the question of the late Dr. James Smith's views of suffrage and, "at the request of some opponents of the American Party, James S. Smith esq. consented to reply to Mr. Miller, and when Mr. Miller had concluded he [Smith] took the stand for that purpose." Miller was reported to have produced the journal of the Convention of 1835 to prove that "the late Dr. James S. Smith ... voted against striking out the word 'Protestant' and substituting Christian." In the ensuing election in Orange County, the No-Nothing candidate, Edward G. Reade, led Democrat John Kerr by a two-to-one margin and was elected to Congress.[30]

Whether or not he met with the anti–Catholic, anti-immigrant Know-Nothing/ American Party in Louisburg, Sidney Smith was his old Democratic self at a convention in Hillsborough's Masonic Hall in June 1856. There he introduced resolutions endorsing James Buchanan and John Breckinridge for president and vice-president. The minutes revealed that "Sidney Smith, Esq., after the reading of the ... resolutions, was called on and in an eloquent manner showed forth the character of James Buchanan to the Convention." Smith spoke of the "cheering prospect that awaits the party, and urged those present, when they returned to their homes, to exert their best endeavors for the cause." Buchanan carried Orange 969 to 747 in November, but Hillsborough voters favored Millard Fillmore, the Know-Nothing candidate, by 266 to 157. In the nation's capitol, sectionalism was so bad that the House of Representatives required 133 ballots to elect Nathaniel P. Banks of Massachusetts as speaker by a vote of 113 to 104. Banks was identified by Dennis Heartt as a member of the "Black Republican" Party.[31]

Twelve years after President Polk's visit to Chapel Hill, another of Sidney Smith's political heroes arrived to participate in two days of festivities, including the delivery of the commencement address at the University. President James Buchanan had no previous association with the institution, but he brought with him Secretary of the Interior Jacob Thompson, an

1831 UNC graduate and native of Leasburg in Caswell County. The slavery issue hung ominously over the nation, but Buchanan was trying valiantly to prevent a breakup of the Union. Smith had worked hard for the visitor in the 1856 campaign, and again his loyalty to the Democratic Party was probably acknowledged by the president of his nation. Very likely fire-eating Sidney Smith was among those who dined under the lofty trees of President Swain's front yard. He also probably was present for a presidential reception under the Davie Poplar, near the monument to Joseph Caldwell, dedicated the previous year; and he certainly would have recognized the name of Francis L. Hawks, his father's antagonist-turned-patient, a copy of whose brand-new *History of North Carolina* the chief executive presented to Elisha E. Wright for the best English composition by a graduating senior.[32]

Faced with the splintering of the traditional political parties and the rapid rise of the Republicans in the North, Dr. Francis Jones Smith by March 1859 had joined his brother's Democratic party, and both were elected to the district convention.[33] Even the Whig editor of the *Hillsborough Recorder*, Unionist Dennis Heartt, warned abolitionists against interference in southern slavery. He coined new names for protest meetings, such as the "Opposition State Convention." John Brown's insurrection at Harper's Ferry sent a chill throughout the South, and the increasing verbosity of both northern abolitionists and southern "fire-eaters" further fanned the flames of sectional animosity. In May 1860, Sidney Smith was one of five members of an Orange County resolution committee that reported, "We regard with deep concern the long, continued, systematic, and alarming aggression of the Northern people upon the rights, property and people of the South and we warn our Northern Brethren if this line of conduct is longer persisted in, it will end in a dissolution of our beloved Union." The minutes continued, "Mr. [Sidney] Smith then addressed the meeting in a few very elegant and spirited remarks, urging the adoption of the resolutions." Both Sidney and Francis were appointed delegates to regional and state conventions along with neighbors John Berry, General James Allison, Paul C. Cameron, Cadwallader Jones, and John U. Kirkland.[34]

The slavery issue, which divided the nation in the presidential election of 1860, dealt a death blow to the national Whig Party, most of whose southern members took a new name, Constitutional Union Party, and nominated John Bell of Tennessee. As a result, Democrat Buchanan only narrowly carried the state over Bell. Stephen A. Douglas, who married a Rockingham County woman, ran as a "northern" Democrat and received only a few thousand votes; the antislavery Republican Party was not even allowed on North Carolina's ballot. The Smith brothers were again on the winning side, but theirs was but a pyrrhic victory. The moderation of the Orange electorate was indicated by the election of old Whigs to the legislature, but it no longer directed its own destiny.

After Abraham Lincoln was elected president, mass meetings were held by the alarmed populace throughout the state. Late in the year at one such meeting in Orange, Sidney Smith railed against the "aggression of the North" and advocated a state convention before his motion was ruled out of order. The *Hillsborough Recorder* produced a broadside reporting that the meeting tried to calm excitement, but it did call for a state convention. At another mass meeting in Hillsborough, speakers included John W. Norwood, David L. Swain, John Berry, Paul C. Cameron, William A. Graham, and Josiah Turner. A resolution introduced by Norwood was so severe that it did not pass. At a similar meeting in Chapel Hill, Sidney Smith, University President David L. Swain, and Professor Samuel F. Phillips were speakers.

A resolution called the "state of public affairs to be in the highest degree threatening and dangerous to our rights and our security, [but] we are not without hope."[35]

At another meeting on February 6, 1861, Sidney Smith made a long speech—published as a handbill titled "Proceedings of a Public Meeting in Chapel Hill, North Carolina"—in which he lamented that "owing to a spirit of Pharissical [*sic*] fanaticism pervading in the North, in reference to the institution of slavery, incited by foreign emmissaries [*sic*], and fostered by corrupt political demagogues in search of power and place, a feeling has been aroused between the two sections of what was once a common country, which of itself would almost preclude the administration of a united government in harmony." Observing that the issue was no longer partisan, he proposed two leading Whigs, David L. Swain and William A. Graham, as delegates to a predicted state convention. Sidney Smith, James Watson, and John W. Carr were named a committee to present the resolution to Swain and Graham. Smith acknowledged Graham's acceptance, adding a personal touch, "Believe me when I say I can never forget your kindness to me in boyhood, when I was your law pupil." A few days later Smith wrote that Swain had accepted and would speak at Durham's Depot and at Hillsborough during February court.[36]

Still, at a referendum on whether a state convention should be called to consider the rapid acceleration toward disunion, the citizens of Orange County voted overwhelmingly, 1,436 to 458, in the negative. For delegates (in the event the statewide vote should require a convention), pro–Union candidates William A. Graham and John Berry ran far ahead of the pro-convention candidates Henry K. Nash and Dr. Pride Jones. Statewide, demonstrating the Unionist sentiment in the western counties, the no-convention forces won by a few thousand votes.

By the time Governor John W. Ellis refused to obey President Lincoln's call for troops, even die-hard Dennis Heartt had given up hope for the Union, and North Carolina was preparing for war. From Chapel Hill a university student named Edward H. Armstrong wrote his father on April 20, 1861, "The Orange Guards left Hillsboro this morning, and I am told that there were few dry eyes in the crowd congregated to see them depart." At a flag-raising on the campus, Armstrong reported, "Two young ladies made speaches [*sic*] and were followed by the following noted gentlemen, S.F. Phillips, Capt. Ashe, Gov. Swain and Sidney Smith, together with quite a number of Students. Gov[.] Swain in alluding to the war said that the south was invincible by any force that our enemies can send against us. He thought that further blood shed could be avoided, by every man in the South shouldering his musket. Lincoln would then see our strength and would know that it would be useless to attempt to coerce us. Such being the case I beg you to let me be one to proceed to Federal Point, and frighten Lincoln out of his witts."[37] Neither President Swain nor Sidney Smith, his student a quarter-century earlier, had an inkling of what lay ahead.

Despite the statewide popular vote opposing a convention, the General Assembly insisted on calling one. Graham and Berry—a lifelong Whig and a lifelong Democrat—again were elected to represent Orange County, and, faced with a national emergency not of their own making, they reluctantly voted for the secession ordinance on May 20, 1861.[38]

Sidney escaped conscription, and little is known of his activities during the Civil War. He was, however, still playing politics, for on February 6, 1864, Samuel F. Phillips wrote to Graham, "I was sorry to hear, upon getting to Chapel Hill from Hillsboro,' that James N. Patterson, Esq. will oppose Captain Berry. This is in great measure the doing of our friend,

S[idney] Smith, who is a sort of Puck in politics, especially when a little in liquor. He was so upon the occasion when he got up a petition to Mr. P., requesting him to become a Candidate, (two weeks or more ago) & was active in getting citizens of Chapel Hill to sign it. I am the more sorry for it, that Mr. P. will hardly get a vote in the County respectable enough to soothe him for his defeat."[39]

Sidney Smith's Last Years

Following the deaths of his parents and his inheritance of the vast Flowers Place in Chatham County, Sidney Smith lost little time in divesting himself of his real estate. Even earlier, on October 22, 1853, he sold to Josiah Turner for $15 all of his interest in a tract in Orange adjoining the lands previously owned by Abel Thompson & others, "the same tract of land formerly owned by William Smith of said county and by him conveyed to Edwin Reade, Ralph Gorrell, and Sidney Smith."[40] Then, on October 6, 1855, quoting within the deed a portion of his grandfather's will bequeathing him the "plantation called the Flowers Place in the County of Chatham on the waters of Newhope and Bush Creek adjoining the lands of Isaiah Cole, William Merritt, and others and composed of several original tracts and supposed to contain from eighteen hundred to two thousand acres," Sidney Smith sold the vast consolidation to brothers Jehial Atwater and Jahaza Atwater for $11,000.[41] The deed, registered November term 1856, was witnessed by Samuel F. Phillips, Smith's former student and later Solicitor General of the United States. That was a large sum in the mid–1800s, and with it Smith became a popular local creditor—a sort of community lender. Entries in a small account book neatly recorded loans totaling $12,720.81 between 1857 and 1865. The largest amount—$5,000—was lent to the prominent county official James C. Turrentine; among the securities was the statesman and Sidney's former teacher, William A. Graham.[42]

When Sidney Smith wrote his will on November 29, 1864, some Southerners still held out hope for victory in the Civil War and the survival of slavery as an institution. The will simply stated: "I give to my sister Mary all my real[,] personal and mixed estate to her, her heirs and assigns forever and I constitute the Revd. Geo. W. Purifoy [sic] Executor of this my last will and testament." The document was witnessed by George H. Haigh and Dr. J. B. Jones.[43] In *Proud Shoes*, both Cornelia Smith Fitzgerald—who would have been 20 years old when the will was prepared—and her biographer were critical of the testator's failure to include his daughter as an heir. In context, however, Cornelia was both a minor and a slave when the will was written in 1864, and under existing law even the private property of slaves belonged, in effect, to the slaveowner.[44] Sidney Smith could more justifiably be criticized for failure to (1) emancipate his daughter or (2) rewrite or update his will following the fall of the Confederacy in April 1865. If he had done either, Cornelia could then have been eligible for property ownership as a free woman of color. Mary Smith, too, may be criticized for tardiness. Although eventually she willed Cornelia a hundred acres of the Price Creek plantation, that gift would have been more beneficial had the land been transferred earlier when, as a young bride, Sidney's daughter was struggling to make a life for herself and her poverty-stricken husband, Union army veteran Robert Fitzgerald. There is enough blame to go around.

Sidney Smith, noted for alcoholism, escaped Civil War military service because of "broken down Constitution & general bad health." He evaded advancing Union forces by disguising himself and hiding in the woods (courtesy Mary Ruffin Smith Papers, Southern Historical Collection, Wilson Library, UNC-CH).

It may be no coincidence that two weeks after he signed his will, Sidney Smith was ruled unfit for military service. The certificate, headed "Head Qrs, 'Select Medical Board,' Camp Holmes, N.C., Dec. 6th, 1864," reads: "Sidney Smith, a 'Senior Reserve' Conscript of Orange county, N.C., has been carefully examined by us, and, in our opinion, is unfit to discharge the duties of a soldier because of Broken down Constitution & general bad health, which we consider permanent. The said Sidney Smith is hereby exempt from service in the Army of the Confederate States, subject to re-examination and enrollment, when ordered by the Board." It was signed by Geo. E. Redwood, Surgeon P.A.C.S., and Edmd. S. Pendleton and H.W. Coffey, assistant surgeons."[45]

Still, Sidney's "broken-down" condition did not prevent his flight from the Yankee soldiers who marched into Chapel Hill in April 1865. Charles Peter Mallett amusingly described the scene: "Frank staid at home, but Sidney took [to] the woods, and with a long beard and mean apparel, passed himself off as the uncle of some poor family in the neighborhood, and Joe [Mickle] says that the more effectively to carry out the deception, that he made a rent in his garment about six inches below the small of his back, out of which protruded the insignia of 'Dicky Dout.'" The reference was to an English children's rhyme often recited in nurseries and on playgrounds: "Dicky, Dicky, Dout/Your shirt hangs out/Four yards in/and five yards out." In the nineteenth century, reference to a person as a "Dicky Dout" implied that he was a fool.[46]

Sidney Smith died April 25, 1867, but no obituary has been found in surviving issues of the *Hillsborough Recorder*. Mary and Frank buried him near their parents at Oakland.[47] The circumstance of the 48-year-old's death—two years after Confederate military officers described him as "broken down"—is not known, but estate papers filed by the Reverend George W. Purefoy (executor of his will) documented the younger son's addiction to alcohol and tobacco—an affinity sadly described by Sidney's great-granddaughter Pauli Murray in *Proud Shoes*: "He took to drinking and brooded his life away."[48] Purefoy, whose farm adjoined the Price Creek plantation, chaired the building committee for the Baptist Church in Chapel Hill in 1854, so he must have whispered a few "tsk, tsks" as he settled accounts with C.S. Cooley, William Patterson, and the firm of Long and McCauley for the deceased's whiskey, brandy, and tobacco.[49]

If Sidney possessed cash at the time of his death, the estate papers fail to identify it. Instead, his wealth consisted almost entirely of about $10,000 in notes signed by more than thirty individuals, some of the debts uncollectible after the fall of the Confederacy. The attorney had lived on interest from the sale of the Flowers Place more than a decade earlier and his intermittent law practice and hire of his slaves. Among the debtors were men already—or soon-to-be—prominent in Orange and Chatham counties, including J.C. and J.A. Turrentine, John Berry, and families with surnames like Carr, Cole, Davis, Gattis, Hogan, and McDade.

Sidney Smith's body was exhumed from Price Creek and reburied at Jones Grove in 1897. For the new tombstone, Kemp Battle may have thought so little of the younger Smith that he omitted the name (Sidney) by which the lawyer was usually known (H.G. Jones collection).

William A. Graham, governor, senator, secretary of the navy, and vice-presidential candidate, was Sidney Smith's law teacher. However, the attorney borrowed so much money from his former student that the debt remained unpaid when the last of the Smith line died in 1885 (courtesy North Carolina Collection, Wilson Library, UNC-CH).

Most of what little is known about Sidney Smith comes from his great-granddaughter, the Rev. Anna Pauline [Pauli] Murray, author of *Proud Shoes*, shown here at her desk. After her mother's early death, Pauli Murray lived from about age two to twelve with her grandmother, Cornelia Smith Fitzgerald, in this house in Durham, North Carolina. Cornelia's stories, as remembered decades later by her granddaughter, also provide much of what little is known about Mary Smith's household (courtesy North Carolina Collection, Wilson Library, UNC-CH, and H.G. Jones, respectively).

Ironically, however, the largest debtor was Sidney Smith's former law teacher, William A. Graham (1804–1875), former nominee for vice-president of the United States. Graham— lawyer, planter, governor, senator, and secretary of the United States Navy—still owed Sidney Smith $3,924.10 plus interest on a $5,000 loan for which J.C. Turrentine, J.S. Leathers, and C.S. Howland had signed as securities. Although he paid $400 to Sidney Smith's executor, a large portion of Graham's debt remained unpaid when his will, written in 1871, directed the payment of any outstanding liabilities, adding, "These I have indeavored [*sic*] to liquidate ... with the exception of one to the Executors of J. Sidney Smith decd. which I hope to satisfy within a year or two from this time." That was a vain hope; the former vice-presidential candidate carried the debt to his grave.[50]

Purefoy's handwriting was so atrocious that his accounts as executor are read with great difficulty. By the date of his final return on June 11, 1870, however, he had recovered for beneficiary Mary Smith $3,049.69 in cash, $4,186.18 in "good" notes, and two Chapel Hill lots (from Richard J. Ashe and his mother-in-law Maria Mitchell, widow of Elisha Mitchell) worth $650. Given up as "cannot be collected" were notes on several neighbors of the Jones Grove plantation, including A.S. and Zinnie Riggsbee and J.J. Ferrington [*sic*]. Expenditures for settling the estate totaled $3,130.24. In addition to Smith's tobacco and liquor bills, the debts included $25 to Foster Utley for the decedent's coffin, $80 federal tax, nearly $100 for three years' state and local tax, $50 for attorney Samuel F. Phillips, $50 for Norwood & Webb attorneys, $413.80 for commissions, and $15 to bring Dr. J.B. Jones to Hillsborough to prove Smith's will. The final settlement resulted in a total payment of $7,885.87 to Mary Smith.[51]

The settlement of Sidney Smith's estate was not without its drama. At least two court cases were played out, one invoking a name of special interest. On December 29, 1860, Richard Blacknall, Thomas B. Morris, and John W. Carr signed an agreement with Sidney Smith to pay him $275 for the hire of "certain negro slaves" for the year 1861. The claim asserted that one slave named Stephen was returned to the plaintiff on the same day, and $25 was deducted from the bond; therefore, $250 was still due the estate. In Superior Court, the defendants answered that of the slaves involved, one named Harriet was "in a pregnant condition, which was unknown to the defendants, in consequence of which pregnancy her services were not of the value to be paid"; that another, named Dupper, was diseased and sick most of the year, though the plaintiff had represented him to be in a sound and healthy condition; and, consequently, the plaintiffs should not recover the amount demanded. Robert Morris, who wrote the original contract, corroborated the account. Apparently the Reverend Purefoy accepted the explanation, and his attorneys, Norwood and Webb, recognized the "insufficiency in not stating facts to constitute a defense, or counter claim." The case was dismissed by Superior Court Judge Albion W. Tourgee and the estate paid the $25 court costs. In another suit against Robert Loader, Jones Watson, and John W. Carr, the judge wrote, "It appearing to the Court that the defendants have settled with the plaintiffs *in fais*, it is ordered & adjudged that the defendants pay one penny & the costs of the court to be assessed by the clerk."[52]

The handwriting on one of the legal documents raises an interesting question. The name "Harriet" was inserted above the line in what may have been a hand different from that which produced the main document. Was the document altered by a historian wishing to identify that particular slave woman as *the* Harriet (the mother of Sidney Smith's daughter and three of Francis's)? The document dates about ten years after the birth of the last of Sidney and Frank Smith's daughters, and *that* Harriet is not known to have produced another child as she aged. If the document was tampered with for literary license, a moving story could be constructed to demonstrate the evils of slavery. For Sidney Smith to have hired out as a slave Harriet—the mother of his own daughter Cornelia, as well as the mother of his brother's three daughters (and now presumably pregnant with another child)—would certainly present a chilling image of the human slavery system. In 1861, Cornelia would have been about seventeen years old, so the question arises whether she too might have been hired out, or whether Mary Smith had intervened and sheltered her mixed-race nieces from the slave lease system. Furthermore, the question would remain as to how Sidney held title to *the* Harriet in 1860 when official records show her as the property of Mary Ruffin Smith in 1845.

Chapter 4

Lecherous Doctor Son:
Francis Jones Smith (1816–1877)

Except for medical account books, Francis Jones Smith left even fewer documentary traces than his brother. Worse, none of his three daughters found a biographer, so he and his progeny have been virtually ignored by historians. His repeated rape of the slave Harriet is known simply because his brother Sidney's daughter married an educated Union army veteran, and the pair's granddaughter wrote a revealing book, *Proud Shoes*. The best reason for remembering Dr. Francis Smith is to cast light upon his descendants, who are equally deserving of recognition.

Born in Hillsborough on August 17, 1816, Frank—as he was popularly called—probably attended one of the male academies in that county seat. That he attended the University of North Carolina from 1832 through 1836 and left without graduating is documented, as is his sharing with Sidney a room in West Building (Old West) and membership in the Dialectic Society. For the academic year 1837–38, Frank followed his father's path to the medical class of the University of Pennsylvania, from where he too left without a degree.[1] As the son of a former congressman then a sitting trustee of both of the universities that he attended, Frank Smith was among an elite cadre of 380 potential physicians. Mere admission to the Philadelphia campus was a distinction that gave father and son respectful acceptance in the Carolina Piedmont. With less than one academic year of training in medicine, Frank Smith returned to Hillsborough and opened practice, presumably as an unofficial partner of his father, although their accounts were kept separately.

"Tall, dark, brooding man"

About three years passed between the birth of Harriet's child by Sidney Smith and the arrival of her second, Emma, sired by the older brother Frank. By Pauli Murray's account, a bloody fight between the brothers confirmed Harriet as "Frank's woman," a condition perhaps welcomed by the attractive light-skinned slave, if for no other reason than protection from further brutal rapes by Sidney.[2] It is not clear, however, whether Frank's initial domination occurred prior to the birth of Cornelia in February 1844. Murray pictures the subsequent relationship between Frank and Harriet as distant, "barren of all communication save that of the flesh. In the Smith house Francis was the silent, remote master who scarcely noticed

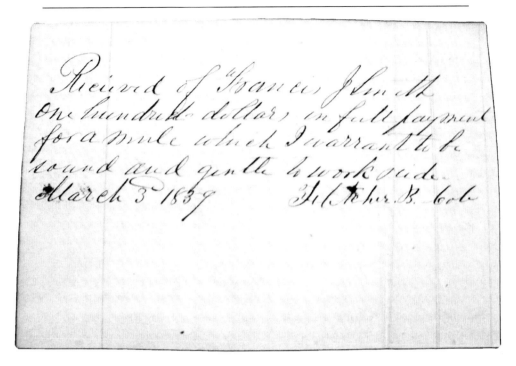

Having spent one term in the medical department of the University of Pennsylvania, Francis Jones Smith returned to Hillsborough and practiced medicine with transportation supplied by a mule (courtesy Mary Ruffin Smith Papers, Southern Historical Collection, Wilson Library, UNC-CH).

Harriet's presence. And she waited upon him with the same impartial deference she showed the other Smiths, giving no sign that she was his mistress." Yet, Murray believed, "over the years Harriet was silently devoted to him and no one ever heard of his having another woman."[3] Meanwhile, "Sidney became an outcast in the family, tolerated because he was blood kin but detested because he sired a scandal." Those quotations, remembered by a young child as told by an aging grandmother, must be considered in context. They seem to imply that, to Frank, Harriet was simply a convenient body to satisfy his sexual desires. However, given the absence of modern contraceptives and the elapsed time between Harriet's birthing over a period of roughly seven years (1844–1851), another question arises concerning the frequency of and conditions under which the conjugal visits occurred. Augustus Long's claim of "a cottage in the corner of the yard" where the doctor "received his concubines"[4] applies only to the period after Emma's birth, which occurred before the family moved from Hillsborough in 1847.

Unlike Sidney Smith's Cornelia, whose memories were reported in the writings of her granddaughter, the three daughters of Harriet sired by Frank Smith left virtually no literary traces. Consequently, even less is known about their father. Still, a few glimpses of Frank can be seen through *Proud Shoes*. For example, Cornelia contrasted her father and uncle in their competition for Harriet: "Sidney had always been a hot-blooded, impetuous little fellow who hurled himself with single-minded fury into whatever caught his interest," while "Francis was by nature more cautious and restrained. Sidney exploded and spent himself, but Frank knew how to wait and bide his time." The description continued, "He [Frank] was a tall, dark, brooding man who seemed withdrawn much of the time. While he said little and seemed calm and self-possessed at all times, he had a terrible temper beneath his quiet exterior."[5] Thus, we have Sidney as a "hot-blooded, impetuous *little* fellow" and Frank as "*tall, dark, brooding*" [emphasis added]—not much on which to formulate images of in-the-flesh adversarial brothers. Unanswered are questions such as eye, hair, and skin color; pitch of voice; choice of dress; circle of friends; and—most of all—strength of character. Were both brothers exclusively heterosexual, and if so, did they run with other women, black or white? Did their consciences bother them when they raped women of another race? Deep down, how did they justify their assaults? Cornelia loved her father Sidney and thought he loved her; why, then, did Frank appear (at least through Cornelia's eyes) to ignore his own children? Is Frank's image less humane than Sidney's only because the latter's daughter found an author to publish her memories? As the poet Horace wrote in *Ars Poetica*, a word once uttered can never be recalled.

Successively, about 1847, 1848, and 1851, Harriet bore three more girls—Emma, Annette, and Laura—each sired by Dr. Francis Smith. The primitive state of birth control procedures in the middle of the eighteenth century raises questions, such as the frequency with which Francis Smith slept with Harriet over a period of at least six years. Were there any familial relations between the father, mother, and daughters, even after the females were emancipated? Other questions remain unanswered not only between the parent couple but also between Harriet, the girls, and Mary Smith. We can only wish that audio recorders had been invented and that Pauli Murray, when she lived with her grandmother, had been old enough and able to record for posterity additional memories of Cornelia Smith Fitzgerald, who carried so many secrets to her grave in 1924 at age 80, when her biographer was just 14.[6]

While Harriet's four girls were under the care of two mothers—herself and the mistress in the big house—her first born, Julius, was relegated to the slave cabins. When the boy was about thirteen, he was caught in a snowstorm, almost froze to death, and was crippled the remainder of his life.[7] Julius Smith would have been forgotten by history had not Mary Ruffin Smith remembered him in her will with a bequest of twenty-five acres of Price Creek lands.

"He was somebody in particular"

A couple of years after the medical student returned to Hillsborough without a degree, an interesting "Card" appeared in the local newspaper reading, "Dr. James S. Smith's health is so far restored as to enable him to resume the practice of his profession. He cannot promise to ride in the night, as his eye sight has so far failed him to render night travel dangerous. He has associated his son F.J. Smith with him, in the practice who will be able to attend to night calls and such as offer in inclement weather." To provide conveyance for those calls, the new doctor paid Fletcher B. Cole $100 for a mule that was warranted "to be sound and gentle to work & ride."[8] Thus, fresh from the University of Pennsylvania, Francis Smith, calling himself a doctor, had filled in during his father's indisposition; now he shared a partnership. Without formal licensing of physicians in the state, the establishment of a medical practice required little more than hanging out a shingle and filling a carpet bag with patent medicine.

The name of Frank Smith infrequently appeared in the *Hillsborough Recorder*, and then usually in connection with his occasional flirts with politics, first as a Whig alongside his father, later as a Democratic follower of his more vocal brother. However, his practice was so slow in 1846 that he and his father advertized the lowering of their medical charges for mileage exceeding one mile in good daytime weather from fifty cents to thirty cents, "and all other charges reduced in proportion."[9]

Dr. Smith's account books, several of which are preserved in his sister's papers, initially were fairly well kept, suggesting an orderly medical practice. However, carelessness increased with the years. One volume, covering early years of his practice and showing most medicines at 25 cents per dose, documents visits to John A. Faucette for venesections and tooth extractions at a dollar apiece. The charges for each visit to William H. Riggsbee was $4.50. Among Smith's better known patients were Josiah Turner and Hugh Waddell. Several students at the University in Chapel Hill, perhaps to escape attention on campus, sought his services. Among them was James H. Viser from Alabama, a "first distinction" graduate in the Class of 1841, to whom Dr. Smith administered "clap medicine" during his junior year. Henry Revels, a free Negro, was charged $10 to treat the same disease. An interesting charge to John Reeves, a Freedman, reads: "To medicine & directions wife in abortion, $2." One account reveals that the young physician was a "soft touch" for both his father and brother; Dr. Frank repeatedly paid his father's debts, and he lent Sidney $40 for the purchase of a horse. In another book, an entry for May 10, 1854, reads, "Edward C. Cole, Dr., at Sam Williams. To visit & instrumental deliver of wife & attendance all day & night. Medicine $30."

Another account book is of special interest because it extends through the Civil War, when issuance of five-dollar "medical certificates"—sought by white men to escape Confederate military service—made up a portion of the doctor's income. By then, farm accounts shared the medical volume, entries for merchandise and farm labor hardly distinguishable from medical services. The emancipation of Harriet and her four daughter was ignored; the mother and daughters were treated no different from others, simply identified as "Colored" or occasionally "Freedman" or "Freedwoman." At least, Frank Smith gave his daughters his surname. An account of Harriet, the mother of the doctor's three daughters, was listed on June 3, 1866, as "Harriet Smith, Colored, Dr., to 1 bushel wheat loaned—1.50 cts loaned"; sixteen days later was entered "Harriet Smith, Colored, Dr., to $3.40 cash loaned. $1.50 loan paid $3." On another occasion, the entry read, "To Harriet Smith, Freedman, to $6.30 loaned."

By far the most poignant entry, dated May 9, 1873, reads, "Harriet Smith, col., $11.50 to pay for Lightning Rod." Sadly, the rod arrived too late, for the mother of Dr. Smith's three daughters had been grievously wounded by a lightning strike on her cabin nine months earlier, and she died from those wounds four months after the purchase.[10]

A unique account of Dr. Frank Smith's dress and demeanor was published when its author was past the age of 75, and his report may have contained as much hear-say as childhood memory. Augustus White Long, a native of Chapel Hill who spent his career in academic institutions outside the state, provided several intriguing comments on the Smiths as he remembered them just after the Civil War. "Dr. [Frank] Smith," he wrote, " lived with his spinster sister in a big house surrounded by a thousand acres of land, their former slaves being their tenants. More strictly speaking, Miss [Mary] Smith lived in the big house with a former schoolmistress as a companion, a prim little lady [Maria Spear] with corkscrew curls.... Life on such a plantation was not only semifeudal, but it harked back to the patriarchal days of the Old Testament." Long described Dr. Frank Smith as "a colorful survivor of what the historical writers of today [1939] call the slaveholding aristocracy. A large landholder and a personage, he was somebody in particular. When he appeared on election day [about 1866], he was always dressed for the part: high hat, frock coat, flowered waistcoat, and gold-headed cane, chin whiskers like Uncle Sam's." Accompanied by his body servant, Candy Parton, one of three local Negroes who voted Democratic, Smith "planted himself before the voting window, legs wide apart, the end of his spinal column resting on the knob of the gold-ended cane padded by both hands. 'Candy, go up to that window and vote,' he said with emphasis, as he scowled at a group of Negroes who seemed inclined to crowd in on Candy. The old darky shuffled up to the pole and voted, looking as if he were not sure he could go through with it, but Dr. Smith never had a doubt. There stood the Old South."[11]

Long's description of Oakland, some time after the death of Mary Smith in 1885, is particularly revealing: "The big house was occupied by a caretaker; the 'office' was locked and boarded up. That pattern of life had faded out. Dr. Smith and his concubines were dust; so were his spinster sister and the little schoolmarm with the corkscrew curls." The comment on an "office" referred back to a previous claim that the doctor "lived out in the 'office,' a two-room cottage in the corner of the yard, his meals being sent out to him, and here he kept his whiskey and received his concubines." Long's assertion that Francis Smith studied medicine but, "following a tradition among the sons of planters," did not practice his profession, is proven erroneous by the survival of the doctor's account books in his sister's papers.[12]

"Dr. Frank" Smith, according to a neighbor's account, took his meals and entertained his "concubines" in this small outbuilding (shown before recent restoration) at Price Creek (photograph by Kenneth M. McFarland, courtesy North Carolina Department of Transportation).

By the time the Census of 1870 was taken, Sidney Smith had been dead three years, and Mary Smith's wealth was listed in Orange County as $20,000 in real estate and $1,000 in personal property, and Frank Smith's was $3,000 and $1,000, respectively. The evaluation for Mary was probably excessive, that for Frank too low. Census figures, like county tax lists, were only as valid as the lister's honesty and objectivity. Living with the siblings in "Dwelling 371" were also Maria L. Spear (68), Mary's friend and teacher; Whitted Eaton (55), a black servant; and Sallie McGuire (37), a black servant, and her four children—Patrick (16), Parthenia (14), Maria (12), and Tippo (9).

The agriculture schedule for the same year provided more—but obviously understated—statistics on Mary's holdings. That year her Price Creek acreage, underestimated at 150 acres improved and 800 unimproved, was valued at $7,500, supplemented by farm implements at $100. Wages in the amount of $500 had been paid the previous year, and the plantation included 2 mules, 5 milk cows, 2 working oxen, 5 other cattle, 2 sheep, 24 swine, all with a value of $550. The farm produced the previous year (in bushels): wheat 150, rye 20, Indian corn 750, oats 150, peas and beans 14, Irish potatoes 30, sweet potatoes 50. Other productions included 250 pounds of butter, 40 gallons of molasses, 15 pounds of wax, and 100 pounds of honey. Animals slaughtered numbered 225, and the estimated value of all production was $1,500.[13]

This was the first census to dignify Harriet and her daughters as free people. The first daughter, Sidney's Cornelia, had already married Robert Fitzgerald but has not yet been identified in this 1870 census. Harriet Smith (age 53 according to the census) was keeping house on Price Creek plantation, "Dwelling 374," and living with or near her were daughter Emma (23), Emma's farmer husband Henry Morphis (25), and the couple's one-year-old son Samuel. Together, Harriet and the Morphises reported personal property worth $300. Annette (20) was keeping house at "Dwelling 292" with her farmer husband Edward Kirby (20), their daughter Laura (1), and one-month-old son Francis; they reported personal property worth $600. Laura (18) was keeping house in Charlotte with her husband, barber Gray Toole (25), and their five-month-old daughter Delia. Living with the Tooles was Gray's brother, 19-year-old Henry Toole, who later became a barber and prominent businessman in Rock Hill, South Carolina. The Tooles reported personal property worth $200. Gray Toole's first name was sometime spelled "Grey"; Morphis as Morphus; and Kirby sometime Kerby. Thus all four of "Miss Mary's Girls"—as gossips in Chapel Hill called them—were now married and beginning their own families. Both Sidney and Frank Smith were grandfathers.

"Violent insanity unto death"

There appears little doubt that, like his younger brother, the doctor became addicted to alcohol and suffered physical, moral, and mental deterioration. Kemp Battle, who with his wife Pattie were Mary Smith's most intimate friends, on several occasions commented on Frank's failing health, both in mind and body. Referring to Mary Pauline (Cornelia Fitzgerald's seven-year-old daughter who lived a short time at the Smith home in 1877), Pauli Murray wrote that the little girl "could not fathom why the servants called the queer old man she saw hobbling about on a cane mumbling to himself 'Marse Frank.' They warned her to stay away from him because he'd had a stroke and lost his mind." Frank's nearest relative, Louisa A. Holt, alluding to his condition, asked Mary Smith if Frank had "acknowledged his Lord & Savior & become a member of the household of faith.... Oh, I do hope he has turned his face to Zionward."[14]

Francis Jones Smith died intestate April 17, 1877, from—according to Battle—"a lingering disease passing through violent insanity unto death." Augustus White wrote, "It was reported in fervently religious circles that Dr. Smith died in great terror, torn with regrets and Remorse."[15] An obituary in the *Hillsborough Recorder*, May 2, 1877, contained enough errors to suggest that Francis Smith's reputation had been confused with that of his father, dead for 25 years: "Dr. Frank Smith, 61, at his residence in Chatham County, 2 weeks ago. Last surviving son of Dr. James S. Smith, physician of this place. At one time Dr. Frank Smith was a member of Congress. He is survived by one daughter." Francis Smith never served in Congress; he was survived by not one but three daughters (Emma, Annette, and Laura); and he died in Orange rather than Chatham County.

Long before Frank died, Mary, with Maria Spear at her side, contemplated her own final days. Her parents and younger brother lay in the ground at Price Creek, and she must have pondered about where her own body should to be interred. After Delia Smith's death, Frank came into ownership of Jones Grove in accordance with his grandfather's will, so it occurred to Mary that she could recognize and respect the affinity between grandfather and grandson by burying Frank in the Jones family plot six miles down the road in Chatham County. Although Maria's mother was interred at St. Matthew's Episcopal Church in Hillsborough, the lonely spinster accepted her longtime friend's invitation to be buried with the Smiths.[16] Together the spinsters decided to bury Frank at Jones Grove and to instruct Kemp Battle to have their respective bodies interred there too when the time came. Mary knew that she could depend upon Dr. Battle to arrange for the disinterment of the bodies of her parents and brother Sidney and for their reburial at Jones Grove. Frank's body, then, joined those of his grandparents (Francis Jones and Mary Parke Jones) and uncle (Ruffin Jones) in the soil once owned by his great-grandfather Tignal Jones, Sr.

A crumbled tombstone at Jones Grove may be reflective of the wasted life of Dr. Francis Jones Smith, who contributed little to society except to hold onto the Jones Grove plantation, which his sister ultimately willed to the University of North Carolina for worthy purposes (H.G. Jones collection).

The Estate of Dr. Francis Jones Smith

Kemp Battle had witnessed spinster Mary Smith's successive care of her father, mother, brother Sidney, and now Francis. He also witnessed Mary's relinquishment of her right to administer the estate of her brother, resulting in the probate court's appointment of Andrew Mickle, a merchant and sometime bursar of the University of North Carolina.

Except for the Dimmock's Mill property owned for a while,[17] no record has been found of real estate holdings by Francis Smith beyond the Jones Grove plantation, bequeathed to him by his grandfather Francis Jones and transferred to his name upon the death of Delia Smith in 1854. Based on Maria Spear's testimony in 1847, the young doctor had been doing "a handsome practice for 6 or 8 years" and often lent money to his father.[18] About that time the bachelor brother moved with the remainder of the family to Oakland, the large new house on the Price Creek plantation, from where his practice was centered in southern Orange and northern Chatham County. The close proximity of Jones Grove may have become more meaningful for him during the next three decades. His Grandfather Jones, however, had abandoned the manor house in 1837 when he moved in with the Smiths in Hillsborough, so the original buildings, inhabited for years by tenants, probably had suffered from neglect, muting the sentimentality of a grandson who viewed the place merely as a source of rental income.

In addition to ownership of the Jones Grove plantation, the deceased brother held a mortgage of several hundred dollars on the land of James Pace and wife Elizabeth in Chatham County, and that property on Rocky River promptly passed to his sister Mary.[19] The record suggests that Frank Smith, like his younger brother, had spent much of his income on alcohol and medicines. He had inherited from Sidney the note on William A. Graham from February 1869 in the amount of $3,299.23, on which only a portion had been paid. In addition, he held a note on Robert Graham, surety for his father, in the amount of $1,500 with seven percent interest from 1872. When Frank's estate was closed in 1891 (by which time the former governor's son John W. Graham had become administrator), it apparently still held a note for $1,500 on Robert Graham.[20] It is noteworthy that the last three Smith survivors played a significant role in providing funds for the very prominent Graham family even after the death of the former governor. Apparently the wide gap between their respective political allegiances—Graham was a Whig, Sidney was a Democrat, and Frank eventually turned Democrat—was no bar to their financial relationships.

The father-son doctors over a period of more than 50 years had built a substantial library of books relating to medicine, and after Frank's death, the entire collection of 200 volumes was promptly given by Mary Ruffin Smith to the library of the University of North Carolina at Chapel Hill. The breadth of the collection is revealed in the variety of titles ranging from anatomical studies to good health practices and proper medications and treatments for physical and mental disorders. The books, most of which were published in the first third of the nineteenth century, provide a measurement of medical knowledge two hundred years ago.[21]

Mary inherited from Dr. Francis Smith—in addition to the 1,740-acre Jones Grove plantation—at least $6,549.23, most of it in notes yet to be redeemed. All that had been preserved from Francis Jones's estate, all that had survived the schemes of her father and two brothers, now belonged to the 63-year-old spinster, the only "legitimate" survivor of the

Jones-Smith family. Many Orange and Chatham county neighbors must have been envious of the rich woman who lived in the big white house on the road from Hillsborough to Fayetteville, virtually within sight of the University of North Carolina, Few of them, however, recognized the tragedies that had already aged her far beyond her years, and none could have anticipated the additional misfortunes that would follow her during her final eight years. Only one—Kemp Plummer Battle—could have imagined that the surviving Jones-Smith fortune would be dedicated to future generations of Mary Ruffin Smith's fellow North Carolinians.

Chapter 5

Saintly Daughter:
Mary Ruffin Smith (1814–1885)

To construct a biography of Mary Ruffin Smith, one must begin by stringing together isolated references from many sources and melding them with the memories of a niece as told in old age to—and reinterpreted by—Pauli Murray, whose book, *Proud Shoes: The Story of an American Family*, was first published in 1956. Even so, Mary Smith remains shadowy during much of her life. The poignancy of the spinster's fading years, however, is revealed more clearly in letters written by her former teacher and longtime companion, Maria Louisa Spear, and in memorial tributes by her most loyal male admirer, Kemp Plummer Battle. Other than her will, few specimens of Mary's own handwriting have been preserved; furthermore, in nineteenth century North Carolina, except for marriage and obituary notices, the names of women seldom entered the public records. Even newspapers like the *Hillsborough Recorder* only occasionally carried names of women.

This we do know: Mary Ruffin Smith was born in Hillsborough in 1814—the exact date is missing on her tombstone, and birth and death records were not officially recorded in North Carolina for another century—the only granddaughter of Francis and Mary Parke Jones of Chatham County and the first child and only daughter of Delia Jones Smith and James Strudwick Smith. Her father was understudying with a local medical doctor and beginning to dabble in assorted business activities before pursuing a life in medicine, politics, and civic affairs. Nothing is known of Mary's childhood, but by the time she reached the age of twelve, she had come under the influence of three men who would gain national significance both in the lay world and the Episcopal Church: Francis Lister Hawks, a rising young lawyer from New Bern who moved to Hillsborough about 1822; William Mercer Green, a minister who moved from Williamsborough to Hillsborough shortly afterward; and Hawks's brother-in-law, Walker Anderson, who ran a private school in the town. Hawks and Mary Smith's father already knew each other; they had served together, not very harmoniously, in the 1821 session of North Carolina's House of Commons.[1] Despite feistiness as a politician—he was known for his fiery oratory—Hawks was senior warden of the new St. Matthew's Church to which Green came as rector. Soon, with Green's encouragement, the young lawyer abandoned his legal duties and studied for the ministry. Together the three men participated in the building of the new church in Hillsborough before going their separate ways to national attention. Hawks achieved fame as an inspiring minister, historian, and educator, including service as the first president of the University of Louisiana; Green, a scholar as well as min-

The Rev. William Mercer Green, founder of the Hillsborough Female Seminary and future Episcopalian bishop, was Mary Ruffin Smith's teacher and lifelong admirer. When Mary was fourteen, the superintendent judged her "first" in all subjects except writing. The teacher would have been pleased with Mary's clear handwriting when she penned her will nearly a half century later (see photograph in Chapter 6) (courtesy respectively Mary Ruffin Smith Papers, Southern Historical Collection, and North Carolina Collection, Wilson Library, UNC-CH).

ister, taught and pastored at the University in Chapel Hill before becoming Episcopal Bishop of Mississippi; and Anderson also taught at the University before moving to Florida and serving as that state's first chief justice. All three would fondly remember Dr. Smith's little daughter.[2]

Mary Smith's scholastic progress at Hillsborough Female Academy was confirmed by her report card for Summer 1828, in which Green rated the 14-year-old student first in arithmetic, rhetoric, chemistry, philosophy, mythology, botany, astronomy, evidences of Christianity, and music. Only in writing was she rated second. Green kept in touch with his student during his travels; for example, when Mary was 19, the teacher sent her a newsy letter from Red Sulphur Springs, Virginia, asking that she remember him to all his "flock." Hawks confirmed their teacher-student relationship when in 1853 he wrote to express to Mary his pleasure for having participated "in your early instruction."[3]

In 1824 when Mary was ten years old, her grandfather Francis Jones gave her "a negro or mulatto girl named Betsey (the daughter of Tempy), aged six years." It is easy to suspect that this was a birthday present, a young playmate to be trained as a personal servant.[4] Betsey was only the first of several slaves to be owned by Mary. Twelve years later, December 1,

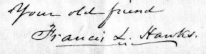

Chapel Hill, June 1. 1853.

Dear Mary,

You have desired of me some memorial whereby you may remember me after my departure. Will you let this note subserve that purpose, conveying to you the assurance that it has afforded me no small satisfaction to have met you again after an absence of so many years; and to find the pupil entertaining feelings of grateful affection toward her old preceptor. Those feelings are quite a sufficient reward for my efforts in your early instruction, and I beg you to believe that you will always be remembered with regard and interest by

Your old friend
Francis L. Hawks.

Another of Mary Smith's teachers in Hillsborough, the Rev. Francis Lister Hawks, rose to prominence in the Episcopalian ministry, serving as historiographer of the denomination, founding the Church Journal, and turning down three bishoprics. Upon Hawks's return to Chapel Hill in 1853, he accepted with appreciation Mary's "feelings of grateful affection toward her old preceptor" (courtesy respectively Mary Ruffin Smith Papers, Southern Historical Collection, and North Carolina Collection, Wilson Library, UNC-CH).

For his granddaughter's tenth birthday, Francis Jones presented to Mary Ruffin Smith "a Negro or Mulatto girl named Betsey (the daughter of Tempy) aged about six years" (courtesy Mary Ruffin Smith Papers, Southern Historical Collection, Wilson Library, UNC-CH).

1836, Dr. Smith, for $800, sold to his daughter "a negro woman named Love aged about 44 years, her daughter Amy about 8 years, her son Jim aged about five years & her daughter Virginia aged about eleven months."[5] So Mary Ruffin Smith in her twenties was already a slaveholder; furthermore, by her grandfather Jones's will written in 1841, the deed to the expansive Price Creek plantation was held in trust for her by her parents. From the standpoint of finances, she was in a position to command respect, even envy, from potential suitors.

Meanwhile, a young light-skinned slave woman came onto the Hillsborough scene and radically affected the life of every member of the Smith family. On September 30, 1834, Dr. Smith paid William Kell $450 current money for "a negro girl named Herritt [*sic*], aged fifteen years past a slave," warranted to be "sound and healthy and clear of any defect whatsoever as to her health." The Smith children were barely older—Mary was 20, Francis 18, Sidney 15—than the attractive new slave who, based on her daughter's memory as told to Pauli Murray, was "one of the most beautiful girls in the county, white or black. She was small and shapely, had richly colored skin like the warm inner bark of a white birch, delicate features, flashing dark eyes and luxuriant wavy black hair which fell below her knees. She was shy and reticent but her eyes talked." Murray added, "I never knew whether she [Harriet] had any Negro blood. Grandmother [Cornelia Smith Fitzgerald] always said she was three-fourths white and one-fourth Cherokee Indian."[6]

With Dr. Smith's permission, Harriet married a local mulatto freedman by the name of Reuben Day, and about 1842 she bore him a son named Julius. Pauli Murray graphically describes a subsequent, horrible scene in which Sidney Smith forced Reuben to flee for his life, then in late 1843 raped Harriet.[7]

Perhaps the marvel is that a decade had passed before the attractive young slave woman was forced to submit to one or both of the Smith brothers. Of course, we have no proof that Harriet remained untouched by a white man that long, because in 1844, when she gave birth to a daughter named Cornelia, sired by Sidney Smith, condoms were not commonly available, and attempts at birth control were primitive at best. More than a century later this daughter provided the subject for Pauli Murray's powerful narrative. It was not uncommon for slave women to bear children sired by white men, but for the birth to occur in the family of Dr. James Smith—a former congressman who counted national figures among his associates—ought to have shocked the neighbors in the Orange County seat. Under existing law, a child took the race of its mother, and since Harriet was a slave, so was her daughter, officially classified as "mulatto" but often simply listed in public records as "Colored" and, by the end of the century, "Negro."

Cornelia's presence in the Smith household must have been a heavy cross for Mary Smith, 30 years old when the child was born. Dr. Smith was under severe strain from his reckless real estate transactions; Delia Smith was frail and in ill health; and their sons were warring with each other over the baby's mother. The honor of the family was at stake. Those conditions combined to dictate Mary's response to the immediate situation. Unable to relegate her own blood-kin to the slave cabins, she chose to keep the child and mother in her own care in the Smiths' Hillsborough home. And, to legitimize her decision, on August 25, 1845, she paid her father $550 for Harriet, by then about 26 years old and encumbered with two children—her boy Julius, aged about three years, and her daughter Cornelia, aged about one year.[8]

Sidney's rape of Harriet and the birth of their daughter no doubt were the determining factors in Mary Smith's decision to exercise the equivalence of adoption by simply purchasing

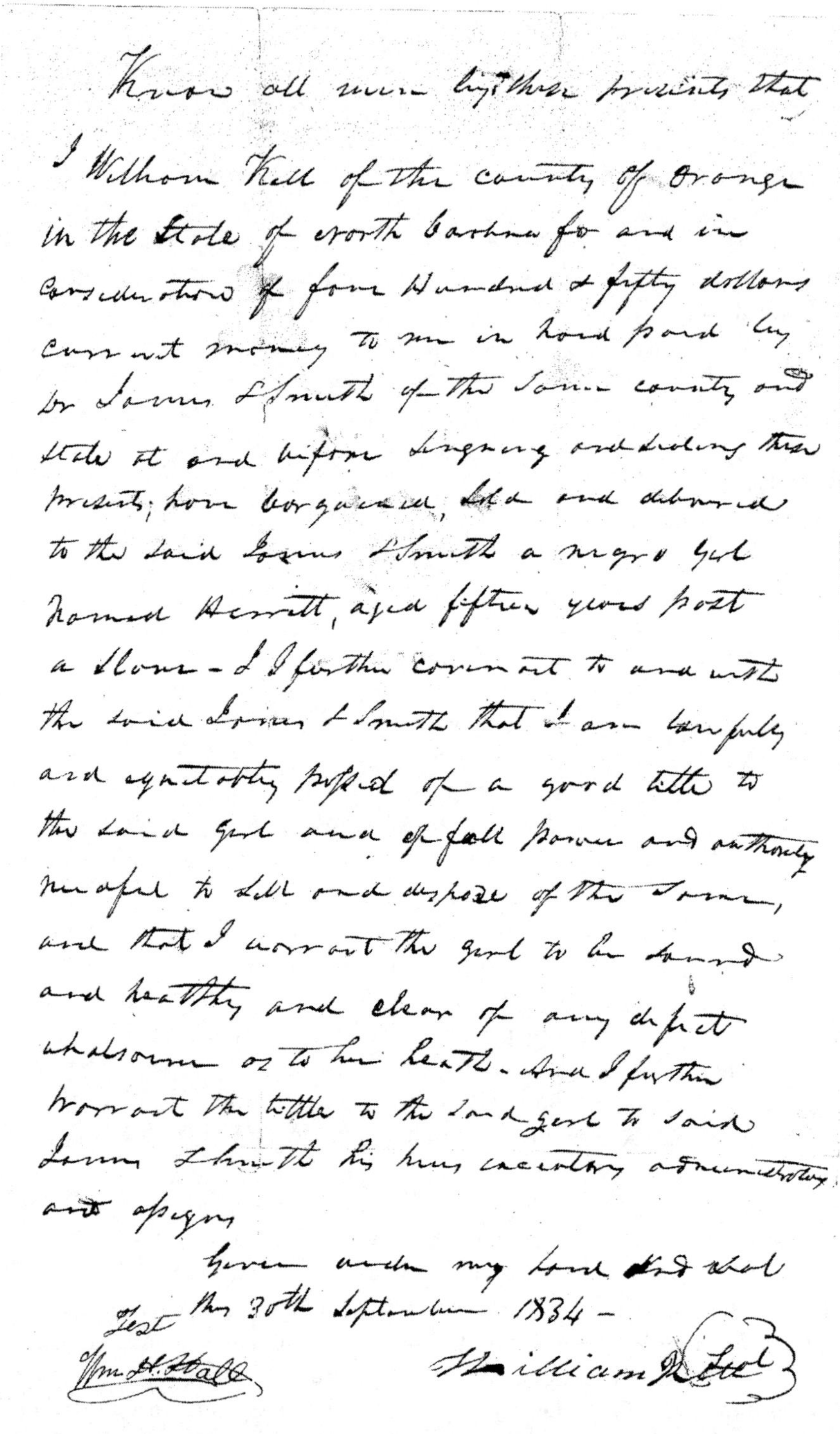
Know all men by these presents that
I William Hall of the county of Orange
in the State of North Carolina for and in
consideration of four hundred & fifty dollars
current money to me in hand paid by
Dr James S Smith of the same county and
state at and before signing and sealing these
presents; have bargained, sold and delivered
to the said James S Smith a negro girl
named Harriett, aged fifteen years past
a slave - & I further covenant to and with
the said James S Smith that I am lawfully
and equitably possessed of a good title to
the said girl and of full power and authority
needful to sell and dispose of the same,
and that I warrant the girl to be sound
and healthy and clear of any defect
whatsoever as to her health - And I further
warrant the title to the said girl to said
James S Smith his heirs executors administrators
and assigns
Given under my hand and seal
this 30th September 1834 -
Test
Wm H. Hall
William Hall (Seal)

Harriet, the slave woman who was destined to play a dramatic role in the Smith family, was first purchased by Dr. Smith in 1834, ten years before she was to bear the first of the four children fathered by Sidney and Francis Smith (courtesy Mary Ruffin Smith Papers, Southern Historical Collection, Wilson Library, UNC-CH).

Know all men by these presents, that I James S Smith of the County of Orange and town of Hillsborough in the State of North Carolina, hath this day bargained, sold, and delivered, and by these presents do bargain, sell, and deliver, to Mary R Smith of the said County and State, a negro woman Harriet aged about twenty six years, and her boy child Julius aged about three years, and her daughter Cornelia aged about one year, for the consideration of five hundred and fifty dollars, to me in hand paid by the said Mary R Smith, at and before the signing, sealing, and delivery of these presents, the receipt whereof I do hereby fully acknowledge.

And I further warrant the title to the said Harriet, Julius, and Cornelia, three negroes to the said Mary R Smith, her heirs, and assigns, against the claims of myself, heirs, or assigns, executors and administrators, and all manner of persons whatsoever.

Given under my hand and seal this twenty fifth of August 1846.

Eleven years later, Dr. Smith sold to his daughter Mary the same "negro woman Harrit aged about twenty-six years, and her boy child Julius aged about three years, and her daughter Cornelia aged about one year." There was no recognition that Cornelia was in fact Dr. Smith's granddaughter and Mary's niece (courtesy Mary Ruffin Smith Papers, Southern Historical Collection, Wilson Library, UNC-CH).

the mother and child. Thus by age 31, her spinsterhood had been determined. Pauli Murray described the awkward situation: "Grudgingly, Miss Mary Ruffin brought the baby into the Smith house and kept a private nurse for her until she was six years old. It was the first of many such battles in her soul in which Miss Mary would be torn between conscience and pride. The decision set her on a course of action from which she could not retreat for the remainder of her life. Like Harriet, she was drawn deeper and deeper into a quagmire. She was to experience a common bonding with Harriet which transcended the opposite poles of their existence as mistress and slave."[9]

Mary Smith's remaining four decades would be spent sharing the mothering not just of Cornelia but also of three additional girls sired by Francis Smith, to whom Harriet submitted, perhaps in her contempt for and protection from Sidney.[10] Judged from Murray's description of the relationship, Dr. Francis Smith used Harriet for sexual purposes, then virtually ignored her and his three daughters both contemporarily and for the remainder of his life.

Just after Emma's birth, the Smith family abandoned Hillsborough and moved to a newly constructed country house, described by Murray this way: a "large white Doric-columned Smith house [that] sat off the road beyond a great iron gate in a grove of giant oak trees." She added, "Grandmother said that when she was a little girl one of her duties in the fall was to rake the oak leaves into great piles and burn them."[11] Mary Smith must have been relieved to escape the confines of King Street. The fresh air and shade trees of rural Orange County, coupled with diversion of attention from Harriet's increasing brood, no doubt gave her some relief from whispered conversations in the closely-knit population of the little town.

Following the deaths of James and Delia Smith and the gradual descent of their two sons into debauchery and alcoholism, Mary and Harriet had their hands full as four girls approached and passed puberty. The women, Murray wrote, "shared a strangest motherhood in which neither could fully express her maternal feelings. The same overpowering forces which had robbed the slave mother of all natural rights had thrust them unwanted upon the childless spinster."[12] Although spinsterhood was by no means rare at mid-century, probably neither the Smiths nor their friends would have suspected that so eligible a relatively young woman as Mary Smith might remain unmarried. Certainly she would have brought a handsome dowry to a marriage.

We have no reliable physical descriptions of Mary Ruffin Smith. Sidney's daughter Cornelia, according to Pauli Murray, remembered "Miss Mary" this way: "She was not beautiful herself—she was a tall, angular, dark-haired, sallow-skinned young woman, inclined to be stiff and awkward—but she commanded another's grace, which was the next best thing to being beautiful."[13] Mary "learned music, art, literature and needlework and spent much of her youth painting with water colors and composing songs and ballads." That interest in music is documented in a manuscript music book formerly belonging to Mary Smith and given to the University of North Carolina Library by Murray.[14] Intriguingly, the book includes loose sheets titled "Gloria in Excelsus" by "MAC," identified by Curator William S. Powell as the handwriting of Moses Ashley Curtis, one of the rectors of St. Matthew's. There are, in addition, an original score "To Mr. James Strudwick" (a name quite familiar to the Smiths), and a poem beside which is written "Chapel Hill Serenade":

Could deeds my heart discover
Could valour gain thy charms
I'd prove myself thy lover
Against the world in arms.

Bow'd fair, thus low before thee
A prostrate warrior's view
Whose love, delight, and glory
Are centered all in you.

Cornelia contrasted Mary and her friend, Maria Spear, by 1866 again living together, this way: "Miss Maria Spear, the governess, was a warm, gentle, compassionate soul whose Yankee heart was opposed to slavery. Mary Ruffin admired and loved her and kept her in the family ... but she never absorbed her gentle ways. She [Mary] grew into a proud, stern, inflexible woman." Murray added, "Miss Mary was stingy with her purse, her patience and her affections, but always in the background was a gentler influence at work. Northern born, thoroughly anti-slavery Miss Maria Spear preached a silent gospel by example. Where Miss Mary was adamant and harsh, Miss Maria came behind her with a kind word."[15] It is not surprising that Cornelia's daughter Mary Pauline, the source of these impressions (who at age seven—probably early 1877—lived for a while with the two spinsters) preferred one over the other. Little Pauline said, "Miss Maria was a dear little old lady who wore black dresses, white collars and cuffs and a little white muslin cap on her head.... Every night before I went to bed, she'd have me sit on her knee and read my Bible.... I liked most of all the trips to the Chapel of the Cross on Sundays with Miss Mary and Miss Maria in the family carriage." The child claimed that Mary Smith was far less patient with her and sometimes in anger called her a "nigger."[16] If so, it was a side of Mary not fully supported elsewhere in the story. Not to be overlooked are the facts that Cornelia by blood was one-half Smith, Pauline was only one-quarter Smith, and Mary Smith was many years older and probably less tolerant when the little girl came into her life. Pauline's presence in the Smith household also occurred during Dr. Francis Smith's incapacitating and final illness.

Kemp Battle believed that Mary's eligibility for matrimony had been trumped by her acceptance of virtual parenthood over the four daughters sired out of wedlock by her brothers. However, in view of the volatility of the race issue, even Battle referred to the women, when grown, as "girls" and looked upon them more as servants than as genuine members of the Smith family. Trained in the oratorical language of the era, Battle wrote, "Miss Smith was one of the best of her sex. Of modest unassuming manners, of superior intellect, of wide information, especially in medical botany, of deep piety, of boundless charity in deed and word, she tenderly nursed with patience and skill the dying sickness of mother, father, two brothers, and a devoted friend, her girlhood's teacher, Miss Maria Spear, and died the last of her race."[17] Unfortunately for history, not one of Harriet's other three daughters found a Boswell to record for posterity her own memories of growing to adulthood in the strange Smith household.[18]

Mary Smith's religious inclination, promoted from an early age by clergymen Green and Hawks at St. Matthew's Episcopal Church, was sustained by subsequent ministers there, including the Rev. Moses Ashley Curtis, who also whetted her interest in the study of botany during his first tenure (1841–1846) as rector. The subject of religion is seldom mentioned among records relating to other members of her family. The funeral of Francis Jones was conducted at the home of his son-in-law, but the handwritten invitation did not identify an officiating minister. Mary's father was an early communicant in St. Matthew's Church; her mother, during her last illness professed her faith and was given communion by the rector of Episcopal Church in Chapel Hill. No mention has been found associating Francis and Sidney Smith with a church.[19]

It was after the Smiths relocated near Chapel Hill and the Rev. William Mercer Green was serving as the founding rector of the Church of the Atonement (later called the Chapel of the Cross) that Mary was fully documented in the local church records. Her name appears as a charter member among 24 communicants in 1848. Delia Smith appears on a revised list of indeterminate date, and Maria Spear is listed on another revised roster for 1856. The Episcopal pastor officiated at the funerals of both of Mary's parents.

Of major significance is an entry for baptisms dated December 20, 1854:

Five Servant Children belonging to Miss Mary Ruffin Smith, viz.

Julius Casar [sic]	aged	12
Cornelia	"	10
Emma	"	8
Annette	"	6
Laura	"	2

(The Mother's name is Harriet.)

Harriet's son, Julius Day, probably was jokingly referred to on the farm as "Julius Caesar." Regardless, it is highly significant that Mary Smith made no distinction between the young man and his half-sisters when bringing them into the church.[20]

Presumably each of the children received from "Miss Mary" a Bible, for Pauli Murray wrote that her grandmother Cornelia "treasured that ragged old Bible Miss Mary Smith of Chapel Hill had given her more than any other article in the house. She said she got it when she was a little girl and was confirmed at the Chapel of the Cross. It was over one hundred years old. It was the one book Grandmother tried to read herself, peering through her glasses and spelling out the Psalms a word at a time."[21]

Chronologically, other entries of interest in the fading records of the Chapel of the Cross include: (1) Under *baptisms*, November 22, 1863: Lucy Battle, colored child belonging to Mary Smith, by the Rev. F.W. Hilliard. (2) Under *confirmations*, April 25, 1864, headed by the names of Bishop Thomas Atkinson and Rector F.W. Hilliard, are "colored" names— David Moore, Cornelia Burnet, Laura Smith, Emma Smith, and Eliza Mallett. Could Cornelia "Burnet" possibly be Cornelia *Smith*? (3) Under *comm____ed first time*, July 3, 1864, is the name Laura, servant of Mary Smith. (4) Under *marriages*, December 22, 1864: Henry [Morphis], servant of W.H. Battle, and Emma, servant of Mary Smith, by the Rev. F.W. Hilliard. (5) Under *communicants* for 1864 and "added at various times" are 23 names including Emma, "col'd Serv't of Miss Mary Smith." (6) Under a revised list of *communicants*, May 13, 1876, are names of both Mary Smith and Maria Spear. (7) Under *Bishop's Assessment and Convention Fund* for 1880 are 12 names with their quarterly payments for 1880–1881. Kemp Battle paid $1.25 per quarter and Mary Smith $1 per quarter; no others paid more than 75 cents each. Maria Spear paid 25 cents each for the July and October 1880 quarters preceding her death. (8) A list of *Communicants at Mission Station at Durham* for April 1880 identifies Cornelia Fitzgerald as the mission's only member described as "colored." Finally, an entry for September 1859—the baptisms of Parthenia and "Maria Spear," both identified as "Ser-

8

Baptisms Continued

1854
October 29 Andrew (born 28th. August 1854)
Infant Son of Andrew & Helen M.
Mickle. The Parents, Sponsors
        also
Amy (about three years old)
Servant of Mr. Mickle.

December 20. Five Servant Children belonging
        to Miss Mary Ruffin Smith
    viz.
        Julius Cæsar   aged 12
        Cornelia   "   10
        Emma   "   8
        Annette   "   6
        Laura   "   2
    (The Mother's name is Harriet.)

1855
January 14. Charles Washington (born 28 Sept. 1854)
Infant Son of Essly & Louisa
Hunt. The parents, Sponsors.

May 6. Kemp Plummer Battle (Adult)
His Father & Mother, Witnesses.

Record of baptism at the Chapel of the Cross of five of Mary Ruffin Smith's slaves—all children of Harriet and four of them Mary's nieces—on December 20, 1854 (Chapel of the Cross, Chapel Hill; courtesy Ernest A. Dollar, Jr.).

vants of Miss Mary Smith"—probably contains a recording error. Maria Spear's name appears on a list of 52 communicants at the Chapel of the Cross in 1856, and she was living with two free women of color in Chapel Hill when the census was taken four years later.[22]

Although Harriet apparently was never brought into the church family—bearing children out of wedlock may have been a bar to membership—references associating her children with the patrician Chapel of the Cross suggest the struggle through which Mary Smith sought to bring up her mixed-race nieces in the twilight zone between slavery and full-fledged citizenship. It is noteworthy that her effort to give the children religious education predated the establishment of schools for Negroes and at a time when many Protestant churches did not accept non-whites as members. It is also noteworthy that Pauli Murray's biography of her grandmother Cornelia, the daughter of Sidney Smith, was written *before* the author herself made history in the same sanctuary. Had it been written after 1977, when (as the first woman of color to be ordained to the Episcopalian priesthood) she celebrated the Holy Eucharist in the Chapel of the Cross, the following matter-of-fact report would deliver an even more emotional impact upon the reader: "She [Mary Smith] might have left them [Julius, Cornelia, Emma, Annette, and Laura] to be 'converted' at one of Uncle Ned Cole's revivals on the plantation. Instead, she elected to send them to the Chapel of the Cross on the University campus in Chapel Hill to be trained in the Episcopal faith. Grandmother said that when she was twelve years old she was confirmed at the chapel along with the daughter of ex–Governor David L. Swain, who was then president of the University." The description continued, "Every Sunday morning the four attractive girls were seen riding along with Miss Mary Ruffin Smith in her beautiful white family carriage on their way to the Chapel of the Cross. People seeing them pass nudged one another and said, 'There goes Miss Mary Smith and her girls.' To keep up appearances, Miss Mary sent them upstairs to the balcony in church while she sat alone or with Miss Maria Spear downstairs in the Smith pew. This only heightened the curiosity of the congregation."[23] That the small congregation at the Chapel of the Cross harmoniously accommodated the unusual carriage load of biracial children was a deed gratefully remembered by Mary Smith in life as well as in her will.

According to the church's website in 2012 (but based on a paper by Mary Arthur Stoudemire written in 1981),

> One most loyal, generous and devout parishioner was Mary Ruffin Smith who lived in a large white house that still stands on Smith Level Road.... Whenever there was a need, Miss Smith gave. A new roof was needed in 1884. Miss Smith gave one hundred dollars which paid for the slate roof, the same roof that is there today. She gave a new organ and bought the lot across the street from the Church when money was needed and no buyers could be found. This is the same lot occupied today [1981] by the new parish house of the Lutheran Church and the ATØ Fraternity house. When Miss Smith died she willed the lot to the Chapel of the Cross. In 1891 the Vestry sold the lot for two hundred and fifty dollars.

Meanwhile, the church reached its lowest ebb in 1884 when Cornelia Spencer wrote that she saw at the church only "the Malletts and Miss Mary Smith." After her death and bequest of additional properties to the church, the Episcopal Diocese of North Carolina bought an Eagle lectern for a hundred dollars and gave it to the parish as a memorial to Mary Smith.[24]

Her own, however, was not the only church supported by Mary Smith. W.C. Cole, her plantation manager and record keeper, wrote Cornelia Spencer, "She was as strictly High Church as one could be without being a ritualist, yet aided every denomination both white and colored in this country in building, repairing &c whenever called upon. Indeed, she has frequently asked me where she could give her money in that way and not retard others in performing their duty. 'Blessings brighten as they take their flight.' She helped us at our church frequently in getting Sunday School literature."[25]

Cornelia Phillips Spencer added both insight and mystery to Mary Smith's religious inclinations: "The almost exclusive companionship with Episcopalians gave her predisposition in favor of their church which without such friendship she would probably have missed. The Smiths and Jones' family had little leaning that way, and Miss Mary's adherence to that form of worship tended to sever her from her own people—though as daughter and sister her loyal affection to her own was genuine and lasting." Spencer added,

> Her own habits and requirements were very simple. She lived without a single article of luxury in dress and furniture or equipage, and was satisfied with a small and select circle of friends whom she did not replace as time thinned them out.... What was remarkable about her life considering her ample means and absolute independence, was its simplicity. She lived comfortably—she kept a comfortable equipage—but she spent nothing on luxury or on ostentation of any sort. Quiet in manner, reserved in speech, and with an air half timid, and a smile half deprecatory, she passed on her way unnoticed, and very few even of those who knew her best gave her credit for the close observation, the intelligence, or the discriminating judgment with which she took of men and women. While Judge [William H.] Battle and his family were residents of Chapel Hill, her association was chiefly with them, and the friendship was afterwards transferred to President and Mrs. [Kemp] Battle, to whom when alone she at last looked for the offices of friendship.[26]

Regrettably, Cornelia Spencer failed to carry out her plans to prepare a more substantial biography of Maria Spear. On January 20, 1881, she wrote: "Miss Mary Smith wants me to write Miss Maria Spear's obituary. I do not want to do it, but of course I have got it to do!"[27]

Mary Ruffin Smith is pictured by Pauli Murray as ambivalent concerning the subject of slavery, on which much of the wealth to which she fell heir had been built. Her niece Cornelia was too young to have remembered much about her first couple of years in Hillsborough, but her memories in growing up on the Price Creek plantation were vivid and well recorded by Murray. Even in Cornelia's young eyes, "As slave life went, the Smith servants were not badly treated. They had their own surnames and were allowed to marry and raise their families on the place. They were well fed, well clothed and thought a good deal of themselves. They even had their own plantation preacher, Uncle Ned Cole, who could read and whose moving sermons attracted blacks and whites alike from neighboring plantations."[28] This judgment, however, came from mulattoes who generally occupied a middle position between the white owners and "darker-skinned field hands" upon whom the hardest work and least rewards fell. Still, in Cornelia's memory, "It [the Smith plantation] represented prosperity, gracious living and social prominence. Like most plantations it was almost entirely self-sufficient. The Smiths had their own mill, blacksmith shop and carpentry shed. They produced most of their food and clothing on the premises. The menservants learned tasks and the women were taught to weave and to sew." Cornelia "talked constantly of their bountiful supply: the great smokehouses in which hung hams, sides of bacon, cured beef and salted pork; the cribs piled high with corn, wheat and rye; the granaries bulging with bins of meal, flour, sugar cane, potatoes, nuts, dried fruits; tubs of lard and butter."[29] The modern reader must keep in mind that this oral history was coming from a woman who had tumbled downward from one society to another—from her "colored" childhood, when as a member of the prosperous white Smith clan she occupied an exceptional place in a multiracial world, to one in which mulattoes were treated as simply a part of an inferior race, listed in the county records along with full-blooded blacks by the designation "N" and forced to remain in their degraded "place." Although Robert and Cornelia Fitzgerald owned their modest home in a segregated area of Durham, memories of the expansive Price Creek plantation with its annual harvest were magnified in the imagination of the aging woman. In terms of her daily life of drudgery, in trying to survive on a soldier's pension, the past may have looked much rosier than her present or future.

Perhaps, then, Cornelia Smith Fitzgerald also exaggerated her aunt's sentiments on slavery when she reported having often heard Mary "complain to her women friends that slavery was the greatest evil on earth and that the true slave was the Southern woman. The men occupied themselves with their professions, hunting and riding, or politics, while the women of the plantation had to carry the main load.... When you come right down to it ... if you weren't in the business of buying and selling slaves for profit, they cluttered up the place and cost more than they were worth."[30]

Either Cornelia Fitzgerald failed to confide to her granddaughter—or Pauli Murray, only in her fifteenth year when her grandmother died, chose not to record—much about conditions at Oakland during the Civil War and the war's effect upon the extended Smith family. Neither brother served in the army. Sidney was rejected by Confederate authorities as "broken down" and unfit for service, and the doctor's practice appears to have been limited to his home community, including the issuance of medical exemptions for men threatened by the draft. No correspondence has been found to document the wartime problems faced by Mary in managing the huge Price Creek plantation and its more than two dozen slave workers. Especially unfortunate is the silence of the four multiracial Smith daughters. In 1865, Cornelia would have been 21, and Emma, Annette, and Laura about 18, 16, and 14 each. What we would not give for Cornelia's memory of her and her sisters' reaction when they were told that they were legally freedwomen!

From her research, however, Murray created a plausible, if not fully documented, impression of the vicissitudes faced by Mary during the war:

> In 1860, three of the thirty Smith servants were in their seventies and no longer able to do much work. Seventeen others were less than twenty-one, and nine of these were under fourteen years of age, hardly able to earn their own living. Sooner or later, everything which happened in the slave quarters had to be resolved by "Miss Mary." She had to look after the old folks, give medicine to the sick, bandage the sores and cuts of slave children, run down to the cabins when a mother was in childbirth. She must order food and clothing and parcel it out among them, find clothes and refreshments for slave marriages, approve husbands for the women and wives for the men, arbitrate in their family squabbles, supervise the training of growing girls, be present at all their prayer meetings, bury them when they died and keep the whole kit and caboodle in smooth working order. She seldom had a minute to herself day or night, since she was 'on call' at all times for any emergency in the cabins.[31]

Even so, we are left with little sense of actual circumstances on the plantations until the end of the war.

As Union General William T. Sherman arrived with his army in Wake County, former Governor David L. Swain and former Senator William A. Graham met him outside Raleigh on April 14 and gained a pledge that Union troops would spare the capital city and the University of North Carolina from the devastation visited upon Atlanta and other southern areas. Two days later, Confederate General Joseph Wheeler's cavalry, after briefly occupying Chapel Hill, retreated, leaving the village the next day to the Ninth Michigan cavalry under command of Union General Smith D. Atkins. On his return to Chapel Hill, Swain wrote General Sherman on the 19th that first Wheeler's men, and afterwards the Federal soldiers, had committed depredations, stripping families of their means of subsistence. He particularly mentioned the plight of the Smiths' adjoining neighbor, the Rev. George W. Purefoy, whose family of over fifty persons, white and black, had been left with "no provisions and not a horse or mule."[32]

Word soon reached town that the Smith farm had suffered depredations. On April 24, Charles Peter Mallett sent Joe Mickle to check on Mary Smith, only to find that she had been "pillaged of every thing, all her bed and table linen and towels [*sic*] not one left." Two days later Mallett reported that after a guard was posted, Mary was "in better spirits and more composed and has had supplies sent to her." Then, on May 10, he wrote that although he had not gone to church and therefore had not seen Mary Smith, he had learned that she met with "another loss and disappointment, having sent all her washing to town by her carriage driver, who has not since been heard from." This statement may imply that one of the Smiths' trusted servants abandoned them and joined other former slaves in following the Union Troops. In another letter dated April 30 to Henry London, Mallett reported, "They [the Union troops] have not on the whole behaved badly in the village where we have a safe guard, but in the country they have done badly, pillaging of every thing they could carry off ... the country is stripped of mules and horses."[33]

Mallett could hardly conceal his amusement when he shared with his son the "Dicky-Dout" story of Sidney Smith's attempt to escape Yankee troops by disguising himself as the derelict "uncle of some poor family" and taking to the woods.[34]

Evidence that the Smith siblings suffered additionally from Union occupation troops comes from the trustees of the Diocese of East Carolina who reported in 1896, "We have agreed with the Diocese of North Carolina to unite in the prosecution of a claim against the United States Government for damages to the property of Mrs. [*sic*] Mary Ruffin Smith, sustained during the war between the States, and we have reason to believe there is a good prospect of recovery of said damages."[35] Several payments from Mary Smith's estate appear to be associated with the claim: $9.40 to D.C. Mangum, commissioner, for "taking depositions in claim against U.S."; $1.50 to Mrs. Mary Partin for "witness"; $2 to W.C. Cole for "services as hunting witness" and $1.50 for "fee as witness"; and 75 cents to G.C. Packard for "sending for witnesses." Of possible significance is the fact that the Partins owned land adjoining the Smith property, including the fork formed by the Hillsborough-Fayetteville and Chapel Hill-Pittsboro roads. No further documentation in regard to the claim has been found.

A picturesque—even fanciful—story is told by Pauli Murray. As the 9th Michigan Cavalry marched into Chapel Hill and a contingent approached the Smith residence, "Grandmother [Cornelia] didn't go to the welcoming! She was too busy helping Miss Mary dig holes and bury the silver and other family valuables. Then they dragged brush over the places they had dug and built bonfires to hide their work." Laura, then 14, was said to have greeted approaching troops with a "Union flag and white cloth of surrender held high above her head." She presented her flags to the captain, who lifted her onto his saddle, then rode to the Smith house at the head of a volume of soldiers "in grand style, looking very delighted and not in the least like one who had just surrendered the Smith pride."[36]

Murray described poignant circumstances at Price Creek:

> Nothing was quite the same again. During the war, Miss Mary had come more and more to
> rely upon the four girls who were the only daughters she had ever known. Now she was almost
> alone with only an eccentric brother, who withdrew into himself, and one or two friends.
> Aged beyond her fifty years and burdened with debts and worthless Rebel bonds, she made a
> proposition to her former slaves. If any of them wanted to stay on and work the crops for her,
> she'd stake them to food and clothes and let them live in their cabins rent free. Most of them
> accepted her proposal and continued much in the same way on the surface, but tentatively and
> with old formalities on both sides. The Smith girls remained with her in the Big House and
> Great-Grandmother Harriet, who was at last free to shut the door of her cabin, stayed on as
> Miss Mary's maid.[37]

As her nieces approached puberty, Mary Smith, even if a virgin herself, was wise to the
temptations of young women, and she was even more wary of the hormonal dangers from
the opposite sex. Murray quotes her cautioning the girls, "Now, don't you go out there in
the blackberry bushes and get a baby." She guarded the nieces from advances of men of both
races, and was adamant for their association only with carefully vetted men, all mixed-race
and of good repute. She was immediately approving when Emma returned the admiring
smiles of Henry, the son of Judge William H. Battle's slave girl Lizzie and Sam Morphis, a
highly respected Chapel Hill slave who was permitted to hire himself out by his nominal
owner, James M. Morphis, who lived in Texas. Henry had been admitted into the Chapel of
the Cross, and he and Emma were married by Rector Hilliard on December 22, 1864. Edward
(Ned) Kirby, a handyman and preacher of sorts and son of Thomas and Judith Kirby, was
also approved by Miss Mary, and he was married to Annette in March 1868 by the Rev.
Charles Phillips of the Chapel Hill Presbyterian Church. Maria Spear, by then living with
Mary Smith, wrote, "All here are busy preparing for Annette's marriage to Ed Kirby tomorrow
even[ing]. Mary & myself are busy icing & trimming five cakes." Laura, the youngest, had
an unsatisfactory marriage with Grey Toole, an established Charlotte barber.[38]

The courtship of Cornelia and Robert Fitzgerald provides an inspiring story as reported
by their granddaughter Pauli Murray. The narrative is too good to be abstracted except for
the revelation that Mary Ruffin Smith, a white woman of the Old South, invited Robert G.
Fitzgerald, a man of color and a former Union Army soldier, to dinner in the Big House and
virtually encouraged him to propose to her oldest niece. However, because there exists no
comparable description of the other sisters, the smitten visitor's impression of the "fine looking octoroon" merits quotation: "And indeed she was fine looking. Grandfather never forgot
how she looked on that first meeting. She was dressed in her best, a beautiful woolen suit
which she had made herself, a high ruche about her neck trimmed with soft white lace, a
fringed scarf tied in a bow and pinned with a large oval breast pin. She wore no other adorn-
ments and she did not have to. She was the most strikingly beautiful woman Grandfather
had ever seen. She wore her hair brushed tightly back in long black curls down her back,
with a forelock cut into boyish ringlets which fell over her brow."[39]

The marriage was performed by Justice of the Peace Archibald C. Hunter on August
8, 1869, at Robert Fitzgerald's Woodside Farm near University Station.[40] The couple's first
child was named for Mary Smith—Mary Pauline Fitzgerald; the second, for Maria Spear.
These free choices, made long after Cornelia had been emancipated and brought to adulthood by the unmarried aunt, give a far more favorable word portrait of Mary Smith and
Maria Spear—particularly the surrogate mother—than appears elsewhere in *Proud Shoes*.

The most influential person in the life of Mary Ruffin Smith was a teacher, Maria Louisa Spear, ten years her senior, about whom mysteries persist nearly two centuries later—mysteries that need to be clarified because of her central role in Mary Smith's life. As "Miss Maria" aged, Mary provided a home for the destitute and near-blind teacher; drafted a will leaving her a large house and plantation; and buried her body next to her own reserved plot in the Jones Grove cemetery. Particularly from 1866 onward, we know little of Mary Ruffin Smith except through letters of her alter ego.

First, to unscramble the evidence. Earlier writers assumed that this young teacher arrived alone in North Carolina in 1826, succeeded Lavinia Brainard as teacher in Hillsborough Female Academy, and during the next half-century became one of the state's most publicized educators. New research, however, reveals that Maria Louisa Spear did not arrive alone, and that some of the recognition previously attributed to her may be due her mother, also named Maria Spear. Like Lavinia Brainard's family, the Spears were probably attracted to North Carolina by Dr. James Strudwick Smith's request for the assistance of Congressman Willie P. Mangum in finding a "Suitable Lady" from New England for the Hillsborough Female Academy, chartered by Smith and others in 1824.[41]

The two Marias are clearly differentiated in the medical account books of Mary's physician father, beginning with an entry of September 4, 1826. Under charges for "Mrs. Maria Spear," most sick calls were for the mother, but several others are noted specifically for "Miss Maria," "Bill" (brother William Wallace Spear), and "Mary Whitted" (the latter presumably a servant). The fact that the accounts of Mrs. Maria Spear were paid "by settlement with Female Academy" and "Trustees Spring Session" give credence to the assumption that the mother was a teacher at, or otherwise employed by, the school. She died December 13, 1835, and her tombstone stands beside that of her sister, Susan Esther Baker (1780–1846), in the cemetery of St. Matthew's Episcopal Church in Hillsborough.[42]

Further contradicting the traditional assumption that there was just one "Maria Spear" is a statement by John Steele Henderson that "Miss Maria Louisa Spear ... resided in Salisbury for a few years," where her brother, William Wallace Spear, served as rector of St. Luke's Episcopal Church in 1835. "Bill" Spear was graduated from the University of North Carolina in 1831 and, with the assistance of the Protestant Episcopal Diocese of North Carolina, attended the General Theological Seminary in New York. He was ordained as a deacon at Hillsborough in 1834 and later married Emily Ewing of Philadelphia. In 1838, only seven years after Spear received his undergraduate diploma, the University of North Carolina granted him a rare degree, "Master of Arts—Special Alumni."[43]

Leaving Salisbury after a year or less, William Wallace Spear became rector of St. Michael's in Charleston, South Carolina, but about 1840 he moved to the rectorship of St. Luke's in Philadelphia. Five years later he became associate editor of the *Episcopal Recorder*, published in Philadelphia; but from 1847 to 1855 he was back in Charleston as rector of the newly consecrated Grace Church, which in 2012 accepted a gift of his portrait.[44]

Henderson, a state senator in 1881 when he wrote the history of the episcopacy in Rowan, reported that the younger Maria "lived in the family of the Rev. Mr. Wright" and that several female members of his own family studied under her. He recorded that Maria was born April 12, 1804, in Paddington, England, and that—as the older sibling—she "educated, both directly and indirectly, her brother and sisters, and became a prominent and useful teacher of many young ladies; and all her pupils have retained through life a grateful sense of the value of her literary instructions and religious influence." He added that Maria "was one of the first persons confirmed by Bishop Ravenscroft, and became an intimate friend and active helper of her pastor, Mr. [William Mercer] Green, of Hillsboro, now the venerable Bishop of Mississippi, who has recently spoken of her as an 'incomparable woman.'"[45]

Writing a few weeks after the death of Maria Louisa Spear in 1881, Senator Henderson performed an additional service by quoting portions of a posthumous tribute written by Cornelia Phillips Spencer and published in the *Church Messenger*: "Miss Maria Spear, having been born an English woman, remained an English woman all her life, possessing some of the most valuable representative characteristics of that nationality. She was thorough, she was sincere, she was quiet, she was conservative, and she was a staunch and devout church woman. Her love for the Episcopal Church, and her delight in its service, was in her blood. She has been teaching in North Carolina for *fifty-six* years, and of the many who have been instructed by her, and the many friends who loved and esteemed her, not one, perhaps could this day remember in her an inconsistency, or an indiscretion or an unkindness."[46]

In the available newspaper advertisements of Hillsborough Female Academy, the name of daughter Maria Louisa Spear does not appear until February 26, 1839, when the *Raleigh Register* announced: "The Exercises of this Institution commenced on the 24th January, for the present session, under the charge of its efficient and accomplished Principal, Miss Maria L. Spear. The services of this lady, for several years past, have been such as to meet the highest expectations of the Trustees, and to deserve for this Academy as great portion of public patronage as has been extended to any similar Institution in the State. Miss Spear has associated with herself in the task of instruction, her sister, Mrs. Elizabeth Smith, whose talents and skill in the departments of Music, Drawing and Painting have been fully tested and are of the highest order." Receipts for student Mary Webb's tuition exist under Maria Spear's signature for January 9, 1835; July 7, 1836; and January 30, 1837; and Maria's name is mentioned as the teacher of Martha Mangum (daughter of Senator Willie P. Mangum) in reports of August 16, 1840, and January 18 and June [no date], 1842. Thus young Maria Louisa Spear's teaching at the Hillsborough Female Academy is documented almost continually from 1835 through 1842.[47]

If the "several years" mentioned by Senator Henderson can be assumed to be an exaggeration, it can be hypothesized that the senior "Mrs. Maria Spear" and her daughter, Miss Maria Louisa Spear, both taught in Hillsborough, but that, in addition, the younger Maria taught a short while in Salisbury prior to or during her brother's pastorate there, returning to Hillsborough and resuming her teaching at the Female Academy before her mother's death in December 1835. There are other mysteries associated with Maria Louisa Spear. In 1840–1841 she roomed in the home of Dr. James Smith and was a "frequent & intimate" visitor at other times,[48] but her whereabout for the next decade is not easily documented. She has not been identified in the Census of 1850 (the first census to attempt to identify by name every living white American), but the Census of 1860 records her living with two mulatto freedwomen—Nancy and Clarice Gooch—in Chapel Hill, next door to the Mallett family, intimate friends of both Maria Spear and Mary Smith.[49]

If Maria Spear's antebellum whereabouts and specific activities are only sketchily known, they are better documented after the Civil War. Some time after being recorded in the Census of 1860 as living with the freedwomen in Chapel Hill, the teacher was introduced to Charles

Beatty Mallett (1816–1872) of Fayetteville, among whose antebellum promotions was the construction of a railroad from Fayetteville to the remote coal fields at Egypt Landing in Chatham County. The introduction came through Mallett's father, Charles Peter Mallett (1792–1873), who, living and operating a bookstore in Chapel Hill during the war, frequently called on Mary Ruffin Smith, a fellow parishioner at the Chapel of the Cross. He wrote a granddaughter in 1866, "I always feel grateful that God allowed me to be the instrument in bringing her [Maria Spear] into your Father's family." The elder Mallett's deep admiration for "Miss Maria" was expressed this way: "I notice your remarks dear Maggie in regard to Miss Maria. She is justly entitled to all the affectionate regards which you and Carrie and Alice and even the boys can feel and which I trust may last with your lives, and I often feel thankful that God allowed me to be the instrument of introducing her into your Father's family. I seem to feel towards her as towards my sister Walker [?] of whom Miss Maria reminds me very much."[50]

It was while living with the Malletts at Fayetteville that "Miss Maria" earned widespread admiration for her skill with a needle. She was already a legendary teacher, but her sewing skills became newsworthy from her participation with ladies of the town in memorializing the Confederate dead. In 1865, after the bodies of several dozen local men killed by Federal forces were hurriedly buried—some in unmarked graves—a group of women, led by Ann Kyle, wife of Captain Jesse Kyle of the Fifty-second Regiment of North Carolina Troops, sought to raise funds for reburial of the bodies in an appropriate place. The movement expanded into a decision to seek additional funds for the erection of the state's first monument to the Confederate dead. Maria Spear's suggestion that the ladies sew a large silk memorial quilt, to be awarded the winner of a raffle, was adopted and—as so often is the case of a winning idea—the consummation of the project fell largely on its proposer. Maria conceived the intricate design and invited other town women, including some school-age girls, into the Mallett home for weekly "quiltings."[51]

New Advertisements.

MEMORIAL QUILT.

The graves of the Confederate soldiers in and near Fayetteville. N. C., are in a neglected condition. Certain Ladies of the town, being desirous of paying the just debt of gratitude which they owe to the memories of these brave men, have made and elaborately embroidered a beautiful silken quilt of the richest and finest material. The designs are all of a different pattern and worked, many of them, on a ground not exceeding a square inch: the colors are contrasted and blended with true artistic skill, — beautiful sprays and bouquets of flowers, and various emblematical designs combine to make up an article which for elegance of design, fineness of materials and superiority of execution has never been surpassed in this or any country. As an example of patient industry and devotion to the memory of departed merits it is richly worth twice the sum named as approximating its value. Prompted by an exalted spirit of gratitude to those who are lying low, many of them in nameless graves, —the ladies have applied themselves to the task with untiring energy; and the result is a complete success. The ladies acknowledge their indebtedness to the indefatigable industry and inexhaustible taste of Miss Maria L. Spear, who invented the unique style of making up the quilt. She also invented and stamped all of the beautiful and varied designs with which it is embellished. She did most of the execution, and rendered valuable assistance to the ladies employed in the different stages of progress.

They have given all they had, the labor of their hands, their time, their utmost skill, in the preparation of this article. They wish to dispose of it and with the proceeds, to collect the honored ashes of their noble dead, to lay them side by side where they can with loving hands decorate their peaceful resting place and to erect above them a fitting monument to mark the spot which shall be sacred to the memory of the loyed and lost.

They offer to sell one thousand tickets at $1 per ticket and as soon as that number has been sold, to raffle the quilt.

Announcement of a planned "Memorial Quilt" to honor the Confederate dead in Fayetteville. Maria Spear was the central figure in the project (*Fayetteville News*, December 10, 1867; courtesy North Carolina Collection, Wilson Library, UNC-CH). See http://moc.pastperfect-online.com/39589cgi/mweb.exe?request=record;id=2 AF5058F-3BAF-48E4-8F71-070834269544; type=101 for an image of the quilt.

According to a UDC report: "The first meeting for this object was held at Mrs. Jesse Kyle's, after that on every Friday afternoon the ladies and the school girls met with Miss Spear at the residence of Mr. Charles Beaty [*sic*] Mallett, Miss Spear being a member of the household, the beloved and revered teacher of his children. The bits of silk of every hue and of every style were contributed by the ladies and were skillfully and artistically blended by 'Miss Maria.' There were 3,000 squares and when the quilt was completed, it was an elegant piece of work."[52]

When she left Fayetteville in June 1866 to live with Mary Ruffin Smith near Chapel Hill, Maria assumed that she had done her part on the quilt, and a trip back to Fayetteville had reassured her that the work was proceeding well. However, not long after Sidney Smith's death dealt a grave blow to his sister Mary, the unfinished quilt arrived unexpectedly at Oakland. Maria moaned to Maggie Mallett, "When I saw the quilt this evening, I felt overwhelmed. How am I to get it done, I don't know." She added disappointingly, "It seems that Mrs. Hooper told Mrs. Battle that it was coming & if Mrs. B[attle] had told me of it, I would have written to say that it was impossible for me to undertake it. But it is here & I must do my best. If Mary gets better, I can finish it, & if not, I cannot—that is all I can say. I shall do what I can—more I cannot."[53]

Once the incomplete work was back in her hands at Oakland, Maria became re-energized as neighbors came to view it: "Every one who has seen the quilt decides that it is the handsomest one they ever beheld." Unfortunately, only three admirers—Mrs. Kemp Battle, Mrs. Sutherland, and Mrs. Martha E. Lewis—offered to surrender a dollar each for a ticket for the raffle designed to raise $1,000 for the ambitious memorial. By November, Maria returned the quilt, and she wrote Maggie Mallett, "I want to express how relieved I feel that the quilt is actually done & on its way to Fayetteville. I had only four dollars to send with it. Several more would have subscribed, but no one here has any money to spare. I stood by the bedside a large part of four days to try to match the squares of the silk, & at the same time avoid working it; at last I found I could do neither." She concluded, "I really am thankful that it has turned out so well, for it was a responsibility that I would not be willing to undertake again. I am working very hard to finish the two pairs of markers." She again expressed emotion toward the stunningly elegant work when shortly afterward she wrote, "I found a tuft of cotton belonging to the quilt—I shall keep it a long time if I can."[54]

On December 10, 1867, the following notice appeared in the *Fayetteville News* under the heading "Memorial Quilt":

> The graves of the Confederate soldiers in and near Fayetteville, N.C., are in a neglected condition. Certain Ladies of the town, being desirous of paying the just debt of gratitude which they owe to the memories of those brave men, have made and elaborately embroidered a beautiful quilt of the richest and finest material. The designs are all of a different pattern and worked, many of them, on a ground not exceeding a square inch; the colors are contrasted and blended with true artistic skill,—beautiful sprays and bouquets of flowers, and various emblematic designs combine to make up an article which for elegance of design, fineness of materials and superiority of execution has never been surpassed in this or any country. As an example of patient industry and devotion to the memory of departed merits it is richly worth twice the sum named as approximating its value. Prompted by an exalted spirit of gratitude to those who are lying low, many of them in nameless graves,—the ladies have applied themselves to the task with untiring energy;—and the result is a complete success.

The advertisement continued, "The ladies acknowledge their indebtedness to the indefatigable industry and inexhaustible taste of Miss Maria L. Spear, who invented the unique style of making up the quilt. She also invented and stamped all of the beautiful and varied designs with which it is embellished. She did most of the execution, and rendered valuable assistance to the ladies employed in the difficult stages of progress."

Early the following year, Maria wrote, "Poor dear Quilt. I am glad to hear news of it too & earnestly wish it success." The ladies had hoped to sell 1,000 tickets at $1, but economic conditions during Reconstruction resulted in the selling of only about 300 "shares." Martha E. Lewis of Tarboro, to whom Maria had sold a ticket, was the winner. Perhaps Maria entertained the hope of winning with her single one-dollar ticket, in which case she would have given it to Mary Smith. Afterward, however, she wrote, "So, the quilt is gone—well—I never felt as if I should get it, but should have been glad if Mrs. Kyle, or Mrs. Britton could have been successful. I did hear that Mrs. Lewis said, if she drew it, she would present it to Mrs. Jefferson Davis. Do not you hope she will? We should all like that." For her work on the quilt, Maria asked only for mementos: two of the unsold tickets and a photograph of the quilt.[55]

Martha Lewis carried out her promise; the quilt was delivered to the former president of the Confederate States of America, and he graciously acknowledged the gift by letter on July 14, 1870, specifically mentioning the roles of Ann Kyle and Maria Spear. The latter was almost euphoric: "I am so very glad that Jefferson Davis has the quilt. Oh, I am so glad!"[56]

That was not the end for the quilt. After President Davis died in 1889, his widow Varina presented the coverlet to what is today the Museum of the Confederacy in Richmond, Virginia, where it is preserved in the North Carolina Room. During the centennial of the Civil War, it was borrowed back for temporary exhibition by the Daughters of the Confederacy in North Carolina.[57]

General Sherman's Federal troops destroyed virtually all of Charles Beatty Mallett's prewar wealth in the Fayetteville area, but by engaging Maria Spear to teach his three young daughters—Caroline Green Mallett (Carrie), Margaret Anderson Mallett (Maggie), and Alice Hazelton Mallett (Alice)—he unknowingly enabled the preservation of a rich body of handwritten correspondence that provides many intimate details about the last years of the lives of both Maria Spear and Mary Smith. Although letters *from* Carrie (age 18 in 1866), Maggie (16), and Alice (9) are missing, dozens of newsy letters from Maria Louisa Spear *to* the girls have been preserved in the Charles Beatty Mallett Papers in the Southern Historical Collection. Had those letters not been saved, little would be known today about the storied bond of friendship enjoyed between—and the anguished experiences suffered by—the two remarkable spinsters in their declining years. The significance of the letters is multiplied by their conveyance of images of Maria Spear and Mary Smith different—sometime starkly different—from those painted by Pauli Murray in *Proud Shoes*. It should be remembered that Cornelia—the oldest of Mary Smith's four multi-race nieces on whose memory the author depended—was 22 years of age when Maria's first letter in the collection was written in 1866. Oddly, her name has not been found in the letters. Emma had married Henry Morphis in 1864, but the other three "girls" were as yet unmarried.[58]

In the first letter in the collection—to Carrie, dated June 19, 1866—Maria described her trip from Fayetteville to remote Egypt Landing aboard a coal-burning, overheated, cinder-plagued, oil-scented railroad car of the Fayetteville and Western Railroad. The 43-mile railroad between Fayetteville and the coal and iron fields of Chatham (now Lee) County had been a major antebellum project of C.B. Mallett, and, although ten miles of track out of Fayetteville had been destroyed by Federal forces in 1865, the rolling stock had been safely retired to the northwestern end. Consequently, the road was soon reopened, and Maria may have been one of its first postwar passengers.[59]

Maria was met at the Deep River landing by Sam Morphis, a legendary former slave from Chapel Hill, with his "old fashioned, low riding" carriage, in which, Maria wrote, "a very agreeable ride I had. Sam could tell me all about Chapel Hill and Mary Smith's family. So I was really entertained. The horses did not do anything amiss, and Sam did not speak a harsh word." Just north of Pittsboro, Sam bought corn and fed his horses at Womack's, while his lone passenger "got out of the carriage & walked about under the trees, eat [sic] plums, & drank some most delightful water out of a nice clean bucket which the head man very politely brought me."[60]

The carriage arrived at Oakland, the Smith's Price Creek home, just after sundown, and Sam was gratefully paid eight dollars for his service. Noting that this was her first visit to Mary's home without bringing a gift, Maria solved the problem by presenting to her hostess her own going-away gift from the folks in Fayetteville. Although she had survived the trip without incident, she reported that in the morning she experienced an intense headache and sick stomach, for which "Frank [Mary's physician brother] gave me a dose of Calomel, which relieved me of a quantity of bile." Blaming the sun and her appetite, she intended to be "very prudent in my eating, sitting up, or fatiguing myself in any way—especially to the sun." She reported visits from the Mallett girls' Chapel Hill relatives, and she could not resist giving a lesson for Alice about the movements of the planets during the summer.

Maria's second newsy letter—to Maggie, dated July 11, 1866—revealed more of the teacher's private thoughts. She was eager to report on one of the girls' favorite hymns: "Tell Alice that I heard the coloured Brethren & Sisters, for I suppose I must not say *negroes*, singing 'I Want to Be an Angel.' I thought of her, & wondered if she would play it yet. The singing was at Harriet's house, one moonlight evening, & you don't know how pretty it sounded through those tall trees." The statement establishes that Harriet no longer lived in the main Smith house after her—and her four daughters'—official emancipation. Then, heartbroken over local conditions a year after the end of the war, she wrote, "Poor Chapel Hill, the Church, & everything else, is dying a slow lingering death." In none of her letters did Maria mention the trials of the University of North Carolina which, following President Swain's death in 1868 and a couple of years under Republican Party control, closed and did not reopen until 1875. The new president—Kemp Plummer Battle—became a major figure in the life and legacy of both Maria Spear and Mary Smith.

A Sunday visit by the girls' grandfather, Charles Peter Mallett (who operated a bookstore in Chapel Hill from 1858 to 1868) provided the subject of a little lecture: "Your dear grandpa rode out one Sunday evening to see me. I was so glad. We were sitting at the front door. Several persons had passed. Mary said, 'Well, here comes a *gentleman*.' We looked as he came clearly in view, & it was a *gentleman* sure enough, for it was your grandpa. How I do love to look at people who bear the unmistakable stamp of Nature's Nobility. Remember, if you do not receive that mark in early youth, you will never have it. Remember that, Carrie & Maggie, Sisters, dear, in your daily intercourse, at your table, in your parlor, in your chamber."

On her way to visit the Mallett home, the teacher witnessed a July 4th celebration for the freedmen. In front of the Chapel Hill Presbyterian Church, "Mr. Guthrey & Mr. Sparrow

& a colored Brother delivered speeches—Guthrey's well enough—Sparrow's bad enough— the colored Brother excellent. He told them that their [the freedmen's] former owners were all the friends they could look to, that they might trust white people, but their own people they could not trust &c." She continued, "Mrs. Spencer & the Fetter girls made the banner. It looked very neat, one side of pink cambric had 'Our Trust Is In God,' the other of white with 'Respect To Our Former Owners'—their own selections." Then, perhaps mischievously, she added "They had a dinner out beyond Mrs. Utley's, at which the town negroes eat [*sic*] up what the county negroes brought; the latter got little or none." The festivities continued: "In the afternoon they had a fair in the long room at Guthrey's [Union Hotel]. Guthrey was married that night to Miss Jane Cave & brought her immediately home. The negroes gave Three Cheers for Mr. Guthrey, Three Cheers for his bride. That was her welcome home."[61]

Maria's presence gave Mary Smith incentive to become more sociable around Chapel Hill and Hillsborough. The elder Mallett wrote Maggie on September 30, 1866, "Miss Maria and Miss Mary spent the day with us yesterday, and altho it was a stormy day without doors we had a very pleasant visit which I believe was mutually pleasant and enjoyed." He added an interesting comment: "I learn that Genl. Atkins and his wife are in town. There has been no demonstration of any sort, and I hope every thing will pass off quietly."[62] A month later, October 17, while Maria was on a visit to Fayetteville, Mallett wrote again: "Miss Maria will tell you of the pleasant visits we had recently made to her and Miss Mary." He alluded again to his high regard to the teacher: "I am highly gratified to notice the kind manner in which you remember her [Maria Spear], and I always feel grateful that God allowed me to be the instrument in bringing her into your Father's family. You girls and especially Carrie will or ought to feel an everlasting love for her. I intend going out to see her often."

In reporting on Bishop William Mercer Green's recent visit, Mallett repeated the bishop's story of his visit with former Confederate States President Jefferson Davis, then in prison: "During the first twelve months of his imprisonment, he was subjected to all the indignity and severe usage which could have been practiced towards a Felon. He was not allowed a pen knife to pair his nails. When they had grown out to an insupportable length on his fingers they grew long and turned down like the talons of an eagle—on his toes they were so long he could not wear a shoe. At last a thunder storm broke in a window and he made use of the fragments of glass to pare them. His condition is now more comfortable."

The following February 8, while Maria was again visiting Fayetteville, "Grandpa" instructed Maggie to tell her younger sister Alice "to use all diligence in improving the time which she will spend under Miss Maria's care. She will probably never have another such opportunity."

Twenty-three years after he fathered an out-of-wedlock biracial daughter and twenty years after he represented Orange County as a Democrat in the State House of Commons, Sidney Smith died April 25, 1867, if not by suicide, then certainly from the effects of alcoholism. Estranged from his brother and sister, the dying 48-year-old lawyer appears to have been shunned also by his neighbors, and the tragedy was magnified by the absence of Maria Spear, then visiting in Fayetteville, leaving Mary to grieve alone. With only Mary, Frank, a sprinkling of friends, and farm hands present, the errant brother was buried near his parents on the grounds at Oakland. Friends in Chapel Hill—the Malletts or the Battles—had taken Mary into their home and cared for her immediately following Sidney's death. On her return to Oakland, Maria wrote Maggie on May 13, "My poor dear Mary requires all of my attention.

The shock is a severe one. She is so sad and frightened, that sometimes I am at my wits' end to know what to do or say.... Not a soul came to see Mary from the time she went home, until my arrival, & on the Sunday that intervened, not a human being, but Mary herself, was in this house or yard, or within sight or hearing, from after dinner, till nearly sundown." On the same date, Maria wrote Carrie, "You may know how necessary my presence here is to my poor distressed and frightened Mary when I tell you, that the Sunday afternoon before I came, there was not one human soul in this house or yard, for hours, but herself. Poor thing, poor thing. When you pray for me, never omit her name for she needs help."[63]

Mary remained inconsolable. Six months later (November 6, 1867) Maria wrote Maggie, "It has been because Mary has been in such distress that I have been at my very wit's end to know how to comfort her. At last when I found nothing but time & God's mercy could do it, I ceased my efforts—but even to do that was a trial. Oh me, those who lose Christian friends can have no idea of what it is to lay a dear object in the grave without the hope of a joyful resurrection. Mary will never get over it." The lament—"without the hope of a joyful resurrection"—can be interpreted in one of two ways: that Sidney Smith actually committed suicide (a sin in the eye of the church), or that he simply died without having accepted the teachings of the Episcopal Church. For devout Mary Smith, the difference was minimal. Mary was still grieving five years later when (July 12, 1872) Maria expressed sympathy for the death of Charles Beatty Mallett: "Mary sends her love to you all. Says she knows what you feel, for death was a bitter trial to her, when Parents & Brother were sent for, & she left behind to mourn."

The health of others was often mentioned in Maria's letters. For example, on November 4, 1867, she wrote Carrie that nearly everybody in the neighborhood had suffered a cold: "Frank has it, & the little house girl is choking and sniffling all the time. Emma's baby came near dying on Saturday. He is so fat & short—needed rubbing his heart & throat with oil of amber & putting his feet in hot water, & believe that saved him. He had taken Calomel &c but almost strangled before they could have time to operate."

In the spring Maria visited Mallett friends in Wilmington and fondly remembered a steamboat ride. To Maggie on May 13, 1867, she scribbled a note about her homeward experience via the Wilmington & Weldon and North Carolina railroads, on which there were few fellow travelers—only two came aboard in Goldsboro and "several" in Raleigh. She paid $3.75 for the ticket plus $2.50 for the sleeping car. At Durham's Station, unable to find passage to Chapel Hill that day, she paid $2.50 for "a good room, a good fire, & a supper & breakfast of fish." The next morning, she was able to proceed to Chapel Hill: "Mr. Huskey thought proper to let me mount into his spring wagon, take a seat upon the mail bags, coats &c. & pay my $4." Her riding companion was Betsy Tolar, a housekeeper to one of her former unnamed scholars in Hillsborough.[64] After dining at Mrs. Battle's, Maria paid $3 for another hack to deliver her to Mary's Oakland. Seemingly relieved to be back "home," she described the contents of her room: a bed, bureau, wardrobe, little table, washstand, looking glass, and easy chair. She joked about "a bright tin cup to dip up my water, but Mary says 'it is paid for.'" She added, "I of course sleep with Mary, but Theny has a fire ready for me & I wash & dress to my heart's content."[65]

Circumstances in 1868 appear to have—at least temporarily—brightened the lives of the two spinsters. "We have a white driver now, George Pendergrast," with whom they had a nice ride, described by Maria to Carrie on January 7. She was disappointed, however, when on two trips to the Chapel of the Cross, the church was not open and no one was present to administer communion. Then on March 19, she revealed to Carrie, "All here are busy preparing for Annette's marriage to Ed Kirby tomorrow even[ing]. Mary & myself are busy icing & trimming five cakes." The ceremony was performed at the Presbyterian Church in Chapel Hill by the Rev. Charles Phillips. Mary was losing another niece with the aunt's blessing. A comment in the same letter, coupled with other expressions from time to time, seems to question Pauli Murray's interpretation of Maria Louisa Spear's feelings about race. After commenting on the cake-trimming, she added, "Negroes hold themselves above white people now, but let them be in sorrow or in joy, how quickly they find their old friends." And, on May 2, following the Republican victory at the polls, she wrote Carrie, "Oh me, does not your heart ache about the election[?] Poor, dear North Carolina, ruined, ruined." On August 4, 1871, she reported to Maggie that on the Smith plantation only one tenant voted "conservative," five did not vote, and the remainder voted "radical." She sighed, "Is it not too bad, so good as Mary is to them all."

The urge to teach began reasserting itself in late 1867 when Maria wrote on a scrap of paper, "If my duties here were not so imperative, I would hunch up somewhere to teach, for I feel that 'Othello's occupation's gone.' Yes, indeed, a new existence at 63—but never mind, this is my place now. Let the future take care of itself." She wrote Carrie on February 13, 1868, "I began to teach forty years ago," adding, "A life of earnest effort to be a friend to my Scholars, to enter into their feelings & to do to them as I thought they most needed, is all I claim."[66]

During the ensuing winter, the teacher's spirits were boosted. In an undated letter, perhaps in December 1868, Maria wrote, "The neighbors want me to take a school & offer to build me a school house, among those rocks & trees, just where you turn into Mary's lane. I have declined, because it would take me all day away from Mary, & because, if they build a house, I should feel obliged to keep up the school, whether it suits me or not. If I conclude to attempt anything of the kind, I will build the house myself. A small log school house would cost me very little, & being on Mary's land, would be useful to her, whenever I stopped. But at present I have not determined." Regardless, she exulted, "Now what do you think: I have a Scholar who comes for two hours every morning & pays me two dollars a month. That is but ten cents for two hours of undivided attention, but you can't think how much happiness I have been enjoying since she began. I felt before as if I had lost myself, & dropped out of my own sphere."

The school house was built as she envisioned, either by herself or by her neighbors, for on March 22, 1869, Maria wrote Carrie, "I am so busy engaging about my little log school house." On May Day, she wrote Maggie, "Surely I have been very happy in my school life, so many pleasures scattered along my path. And my little log cabin school is a source of great pleasure to me. The girls come with little baskets of flowers every day." On December 3, she wrote Carrie, "My little school closed for the winter yesterday, when we expected a snow storm every minute—but it did not snow." The following April 11 (1870), she wrote Carrie that she had a cold and "could do nothing but teach my four little Scholars sometimes over at the school house & sometimes here [in the house]," and on November 12 she complained to Maggie that a frost had killed as many as nineteen of her Morning Glories around her "school room door." Her school was mentioned again on August 27, 1872, when lightning struck two trees nearby, and on April 29, 1873, when she told Maggie that she would have to postpone a visit because "I cannot break up my school." It is not clear how long her eyes allowed Maria Spear to continue the work that gave her life meaning.[67]

As she did in most of her letters, Maria reported on visits to, and the health of, the Mallett girls' relatives and friends in Chapel Hill and Hillsborough, often mentioning members of the Mickle family, who were especially close to Mary Smith. Almost invariably, the teacher worked in a few moral lessons, along with recommendations of books. Maria's comments on Mary's strict character judgments were often revealing; for example, on October 6, 1869, she reported a compliment paid to Carrie, adding, "Praise from Mary, is Praise worth having." In extending sympathy for a death in the Mallett family, Maria wrote Carrie on November 12, 1870, "Mary sends her love to you & all the family & is truly sorry for all the pain you suffer. She knows what pain is, for hers has been in many senses, a painful life."

Maria Spear was not habitually chatty, but on August 4, 1871, she could not resist telling the 18-year-old Carrie about a humane resolution of a canine problem: "Our little dog Sprite has two fine little puppies. She is happy enough. She had three, but could not nurse so many, so we got Emmaline who has a young baby, to take it, and I wish you could have seen the little thing, at three days old, sucking away, swallowing down the good rich milk, as if it belonged to her. I heard from her yesterday. She was doing as very well." Emmaline was one of the mulatto women on the plantation, and perhaps human nursing of a valued animal was not out of the ordinary in cases of favorite pets. Loneliness in the large house was expressed a year later (August 7, 1872, to Carrie): "My garden is my only pleasure, since our dear little Sprite was taken from us. She died at daybreak, the very same Sunday that your trial came upon you. The house has felt large & empty ever since." Based on Maria's testimony concerning the parsimoniousness of Dr. Smith, it is easy to picture Oakland, large and imposing, as a sparsely and perhaps shabbily furnished home—a far cry from the elegantly furnished mansion seemingly implied by Cornelia's memories. Such conflicting pictures of ostentation and humility can be seen in the South following war and its devastation to land-rich but poor families.

A tragedy of enormous effect upon Mary Smith and her four nieces occurred on the plantation in August 1872 when lightning struck Harriet's cabin, killing a 12-year-old boy named Dennard, injuring Harriet and Mary Cole, and stupefying Ed Cole. In accounts to each girl—Carrie on August 26 and Maggie the next day—Maria told essentially the same story, the fullest being to Carrie: Lightning struck in seven places on the plantation. One large tree, near which the farm hands had been working, she wrote, "was torn all to pieces, but John had sent all home at the beginning, for he said there was no place to fasten the mules, except to trees, & he remembered how much Miss Mary had said about the danger. So, they [the mules] were all saved. Of the three flashes, two struck two trees, half way between my school house and Harriet's." It was in Harriet's cabin that the carnage occurred. Dennard and Mary Cole had just returned from school, and as they ducked into the cabin, two trees were struck, and Dennard remarked, "There, Mary, what a good thing we got in here, we might have been killed." Hardly had the boy finished the sentence when the third flash struck Harriet's chimney, ran down it, came through the fireplace, struck Dennard on the head, ran down his back, killing him instantly. The bolt paralyzed Harriet and Mary Cole, stunned Ed, and ran out through the front door. Adding to the tragic picture, the bolt hit Dennard so quickly that the boy did not have time to swallow the melon that he was eating. Additionally, most of the chickens, which had run under the cabin to escape the rain, were also killed. Remarkably, Annette and her baby, cowering on a bed, and several children playing on the floor, escaped injury. A half hour passed before Ed Cole sufficiently regained his senses to run to Mary's house and fetch her brother, Dr. Frank Smith, whose own health was such that he could be of little help. The storm and resulting rains were so bad that the dead boy's father, who lived in Hillsborough, could not retrieve the body from Harriet's cabin until the following Saturday. Uncharacteristically, Maria attributed blame: "It seemed as if ignorance & self-will in one of the persons invited the danger, for he insisted on opening the door, & their all coming round the table to eat melons, which he had brought."

While Harriet remained an invalid for more than a year, Mary and Maria, ignoring their own decrepitude, returned the tender care that the faithful servant had given them. Maria told the remainder of the story to "My dear Girls" on September 10, 1873: When Herbert Mallett's letter arrived, "it found Mary & myself fully occupied attending the dying bed of her old faithful servant Harriet, and as the weather has been almost incessantly rainy, we have had, in the wet, to cross three fences, & go through two cotton fields, every time we went. I picked my times, & so got along very well, but Mary went every day in the rain & the dew, & nearly laid herself up. It is all done now, & I hope Mary will have no more such trials to her feelings and exposure to her health. I have just sent over the flowers, to go in the coffin, or on the grave as they like. I shall not go." Two months later (December 13), Maria wrote that Mary had "never had time to get well of the severe cold she took when Harriet died." Besides, she was worried with changes among her tenants. Harriet and Ed Cole appear to have been the glue holding the tenants—perhaps the entire plantation—together.

Next to teaching school, the use of her delicate fingers was Maria Spear's favorite pastime. Painting, sewing, and pressing flowers provided both pleasure and income—much of the former, precious little of the latter.[68]

According to her niece Cornelia, Mary Smith also painted. Pauli Murray wrote about a "gilt-framed painting by Miss Mary Ruffin Smith called 'The Silver Fountain' which hung just ... over the mantelpiece and which Grandmother counted among her most treasured heirlooms."[69] Maria honed her talent throughout life, but in later years these activities—next to caring for Mary Smith and until her eyesight failed—were her greatest pleasure. Repeatedly she enclosed small pieces of embroidery or pressed flowers in her letters to Carrie and Maggie, and she delighted in similar gifts in return. For example, she acknowledged a tiny gift from Carrie [April 1, 1874]: "Mary sat down by me on my 'Rustic Seat' (two logs with an old chair back) & as I opened the letter, we were both struck with the beauty & brilliance of the little bunch of flowers. It was pressed so flat that it looked like a rich piece of embroidery." Above almost anything else, Maria valued her silver thimble and scissors. She wrote Maggie (December 18, 1867) about almost panicking when she misplaced the little pair of scissors on which the name "Maria" was engraved. A thorough search left only one place unchecked, the fireplace, but Theny had already carried the refuse to the "ash house." Remembering that "Mr. Saunders exchanges a box of concentrated lye with three bushels of ash," Mary instructed Julius to sift the ashes as they were measured. Sure enough, Harriet's son, then a grown man, retrieved the precious scissors. They had lost their brilliance and sharpness, and her name was hardly legible, but Maria happily greased, rubbed, and resumed using them.

In her own travels, and when friends offered to shop for her, Maria provided detailed specifications for sewing materials. She made most of her own clothes but occasionally accepted hand-me-downs. In an undated note [probably 1867], she exulted: "Mary has given me her parasol, her black silk dress, her pompadour muslin, & the skirt of a light worsted dress, to wear with a white body—besides collars &c. Have I not been fortunate?" Such comments, along with repeated references to her poverty—for example, she wrote Carrie (March 19, 1868), "I ... do not possess a cent in the whole world"—make clear that Maria Spear was a guest in Mary Smith's home, not a paid companion. Time and again, the teacher wrote of her embarrassment in accepting occasional support from her brother William and sister Elizabeth. Mary Smith was one of the largest landholders in two counties, and she inherited collectible loans from Sidney's estate (and, after 1877, Frank's); yet the two spinsters lived so frugally that neighbors must have considered them as misers. The irony may never have occurred to either of the women, for they lived in an economically-distressed era when ostentation and high living were uncommon. Theirs was a bond, each independent of the other, yet inextricably bound by love. Maria would no more have asked Mary for money than Mary would have offered her a salary. If in the eyes of neighbors they lived as misers, they were—in their individual minds—simply prudent. By living without ostentation, each looked for a better tomorrow. No wonder, then, that Cornelia Fitzgerald—and probably the other three sisters—felt short-changed when out of Mary's vast holdings, each was bequeathed only one hundred acres of land, a house, and a few household goods.[70]

Thus, Maria's few students at Oakland may have satisfied her devotion to her profession, but the few dollars earned from her fingers helped maintain her sense of independence. Local women, including Pattie Battle, used her talents. Although sewing helped produce the little income on which she depended after moving in with Mary Smith, Maria was reluctant to charge personal acquaintances the fair value of her work. For example, on November 7, 1868, she sent Pattie—another Mallett sister—a "little Sacque," with a note reading, "I hope you will not think Two Dollars an exorbitant charge. I am very much obliged to you for giving me the job, as I am greatly in need of money, that even that little is a comfort." In addition to small jobs for members of the Mallett family, she had an arrangement with a "Baltimore Depository"—perhaps associated with an Episcopal diocese—for clothing work. Materials and orders were received irregularly, and remuneration was low. In 1868 [February 13] she reported having spent six weeks to finish a "Baltimore cloak"; still, she was eager for more work: "So, if The Depository does not give me more work this year than last, I shall have to try doing without gain—so be it, but I still 'hope on, hope ever.'" A few months later [May 2, 1868] she received a bundle of materials for the sewing of three cloaks for which she was paid only $6 each by the depository.

A letter of November 8, 1872, indicated that either Mary or her tenants were paying Maria a bit for her sewing: "I am very busy altering & making dresses for the colored [written "coloured" but with the "u" deleted] ladies on this plantation, & am very thankful to make a little in this way, because I have no school, & do not like to throw myself down entirely on the charity of my dear brother & sister, who lovingly aid me to the utmost." Making clothes for hired hands required less talent than she had displayed in making the famous quilt honoring dead Confederate soldiers, but Maria gladly accepted the task.[71]

An unusual local custom was divulged by Maria in a letter dated December 13, 1873: "Our old, blind, bed-ridden neighbor, Mrs. Pendergrass, died this week—94 years old. I had to give her a cap. That is a rule in this neighborhood, a cap for the old, & flowers for the young, are always expected."[72]

Maria was happily surprised when Mary honored her friend by splurging on "an eighty-five dollar Wilson & Wheeler's Sewing Machine."[73] Unfortunately, the generous gift came too late for Maria to enjoy very long, because her eyesight had already begun to deteriorate. On March 7, 1877, she confided to Carrie, "The fact is, my eyes have failed me so rapidly in the last year or two, that I cannot do anything at night & even then, I do not see the lines, nor catch the glimpse of one now and then."

For two aging spinsters, occupying a huge dwelling in which Mary's parents and two brothers had suffered and died, their scattered cabins inhabited by black and mixed-race tenants hanging on as white Southerners began chipping away civil rights recently guaranteed by constitutional amendments, life was contradictory. In terms of real estate and notes held on the farms of neighbors, Mary Smith was rich. Agriculture, however, was ailing, and lenders were hard pressed to meet even interest payments. Besides, both women were accustomed to hard times, and the thought of ostentatious living was beyond their experience. Now Maria's eyesight, so crucial to her joys in life—writing, sewing, knitting, drawing, painting, and helping her friend Mary—was threatened.

The following year Maria wrote that she was "no account" and of "little use I am to myself or any one else. My eyes are failing so fast, that I do no work but don [darn] stockings, or some such thing." She was particularly saddened by her inability to take much advantage of the sewing machine that Mary gave her. In a letter to Carrie written on August 25, 1879, Maria reported that her cataract was getting worse. The absence of any additional letters from Maria in the Mallett papers may suggest that she was unable to write further. If so, it is not difficult to imagine the sadness shared by the companions during the last year and a half of the teacher's life.

Maria's letters reveal more about herself than about Mary, and they provide disappointingly little about personnel and daily activity on the Price Creek plantation. However, basing her judgment on Cornelia Fitzgerald's memories, Pauli Murray wrote that Mary "made a proposition to her former slaves. If any of them wanted to stay on and work the crops for her, she'd stake them to food and clothes and let them live in their cabins rent free. Most of them accepted her proposal and life continued much in the same way on the surface, but tentatively and with odd formalities on both sides."[74] The difference lay in the substitution of the status of tenant—free to leave—for that of slave—legally bound to an owner. Maria occasionally referred to yard activities, as on August 7, 1872, when she wrote, "We are as usual, Mary as busy with her cows, chickens & turkeys as possible," but except for dry weather and fires that occasionally burned cabins and crops, little was said about farming activities on the Price Creek plantation. Maria appears to have been completely unacquainted with the Jones Grove plantation. However, she divulged information important to the history of Oakland when on November 8, 1872, she wrote, "Mary has been so busy building a cotton house, moving and rebuilding a crib, gathering her crops, which all have to be measured & divided, changing some old tenants for new, moving others, having the front Piazza new roofed & floored that she hardly has time to breathe." She added a sad report: "In the middle of the last named job [on the piazza], the man, who lived about three miles off, received notice that his house & everything in it, was burned up, so he had to go home & build one for himself. Two other houses in the neighborhood have been similarly destroyed, in one, two negro children, & in the other, two white children perished. The parents being off, picking cotton, the white man got home, just in time to see his poor children in the flames, & to hear their cries, but could not reach them." The following spring [April 29, 1873] Maria again described dry weather that allowed fires to sweep through the community, burning the wheat crop of one tenant and threatening homes.

For many years, Mary Smith sought to run the plantation with the help of trusted tenants, but as her brothers died off and her health deteriorated, she eventually recognized the need for a farm manager. Maria divulged the good news to Carrie on August 25, 1879: "We have been so fortunate as never to spend a night alone. It is seldom, however, that such a gentleman as Mr. Cole can be procured."[75]

Nearly twenty years after Mary had brought Julius, Cornelia, Emma, Annette, and Laura into the Chapel of the Cross,[76] she performed the same duty for the daughters of Emma plus Julius and the little son of Theny [Parthenia], another of her mulatto servants. The happy event provided the subject of a descriptive letter from Maria to Carrie on July 9, 1874: "They are all fine little darkies, were dressed in white frocks, sleeves tied up with blue ribbon, & a blue bow behind, & behaved as pretty as they could. Julius & his wife, Mr. Richard Saunders' daughter, & Mr. Mickle's youngest son were confirmed." The account continued, "The Bp. let them go to their seats, & then gave an address on infant baptism & confirmation. The Ch. was crowded, the galary [sic] so full of colored people that there was not room even to stand & many stayed out in the yard & at the window." Then, excited with the success of the ceremonies, Maria added proudly, "We were in all the principal stores the next day, & every one we met, white & colored, could talk of nothing else. Even a Baptist said he never understood infant baptism before." Mary and Maria accompanied Bishop Thomas Atkinson to the Mickles' home, where multiple sicknesses placed the bishop in the hands of the two women friends: "So Mary & I took charge of the Bp. & we kept him talking, I do assure you. It seemed as if we had known each other for years. He is going to visit Bp. Green this summer, & I expect him to tell him we were two as amusing women as he had often met." Maria concluded with a profound observation: "You can imagine what a gratification this was to Mary to see the children that she had baptized in their infancy, now bringing up theirs to the same altar."

A month later, apparently in response to Maggie's concern that she might never marry (in fact, she never did), spinster Maria Spear consoled her and in doing so, revealed her own virginity:

> I should be distressed if I thought that I had encouraged any woman to lead a single life, for the perfection of our nature can exist only in the state of Wife & Mother, but I do hope I have shown, that when circumstances require maidenhood, be the reasons what they may, it is possible to lead a happy & useful existence. I hold myself & my sex too high up in creation to hang my head like a Bulrush, or to salve my temper, because my Heavenly Parent, Lord and Master, forbid me the blessing of a Husband & Children. A woman's motto in this & all other subjects must be,
>
> > "Thou knowest best what I need most,
> > And let Thy Will be Love."
> > Have you those words, they begin,
> > "Searcher of Hearts" by G.P. Morris.

In January of the following year,[77] Maria's "favorite" nephew, the Rev. Columbus Smith—the son of Elizabeth and Samuel Bryan Smith—died in Key West, leaving seven children including daughters named for both Mary and Maria. Mary remembered her namesake in her will. Unlike the remainder of the family, Columbus Smith was a Baptist; he served a church in Alabama for a while.

Mary's surviving and live-in brother, Dr. Francis Jones Smith, had seldom been mentioned in Maria's correspondence until 1875 when on December 29 she wrote Carrie that both she and Mary had been unwell. Regardless of health, Mary had to continue attending to the business of the farm "and waiting incessantly on her Brother, who was taken alarmingly ill in June, & has never been safe from a recurrence of the attack. He is going about now with two sticks, surprisingly [illegible] but will never in my opinion be well again.... How Mary has gone through it all is known only to the Merciful God." The next summer, Maria wrote Carrie [July 25, 1876], "The Dr.'s situation renders it too inconvenient & uncomfortable, both to her [Mary] and her visitors, to ask anyone to come.... My dear Mary's health cannot improve so long as the Dr. remains in his distressing situation." Apparently Frank's mental health failed even before he suffered a disabling stroke.[78]

Frank's condition continued to deteriorate. On March 7, 1877, Maria wrote Carrie, "During the cold weather, Mary was so uneasy about F[rank] that we moved our bed down into the dining room, & while the snow lasted cooked in there also. So we had bed chamber, kitchen, dining room & parlor all in one." She continued,

> We were up till some time after twelve last night. Frank had one of his bad attacks, each one of which brings on the last sad hour, fierce behavior. He has now lost the use of the one hand which has long been his only dependence & cannot feed himself. I don't think he has attempted to speak today. I have not been able to understand a word he said for many months. What a terrible drain all this is upon Mary, I leave you to imagine. She & I have regretted so often that your visit came at a time when he was so violent that it was impossible for us to have children in the house. For some months he has never left his chair (your dear grandpa's parting gift to me the day I went to bid them farewell). He is lifted from it to the bed morning & evening & neither knows nor cares who is in the house. The truth is Dr. F's derangement has been coming on for years, & we have been so frightened, I for Mary, for as to myself, I could generally keep out of danger, that we had no heart to do anything, but if ever we do get settled, I am going to pay you all a visit, that I have made up my mind to do.

The plight of the two women and a mentally-ill man was made even more dire by the neglect of the plantation and the temptation for the women to abandon Oakland. Maria continued, "Every thing here, house, farm &c. has been going to rack & ruin, all this time, for Mary held herself in readiness to move at anytime, but we have all calmed down now, & she & I both think that she will be happier here than anywhere else, & I know I should, so she is making up her mind to get comfortable here, & if possible enjoy a quiet rest, before she too has to leave also. During all this time, I have watched her from day to day, failing continually.... But I trust the worst is over."

Francis Jones Smith, M.D., died April 17, 1877. Augustus Long wrote, "It was reported in religious circles that Dr. Smith died in great terror, torn with regrets and remorse."[79] No mention of the funeral has been found in the correspondence, but Mary decided against burying her older brother at Price Creek, the scene of so much sadness. Instead, she chose the Jones Grove plantation, which Frank had inherited from his grandfather, Francis Jones. The decision was undoubtedly a joint one by Mary and Maria, who planned to exhume and move the bodies of Mary's parents and younger brother, thus establishing a cemetery for the entire family—minus, of course, the born-out-of-wedlock daughters of the two brothers.

Frank had been out of public view so long that in its issue of May 2, 1877, the *Hillsborough Recorder* mangled his obituary: "Dr. Frank Smith, 61, at his residence in Chatham County, 2 weeks ago. Last surviving son of Dr. James S. Smith, physician of this place. At one time Dr. Frank Smith was a member of Congress. He is survived by one daughter."[80]

There was no will; consequently Frank's *three* daughters, free and of age, received nothing from his estate. Instead, Mary inherited everything—the Jones Grove plantation of more than 1,700 acres plus about $6,500 in cash and personal notes valued at $15,000. Thus by 1877 she possessed everything left of Francis Jones's worth that had escaped her father's profligacy and her brothers' self-indulgence. In Orange and Chatham county terms, Mary Ruffin Smith was a wealthy woman.[81]

With the "girls" out on their own, it may have been Maria Spear's influence that led Mary Smith to open her heart, loosen her purse strings, and begin making loans following Frank's death. It was the neighborly thing to do. Besides, Mary had never been accustomed to luxurious living in a family whose male members controlled all finances. Her decision would lead to an earned reputation as a good neighbor and an unwanted image as a rich woman. In Chatham County alone, from the year of Frank's death until her own death in 1885, Mary Smith assisted at least seventeen neighbors with loans totaling more than $9,000, each backed by a mortgage:

1877	James Pace	$800	AV/368 owed FJS	Rocky River
1878	Stephen E. Cole	$400	AV/483	Cub Creek
	James Pace	$10	AV/563	Rocky River
	Daniel T. Tilmon	$2,000	AX/330	Morgan Creek/county line
1880	Silas J. Riggsbee	$250	BA/139	East side CH-Pittsboro Rd.
1883	Edward H. Ward	$500	BF/376	Adj. Jones Grove/J.W. Hackney
1884	Stephen E. Cole	$300	BH/300	Cub Creek
	Charles D. Hackney	$500	BH/342	Price's Creek/Pritchard's Mill
	P. M. Pearson	$500	BH/384	Where he lives
	M. S. Hackney	$550	BH/537	Hackney's Quarter
	J. G. Bennett	$500	BI/192	Bush Creek
	J. Q. Bryant	$525	BI/194	Haw River
	B. M. Ray	$150	BI/199	Lystra Church/Cub Creek
	D. Tilmon	$500	BI/240	Morgan Creek
	M. T. Horton	$800	BI/295	New Hope Creek
1885	W. C. Pearson	$200	BL/13	Hearndon Creek
	M. S. Hackney	$550	BN/201	New Hope Creek

One of the listed mortgages was outstanding as late as July 16, 1901, when Mary Smith's executor Kemp Battle foreclosed on Charles Hackney and wife Antoinette's mortgage of February 12, 1884. At a public sale, the 77 acres on Price Creek and Pritchard's Mill Road was sold for $255 through William C. Cole, Mary's agent.[82]

There were several other real estate transactions. The debt of $650 owed by R.I. Ashe and Mariah Mitchell to the estate of Sidney Smith was repaid in 1868 by transferring jointly to Francis and Mary Smith two lots in Chapel Hill, each partially touching College Street [Cameron Avenue]. On February 9, 1881, Mary sold to James B. Mason, for $825, a one-acre lot on the south side of Chapel Hill's Franklin Street, "being the lot conveyed to said Mary R. Smith by Thomas M. Argo as assignee in bankruptcy of Wm. J. Hogan." And on November 14, 1881, she sold to Fendal Hogan, for $1,500, a one-acre lot on Cameron Avenue near Mallett Street in Chapel Hill conveyed to her by James B. Mason and wife by deed dated February 9, 1881.[83]

A gift of 52 acres on Morgan Creek in 1882 spoke clearly of Mary Smith's favoritism toward her niece Emma Morphis and Emma's first-born son, "Little Sam." Emphatically, however, the deed restated the spinster's distrust of men. The property was limited to Emma's ownership during her natural life as "her sole and separate property free from the debts, liabilities or contracts" of her husband, and, upon her death, to "her son Samuel Morphis & his heirs and assigns in fee simple."[84] Except for the bequests in her will, this appears to have been Mary Smith's sole gift of real estate to a member of the household.

The toll that Frank's wasted life and illness had taken on the two women during the past eleven years was intimated by Maria to Carrie and Maggie on June 27, 1877: "I am not sick, but I am worn out. The constant fears & anxieties of the last two or three years have made Mary prematurely old, & taken away what powers age had left me.... Mary has some comfort in her brother's death, for which I know you will return thanks with us. It all seems like a sad, strange dream, more than a reality." To explain her reluctance to plan a visit to Fayetteville friends, she promised, "I will certainly do so when I can feel satisfied to leave Mary. She feels her loneliness so severely, that I do not think it would be right to leave her alone." With relief, she added, "We have a very gentlemanly & kind young man to live with us, but he is absent from the house nearly all the day, & she requires some one who can enter into her feelings & soothe her stresses."[85]

Usually so demure, Maria revealed a lighter side of her existence when in the same letter she acknowledged a birthday gift from the Mallett girls—two bottles of "Ochiltree" wine, made by mutual friends: "I was very much fatigued & poorly, the day they came (I mean the 2 bottles) & I opened that one immediately, & regaled myself freely. I don't know that I ever felt more relief than it afforded me, & I wished that you could know what a change it made in my feeling. Several times since, I have resorted to the same, & always with success. I should have liked dear old Mrs. Ochiltree to know what good the bottle she gave me to travel on did me."

Again declining an invitation to Fayetteville, Maria wrote jointly to Carrie and Maggie on November 5, 1877:

> Miss Mary's health will not permit me to leave her at night, or allow her to stay all night at a friend's house. Poor Frank's painful situation for two or three years was a fearful strain upon his sister's heart, mind, & health. I feared that she would sink before him, but necessity & affection kept her up so long as he needed her. Since then, she has been failing, reviving so far as to go to town for a day at a time, & spend several days afterward at home in recovering from the fatigue & excitement. Various medicines seem to improve her for a while, but the least thing upsets her again. Last Sat. night she was worse than I have ever seen her, & for some hours, the usual medicines entirely failed. Next day (Sunday) she was better. I wrapped myself in blankets, & lay down & slept nearly all day. Last night she slept, & so did I. Today she is about, attending to her family, & my cold is going away. You see, my dear children, that for me to leave her is an impossibility. You & I have had the pleasure of anticipating this visit, but we must give it up & be *very, very thankful* that my dear Friend is still spared to me, & that the quiet home provided for my old age is still my refuge & comfort. I am feeling the infirmities of the period of life at which I have arrived, 73½—and am daily receiving the rest & leisure which dear Mary affords to me.

Mary and Maria's devotion to the Chapel of the Cross, which was preparing for a visit by the bishop, was again exhibited in the same letter. "We have sent for a carpet—I say *We*, tho' in truth, I could give only one dollar toward the purchase—but I was glad to be able to do even that little. Mary has sent five dollars for a vase to place on the Altar, & $2.50 for an alms plate—I hope all will come in time."

Maria's letters, filled with her concern over the health of her friend and companion, also recorded her own health, always delicate but under enormous strain in a big house on a big plantation governed by an ailing spinster. On July 18, 1878, as she had so often done previously, she poured out her feelings:

> I have not been well for months—& will in all probability never will again. I am particularly grieved about all this, because I am of no use to Mary with her sewing, & not much in her housekeeping. I am using a pencil because it is so much easier to write with that, than with a pen. Dr. Lewis does not think that at my age it will ever be necessary to operate on my eye. It is the right [one] over which the cataract is growing. No pain at all, but a veil between it & every thing I look at. If the left eye is covered, I cannot tell who is at the table with me & so on. My sister is so distracted, fearing that I shall not be able to write to her, that I determined to learn to write with my eye both closed—& I am happy to say that I can do it.

Even in that letter, however, Maria was able to send some good news: She and Mary in the spring had spent a month with the girls' uncle, Dr. William Mallett: "It was very pleasant to us both & of great benefit also, for I fattened enough to require all my clothes to be let out, & Mary started up hill again & learned to eat once more. She thinks, & so do I, that going there saved her life. She was starving with Dyspepsia, & the change, lively company at the table, &c. worked a wonderful change in her. All the family, even the little man servant, were as kind to us as they could have [been]. Your aunt & the girls could not have been more devoted to us than they were." Shortly afterward, Maria wrote again, "Mrs. Bryant will tell you that she met me & that I look remarkably well, & so I do, wonderfully for a person 74¼ old, but she does not know how no account I am, & how little use I am to myself or any one else. My eyes are failing so fast that I do no work but don [darn] stockings, or some such thing."[86]

The last of Maria's letters preserved in the Mallett Collection was dated August 25, 1879. She and Mary had the pleasure of taking communion from "Rev. Dr. Cheshire," whose son, Joseph Blount Cheshire, Jr., although only a deacon, had recently come as rector of the Chapel of the Cross. Neither Maria nor Mary lived long enough to see this son, within fifteen years, elected Bishop of North Carolina or in his later role in saving St. Mary's School through the use of funds from Mary Ruffin Smith's estate that had originally been willed to Maria Louisa Spear.[87]

Maria Louisa Spear died January 6, 1881. The *Orange County Observer* of Hillsborough on January 15, carried this notice under "Chapel Hill in Brief": "Miss Mariah Spear, living with Miss Mary Smith 5 miles south of this place, was found dead in her bed, Wednesday morning, Jan. 5. She [had] retired in apparent good health, Tuesday night, and died during the night." Cornelia Phillips Spencer wrote her daughter the next day, "Think what a shock! They [Mary and Maria] used the same room, though separate beds. Both went to bed in usual health.... A dear and admirable old lady is gone—a long & useful & excellent life is ended. I cannot doubt that she was ready for the messenger." She continued, "Miss Maria Spear had a remarkable presentiment of an approaching death. She had arranged all her little affairs, given every direction & so to speak, had bid the world good night for 2–3 weeks before the messenger came. She was in her usual health too. She seemed to have died as she slept. Not a pang—nor a struggle. I shall always love to recall her as one of the loveliest old ladies in the world." Two months later, Spencer described a visit with the grieving Mary: "Thence to see Miss Mary Smith, who has the Ledoux parlor for her bedroom at present—

Report of Maria Spear's death, issued by the Chapel of the Cross, of which she was a faithful attendant (Chapel of the Cross, Chapel Hill; courtesy Ernest A. Dollar, Jr.).

is very lonesome & unhappy." The reference is to a style of interior decoration associated with the French architect Claude Nicolas Ledoux (1736–1806), described by one writer as "a highly imaginative and often fantastic way."[88]

By a sad coincidence, the penultimate letter in the Mallett Collection, one of the few extant letters penned by Mary Ruffin Smith, described that terrible morning. Dated January 20, 1881, it read:

My dear Carrie,

I feel so unhappy I do not know what to do with myself. You & Maggie can understand how I feel, for I know your love to my dearest best friend. I am alone in the world. How I wish you two were near enough for me to see & talk with you. I cannot tell you anything about my dear friend's end that you do not know already, as your Aunt has written to you. She was in usual health the night before, so when I woke in the morning I called her, as I often did, & she did not answer. Then I started to the bed but my heart gave way, & I called to Mr. Cole to come & see what was the matter. He burst out crying & I knew all was over. If you could look at her, but everybody said she looked just as if she had fallen asleep & as she [illegible] "Asleep in Jesus." Oh! If I only could say that is enough—but I miss her too much.

I hope you can read this. I am too nervous to write. The hymn, her favorite one, "Rock of Ages," was sung at the Funeral. She is buried in our Grave Yard, & when my time shall come, I shall lie beside her. I know you all pray for me. I am so lonely. All are gone. I am staying at Mr. [Kemp] Battle's. I really don't know what I shall do. I can't make up my mind, to stay where I am is too lonely, & yet, I hate to leave a place associated with all who were dear to me. I don't know what to do. Mr. Battle & Pattie have kindly offered me a home with them. I really do not know yet what I want. My God & Lord has to [decide] what is best for me. Dear, dear Miss Maria was so pleased with the flowers you sent. I am so glad they came in time to give her pleasure. She kept them as long as she could.

Now, dear girls, it has been an effort to write this, but I thought you would be pleased to hear from me. I love you both for her dear sake, as well as your own. Whenever you can come, I shall be glad to see you if I keep [the] house. Oh! My heart is broken. Pray for me. My best love for you all & Mrs. Birdsall.

Your affectionate friend,
Mary R. Smith.[89]

In January or February 1881, after a death in the Mallett family, "M.R. Smith" again addressed "Dear Girls": "I can't think of anyone's loss but my own. I know you all loved Miss

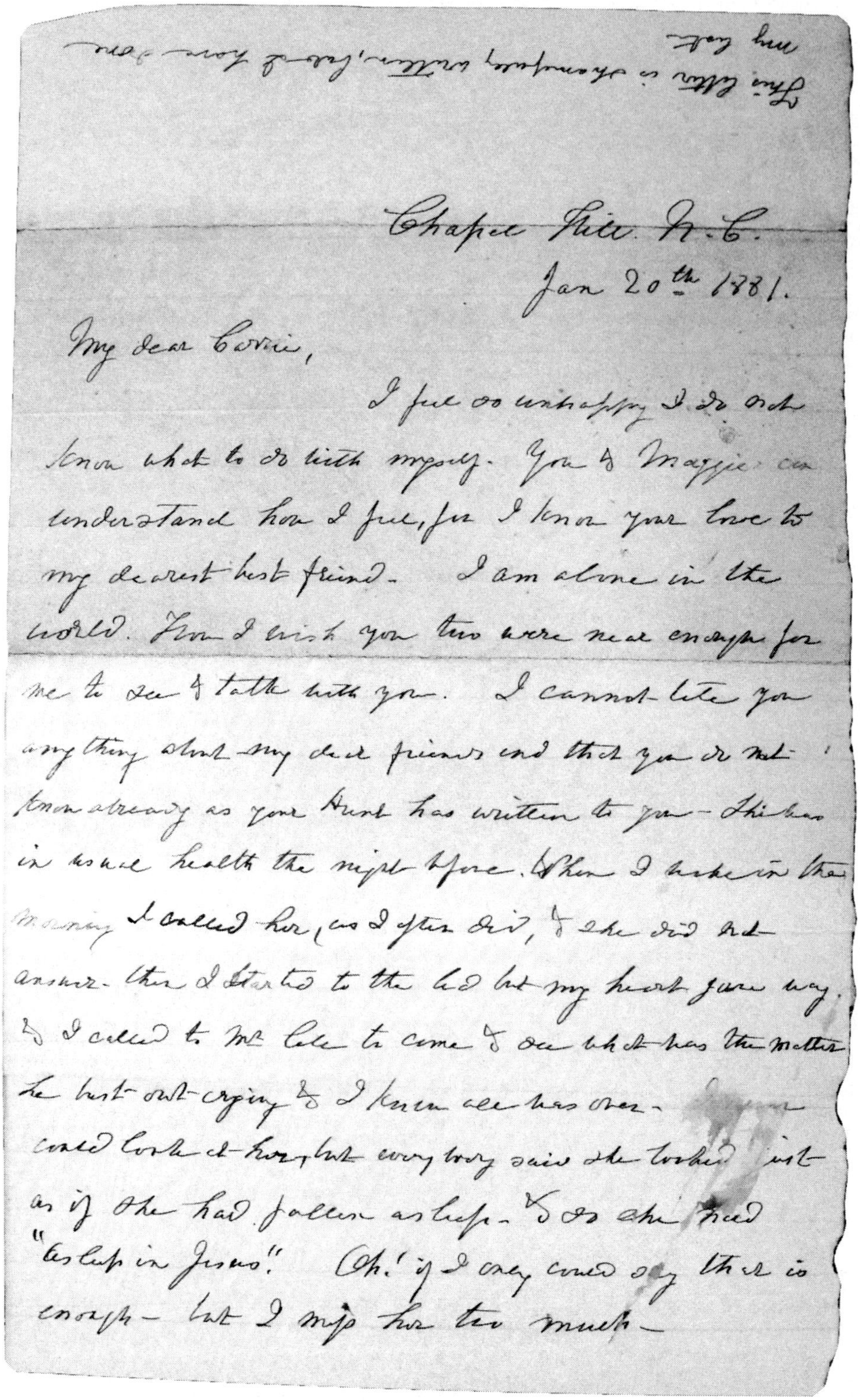

This letter is shamefully written, [illegible]

Chapel Hill N.C.
Jan 20th 1881.

My dear Carrie,

I feel so unhappy I do not know what to do with myself. You & Maggie can understand how I feel, for I know your love to my dearest best friend. I am alone in the world. How I wish you two were near enough for me to see & talk with you. I cannot tell you anything about my dear friend and that you do not know already as your Aunt has written to you. She was in usual health the night before. When I woke in the morning I called her, as I often did, & she did not answer. then I started to the bed but my heart gave way. & I called to Mr Cole to come & see what was the matter he burst out crying & I knew all was over. [illegible] could look at her, but everybody said she looked just as if she had fallen asleep. & so she died "asleep in Jesus." Oh! if I only could say that is enough — but I miss her too much —

First page of Mary Ruffin Smith's letter to Carrie Mallett, January 20, 1881, describing the death of her longtime friend and companion, Maria Louisa Spear (courtesy Charles B. Mallett Papers [3165], Southern Historical Collection, Wilson Library, UNC-CH).

Maria. I know how much interest she took in you—& I do for you too. I hope you can come up sometime this year so we can talk about her."

Unfortunately, any further correspondence between the Mallett sisters and Mary Smith appears to have been lost. However, letters among the Malletts repeatedly revealed the teacher's influence upon their family. When Maria had left Fayetteville to live at Oakland, John Wright Mallett wrote Maggie on June 8, 1867, "She was a great comfort to you and Carrie, but my dear sister I am truly thankful & happy to see you actuated by a spirit so noble & Christianlike," and upon Maria's death, a cousin in Louisiana wrote to Carrie on December 18, 1881, "Dear Miss Maria, how you will miss her, but let us make her example and precepts our guide. She sweetly sleeps but speaks to us through her useful and patient life. I feel for Miss Mary [Smith], but she has many friends and will doubtless find a pleasant home."

Having made the joint decision upon Frank's death, Mary buried her friend in the Jones Grove cemetery, and a handwritten note in records of the Chapel of the Cross reads "Jany. 7th, 1881—Miss Maria Louisa Speer [*sic*] aged 76 yrs. died Jany. 5th 1881 at residence of Miss Mary R. Smith, Orange County. Buried at the Smith Family Burying Ground, Jones's Grove, Chatham County by the Rev. Edmond [Edward?] N. Joyner of St. Bartholomew's Church, Pittsboro, in the absence of the Rector of this Parish."[90]

The effect of Maria's death upon Mary Smith was perhaps described best by Cornelia Spencer: "While Miss Maria Spear lived she hardly felt how alone she stood. After that lady's death in January '81, her interest in life, beyond its daily duties, visibly slackened. Her health failed, and less and less frequently her carriage was seen at the door of the 'Chapel of the Cross.' We, all of us, may reckon on dying pretty much as we have lived. Miss Mary Smith knew her end was near, but she spoke no word of it to anyone, and finally when the supreme hour came, she died as she had lived, quietly, silently, and almost alone."[91]

In an undated note, Kemp Battle wrote Mary, "I think of you often in your loneliness." In that loneliness following Maria's death, Mary Smith was shown many kindnesses by citizens of Chapel Hill, but no one was more solicitous than Kemp and Patty Battle, who again opened their own home to her. The university president wrote, "I suggest to Patty to give you the choice of the upstairs rooms. One, which appears to me best, lets you have your old room and also that adjoining, in which the new China stays. By curtaining the window this would be a comfortable room and would be kept warm by having a good fire in the bed room & leave the door open. We want you to be comfortable." He gave an after-thought, "In the winter a small stove could be used to heat this [second] room."[92]

Cornelia Phillips Spencer, Chapel Hill's most prolific female writer, provided the best biographical sketch of Mary Ruffin Smith (courtesy North Carolina Collection, Wilson Library, UNC-CH).

Mary appeared to be living with the Battles—or perhaps with a servant in one of her sparsely-furnished houses on Cameron Avenue—when Elizabeth Spear Smith (Maria's sister to whom Mary had recently shipped the sewing machine bought earlier as a gift for Maria) offered to become her live-in companion. Provided Mary would move back to Oakland, Elizabeth Smith offered—almost begged—to come and stay with her "till you are tired of me and want to make a change, then say so in plain terms—I love straight forward dealings—& I believe you do too." Referring to her late sister, Elizabeth wrote, "I am not worthy in any respect to wipe the dust from her shoes."[93] Maria's brother, the Rev. William Wallace Spear, lamented to Cornelia Phillips Spencer that "there is no memorial of her [Maria's] great services to M[ary] & her gratitude &c save the stone wh[ich] marks her grave wh[ich] very few of her friends will ever see. The liberal provision wh[ich] she made in her will lapsed entirely at Sister's death." He referred to paintings by his sister, some of which had been lost. He added, "I am glad that some of the pictures I sent her are preserved in the Coll. Library."[94]

Despite the kindness of her friends in Chapel Hill, Mary's last four years must have been the loneliest of her life. Except when spending time with the Battles and others, she was alone at Oakland with perhaps a live-in servant and assistance from the families of Emma Morphis and Annette Kirby, who remained nearby. Little is known about circumstances surrounding her death. Raleigh's *News & Observer* initially reported it this way: "November 13th, 1885, at her residence near Chapel Hill, Miss Mary Ruffin Smith, aged 72 years. Miss Smith was a lady of uncommon strength of mind, lofty character, large charity, unaffected piety and earnest Christian life." Four days later, however, the same newspaper published a longer memorial, either written by Kemp Battle or from information provided by him. It contained the following paragraph: "The community in and near Chapel Hill lost one of its best and most intellectual women. She inherited from her father, Dr. James S. Smith ... a clear,

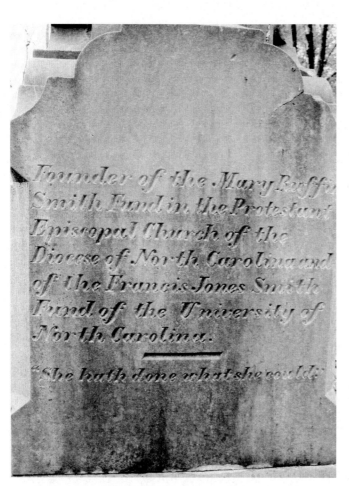

The center block of Mary Ruffin Smith's tombstone was designed by her friend and estate executor, Kemp P. Battle (courtesy J. Boyd Webb).

strong mind, and under such preceptors as the late Miss Maria Spear, the Rev. Dr. Francis L. Hawks, and others, and such spiritual advisers as Dr. Hawks, Dr. (now Bishop) Green, the late Dr. Curtis and others, she became a woman of learning and a pious Christian, earnestly devoted to the Episcopal Church, of which she was a devout member for forty or fifty years." The writer estimated the value of Mary's estate at from $40,000 to $50,000, all reportedly left to the Episcopal Diocese of North Carolina and the University of North Carolina, exclusive of 425 acres of land devised to former slaves and several small cash bequests. No mention was made that four of the "former slaves" were in fact Mary Smith's nieces.[95]

Among those who made claims on Mary's estate for attendance in her sickness and death were Dr. T.W. Harris and nurses Mary Johnson, Jane Pendergrass, and Adeline Snipes; Richard Johnson also provided night service. Although he may not have been present during her final sickness (and he never made a claim on her estate), it is known that Dr. William P. Mallett was another of her physicians. When Dr. Mallett prescribed one of Mary's favorite

Historian Jean Bradley Anderson, who contributed substantially to this book, stands beside the monument memorializing Mary Ruffin Smith in the Jones Grove cemetery. The finial originally atop the cross is missing, and the cemetery, owned by the University of North Carolina but neglected for more than a century, has been cleaned off and made accessible by Chatham County cemetery census-takers and more recently by John Row, a resident of Galloway Ridge. The other tombstone visible in the picture is for Mary's teacher and live-in companion, Maria Louisa Spear (H.G. Jones collection).

foods—squirrel soup—the spinster offered to give a shotgun to James Morphis if Emma's thirteen-year-old son would go into the village, retrieve it from a gunsmith, and shoot some squirrels for her soup.[96]

Mary's body was washed and shrouded by Mrs. Long and Miss Johnson; the coffin was made by Foster Utley; and S.J. Lamb provided carriages. Ironically, both the rector of the Chapel Hill's Chapel of the Cross and Pittsboro's St. Bartholomew's Episcopal Church were away, so the funeral service was conducted by the Rev. Franklin Leonard Bush of Durham, the white minister in charge of Pittsboro's St. James's Chapel for blacks. His subject was "The maid is not dead, but sleepeth."[97] Cornelia Spencer gave a better description: "A large gathering of her tenants, neighbors and old friends assembled at her house on Sunday, Nov. 15th, 1885 to pay her the last offices due. The Rev Mr. Bush, of Pittsboro, officiated, and after the services at the house was ended, a long procession followed the hearse to the old family burying ground at Jones' Grove six miles distant in Chatham. There she was laid among her own once more, and by the side of her friend, Miss Maria.... Miss Mary left no relations nearer than cousins, second or third."[98]

But she left friends, especially neighbors whose farms she had saved by lending money that could have been spent on her own comfort, and Kemp Plummer Battle, in whom she trusted and who in turn battled bureaucracies for more than twenty years to assure that her beneficences were applied to the public purposes that she chose (and some that she had not envisioned, but for which she would have approved). Most of all, her life justified the faith of her grandfather Francis Jones and at least partially atoned for the personal faults of her father and brothers.

Mary Smith's great-grandniece, Paula Murray, recently achieved sainthood in the Protestant Episcopal Church in the United States. If sainthood were conferred upon lay persons for their service to humanity, Mary Ruffin Smith would have been another worthy candidate.[99]

Chapter 6

Beneficiaries: Church and State

When the Federal census was taken in 1880, Mary Smith was living at Oakland in Chapel Hill Township with Mariah [*sic*] Spear (76), "tutoress"; Sally McGuire (50), black servant; and Reuben Durham (22), a mulatto hireling.[1] Mary's four nieces—born slaves but after emancipation freedwomen—were by then married and raising their own families: *Cornelia* and brickmaker Robert Fitzgerald with children Mary Pauline (9), Maria (7), Thomas (6), Sarah (5), and Agnes (6 months); *Emma* and farmer Henry Morphis with children Samuel (12), Thomas (10), James (8), Harriet (7), Una (6), Mary (3), and Julius (1); *Annette* and hack-driver and lay preacher Ned Kirby (30) with children Laura (11), Francis (10), Harriet (8), Oscar (6), Thomas (4), and Kemp (2); and *Laura* and barber Grey/Gray Toole (38) with children Delia (10), Sidney (7), Lizzie (5), and John (3). The Fitzgeralds lived in Durham, the Morphises on the premises at Price Creek, the Kirbys also nearby, and the Tooles in Charlotte. Choices of first names for some of their children—Mary, Maria, James, Harriet, Francis, Delia, and Sidney—suggest that the nieces, born in slavery and out of wedlock, retained affection for their Caucasian kin. Therein lies one of the many ironies and complexities in the relationship of the nieces and their former owner.

Thus, Mary Smith was blessed with a multitude of nieces and great-nieces and great-nephews, but under the law, she had no heirs. The progeny sired by Mary's brothers were legally defined as bastards, and as such they could claim no inheritance through their fathers. Furthermore, each lacked classification as a white American during an era of discrimination against nonwhite citizenry. So the substantial estates left by grandfather, parents, and brothers rested solely in the hands of Mary Ruffin Smith. Without statutory heir, the aging survivor had choices to make.

On April 27, 1877, exactly ten days after her brother Frank's death and four years prior to Maria Spear's death, Mary Smith sat down and, in the presence of Maria, Kemp P. Battle, and W.C. Cole, signed her last will and testament. Originally drafted in Battle's difficult-to-read handwriting, she had copied it in her own hand, just as he had instructed. It read:

> 1st. I devise the tract of land on which I reside, about 1,500 acres, of several tracts originally, but now used as one tract, including all the lands in Orange County I own outside of Chapel Hill, & also all the stock & farming implements used on said land, to my dear friend Maria L. Spear during her life, & after her death, to the Board of Trustees for the Protestant Episcopal Church in the Diocese of North Carolina.... This devise, however, subject to the exceptions hereinafter mentioned.
>
> 2nd. Out of the aforesaid [Price Creek] tract I devise to Cornelia Fitzgerald, wife of Robert

I Mary R. Smith of the County of Orange, do declare
the following to be my last Will & Testament.

1st I devise the tract of land on which I reside, about
1500 hundred acres, of several tracts originally, but
now used as one tract, including all the lands in
Orange County I own outside of Chapel Hill, & also
all the stock & Farming implements used on said
land, to my dear friend Maria L. Spear during
her life, & after her death, to the Board of Trustees
for the Protestant Episcopal Church in the Diocese of
North Carolina, appointed to hold the property of
the Diocese not otherwise provided for by the Gen.
Convention of said Diocese, as authorized by act
of the Gen. Assembly of North Carolina in such case
made and provided, said Trustees to have full
power to dispose of the same in fee simple and
absolutely as said Convention may direct specially
or by general ordinance. This devise however,
subject to the exceptions hereinafter mentioned.
2nd   Out of the aforesaid tract I devise to
Cornelia Fitzgeral, wife of Robert Fitzgerald (colored)
for her life free from the control or debts of her
said husband, & after her death to her children,
one hundred acres of land out of the aforesaid
tract.
3rd I devise to Julius Smith (colored)
likewise of out of the tract on which I now live,

Mary Ruffin Smith's will left the Price Creek property to her friend and live-in companion, Maria Louisa Spear. When Miss Spear died, the legacy fell to the "Protestant Episcopal Church in the Diocese of North Carolina." Meanwhile, however, the statewide diocese split into the North Carolina and East Carolina dioceses, leading to a faulty State Supreme Court ruling that forced a division of the estate (courtesy Mary Ruffin Smith Papers, Southern Historical Collection, Wilson Library, UNC-CH).

Fitzgerald (colored) for her life free from the control or debts of her said husband, & after her death to her children, one hundred acres of land out of the aforesaid tract.[2]

3rd. I devise to Julius Smith (colored) likewise out of the tract on which I now live, twenty-five acres in fee. It is my will, that the devise to Cornelia Fitzgerald & to Julius Smith shall take effect at my death & the tract given them be good land, equal to the average of the whole tract, with a fair proportion of wood & arable land....

4th. All the real estate owned by me in the village of Chapel Hill, except the Sam Morphis lot, hereafter mentioned, I devise to the Trustees to hold property for the Diocese of North Carolina aforesaid, in trust for the Chapel of the Cross in Chapel Hill ... to sell or dispose of as they may deem best for the same.[3]

5th. The debt due by Sam Morphis to my brother Frank's estate & also whatever interest I now have, or may hereafter acquire in the house & lot in Chapel Hill on which said debt is secured by mortgage, occupied by Sam Morphis, I devise & bequeath to the little son of Henry Morphis named Sam. If said debt should be paid to said estate and the house and lot redeemed, I bequeath the principal thereof to the same Sam....[4]

6th. Whatever of my household & kitchen furniture Miss Maria Spear wishes to have, I bequeath to her absolutely; what she does not want I give to Cornelia Fitzgerald, Emma Morphis, Annette Kirby, & Laura Toole, all colored, equally to be divided between them.

7th. I bequeath out of any monies on hand, or due me to Ed Cole (colored) one hundred dollars, & to Sallie Jones [McGuire] (colored) one hundred dollars, & to my name sake Mary Ruffin Smith, daughter of Rev. Columbus Smith, deceased of Mississippi, two hundred dollars. The residue of all moneys due me & also any property not specifically willed, I give to the Trustees of the Episcopal Church aforesaid, in trust for the Diocese of North Carolina."

8th. I devise out of the Jones Grove tract in Chatham lately owned by my brother Dr. Francis J. Smith, to Emma Morphis, wife of Henry Morphis (colored) one hundred acres; to Annett Kirby, wife of Ed Kirby (colored) one hundred acres, & to Laura Toole, wife of Gray [*sic*] Toole (colored) one hundred acres of land for their respective lives free from the control or debts of their said husbands, & after their deaths to their children in fee. If either said Emma, Annette, or Laura, shall make conveyance of their estates for life or give a lien on the same by mortgage or otherwise, their estates shall cease & their children respectively shall become immediately entitled to the land of their mothers. Said tracts shall be laid off out of said Grove tract by three white commissioners, one to be chosen by the parties entitled. The mother, if living, to choose for herself & children, another by the Trustees of the University of North Carolina, these two to choose a third. My Executor to make deeds to the said parties, according to the terms of this will & the report of the commissioners, or a majority of them, said commissioners are to lay off good land of the average of the whole tract, with a proper proportion of wood & arable land, but their decision or that of a majority in any event shall be final.[5]

9th. All the residue of said Jones Grove tract late the property of my brother Dr. Francis J. Smith, I devise to the Trustees of the University of North Carolina, not to be subject to any of their debts at anytime contracted, with liberty to sell the same in fee & invest or reinvest the proceeds in trust, to hold the property or proceeds as a perpetual fund for education at the University, of such students as may be designated from time to time by the Bishop or Ecclesiastical authority of the Diocese of North Carolina, the interest or income of said fund only, to be expended, such students to be subject to the general rules & regulations of the University.[6]

I appoint & request my friend Hon. K.P. Battle to be the Executor of this my will, written this seventh of April, eighteen hundred & seventy-seven.

Witnesses   Mary R. Smith
Kemp P. Battle
W.C. Cole[7]

Kemp Battle's extraordinary experience—attorney, historian, state treasurer, delegate to a secession convention, and president of a bank, railroad, and university—failed to prepare him for the complexities and the aggravations that accompanied his role as executor of Mary Ruffin Smith's estate. What should have been one of the most enjoyable undertakings of his illustrious career—the dispensation of charity—evolved into two decades of tedious and in some instances contentious work. He left no evidence, however, that he ever regretted serving as a surrogate in assuring that Mary Smith's bequests were used for purposes for which she had intended them.

The executor probably was introduced to Mary Smith when, during his student days at the University of North Carolina, the family of the aging James Strudwick Smith—a long-time trustee of the University—moved into the large new house on the Price Creek plantation. Upon the return of Battle and his wife Martha Ann (Pattie) to Chapel Hill in 1875, they joined Mary as pillars of the Episcopal Chapel of the Cross. By then Maria Louisa Spear, the fabled teacher, was living with Mary and Frank, and she broadened Mary's acquaintances in the local society that featured families such as the Battles, Malletts, and Mickles. The friendship between the Battles and the two spinsters grew, and Mary more and more depended upon Kemp Battle as her attorney and advisor, roles that the university president—remembering that the Jones Grove land had been considered for the location of the

University of North Carolina nearly a century earlier—welcomed. It would not have been unusual if Battle, an Episcopalian and head of the neighboring educational institution, envisioned the eventual disposition of Mary Smith's estate for benefit of his favorite charities, church and state.

As rockaways made more frequent trips between the president's house and the big Smith home, visits became common between town and country.[8] Members of the Mallett family, for example, occasionally spent weeks with Mary and Maria out in the country, and at least once the two women spent an entire month in the home of Dr. William Mallett.[9] After Maria's death, the Battles for an extended period provided a home for Mary. The farm on Price Creek furnished the president's house with home-grown fruits and vegetables, and one of the first debts collected for the estate was $7.15 owed by Pattie Battle for butter. Even the University borrowed money from Mary Smith; in 1883, for example, part of its own $500 debt was repaid; and other officials, including no less than Battle himself, were her debtors. Borrowing—with or without a promissory note—was common in the nineteenth century, and through her wealth, a

Kemp Plummer Battle, president of the University of North Carolina, spent more than a quarter of a century meticulously handling the settlement of Mary Ruffin Smith's vast estate. From time to time, he and his wife Pattie provided the aging spinster living quarters in their own home in Chapel Hill (courtesy North Carolina Collection, Wilson Library, UNC-CH).

strong bond developed that gave Mary Smith hope and strength even when her health was precarious.

Mary's original 1877 will had been so carefully crafted that the death in 1881 of her main beneficiary, Maria Spear, necessitated few amendments to the document, and those were easily made for her by Battle. For the Price Creek tract, the Episcopal Diocese of North Carolina automatically succeeded to the life interest of the deceased friend, and only minor changes were required in other provisions. Shortly afterward, Kemp Battle prepared four codicils requested by Mary. In addition to the one-hundred-acre tracts previously devised each to Cornelia, Emma, Annette, and Laura, *Codicil 1* instructed the executor—if it had not been done prior to her death—to pay for the construction of a house on each of the tracts previously willed, the cost not to exceed $150 each. *Codicil 2* requested that the endowment to be established at the University of North Carolina be known as the "Francis Jones Smith Fund." She revoked the right of the Episcopalian ministers to choose the recipients of student aid and transferred that authority to the faculty, and she instructed that "if from any cause such tuition cannot be paid, then I desire such profits or interests be used exclusively for the maintenance and equipment of the university, not to be liable for any of its debts."[10] *Codicil 3* bequeathed $800 to be divided equally between William C. Cole (her farm manager), Emma Morphis, Laura Toole, Sallie McGuire, Annette Kirby, and Cornelia Fitzgerald.[11] Finally, *Codicil 4* modified the fourth provision of the original will by leaving to the wardens and vestry of the Chapel of the Cross, Chapel Hill, "whatever real estate I own at my death in the corporate limits of the village of Chapel Hill to be held or disposed of as they may deem best for the Parish."[12]

In November 1885 the will was probated in the county courthouses of both Chatham and Orange, and Battle promptly gave newspaper notice of his role as executor and commenced his duties.[13] His task appeared uncomplicated because Mary's will—written with his assistance and witnessed by him—seemed to leave no detail unaddressed. There were only a few individual bequests, all in small amounts, and the household goods and personal items were to be divided by her nieces and close friends. The real estate, after apportionment of 425 acres for Harriet's five children, was willed to three corporate bodies—the personal property and Price Creek land to the Protestant Episcopal Diocese of North Carolina, the Jones Grove land to the University of North Carolina, and the Chapel Hill real estate to the Chapel of the Cross. The coincidence that the executor was a principal of all three benefactors—president of the University and influential member of both the diocese and the local church—was not overlooked, and, fearing criticism, he raised the issue with his brother, attorney Richard H. Battle, who replied, "I do not understand why you have *the slightest* anxiety about a contest—on ground of undue influence, or any other ground. Dismiss it at once."[14] During the next dozen years, Kemp Battle may have chided his brother for being so naive. Neither of them could have imagined the amount of time required and the extent of legal complications that would arise before Mary Ruffin Smith's benefactions eventually reached their destinations.

The annual convention of the Diocese of North Carolina was not scheduled to meet until May 1886, six months after Mary Smith's death. However, with his authority as executor, Battle could not wait to begin what he expected—at the time—to be a pleasurable and uplifting experience in carrying out his friend's generous benefaction to the major legatees, both of them so close to his heart. The first entry on Battle's inventory reflected the degree of trust between the executor and his deceased client: "$323.07 in cash of dec'd deposited in my safe." In effect, Battle, Mary's closest confidante, had been handling her personal affairs and money for an indeterminate time. Only 40¢ was found in Mary's pocketbook, and her bank account showed $454.34 on deposit. Handwritten promissory notes revealed the degree to which neighbors and friends had depended on Mary's financial assistance. Aside from land, personal notes backed by mortgages constituted the greatest portion of the initial inventory—$11,804.69, of which $9,419.12 plus interest was still due. Most debtors bore familiar surnames—Barbee, Bennett, Bryant, Burnett, Cole, Hackney, Horton, King, Lindsay, McCauley, Merritt, Parker, Pearson, Ray, Rigsbee, Wilson, Womack. The Rev. George W. Purefoy, an adjoining neighbor who earlier had served as administrator of Sidney's estate, had already paid off most of his notes. However, there were surprises: John Manning, who later had responsibility for accounting for that portion of the estate devised to the University as the Francis Jones Smith Fund, owed nearly half of his loan; and Bynum Manufacturing Company owed $878.75 plus 8 percent interest dating from 1883. Near the Bynum entry in his accounts, Battle wrote, "Miss Smith agreed that this might be used in buying the property." In other words, she was not averse to owning the manufacturing plant in the Jones Grove neighborhood. Notes reflected a variety of surety; for example, Manly Lindsay's notes were backed by a mortgage on a mule and the following year's crop of tobacco and wheat. The Smith estate also held 32 shares (par value $3,200) of Rocky Mount Mills No. 38, owned by W.S. Battle, one of Mary's debtors. When the mill shares were surrendered in October 1888, they brought only $1,600.[15]

Wisely, Battle authorized W.C. Cole to serve as agent for the estate with a salary of $150 per year and 10 percent commission on receipts that he collected. An adjoining landowner and good neighbor, Cole had been depended upon heavily by Mary Smith in her final years, a dependency recognized by her modest cash bequest to him. Cole's admiration for his benefactor was expressed in a letter to Cornelia Phillips Spencer: "As she has no near relatives to appreciate and express gratitude for your 'labor of love,' please rest assured that there is no one in an humble walk of life who [so] highly appreciates and fully attests the many pleasant things you have written in regard to her."[16] Cole's standing in the community and his personal acquaintance with most of the debtors were of great benefit to Battle, who wore more responsible hats than four normal men in the community.

Since the real estate had been willed respectively to the Episcopal Diocese, the University, and the Chapel of the Cross, the executor was able to give attention almost immediately to the payment of debts, distributions of devised personal property, and the collection of rents for the legatee institutions. Ultimately, of course, he faced the task of selling or managing altogether more than 3,000 acres of the most desirable land in two counties and accounting for every cent to the separate corporate bodies, each of which had its own trustees and constituency. But that would have to wait until the personal estate was settled.[17]

Shortly after the funeral, Battle proceeded with the distribution of personal property that had been willed to Maria Spear with provision that any household items that she did not want would be divided equally between the four nieces. With Maria dead, Cornelia, Emma, Annette, and Laura appointed Foster Utley of Orange and M.S. Hackney of Chatham "to assess & divide into fair lots of equal value" the household and kitchen furniture.[18] On February 12, 1886, Battle entered into his accounts, "The household & kitchen furniture & piano have been divided among the legatees under Miss Smith's will. The books have been

Because of the literary and religious career of her granddaughter Anna Pauline (Pauli) Murray, one of the four sisters to whom Mary Smith left property—Cornelia—is prominently recognized in the literature. This daughter of Harriet and Sidney Smith is shown around the turn of the century with her husband, Civil War veteran Robert Fitzgerald, and four of their children—Mary Pauline, Agnes Georgianna (Pauli Murray's mother), Sarah Ann, and Roberta Annette (courtesy Schlesinger Library on the History of Women in America, Radcliffe Institute, Harvard University, Cambridge, Massachusetts).

turned over to the Trustees of the Episcopal Church, residuary legatees under the will. According to Miss Smith's directions in writing shortly before her death, 1 watch & chain were delivered to Mrs. Louise Holt."[19] The executor also gave a watch, seal, and gold spectacles to Rufus H. Jones of Cary; and a set of plated casters, two counterpanes, and an earthen pitcher to others. He added, "I also delivered 1 ladle (silver), 1 side board, 7 old chairs, to parties to whom she gave them by mouth. Her clothing and a breast pin of small value were given by me to her relations & country neighbors. These dispositions were made with the consent of the residuary legatees." Battle elsewhere mentioned a pitcher given to his wife

Pattie and a sideboard and chair to "Mrs. Dr. Mallett" (Caroline DeBerniere Mallett, wife of Dr. William P. Mallett). The books subsequently were transferred to St. Augustine's Normal School (now St. Augustine's University). Unless it was the Chapel of the Cross, the heir to the piano, described by Maria Spear on September 27, 1847, as of "considerable value," is not known. Disappointingly, neither a Bible nor artwork was mentioned to illuminate references by Cornelia Fitzgerald and Maria Spear's brother to those items.[20]

The appearance of the name of Rufus H. Jones as inheritor of Mary Smith's personal items raises the question of whether there may have been a family relationship between him and Delia Jones Smith. Rufus Henry Jones attended Hillsborough Academy in 1839, graduated from the state university in 1843, and served in the House of Commons from Wake County in 1848–9. A leading businessman in the new village of Cary, he served on its governing board and as a founding member of the Methodist Church; and two of his daughters, Loulie and Sarah Rencher Jones, operated Cary Academy toward the end of the century. The Census of 1870 listed the father as a 50-year-old farmer in White Oak Township of Wake County. Perhaps significantly, Dr. William Peter Mallett (1819–1889), with whom Mary and Maria frequently visited, appeared in the next entry of this census, indicating that the doctor moved his family from Chapel Hill to Wake County after the Civil War. Future research may reveal a family relationship between Mary's grandfather Francis Jones with these Joneses of Cary.

More valuable property—Mary's rockaway and harness, one-horse wagon, livestock (one horse, 6 head of cattle, 28 hogs), farm produce (50 bushels of wheat, 110 barrels of corn, 200 pounds of sheaf oats, 1,500 pounds of shucks, 1,000 pounds of fodder, and 4 bales of cotton), and farming implements—was sold by Cole but was seldom identified individually. An exception was an entry showing that Emma Morphis paid $15 for her favorite cow.

An early task of the executor was the collection of thousands of dollars in notes, most of them backed by mortgages on farms. Despite hard times among farmers, most of the debts were eventually repaid in installments meticulously accounted for in Battle's own unique and often difficult-to-read penmanship. Two of them, however, required legal action, and the court ordered a public sale of the property of J.Y. Merritt and wife. There being no satisfactory offer, Battle as executor bid in the property for $400 but afterward sold it to Henderson Oldham for $300, a figure deemed a fair price. The property of Baxter King, whose notes totaled more than $2,200, was advertised as a "Valuable 3 Horse Farm and Mill," including a dam and mill house in working order on Morgan Creek near Chapel Hill.[21] At auction it brought $1,200, also from Henderson Oldham. This property was formerly called (in reverse order) King's, Cave's, and Barbee's Mill. Significantly, Henderson Oldham was, in Battle's estimation, "an excellent colored man," whose residence on a hill near Williams Chapel provided "one of the finest prospects around Chapel Hill."[22] Not surprisingly, lawyers were generously compensated for a variety of assistance. Unfortunately, Battle did not keep separate books for loans incurred before Mary's death and the payments that came from later sales of tracts.[23]

With cash on hand and some of the notes redeemed, Battle distributed payments totaling $979.95 to specific legatees, including $133.33 each to Cornelia, Emma, Annette, Laura, and W.C. Cole; and $100 to the aforementioned local black preacher on the farm, the Rev. Edward H. Cole. The estate also paid $213.39 to W.S. Jordan, guardian of a young namesake, Mary Ruffin Smith, to whom the deceased Mary Ruffin Smith devised $200. This younger Mary

Ruffin Smith was born February 25, 1873, the daughter of the Rev. Columbus Smith of Mississippi, who was the deceased son of Maria Spear's sister Elizabeth Spear Smith. Interestingly, another daughter of the minister was named Maria Spear Smith, born March 15, 1871. Not surprisingly, in his haste, Battle mistakenly called the younger Mary a niece of the elder Mary.

Battle made a number of other small payments: $5 to the Rev. Ed Cole for his church; $46.60, previously pledged by Mary, to the Church Sewing Society; and $100 to R.S. McRae, treasurer, "for memorial in Chapel of the Cross, by order of the Convention."[24] An interesting charge in 1896 was $3.50 for "Horse & buggy to Hillsboro & dinner for self & driver," likely for courthouse transactions.

The accounting of funeral expenses cast further light on Mary Smith's last illness. Dr. T.W. Harris was paid $40 for medical services; and payments for nursing included Mary Johnson $7, Jane Pendergrass $5, Adeline Snipes $7, and Emma Morphis $12.50. Richard Johnson received $7 for "night service for Miss S." Annette Kirby was paid $10.50 and Emma Morphis an additional $5 for cooking and $15 for "nursing the last illness." Of Mary Smith's four nieces, Emma and Annette had remained at or near Price Creek, faithful to the end. Mrs. Long and Mrs. Johnson were paid $5 for preparing the body, Foster Utley (the University's carpenter and cabinetmaker) $40 for the coffin and arrangements, S.J. Lamb $15 for carriage hire, and the Rev. F.L. Bush $20 for officiating at the burial.[25] An indication that Mary Smith had not contemplated an early death appears in the payment of $4.50 to Hooper and Thomas for "fruit trees ordered by Miss Smith." F.A. Watson was paid $6.30 for a frame for a portrait of Mary's father, Dr. James S. Smith.[26]

There remained a very special obligation for Kemp Battle to perform: assure the permanent recognition of the beneficence of Mary Ruffin Smith. That he accomplished in July 1886 by paying Durham stonecutter Robert J. Rogers $202.50 to execute and install an impressive memorial in the Jones Grove Cemetery, around which was built a three-foot-high wall of rocks with an iron gate. Mounted on a multi-level square granite base, a pedestal, square with scalloped top, contains the following inscription on the front:

In memory of
Mary Ruffin Smith
Who died
Nov. 13, 1885
Aged 71 Years.

On another side are engraved these words:

Founder of the Mary Ruffin
Smith Fund in the Protestant
Episcopal Church of the
Diocese of North Carolina and
of the Francis Jones Smith
Fund of the University of North Carolina.

Then, in quotation marks,

"She hath done what she could."

A large granite cross reaches toward the sky.

Another of Mary Smith's wishes was fulfilled eleven years later. She had intended to move the remains of her parents and younger brother to Jones Grove, and Kemp Battle faithfully carried out the promise in 1897. His account shows, "Paid Wm. Craig, making coffins, disinterring, transporting (six miles) and re-burying three bodies 9.00." In addition, G.C. Pickard was paid $3 for the hire of a carriage and driver to take Battle and the "commission-ers" to the reinterment ceremony.[27]

For a woman with a big heart, who lived frugally and left an unprecedented legacy to her church and state, the granite obelisk—hidden in the woods for more than a century—today stands as the only conspicuous physical monument to the name of Mary Ruffin Smith. Around her lie the only "legitimate" members of the Francis Jones-Delia Jones Smith line. With the new pedestrian access to the cemetery from Galloway Ridge, the time has come for the hundreds of descendants of Cornelia, Emma, Annette, and Laura—Mary's nieces—to make a bittersweet pilgrimage to their origins.[28] Within the walls are nine graves with tombstones (some broken) containing the following abstracted interpretations: Francis Jones, died Feb. 22, 1844, aged 84 years [born 1760]; Mary, wife of Francis Jones, died Mar. 20, 1811, aged 50 years [born ca. 1761]; Ruffin Jones, died 1836, aged 42 years [born 1794]; James S[trudwick] Smith, born Sept. 8, 1787, died Dec. 7, 1852 [Masonic insignia]; Delia [Jones], wife of James S[trudwick] Smith, born May 3, 1787, died Nov. 8, 1854; Mary Ruffin Smith, died Nov. 13, 1885, aged 71 years [born ca. 1814]; Francis J[ones] Smith, born Aug. 17, 1816, died Apr. 17, 1877; James S[idney] Smith, born Mar. 20, 1819, died April 25, 1867; Maria Louisa Spear, born Apr. 12, 1804, died Jan. 6, 1881.[29]

Chapter 7

Warring Episcopalians:
The Battle for Price Creek

News of the bequest of the Price Creek property to the Episcopalians had been widely circulated in the press, so the annual convention of the Diocese of North Carolina in Tarboro's Calvary Episcopal Church on May 19, 1886—six months after Mary's death—was eagerly awaited. Kemp Battle officially presented to the delegates a lengthy report describing in detail the devise: real estate of more than 1,500 acres with a "handsome home" and several tenant houses in fair repair; stock in Rocky Mount and Bynum mills; thousands of dollars in notes; and farm stock and products. He estimated, "The land should bring at least fifteen thousand dollars, many think more, the personalty, I think, nine or ten thousand dollars, making a reasonably probable amount of twenty-four or twenty-five thousand dollars in the total." He described the farm as "a most beautiful one," adding, "Price's Creek runs nearly a mile through it, well canalled [*sic*], and the first, second, and third low grounds, mostly of good fertility, rise on both sides to forests of as magnificent oaks and hickories as it has been my fortune to see. I have traveled extensively in North Carolina, and I am sure I have not visited a farm having more natural resources for production of agricultural wealth." He added, however, "The tenants now in possession, with whom Miss Smith had made contracts for the present year, are on an average not of the best and some of them should not be allowed to remain longer than the expiration of their tenancy."

Battle's moving tribute to the benefactor would be widely quoted by subsequent commentators. He began,

> Miss Smith faithfully and tenderly served and nursed, until they were taken from her care, her mother, her father, her favorite brother, and then the last of her family, her brother Frank, [who] was seized with a lingering disease passing through violent insanity unto death. It was from him she inherited the land devised to the University. She never visited it—regarded herself merely as trustee to carry out her brother's wishes. The bulk of that tract, or if sold, the price is to be a perpetual fund of the University called by his name. To the Church her own property, likewise regarded as a trust fund, not to be diminished by extravagance or luxurious living, she renders up to God, for whom she was the good and faithful steward, to be administered by you, His agents, for the best interest of His Church on earth. With entire forgetfulness of self she does not ask that her name shall be known in connection with it. She sank into her grave willing to be forgotten on earth in the assured hope of living forever in the courts of her Maker.

He continued,

I ask with confidence that the Convention accept these bequests. They are clogged with no burdensome or whimsical conditions, such as have been often imposed by testators with apparently a greater desire for their own notoriety than for the good of mankind. Miss Smith had the most implicit child-like faith in the God of that Bible, which she studied constantly and with a clearness of understanding vouchsafed in few among mankind. She had the same faith that our Church is the best representative on earth of that God whom she adored, and to that Church she gives all which she considered herself at liberty to give, excepting only such small amounts as she felt obliged to devote to others, having peculiar claims on her bounty.

Neither Mary Smith nor Kemp Battle could have foreseen that the absence of "burdensome or whimsical conditions" was a mirage, and that it would be beneficiaries of her bounty—fellow members of the Protestant Episcopal Church—who would go all the way to the State Supreme Court to contest her intentions concerning the Price Creek property. Her executor would regret many times this statement: "The death of Miss Spear, in the lifetime of the testatrix, caused the devise to her to lapse, so that there is nothing in the way of the Convention taking immediate charge of the part of the land devised to the Diocese."[1]

Battle concluded with a personal testimony to Mary Smith's character:

It has been my good fortune to have been an intimate friend of this excellent woman for nearly forty years. She was brought into the Church by the instructions and influence of the teachers of her youth, Rev. Dr. Francis L. Hawks and Miss Maria L. Spear, and by one of the earliest rectors of the Church in Hillsboro, now the venerable Bishop Green, of Mississippi. She was gifted with uncommon mental powers, and had unusual attainments in certain branches of history and science. Especially she made extensive excursions into the field of Medical Botany, studying under the learned Dr. M.A. Curtis, whom she greatly admired and loved. Her judgment was quick, accurate and sound. Her moral sense detected at once all sophistical reasoning, and went straight to the truth. Her insight into character seemed intuitive and seldom deceived her; in fact, I recall no instance of such error. It has often amazed me to discover how rapidly she read the natures of those whom she casually met. When she formed a friendship it was for life. She was entirely free from unkind feelings towards those, who had in her opinion treated her or her family with injustice. She had in largest sense a charitable nature. Afflicted with an unusual amount of bitter trials, she bore them with serenity and unshaken faith in the goodness of God. She was charitable without ostentation, self-respectful without pride, doing her duty always, but claiming no credit and desiring no praise. Quiet, gentle, reserved, she was firm as a rock in matters of principle; afraid of nothing but doing wrong.

Richard H. Battle's motion—"That the pious act of the late Mary Ruffin Smith, in selecting as objects of her bounty the church of her love, should be held in grateful remembrance by every true member of our branch of the Church Catholic"—was endorsed by a rising vote. The convention enthusiastically accepted the bequest and appointed a committee chaired by the Rev. Robert B. Sutton—one-time rector of Pittsboro's St. Bartholomew's Church—to recommend disposition of the legacy. The committee suggested that a determination be made on whether to hold the land or sell it and invest the funds, that any decision on the permanent use of the income be delayed, that in the meantime rents be applied to the Diocesan Missionary Fund, that the latter committee devote "such part" of the income as it determined "to secure the support of a Rector of the 'Chapel of the Cross,'" and that a "suitable memorial tablet" honoring Mary Ruffin Smith be placed in the Chapel of the Cross. Thus was established at the outset the close association of Mary's bequest with her local parish.[2]

The specific Price Creek devises of 25 acres to Julius Smith and 100 acres to Cornelia

Fitzgerald were quietly attended to. Nowhere more clearly than in her will did Mary Smith acknowledge the potential for white men to treat nonwhites unfairly. Fearing that the least valuable portions of the Price Creek tract might be designated for Julius and Cornelia, she specified that each receive "good land, equal to the average of the whole tract, with a fair proportion of wood & arable land." To assure fairness, her will deliberately structured the three-man committee charged with laying off the land: One member was to be chosen by the Episcopal Diocese and one by the devisees, and a third selected by the previous two. Julius and Cornelia chose E.W. Atwater; the diocese chose W.C. Cole; and those two agreed on the third member, G.W. Foushee. After laying off the two tracts, on June 18, 1886, the commissioners entered in Book M [51], pages 148–150, of the Orange County registry the metes and bounds for Julius's Lot 1 and Cornelia's Lot 2. The differential in the acreage of the two bequeathed tracts is easily explained: Julius's father was a free colored man; Cornelia's was Sidney Smith.[3]

The tracts devised to Julius and Cornelia were located south of the Cole-Womble Cemetery across from the junction of present-day Smith Level and Damascus Church roads. Julius's 25-acre bequest adjoined land owned by Wesley Cole at the northern edge of the Price Creek plantation; Cornelia's 100 acres lay just to the south. On the east, each tract bordered lands of the late Rev. George W. Purefoy, which by 1886 was owned by Eugene Wilson and in 2014 is part of Southern Village. The fact that both of the gifted tracts fronted on the Hillsborough-Pittsboro Road was further evidence of the fairness exercised by Mary Smith's instructions; Julius received road frontage of about 215 feet, Cornelia, 1,237 feet.[4]

Of major significance is the simple fact that, except for the original devise to Maria Spear, Harriet's five children were the only human legatees to be substantially recognized in the will of Mary Ruffin Smith. Except for small bequests mentioned elsewhere, all else was left to charity.[5]

Kemp Battle returned to Chapel Hill from the exciting diocese convention in Tarboro and enthusiastically resumed his role as executor for the estate of his deceased friend. He had no clue about the complications lying ahead, certainly not that much of his already busy life would be consumed for nearly two decades in collecting debts and selling land while serving three masters. His early payment of specific bequests and the disposition of Mary Smith's intimate possessions, therefore, were delightful chores compared with the complexities that he would encounter in collecting loans, selling real estate, and dividing shares between the Episcopalians and the University.

The spinster's generosity drew widespread attention throughout the state, and Episcopalians and friends of the University applauded and complimented each other as estimates of the estate's value circulated in gossip and print. Cornelia Phillips Spencer's newspaper and magazine articles pointed to the legacy of a modest woman as an example for men of the state to follow. In response to one of those stories, William Hyslop Sumner Burgwyn, president of the Bank of Henderson, wrote: "What an example to the men of the State this quiet modest secluded woman has set. What a volume is conveyed in the simple monument that 'she gave all she had to church and state'; and it was no mean gift at that." He hoped that "some future Historian of the State will perpetuate her noble act in fitting words to be recorded along side of those of David Caldwell, Swain & Cameron."[6]

The provisions of Mary's bequest piqued no one's interest more sharply than that of officials of the Diocese of East Carolina, which in 1883 had separated from the Diocese of

North Carolina. A number of issues, not the least of which was geography, had led to the "amicable" division, and a resolution adopted at the first meeting of the new diocese declared, "We part as brethren. Not as rivals." The new diocese encompassed 32 counties—Hertford, Bertie, Martin, Pitt, Greene, Wayne, Sampson, Cumberland, and Robeson, and those to the east. Originally the new diocese was called by the name of Wilmington, but at its primary convention on December 12, 1883, the designation "East Carolina" was chosen over names like "Carolina," "Albemarle," and "Roanoke." Although the Episcopal denomination had traditionally been strongest in the east, 3,020 communicants remained in the Diocese of North Carolina against 1,809 in the new eastern diocese. In terms of annual contributions at the time of division, the two dioceses were more equal, the old one raising $36,595.55 and the new one $30,143.69.[7]

Money can divide even "Brothers in Christ," so officers of the new diocese—observing that Mary Smith's will was written in 1877, that the Diocese of North Carolina became the residuary heir upon Maria Spear's death four years later, that the will was executed in 1881, and that the authority of that diocese in 1881 extended over the entire state—were quick to raise an interesting question: Was it Mary Smith's intention to limit her bequest to Episcopalians in only one geographical area of the state?

(In the following chronology, it is important for the reader to keep in mind that the governing body of each diocese met only once a year and that the Diocese of North Carolina usually met a week or so before its sister diocese held its annual council. Consequently, nearly a year usually passed between the annual meeting of the Diocese of East Carolina and the next convention of the North Carolina diocese.)

Exactly one week after euphoria swept over the delegates attending the seventieth convention of the Diocese of North Carolina in Calvary Church in Tarboro, a different mood prevailed in St. Stephen's Church, Goldsboro, where at the third annual convention of the young Diocese of East Carolina a resolution was adopted on motion of Major John Hughes to establish a committee of three for the purpose of "ascertaining what, if any, are the rights of this Diocese [of East Carolina] to the property devised by Miss Mary Ruffin Smith to the Diocese of North Carolina, by will published before the division of said Diocese into two Dioceses." The resulting committee was composed of Hughes; George Davis, a former state attorney general; and Duncan K. McRae, a keen lawyer and former diplomat.[8]

Answering that troubling turn of events, at the 1887 convention of the Diocese of North Carolina eleven months later, a committee headed by Thomas Ruffin, Jr., a recent state supreme court justice, confidently concluded that "so far as the property devised from Miss Smith is concerned, they are satisfied after due inquiry into the facts of the case, that any division of the property given by her, if agreed to by the authorities of this Diocese, would be to defeat the intent and wishes of the testatrix." Still, to "avoid unseemly litigation and contention between the two [dioceses]," the Ruffin committee recommended that a special committee of his diocese meet with a similar committee from the East Carolina diocese to bury the issue. If the easterners refused to retreat, it was suggested that the North Carolina diocese "with the least appearance of unfriendly litigation, bring said matters before the Courts of the State to be judicially determined." Confident in its rights, the diocese assigned interest and rents from the real estate to the Executive Missionary Committee, which reported that it had already received $1,125 from the legacy, from which an appropriation of $500 per annum had been pledged to the Chapel of the Cross, the testatrix's beloved church.[9]

During the year, no doubt there had been informal—and perhaps spirited—discussions when Episcopalians from one diocese met their brethren from the other, but the issue became more contentious and burst into public view when, at the meeting of the eastern diocese a week later, the Hughes committee announced that its members were unanimously of the opinion that the Diocese of East Carolina had "a valid and valuable interest in the real and personal estate ... devised and bequeathed by Miss Mary Ruffin Smith ... and that the said interests ought to be claimed and asserted." The report continued, "In the interest of peace and Christian good will, your Committee respectfully recommend that a committee be appointed by each of the said Dioceses, with full powers to adjust and settle their respective rights in the premises; and in case such a committee shall fail to be appointed by either Diocese, or having been appointed by both, the two Committees shall fail to agree upon any adjustment, then that an amicable suit be brought by the Diocese of East Carolina for the purpose of establishing its rights." Accordingly, Bishop Alfred Augustine Watson appointed a committee charged with meeting with a parallel committee representing the Diocese of North Carolina "to secure to this Diocese its rights in the premises" and, in case of disagreement, "to institute such proceedings at law as the said committee ... shall deem best."[10]

Poor Kemp Battle: With the approval of his own diocesan officers, he had already spent a year and a half carrying out his friend's instructions, including paying cash bequests, and was well into handling the myriad tasks required in collecting the many debts due the estate and managing the extensive holdings at both Price Creek and Jones Grove until their use or disposition could be determined. Already he had collected for the estate over a thousand dollars, of which more than half had been promised to Chapel Hill's Chapel of the Cross.[11] Before the typewriter was introduced in Chapel Hill, and without the assistance of what would later be called a secretary, the university president personally was juggling many responsibilities, any one of which could have occupied the full time of a single officer. Now he was facing a lawsuit—brought by his own fellow Episcopalians, no less. A man of peace, not known for profanity, he may have wished that he had declined Mary and Maria's request that he serve as the executor of the substantial estate. Kemp Battle was, however, from a family of attorneys, so at least he was not without legal cover.

As lawyers representing the two dioceses argued, the Rev. W.S. Bynum introduced a provocative motion at the 1888 convention stating emphatically, "This Convention believes the Diocese of North Carolina [is] entitled to all the Mary Ruffin Smith Legacy," but suggesting that the inter-diocesan dispute be settled by having both dioceses agree to "invest the whole sum involved in an Atkinson Memorial Farthering School at Asheville, North Carolina, so arranged as to give equal privileges to North and East Carolina." Not wanting to add fuel to the dispute between the two dioceses, delegates promptly tabled the motion.[12] Instead, the diocese appointed a committee to meet a similar committee from the East Carolina diocese to resolve the question. A motion to pay the indebtedness of Thompson Orphanage with the "first payments of the principal of the Smith fund" was rejected also; instead, a committee composed of Kemp Battle and John Manning was authorized to handle the diocese's interests in the estate and report to the next convention.[13] The eastern diocese simply dug in its heels, continued its committee, and hoped for a judicial determination in its favor.

When the opposing committees met, however, each "maintained unyieldingly the claims of its own Diocese." With nothing more to negotiate nearly three years after Mary Smith's death, members of both committees concluded that the best procedure was to institute an "amicable suit in the shape of a controversy without action before the courts of the State in order to the determination of their respective rights."[14]

So, with agreement between the two dioceses to disagree, the resulting case was argued in Superior Court, which ruled in favor of the plaintiffs, the Diocese of East Carolina. Dissatisfied with the verdict, attorneys for the Diocese of North Carolina appealed to the State Supreme Court. The case was heard at the February 1889 term, with George Davis and John Hughes representing the plaintiffs and John Manning and Richard H. Battle arguing for the defendants. The tortured six-page decision, prepared by Justice Augustus S. Merrimon, upheld the lower court's ruling largely on the grounds that Mary Smith, when publishing her will in 1881, had no idea that the Diocese of North Carolina would be divided two years later. Furthermore, the court held that, by devising the estate to "the Board of Trustees *for the Protestant Episcopal Church* in the Diocese of North Carolina," Mary Smith was referring to the Protestant Episcopal Church within—that is, throughout—the *state* of North Carolina, not limited to the Episcopal churches within a single geographical jurisdiction. The justices concluded, "We can only know her intention as expressed in her will." The plaintiffs, the Diocese of North Carolina, were assessed the costs of court, and on March 21, 1889, Battle wrote checks to the Wake County Superior Court and the State Supreme Court in the amounts of $9.90 and $22.05, respectively.[15]

If Kemp Battle had not been a man of honor, he might have prevented the State Supreme Court from rendering its faulty verdict. Both he and Mary Ruffin Smith, as active Episcopalians, had followed with interest the need for and accomplishment of division of the state into two dioceses, and it would have been the subject of conversation during the frequent visits of Mary to Chapel Hill and Kemp and Pattie's visits to the Price Creek plantation. No good church-going Episcopalian would have been ignorant of the momentous decision to divide the old diocese. In announcing the bequest in the *University Magazine* shortly after the will was recorded at the courthouse, Battle made Mary Smith's intent crystal clear: The property, he wrote, was "bequeathed to the Episcopal Church in North Carolina, that is, to the Western Diocese, under Bishop Lyman, which is called the Diocese of North Carolina, that part under Bishop Watson being called the Diocese of Eastern [*sic*] Carolina."[16] Unfortunately, Battle's positions both as Mary's confidante and executor of her will—of which both his local parish and his university were beneficiaries—put him in jeopardy of having— or being suspected of having—more than one conflict of interest. Thus privately, he knew that Mary did not bother to alter her will in 1883 because she intended for her estate to benefit the area of the state in which her family had lived for at least three generations. To have divulged that knowledge in court, however, could have cast a pall over the confidence in which the executor was held by the contesting parties. He paid a high penalty for his silence by spending nearly two decades of careful and tedious work in an effort to please multiple masters.

At the next council of the eastern diocese in 1889, its trustees gleefully reported, "The result has been the acquisition by the Diocese of East Carolina of one-half of Miss Smith's estate. The exact value of this half cannot yet be ascertained, the property consisting in part of land, which it may be best to sell, and in part of debts due the estate." Profuse thanks were extended to the victorious committee—George Davis, John Hughes, and William B. Rodman. To simplify the process of transfer by making one signature suffice for receipts, the eastern diocese authorized its treasurer to receive and receipt for funds paid from the estate. Battle had already acted to placate the impatient easterners by paying about $4,000 from collections on hand, monies that the Diocese of North Carolina originally had planned to apply to its own purposes.[17]

The report of the eastern diocese, in view of the "great difficulty of giving adequate attention to landed property at such a distance, and the expenses of a reliable agency," recommended that the diocese's share of the land be sold as quickly as possible, and offered to cooperate with the Diocese of North Carolina toward that end. It was acknowledged that Battle had lost little time in sending part payment of the new diocese's share of income previously collected.[18] By its original decision to devote all of its income from the Smith estate to its Permanent Episcopal Fund, the eastern diocese made Battle's reports and payments more easily traceable in future annual reports. The Diocese of North Carolina was less consistent in the distribution of its portion, so, unfortunately for researchers, its share was not as fully and carefully accounted for in its own journal, the fault for which lay in the diocesan office rather than in Battle's reports.

Many members of other Protestant denominations looked on amused, perhaps gleeful and jealous, as Episcopalians—sometimes described as "high-church"—fought fellow churchmen over lands that began with Samuel Parke's colonial grant, passed down through his son-in-law Francis Jones, were almost frittered away by Parke's grandson-in-law James S. Smith, and were salvaged by the last living heir, Mary Ruffin Smith, who survived her father's reckless real estate speculation and the embarrassingly lewd conduct of her two brothers. Despite strained disagreements between members of the contesting dioceses, Kemp Battle sought to play a neutral role in carrying out the responsibilities imposed upon him by a faulty Supreme Court decision. That same sensitivity to human nature—suspicion that he might favor one master over the other—appears to have guided him throughout his years in settling the Smith estate.

Fortunately, Battle remained on good terms with the treasurers of the two dioceses, Armand J. DeRosset for the easterners, John Manning and (upon Manning's death in 1899) Charles E. Johnson, for the North Carolina diocese. The executor's first success was to win approval of the eastern diocese for distributions already made from the estate; otherwise his role as executor would have been untenable. Perhaps with tongue-in-cheek, the monument that Battle had constructed at Jones Grove in memory of Mary Ruffin Smith does not mention the Diocese of East Carolina.[19]

Even as the court's decision was being scrupulously carried out, there remained tensions between the dioceses. A controversy over a North Carolina scholarship at the General Theological Seminary, which the old diocese refused to share with the new one, still festered, and the Chapel of the Cross in Chapel Hill, in which Battle was a principal member, remained for several years a particular divisive issue. Previous to the court's decision, several authorizations had been made by the Diocese of North Carolina on behalf of the chapel in the university town, and in 1887 and 1888, an appropriation of $500 per annum was authorized for the church "to be paid out of the income of the Mary Ruffin Smith legacy." In the latter year, the executor was "allowed to expend the sum heretofore voted for a tablet in memory of the Testatrix, for such articles of Chancel furniture for the 'Chapel of the Cross' as the Vestry shall desire."[20]

After the court's decision in 1889, the Rev. William M. Clark at the convention of the

Diocese of North Carolina introduced a resolution that again raised tempers in the east: "WHEREAS, This Convention recognizes the very great importance to the Church in North Carolina of keeping a clergyman constantly in charge of the Parish at Chapel Hill; in consequence of the judicial decision in the Mary Ruffin Smith will case, this Diocese is no longer able to continue a sufficient appropriation for this purpose; therefore, *Resolved*, That the Hon. K.P. Battle be appointed a committee to attend the meeting of the Council of East Carolina and lay this matter before the Council of that Diocese and urge upon that Diocese the necessity of aiding in this important matter." The executor probably begged off, because a committee composed of William M. Clark, Richard H. Battle, and Henry A. London drew up a more diplomatic resolution that read:

> WHEREAS, Miss Mary Ruffin Smith resided at Chapel Hill and was for many years inter-
> ested in the Parish of the Chapel of the Cross, and a leading contributor to its support; and
> whereas, the principal duty of the Rector of the Chapel of the Cross at Chapel Hill, is to min-
> ister to the spiritual welfare of the students of the State University, quite a large proportion of
> whom reside in the Diocese of East Carolina; *Resolved*, That in the opinion of this Conven-
> tion, in view of the supposed wishes of the testatrix, and for the reasons aforesaid the Diocese
> of East Carolina be and is hereby respectfully requested to make an annual Appropriation to
> the support of a Rector at Chapel Hill from its share of Miss Smith's estate.[21]

A cold rebuff was not long in coming:

> While fully impressed with the importance of the work at that point [Chapel Hill], and sure
> that this Diocese would gladly aid in its maintenance, if our own needs were less imperative
> than they are, or were more fully provided for, they do not think any obligation to do so rests
> upon us, as we find, upon examining the will of the late Miss Mary R. Smith, that she left a
> certain amount of property in fee to the Wardens and Vestry of the Chapel of the Cross at
> Chapel Hill, and that therefore it would seem that she had in that bequest provided what she
> thought was proper for that purpose, and intended the remainder of her bequest to be used to
> extending the work of the Church in the whole State.

Then a firm rejection: "this Diocese [of East Carolina] respectfully declines to accede to the request of the Diocese of North Carolina to make an annual appropriation to the support of a Rector at Chapel Hill."[22]

Faced with paying the entire amount out of the Diocese of North Carolina's own half of the estate, the appropriation was reduced to $400 in 1890, and the next year a motion was made to reduce the salary to $300, accompanied by a "special appeal ... to the parents of the boys and the Alumni connected with the Church." For the next several years the salary seldom surpassed $400 per year, and the task of keeping a rector at the Chapel of the Cross fell entirely upon the Diocese of North Carolina.[23]

As a loyal member of the Chapel of the Cross, Kemp Battle could hardly have felt neutral in the diocesan disputes, but there is no evidence that he used his position as executor to favor one over the other in carrying out the Supreme Court decision. He carefully sub-mitted to and received validation from the Diocese of East Carolina for all actions performed before that diocese was declared eligible for a share of the estate. Any objection to, for instance, his distribution of personal items to a few individuals, chosen on his personal acquaintance with Mary Smith's wishes, could have led to exceedingly embarrassing inter-diocesan controversy. Even so, it was not until 1890, nearly five years after Mary Smith's death, that the eastern trustees officially approved payment of her specific bequest of "a certain number of acres of land, not described by metes and bounds, [which] was made to a family of colored persons." The approval seemed somewhat petulant: "In the execution of said will, this land was set aside and deeded to these persons by the Trustees of the Diocese of North Carolina, prior to the decision of the Court declaring our Diocese equally interested with that of North Carolina in the provisions of the will. Such being the case, the Trustees of this Diocese have executed a paper ratifying the action ... and consenting to the appropriation of the land heretofore set aside...." Calling Mary Smith's nieces simply "these persons" seemed to veil a bit of condescension, if not racism.[24]

DeRosset reported to the eastern council in May 1889 that he had received part payment of its share in the estate. The payment included 4 percent bonds with par value of $3,400 and other payments—$1,000 in cash, $68 collected on coupons, and $241.25 from rent of lands.[25]

Battle's patience was not inexhaustible. It showed at the 1890 convention of the Diocese of North Carolina when he complained that his committee to audit W.C. Cole's accounts had been delayed because the East Carolina diocese had not appointed its members to cooperate, and that "in regard to the disposition to be made of the land devised to this Diocese by Miss Mary R. Smith, I beg leave to report that it has been found impossible to take any action because no Committee has been appointed by the Convention of the Diocese of East Carolina to co-operate with the Committee of this Diocese." He added that he had taken measures to "secure" such co-operation and hoped that action had been, or would be taken, during that week. He also introduced a resolution asking for a joint committee from the two dioceses "to subdivide the land and to sell in parcels, or in the whole, as they may judge most expedient, to the highest bidder or privately.... In the event that the Diocese of East Carolina shall decline to sell its part of said land, said Trustees shall have power to secure partition thereof and to sell the portion assigned to this Diocese as above mentioned." The eastern diocese received from Battle in 1889–1890 $5,341.01, all of which was added to its Permanent Episcopal Fund. The fact that the diocesan conventions met only once per year, and that reports were often abridged in their journals, delayed official interactions and formal responses.[26]

Despite continued suspicions on the part of some officials of the eastern diocese, Battle proceeded with the tedious effort to collect on the notes due. It was like coaxing cold molasses from a narrow-necked bottle. That he gradually succeeded was a tribute to his and W.C. Cole's patience and understanding of the economic distress being felt by agricultural interests. In May 1890, for example, Battle reported to the dioceses, "It was my hope to settle the [personal] estate of Miss Mary R. Smith before the meeting of this Convention. Unfortunately, however, there was only about a third of a crop made in the section where the debtors of the estate reside. If I had forced sales on mortgages they would have been greatly depressed and probably ruined."[27]

Battle faced all sorts of problems in accounting for receipts, for he had to keep separate books for loan repayments, rents, and sales of personal property, then divide the categories, after expenses, for remittance annually to the treasurer of each diocese. For sales of real estate, entirely different books had to be kept. Annual income from the personal estate was often meager; for example, payments for $150 from collections and $426.68 from rents were received by the eastern diocese during the year ending in 1893. Three years later the total receipts for the same diocese amounted to only $133.95. Not surprisingly, impatience was felt by leaders of both dioceses.[28]

By April 16, 1902, the executor had collected $18,134.20 for Mary Smith's personal estate, which came mostly from the payment of mortgage notes. Expenditures—largely taxes and attorney fees—amounted to $2,385.21, leaving the joint legatees $15,748.99 less commissions of $1,051.04, or $14,697.95. The reader is reminded that this is only for the personal estate—cash on hand, collection of notes due, and sale of farm equipment and produce. Battle explained why it had taken fourteen years to settle: "according to my own judgment, and that of many intelligent neighbors, much loss to the Church, and suffering to the mortgage debtors of the estate, would have ensued if I had enforced speedy payments. In accordance with the wishes of Miss Smith, verbally expressed to me not long before her death, and with the approval of the Trustees of the two Dioceses, I gave time to the debtors, and so succeeded in my collections better than was possible otherwise." In another letter to Bishop A.A. Watson of the eastern diocese, he reiterated his point: "Miss Smith asked me not long before her death to be as indulgent as possible to the debtors, and the authorities of both Dioceses instructed or allowed, me to carry out her wishes. The indulgence was of great advantage to the estate. Experienced business men assure me that much loss to the estate and suffering to the debtors would have been incurred by a harsher course." The journal added a copy of the certificate of the Clerk of Superior Court of Orange County.[29]

Battle added a note summarizing the distribution of personal items, most of which had previously been listed; for example, upon instruction of the dioceses he had given books that remained in the house to St. Augustine's Normal School and a "sideboard & chair to Mrs. Dr. Mallett, 6 common chairs, not included in the will but delivered by request of Miss Smith made shortly before her death."[30]

All the while, with another set of books, the executor was trying to sell the Price Creek land, more than 1,500 acres. By 1893 John Manning, chairman of the committee to which the joint dioceses had finally delegated that task, reported, "we have not sold these [tracts], for the reason that, owing to the bad crops and general depression of agriculture, we have been unable to find purchasers for the same at what we regard as fair prices."[31] To the 1897 council of the eastern diocese, Battle similarly reported that there had been no sales "for want of purchasers." He also explained that owing to bad crops and low prices, the mortgage debtors had been unable to pay.[32]

In light of the times, Kemp Battle and his committee had wisely moved slowly in attempting to sell the Price Creek land. Although an academician, he knew that economic conditions were unpromising in rural areas. Counting on an improved economy, he chose at first to rent out the Price Creek lands. Soon, however, concluding that the Smith land could not be "made profitable" as rental property, he recommended its sale. In May 1890, he and Manning recommended that the land, properly subdivided, should be sold during the coming fall for "one-third cash and on reasonable terms as to time for the residue...."[33]

To stimulate interest in the land, Battle engaged George W. Tate, noted for his large scale map of Orange County in 1891, to lay off the Price Creek property into 15 lots, ranging in acreage from 23 to 386.25. In November 1897, Battle, Manning, and London advertised for sale "the excellent home farm of the late Miss Mary R. Smith ... containing about 1400 acres," which they described as "one of the best plantations in middle North Carolina and a rare opportunity is offered to investors." In the initial auction, only three tracts were sold: Lot 1 to John W. Cole, 53 acres for $265[34]; Lot 2 to William F. Cole, 78.25 acres for $504.41[35]; and Lot 3 to J.W. Crabtree, 37.75 acres for $360.[36] Crabtree later changed his mind and purchased instead Lot 4, 57.75 acres for the same amount ($360).[37] Each purchaser paid one-third cash, one-third in one year, and the final third in three years, "deferred payments drawing interest from date, payable annually." The average price of these three tracts—less than $7 per acre—reflected economic conditions during the Panic of 1893, the splintering of the Democratic and Republican parties during the disruptive 1890s, and a virtual race war in

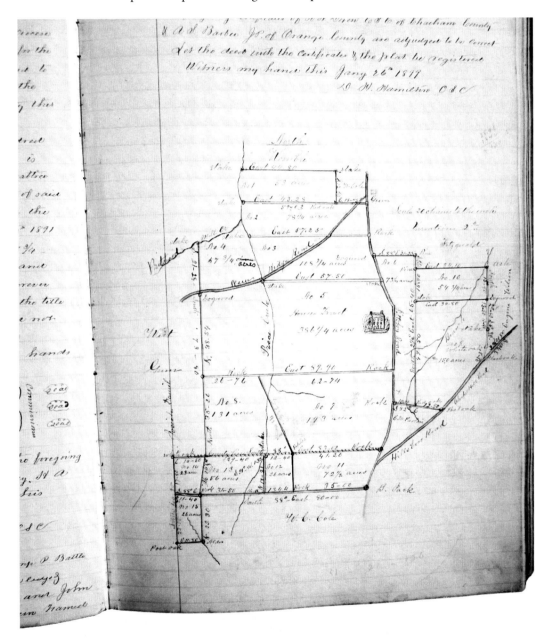

The Price Creek plantation of more than 1,600 acres was surveyed by George W. Tate into fifteen tracts, each of which was sold individually. Cornelia's one-hundred-acre tract (upper right) had already been surveyed (Orange County Register of Deeds, Hillsborough, courtesy David Southern).

"Oakland," the house occupied by the Smiths in 1847, as it appeared after Mary Smith's death in 1885 (courtesy Ernest A. Dollar, Jr.).

North Carolina. However, it is worth remembering that one dollar in 1890 value was the equivalent of many dollars in today's prices.[38]

After another sale in 1898, Battle and London (the remaining committee members after Manning's death) reported the sale of only "very badly situated and rocky land not fit for cultivation containing forty-nine acres, for which $125 was bid and accepted."[39]

The October 26, 1899, issue of the *Chatham Record* advertised an "Important Sale! One Thousand Acres!" to be held in front of H.H. (Hoot) Patterson's Store in Chapel Hill, of the "unsold part of the Price tract of the late Miss Mary R. Smith's land." Apparently no sales were recorded. Two years later the Diocese of East Carolina was informed that Battle and London had been able to sell only two small additional tracts for the sum of $450, leaving 989 acres of the Price Creek lands still to be disposed of.[40] At the next diocesan convention, the commissioners reported that again they had offered the remaining land, in the whole and in parcels, at public auction and private sale, and that no reasonable offer had been obtained. The commissioners added, "Owing to repeated partial failure of crops[,] there has been stagnation in the real estate market in this part of the State." They reminded the delegates, however, that the cultivated portions of the unsold land were being rented under the management of W.C. Cole.[41]

The *Chatham Record* of October 30, 1902, announced that still another public sale would be held in front of the post office in Chapel Hill of "that valuable farm near Chapel Hill formerly belonging to Miss Mary Ruffin Smith, deceased, containing nearly one thousand acres." There appear to have been no acceptable bids.

"Oakland" as it appeared after it was purchased and occupied by the William C. Cole family around the turn of the century (courtesy Ernest A. Dollar, Jr.).

"Oakland" as it appears after a recent restoration (H.G. Jones collection).

Finally, however, in 1904, Battle and London triumphantly reported, "after many unsuccessful attempts, we have succeeded in selling at good prices all of the land devised to the Diocese by Miss Mary Ruffin Smith."[42] In March the home tract—Lot 5 containing 386.25 acres and the handsome three-story house built in the 1840s—was purchased for $3,600 by Barnes & Company (O.B. Barnes, J.F. Pickett, and A.E. Lewis), and that price included also Lot 8—131 acres stretching along Price Creek[43] That was less than $7 per acre for land that included one of the finest homes in the county. Battle was deeply disappointed; he felt a kinship to Mary Smith's large residence, "Oakland," and he had held out for years, hoping for a more satisfactory bid. Lot 7 of 193 acres desirably bordering the home tract and the Hillsborough-Fayetteville road, was taken by Rufus and Zebedee Johnson for $1,200, paid over several years.[44] Perhaps the best buy was by S.W. Crabtree, Lot 6 (73.25 acres for $730),[45] elongated and facing the home tract and stretching a half mile along the east side of the road and abutting the tract previously bequeathed by Mary Smith to her niece and brother Sidney's daughter, Cornelia Fitzgerald.

Purchases not previously mentioned were: Lot 3 (108.75 acres for $775) by Walter C. Womble[46]; Lot 4 (57.75 acres for $360) by Jerome W. Crabtree[47]; Lot 9 (150 acres for $600) by Leonidas L. Merritt[48]; Lot 10 (53.75 acres for $330) by S.W. Crabtree[49]; Lot 11 (72.5 acres for $376.16) by Martha A. Partin[50]; and Lots 12 (26 acres for $115) and 14 (56 acres for $146) by William C. Cole.[51]

309

A. P. Battle, Ex^r of Miss Smith (Mary R.)

Settled May 24, 1902.

Rec'd in full	18,134	20
Expenditures in full.	2,385	21
Balance .	15,748	99
Deduct Commissions, $1,026.04		
" Clerk expenses, $ 25.00	1051	04
Total deductions .		
Balance for distribution.	14697	95
Deduct specific Legacies	979	95
For Residuary Legatees.	13718	00
Heretofore paid as per rects.		
To Diocese of N.C. : $6,682.24		
" " " E. Carolina 6,682.24	13364	48
Bal. due each $171.76	343	52

Kemp P. Battle
Ex^r

Subscribed & sworn
to before me Apl. 24th 1902
W. H. Hamilton
C.S.C.

Kemp Battle's final settlement between the two dioceses for the Price Creek property. One can imagine his relief after seventeen years of painstaking bookkeeping and reporting to two squabbling dioceses (courtesy University Papers, University Archives, Wilson Library, UNC-CH).

Battle added, with relief, "We have collected and paid to the Treasurers of the Dioceses of North Carolina and East Carolina all the proceeds of the sales, less expenses, that are due, amounting to about $7,800. The deferred payments, amounting to about $1,600, are well and safely secured and will be promptly collected and accounted for when due." There remained, of course, the difficult task of collecting the remaining payments on the principal and interest. That job would require five more years.

At last, in May 1909—more than two dozen years after beginning the task of settling one of North Carolina's largest bequests to eleemosynary institutions—Kemp Plummer Battle submitted his final report to the two Episcopal dioceses. His debt to Mary Ruffin Smith, if he ever had one, had been paid many times over. The land, as surveyed into 15 lots by George W. Tate, brought in only $9,703.77, including interest collected from those who paid in installments. In summary, Mary Ruffin Smith's Price Creek lands (excluding the total of 125 acres bequeathed to Julius Smith and Cornelia Fitzgerald) encompassed 1,488.75 acres, which sold for $9,126.87. The latter figure is based on the price shown on each deed; it is somewhat less than the figure shown in Kemp Battle's total ($9,703.77) that included interest. Adding the lots given to Julius and Cornelia, the Price Creek lands totaled 1,613.75 acres.

By resolution on May 13, 1909—nearly 24 years after Mary Ruffin Smith's death—the Diocese of North Carolina accepted the final report of the sales of the real estate and approved deeds executed by Kemp P. Battle and Henry A. London to the purchasers. The committee was released and discharged with thanks.[52] The Diocese of East Carolina kept better records, reporting annually, and was careful to publish Battle's final report, which accounted for all land receipts ($9,703.77) and all expenditures, including payments to the dioceses, of $9,681.93, with $21.78 yet to be divided between the two.[53]

Added to the personalty ($13,718, or $6,859 each), the two dioceses shared, after deduction of expenses, a total of $23,461.71—for each diocese $11,710.86 (or $11,710.85, depending upon which one drew the short straw). At the end, Mary Ruffin Smith's estate yielded to the Episcopalians an amount not much less than Battle predicted in 1886—the personalty more, the real estate less—all this during one of the most politically-divisive and agriculturally-depressed eras in American history. Kemp Battle could finally heave a sigh of relief.

A cursory review of the expenditures of the committee (on the sale of the land only) reveals that little but time and aggravation was expended by the land committee. Advertising cost $107, both in newspapers and in printed circulars. Although a number of the advertisements appear in extant newspapers, none of the broadsides advertising the Price Creek property have been found. (There is a poster in the North Carolina Collection describing the various lots in the Jones Grove lands.) Purchasers were responsible for payment of registrations, but about $30 was spent in taxes and legal work. The commissioners appear to have paid themselves slightly under $250 each for more than two decades of labor (their actual total, $478.61). Their thrift and selflessness, in themselves, were tributes to the frugality and simplicity of the life of Mary Ruffin Smith.[54]

Chapter 8

Saving St. Mary's School

Frigid relations between the two dioceses over the court-ordered division of Mary Ruffin Smith's bequest were not easily thawed. Many church members in the Diocese of North Carolina were convinced that a faulty decision by the State Supreme Court had over-ruled the testatrix's intentions, while some eastern Episcopalians, particularly laymen, failed to understand why nearly a quarter of a century passed before all rents and mortgages were collected, lands sold, and receipts divided.[1]

Through the good fortune of timing, the names "Mary" and "St. Mary's" helped bring healing and warmer cooperation between the dioceses. The educational institution around which Episcopalians in two states rallied was St. Mary's School in Raleigh, and Mary Smith's money played the pivotal role in galvanizing the dioceses in a successful effort to save and give new life to an honored but financially-distressed institution. Although the school was not named for her, until recently it preserved the only living memorial bearing the name of Mary Ruffin Smith.

"This was the greatest enterprise ever undertaken by the Diocese," proudly asserted the bishop of the Episcopal Diocese of North Carolina a quarter of a century later. Bishop Joseph Blount Cheshire, Jr., was explaining how, back in 1897, Mary Smith's bequest saved St. Mary's School from extinction. "[T]he Diocese had in the treasury ten thousand dollars of a legacy left to the Diocese by an old parishioner of mine, Miss Mary Ruffin Smith, of Chapel Hill," he said, adding, "This was all the money in sight" with which to make the required twenty-percent down payment on the $50,000 needed to purchase the land and buildings for which the Rev. Aldert and Bennett Smedes, father and son, had paid rent to the Duncan Cameron family for more than half a century.[2]

Bishop Cheshire's recollection of the exact dollar amounts was a little faulty—Mary's money actually provided a greater portion of the down payment—but he remembered the larger picture correctly. Regrettably, he did not say more about his relations with Mary Smith and her friend Maria Spear when he served as their youthful rector at the Chapel of the Cross from 1878 to 1881. He would have known them well, and if he had not already moved to St. Peter's in Charlotte so soon, he would no doubt have officiated at the funeral of both Maria and Mary.

Historically, in the 1830s an Episcopal School for boys in Raleigh operated in buildings appropriately called West Rock and East Rock because they were constructed with stones rejected during the simultaneous erection of the State Capitol a few blocks away. After the boys' school failed, the Rev. Aldert Smedes, a native of New York, rented the property in

Bishop Joseph Blount Cheshire, Jr., who once served as dea-
con of the struggling Chapel of the Cross in Chapel Hill,
credited Mary Ruffin Smith's money with saving St. Mary's
School in 1897 (courtesy North Carolina Collection, Wilson
Library, UNC-CH). Smedes Hall, the main building at St.
Mary's, is shown after the school's resuscitation (courtesy
Knowles Collection, State Archives of North Carolina).

1842 and opened St. Mary's School for girls. Although patronized by prominent Episcopalians, St. Mary's remained privately owned by its founder and later by his son, the Rev.
Bennett Smedes, who succeeded to the presidency in 1877. Its sterling reputation notwithstanding, the institution was perpetually in debt, partially because of the soft hearts of the
Smedeses, who admitted too many students—especially daughters of the clergy—without
charging adequate tuition. For 55 years, while the school was operated and financed by the
father and son, fellow Episcopalians in the Carolinas bore no responsibility for—but reaped
untold benefits from—St. Mary's School.

As debts increased and Bennett Smedes's personal finances deteriorated, the future of
St. Mary's was gravely in doubt when in 1896 its students and alumni association presented
a memorial to the Episcopalian dioceses outlining the history, value, and precarious financial
condition of the school. The document ended with an appeal for the Episcopal jurisdictions
"either to endow the School, or to erect for it suitable buildings in Raleigh or elsewhere, and
thus relieve it of one great drain, its heavy rent." The opportunity found a responsive ear in
Cheshire—by then the bishop of the Diocese of North Carolina—long an admirer of the
school, who in his annual address said, "Probably all persons at all acquainted with our
history will agree that we owe more to St. Mary's and to its founder than to the work of any
other one man. The time has come when we should not only recognize this debt, but set
about paying for it." He continued, "If St. Mary's is to remain the glory of the Diocese, the

source of Christian womanhood, the conservator of the best and most gracious qualities of our social and religious culture, the Churchmen of North Carolina must rally to the support of the faithful and generous man who worthily occupies the place of his noble father, and hold up his hands while he maintains our cause." The result was the establishment of a committee with authority to "purchase suitable school buildings or to acquire land and erect suitable buildings for a girls' school at any suitable place within the Diocese."[3] Diocesan officials moved rapidly by sponsoring a legislative act establishing a corporate body called "Trustees of St. Mary's School" with authority to assume proprietorship and operation of a reorganized institution.[4]

The trustees at their very first meeting in 1897 agreed to raise $50,000—$10,000 of which was to be paid immediately—to purchase from the heirs of Duncan Cameron the buildings and 25-acre campus, for which the Smedes had been paying rent for more than a half-century. Of the initial amount, $3,883.65 was promptly paid from the North Carolina diocese's Mary Ruffin Smith funds "on account of purchase of St. Mary's property."[5]

Despite continuing tensions between the two North Carolina dioceses over other aspects of the Mary Smith bequest, the easterners were also anxious to save the school, the alma mater of many of the young women of their area. Bishop Cheshire was careful to cultivate the cooperation of his counterpart, Bishop Alfred A. Watson, and early on a complicated agreement was reached under which the two dioceses—North Carolina and East Carolina—contributed some of their respective Mary Smith funds in return for the establishment of scholarships in the names of two benefactors.

At the first meeting of the trustees, Kemp P. Battle, Jr. (son of the university president), was called upon to chair a committee of the whole, at which the following resolution was adopted: "That the fund in the hands of the Treasurer, known as the 'Fund for the Education of Children of Deceased Clergymen,' be increased to three thousand dollars from the Mary Ruffin Smith fund, and that said fund, so augmented, be put at the disposal of the Trustees of St. Mary's School, upon condition that they shall establish in the school a scholarship to be known as the Mary E. Chapeau scholarship" for the free education of a daughter of a deceased clergyman of the Diocese of North Carolina. A second resolution authorized that the "remaining portion of the Mary Ruffin Smith fund be placed at the disposal of the Trustees of St. Mary's School, and that, in consideration of the use of this fund, they shall establish one free scholarship in said school for residents of the Diocese of North Carolina for each three thousand dollars received from said fund, to be called the 'Mary Ruffin Smith Scholarships.'" Nominations for the scholarships were placed in the hands of the bishops.[6]

Under Bishop Cheshire's lead, by 1899 all three Episcopal bodies within the state—the two dioceses plus the new Jurisdiction of Asheville—had become partners in the ambitious undertaking. In these efforts, Mary Ruffin Smith's money, so laboriously and sometime contentiously accumulated and shared by two dioceses, provided an essential portion of the funds that resuscitated St. Mary's School. The exact proportion of the costs of acquisition borne by Smith funds is difficult to ascertain, but several specific additional examples can be cited. In 1900, the Diocese of East Carolina offered to contribute $4,000 from its Mary Ruffin Smith fund on condition that the trustees "guarantee to this Diocese a perpetual scholarship" of $200 per year. In the school year beginning in 1900, it was reported that the scholarships had been held by "worthy and promising pupils."[7]

Additional Smith funds contributed by the Diocese of North Carolina in 1905 included

$3,000 "on account of St. Mary's School debt," along with another payment of $500. The following year the same diocese paid $2,500 more from its Smith Fund, and the Diocese of East Carolina paid a similar amount from its own "Mary Ruffin-Smith" [sic] Fund.[8]

In his position as president of St. Mary's board of trustees, Bishop Cheshire reported proudly, "It will be observed in the report of the Treasurer that $1,000 was paid during the year covered by the report upon the principal of the debt remaining due to the Cameron Trustees. This sum was made up of $500 given by Mr. Thomas Atkinson of Richmond through Bishop Strange, and $500 from the Mary Ruffin Smith Fund. This reduced the principal of said debt to $13,000.... We are informed that an additional sum of $2,500, since the Treasurer's report was made out, has been paid to him from the Mary Ruffin Smith Fund to be applied to the principal of the debt which will thereby be reduced to the sum of $10,500." The remainder of Mary Smith's money (and its earned interest) in the Diocese of North Carolina—nearly $5,000—was eventually added to the Permanent Episcopal Fund.[9]

In the report for the year ending May 1, 1906, the trustees of St. Mary's triumphantly summarized their success:

> The payment of the debt for the purchase of St. Mary's School property marks the attainment of the first goal in the progress of this institution. Nine years ago this month the Convention of the Diocese of North Carolina passed a resolution endorsing the scheme of purchase proposed by the Trustees, and out of its very limited resources appropriated six thousand dollars of the ten thousand dollars required as a cash payment to secure the property. For the forty thousand dollars remaining we asked a credit running over the period of twenty years. Nine years have passed, and the whole balance has been paid off. Moreover, we have spent above twenty thousand dollars in improving the property, and adding to the accommodations and equipments for the school. In this work the Church in all the Carolinas has co-operated, but the principal part of the burden has been borne by North and East Carolina. The Treasurer has now in hand thirteen thousand five hundred dollars, as was mentioned above, for the erection of a beautiful and commodious Auditorium which has long been needed.[10]

The earliest mention of the resulting scholarships in St. Mary's publications is found in the school's catalog for 1905. The entry reads: "Mary Ruffin Smith Scholarships. In compliance with conditions of the Mary Ruffin Smith bequest to the Diocese of North Carolina, St. Mary's maintains four Diocesan Scholarships—three in the Diocese of North Carolina and one in the Diocese of East Carolina. These scholarships include board, fees and tuition in the Academic or Business Departments and are of the approximate value of $25 [sic] each. Each scholarship is filled by the Bishop of the Diocese to which the scholarship belongs."[11] The following year the school's bulletin gave two slightly different readings: One tuition scholarship, "established from the Mary Ruffin Smith Fund," and from the Diocese of North Carolina, two board and tuition scholarships from "the fund left the diocese by Miss Mary Ruffin Smith." By 1923, the bulletin listed three Smith scholarships: one non-competitive Mary Ruffin Smith Scholarship of the Diocese of North Carolina $50), and two competitive scholarships "from the fund left the diocese by Miss Mary Ruffin Smith."[12] In each instance, the bishop nominated the candidate. As late as 1998, the last year that St. Mary was both a high school and college, the "Mary Ruffin Smith Endowed Memorial" was offered, the holder of which was selected by the bishop of the Diocese of North Carolina.[13]

There remains another thread leading back to Mary Ruffin Smith. Bishop Cheshire said that the trustee largely responsible for handling the purchase of the St. Mary's campus in 1897 was William A. Erwin, a step-grandson of William Rainey Holt's second wife, Louisa

Allen Hogan Holt, who was said by Kemp Battle to have been the closest living relative of Mary Smith. Three decades later, William Erwin financed the construction of the new Chapel of the Cross in Chapel Hill in memory of his grandfather Holt.[14]

From 1897 until today, St. Mary's School—initially rescued by Mary Ruffin Smith's legacy—has survived additional hard times, and it remains one of the stellar female schools promoting Christian education in the South. The "Mary Ruffin Smith Endowed Memorial" scholarship stood out for years as the sole living memorial in the name of the saintly spinster who devoted her substantial fortune to charity. Despite her request that her name not be perpetuated though her gifts, it is difficult to believe that she would have been displeased with at least one tribute to her eleemosynary impulse.[15]

Chapter 9

Healing the Wounds:
The Chapel of the Cross

As long as her family resided in Hillsborough, Mary Ruffin Smith's religious life was centered in St. Matthew's Episcopal Church, so intimately associated with rectors William Mercer Green, her first teacher, and Moses Ashley Curtis, from whom she developed a keen interest in botany.[1] When her family occupied the handsome new home near Chapel Hill in 1847, Mary was reunited with Green, who had organized a new congregation, the Church of the Atonement, soon renamed Chapel of the Cross. That parish at the edge of the university campus was her church home for the remainder of her life, and her Sunday morning arrival with her biracial nieces in a "beautiful white family carriage" became a picturesque image for townspeople and future commentators.[2]

The handsome Gothic-styled chapel, much of the cost of which came from Green's own pocket, was a local showplace with few parishioners. Its construction was accomplished at the very time when Dr. James Strudwick Smith was on the verge of losing the vast holdings placed in his care by his father-in-law, Francis Jones. Almost certainly, therefore, little or no Smith money went into the fine church building that would become a focal point of Mary Ruffin Smith's life during her remaining decades.

With Green's departure to accept the bishopric of Mississippi, the parish struggled. Its rector, Aaron F. Olmsted, was soon succeeded by Thomas Frederick Davis, who lasted only three years. A succession of men served the parish short terms until well after the Civil War, in the intervals sometimes by the Rev. Robert B. Sutton of St. Bartholomew's in Pittsboro. The most notable event at the Chapel of the Cross during those years was the meeting of the Forty-sixth Annual Convention of the Diocese of North Carolina in 1862. The parish survived the tragic years of war and reconstruction only by the continued support of a few families such as the Battles, Malletts, and Mickles, and of individuals like Mary Ruffin Smith.

In 1878 a young Joseph Blount Cheshire, Jr., arrived as shepherd of the languid parish. Cheshire had studied law under the Ruffin legal firm in Hillsborough, but, at age 26, he turned to the ministry and was called as deacon to the Chapel of the Cross. He married into the prominent Webb family of Hillsborough, and he developed a lifelong friendship with Kemp Battle, the president of the recently reopened University of North Carolina. Among his parishioners were Mary Ruffin Smith and her friend and housemate Maria Spear. Had he not been called to the much larger St. Peter's parish in Charlotte, Cheshire probably would have preached at the funeral of both Maria and Mary. His youthful association with Mary Smith would be remembered when, as bishop of the Diocese of North Carolina in 1897, the spinster's money enabled him to save St. Mary's School in Raleigh.[3]

Mary's love for the struggling church in Chapel Hill was demonstrated by gifts during her lifetime[4] and especially by her will, which left to the parish her real estate in the village.[5] Even that property, however, did not provide the annual operating expenses for the ministry near the campus, and she expected additional assistance to be given the parish by the Diocese of North Carolina, to which she willed most of her personal estate and the Price Creek lands. The parish's humble condition was revealed in its report to the diocese in 1885, the year of Mary Smith's death: Expenditures were $100 for the unfilled rector's salary, $370 for other parish expenses, and $25 each toward the bishop's salary and diocesan needs. However, Kemp Battle, wearing still another hat as the church's senior warden, reported proudly that the parish occasionally welcomed the bishop and visiting ministers, and that lay readings had been regularly kept up, in the absence of a clergyman, by John Manning and himself. Even more dismal were the statistics for the following year: no minister; 35 communicants; offerings totaling $171.74 for parish expenses; $25 toward bishop's salary; and $28 for diocesan missions. Church property was valued at $1,600.

In September 1886 W.M. Clark became rector at a salary of $165, and Bishop Theodore B. Lyman expressed the hope for a plan "by which the limited resources of the congregation can be supplemented." Accordingly, the diocese made a $400 allocation to the parish in 1887 and 1888 "to be paid out of the income of the Mary Ruffin Smith legacy." The $100 previously granted by the diocese from the personal estate for a memorial to Mary Smith was later devoted to chancel furniture.[6] Three years later—after the court ordered a division of the Smith bequest—the Diocese of North Carolina allocated only $125 to the parish, and Augustine Prentiss served as rector until October 1890, followed for a year by E.M. Gushee of Massachusetts. The vestry, wrote Kemp Battle, regretted that it had been unable to attract a permanent rector, adding, "The Parish is essentially weak in numbers and resources, but the presence in the University of a considerable number of sons of the Church renders it, in some respects, one of the most important in the Diocese. The Parish is greatly indebted to the Reverend Mr. Gushee for his active and efficient aid in securing a beautiful recess chancel and other improvements to the church edifice."[7]

It was at this point that the Diocese of North Carolina, stung by the State Supreme Court's requirement that it give up half of Mary Smith's estate, called on the Diocese of East Carolina to share in the cost of keeping up the Chapel of the Cross, which was attended by Episcopalian students without regard to residence. The request was eminently fair, but the response was swift and sharp: According to their interpretation, Mary had relieved the easterners of any obligation for help because she bequeathed directly to the Chapel of the Cross her modest real estate holdings in the village of Chapel Hill. The original diocese again in 1890 offered the sister diocese the privilege of sharing the management of the Chapel of the Cross; the invitation apparently was simply ignored.[8]

Left on its own, the Diocese of North Carolina reduced its supplement to the Chapel of the Cross in 1890 to less than $400 per year.[9] Augustine Prentiss served a short time as rector. A resolution to increase the supplement to $500 "toward the support of a resident Rector at Chapel Hill" the following year was amended to $300, accompanied by a special appeal to the "parents of boys and the Alumni connected with the Church." That year the church counted 13 families, $168.50 in rector's salary, and property values of $5,250 for the chapel, $800 for the rectory, and $300 for the other church property.[10]

Frederick Towers became minister in charge in September 1891, and the sale of a lot given by Mary Smith, together with a fundraising campaign, provided moneys for repairing the church and rectory, bringing the value of the buildings to $6,275. The minister's salary was still only $312.50 for a local congregation of 57 plus 45 students who regularly attended services. It appears, however, that the following year Towers's salary ($316.94) was "exclusive of the appropriation of $500 by the Executive Missionary Committee." In 1895, a two-manual organ was purchased and presented to the parish by students of the University; by then Louis H. Schubert was rector.[11]

Bishop Lyman had given verbal support for the Chapel Hill mission—for example, as early as 1886 he had expressed hope for a plan "by which the limited resources of the congregation can be supplemented"—but he had no success in getting assistance from his counterpart in the Diocese of East Carolina. Although a native New Yorker, Bishop Watson became so sympathetic with the Southern cause in the Civil War that, when his church in Wilmington was occupied by the Federals, he was expelled from the city for refusing to deliver a public prayer for the President of the United States. Even though the University of North Carolina had conferred an honorary degree on him in 1868, Watson still gave no effective support toward helping the struggling church at Chapel Hill.

Happily, the outlook improved greatly with the election of Joseph Blount Cheshire, Jr., to succeed to the bishopric upon Lyman's death late in 1893. Cheshire, remembering fondly his youthful deaconate in Chapel Hill and the subsequent bequest of his parishioner, Mary Smith, was warmly sympathetic toward diocesan support for the struggling ministry. But as long as Watson was bishop of the eastern diocese, he could get little support from that quarter.[12]

Another decade passed with little progress in strengthening the financial status in the Chapel Hill parish. There was, therefore, no assurance of a friendly response when the Diocese of North Carolina in 1905 established a committee "to secure, through the assistance of the Diocese of East Carolina, the District of Asheville and the congregation of the Chapel of the Cross, at Chapel Hill, a salary for the support of a Chaplain of the Church at the University of North Carolina, the salary of a University professorship being considered as adequate stipend for such an office...."[13]

Fortunately for the Chapel of the Cross, long-awaited help came from the Rev. Robert Strange, who succeeded to the East Carolina bishopric upon Watson's death in 1905. Having attended two military schools in Hillsborough, Strange was graduated from the University, was prepared for the ministry by the Rev. Robert B. Sutton of the Episcopal parish in Pittsboro, and was confirmed by Bishop Thomas Atkinson in the Chapel of the Cross. In his very first bishop's address to his diocese, Strange revealed that he had recently visited the campus, preaching to the students and talking with them personally, and announced that he planned "to do this work at the University every year." Delegates to the next council endorsed this new attitude by adopting a resolution recognizing that "Chapel Hill is a most important point for Missionary work among young men, and the Council is pleased to learn that our Bishop proposes to devote a portion of his time to that special work."[14]

Meanwhile, the number of students in the University had grown rapidly (reaching 790 in 1908), and the Chapel of the Cross—the only church in the community for the eighty

Episcopalian students, about equally divided between western and eastern portions of the state—became an increasing concern of individual members of the denomination throughout North Carolina. A "Committee on Church Work at the University of North Carolina," chaired by Francis M. Osborne, began collecting pledges in the Diocese of North Carolina and reported that it already had collected $94.25 and that the Chapel of the Cross vestry had increased its pledge to $500 for the rector's salary for the next year. But more was needed. By resolution, the convention urged every congregation to take up a special collection for the fund on the first Sunday in September each year.[15]

Bishop Strange energetically supported a similar fundraising effort in his diocese, adding a personal note, "We ought to thank God that we have such a place in our own State to send our boys. My own son goes there in the next two years and every young man looking to the Holy Ministry in this Diocese shall do his academic work chiefly at the University." He appointed a com-

The election in 1905 of the Rev. Robert Strange as bishop of the East Carolina Diocese warmed relations between the two ecclesiastical bodies and encouraged stronger support for the Chapel of the Cross (St. James Episcopal Church Collection, University of North Carolina at Wilmington, courtesy Susan T. Block).

mittee seeking to raise annually $500 from the churches in his diocese "for the support of a Clergyman at Chapel Hill." By the next May, the committee had raised $365.42 from 22 parishes and mission stations, and its chairman believed that the remainder would be obtained. The following year the committee recommended that the collections for the first Sunday in December each year be set aside for the salary of the rector at Chapel Hill. And to prove its seriousness, the Diocese of East Carolina assigned a quota to each parish for the support of a rector at Chapel Hill, ranging from $1 for St. Joseph's in Camden County and $1.77 for Emmanuel in Farmville to $50 for Christ Church, New Bern, and $150 for St. James's, Wilmington. There was, of course, no penalty for noncompliance, but contributions to the fund in the year June 1909–May 1910 totaled $584.67 from 32 parishes, ranging from $2 to $150 (the latter amount was from St. James's, Wilmington, and there were further contributions for another $100 from "Wilmington Friends"). The most significant recommendations of the report were (1) that the annual contribution be increased to $600 and (2)

A grand new Chapel of the Cross, financed largely by William Allen Erwin, is shown under construction about 1925 (courtesy North Carolina Collection, Wilson Library, UNC-CH).

The original Chapel of the Cross, built in 1848 largely by the Rev. William Mercer Green, appears in the foreground of this recent view. The 1925 building is at left (H.G. Jones collection).

that it be "put upon a permanent basis."[16] Meanwhile, individuals and churches of the Diocese of North Carolina contributed $334.97 and pledged $600 per year in the future. The young District of Asheville pledged $200 annually, which, when added to $600 each from the two dioceses and $600 from the local parish, gave a promise of $2,000 annually for the support of the Chapel of the Cross. The rector's annual salary reached $600.[17]

Finally, good relations between North Carolina Episcopalians—impaired for two decades by an unseemly controversy over the magnificent generosity of Mary Ruffin Smith and a faulty State Supreme Court decision—were restored. The permanency of the Chapel Hill parish—that meant so much to Mary Smith, Kemp Battle, Bishop Cheshire, residents, and former students of the University—was assured. By 1925, when an impressive new church was dedicated, the congregation counted 224 baptized persons, annual expenditures of about $4,000, and a physical plant valued at $163,000 minus $17,000 indebtedness. Uncounted were the hundreds of former students at the University who had benefitted from that same generosity.[18]

For the second time in its 109 years of existence, the Convention of the Episcopal Diocese of North Carolina met at the Chapel of the Cross in 1925. On that occasion the splendid new church was dedicated beside the gothic structure built by William Mercer Green and a few loyal Episcopalians nearly eighty years earlier. This was a very special occasion for Bishop Cheshire, who reminisced: "Forty-seven years ago this month, in the week following the Fourth Sunday after Easter, I came to Chapel Hill to serve my Diaconate in this parish, sent here by Bishop Atkinson, who on Easter Day preceding had ordained me in Calvary Church, Tarborough.... I look at yonder structure, the church of my first cure, and think of the holy and blessed lives to whom I ministered within its walls. I am not sad, when I dwell on those memories. I am happy and thankful for my associations with them, and I know that they have passed on to a better and more blessed state." Among the images evoked on that occasion were certainly those of Mary Ruffin Smith, Maria Louisa Spear, and Kemp Plummer Battle.[19]

There were additional occasions on which those names were spoken. Kemp Battle's enormous service to the community—including his steering of Mary Smith's estate to his church and his university—led to the naming of a new parish house in his and his wife's honor. The magnificent new church building, designed by architect Hobart Upjohn and occupied in 1925, was a gift of William Allen Erwin in memory of his grandfather, William Rainey Holt. Holt's second wife—and thus Erwin's step-grandmother—was Louisa Allen Hogan Holt, characterized as Mary Ruffin Smith's closest living relative in 1885. And Erwin, whose wife Sarah was the daughter of the Rev. Aldert Smedes, played a leading role with Bishop Cheshire in applying Mary's money to the 1897 purchase of St. Mary's School, founded by Erwin's father-in-law. The associations with Mary Ruffin Smith and the good work accomplished through her benevolence appear endless.[20]

Chapter 10

Cleaning Up, Warming Up, and Lighting Up the University

The tradition remained strong that Jones Grove in Chatham County might have become the site of the University of North Carolina in 1792 if the senior Tignal Jones had supplemented the one thousand acres offered jointly by his son Tignal Jr. and his neighbor Robert Cobb.[1] Regardless of the disappointment, the Jones-Smith family developed a close association with the new institution at New Hope Chapel Hill. Francis Jones for several years owned interest in the University's original Lot 9 on Franklin Street; Dr. James Smith served thirty-one years as a trustee of the institution; and both of the doctor's sons attended (but did not graduate from) the college. The relationship was cemented years later when President Kemp Battle became virtual guardian of the family's last surviving member, Mary Ruffin Smith.[2]

From its original 700 acres on Pokeberry Creek, in time the Jones Grove plantation grew to more than 1,700 acres and became a social center of the area, complete with a store and a popular horse race track.[3] Francis Jones, with the title "Captain" reflecting his Revolutionary War service and holding more than 3,000 additional acres in the Price Creek and Flowers plantations, thus became one of the area's largest landowners.

Mary Parke Jones died in 1811 and was buried in the yard at Jones Grove, thus beginning a cemetery that eventually would provide the final resting place for—with four notable exceptions—all of Francis and Mary Jones's next-generation descendants.[4] Very likely, slaves—Jones owned 20 at one time—were buried in unmarked graves nearby.

Jones's only daughter Delia in 1813 married James Strudwick Smith, the Orange County physician who later served as United States Congressman (1817–21), state legislator in 1821, and member of the 1835 state constitutional convention. The Smith couple established a home in the Orange County seat of Hillsborough, leaving widower Francis Jones and his bachelor son Ruffin with their slaves at Jones Grove in Chatham. Ruffin Jones died in 1836 and also was buried in the family graveyard. The following year the aging veteran of the Revolution moved in with the Smiths in Hillsborough; there he died in 1844, leaving all of his property to James Smith in trust for Delia, Smith's wife and the testator's daughter. The will required that upon the death of Delia, the three plantations were to become the property of her children: the Price Creek tract for Mary Ruffin Smith, the Jones Grove tract for Francis Jones Smith, and the Flowers Place for the younger son, James Sidney Smith.[5]

Dr. James Smith, too busy with his on-again-off-again medical practice, roller-coaster political career, and near-disastrous real estate schemes, paid little attention to the Chatham County lands except to collect rents. The Jones Grove mansion house, occupied by tenants, and the race track, no longer attracting elite neighbors, gradually deteriorated, and even the cemetery was neglected. Almost immediately after Francis Jones was buried at Jones Grove in 1844, Smith, with money from lands in which he only held a lifetime interest, began construction of a large three-story house—a mansion in the eyes of neighbors—on the Price Creek plantation six miles north of Jones Grove and three miles from Chapel Hill. The 700-acre core of the Price Creek farm had originally been granted by Lord Granville to Samuel Parke, who gave it to his son-in-law Francis Jones.[6]

Dr. James Smith died in 1852, Delia Jones Smith two years later. In accordance with Francis Jones's will, the three siblings assumed ownership of their respective tracts. Three years after his mother's death, Sidney Smith, an attorney and former state legislator, sold the Flowers Place to Jehail and Jahaza Atwater, brothers who between them owned 58 slaves.[7] Sidney died in 1867; his will, not mentioning his daughter Cornelia, left everything he owned to his sister. The older brother, Dr. Francis Jones Smith, held onto his Jones Grove tract but did little more than collect rents from its tenants and neighborhood renters. He died intestate in 1877. His three daughters (Emma, Annette, and Laura, who, like Cornelia, were born in slavery but gained their freedom in 1865) might have gone to court to claim a share of his estate. Instead, every dollar and every acre that Francis Smith owned passed to his sister, Mary Ruffin Smith, the last "legal" member of the Jones-Smith family.

Unmarried Mary Ruffin Smith, inheritor of all of the Jones-Smith property, died November 13, 1885, willing to the University of North Carolina the Jones Grove plantation from which the proceeds established a permanent Francis Jones Smith Fund, the earnings from which provided scholarships for indigent students. Thus the plantation, part of which nearly a century earlier was offered as the site of the University, finally came into ownership of that well-established public institution.[8]

The president of the University of North Carolina, Kemp Plummer Battle, had befriended spinster Mary Ruffin Smith and for many years was her most trusted advisor, drafting her will and acceding to her request that he serve as executor of the estate. Having been both intimately associated with the testatrix and in a position to clarify questions that arose in connection with the bequests, he felt himself "on the spot" because he played official roles in all of the charitable institutions directly benefitting from Mary Smith's generosity. As a leading lay leader in the Protestant Episcopal Diocese of North Carolina, he had both personal and official interests in the Price Creek legacy. In addition, his own University was the beneficiary of the Jones Grove property. It is no wonder, then, that he expressed concern that his dual roles might be viewed as conflicts of interest. Reassured by his attorney brother, he proceeded with his arduous task with confidence that he could objectively carry out Mary Smith's wishes.[9]

Although he promptly notified top officials of the Episcopal Diocese of North Carolina of their good fortune, Kemp Battle—with no foreknowledge of legal issues that would arise among his fellow churchmen—could wait until the annual convention of the diocese in May 1886 to submit full details and propose the orderly disposition of the Price Creek bequest. That land was already rented for the next year, and the executor could leave the day-to-day management to W.C. Cole, who had previously served as Mary Smith's farm manager. Until a decision was made by the diocese on the question of sale or continued ownership, rents from that land could simply be collected and transmitted to the treasurer of the diocese.[10]

More pressing was Battle's task of settling the bequest of the Jones Grove plantation to the university of which he was president. While Cole's farm adjoined the Price Creek property, Jones Grove was located six miles south in another county, less convenient for the caretaker's close supervision. Besides, the University was sorely in need of financial support, and the prompt sale of the real estate was difficult to resist. Despite its constitutional foundation, the oldest state university to open its doors had struggled from its beginning. Now, only ten years after its revival following closure during the debacle of Reconstruction, the institution found virtually no support from a miserly legislature of a poor state in which advocates of denominational colleges looked upon the Chapel Hill campus as a competitor for the hearts and minds of students.

Battle lost little time in carrying out Mary Smith's bequests to her five former servants and dividing those portions of her personal property willed to neither the Episcopal diocese nor the University.[11] Fortunately, those pleasant tasks were accomplished before a State Supreme Court decision forced the executor to divide the Price Creek income between two dioceses, immensely complicating the administration of that portion of the estate. Even so, Battle served three masters in the management and disposal of, and accounting for, the Price Creek and Jones Grove properties. For two decades, much of his time and many of his worries involved the sharing of Mary Ruffin Smith's benevolence with the institutions to which he was most closely attached—his church and his college.

At a highly anticipated meeting of the Board of Trustees of the University on December 2, 1885, Battle read Article 9 of the will of Mary Smith, to whom he paid tribute: "A more intelligent, wise, noble, pious and duty loving woman never existed.... Her modesty was as great as her worth." He added, "She is the first woman who has ever increased the endowment of the University and her donation is the largest ever made by one person." Many years later, Battle wrote, "Miss Smith was one of the best of her sex. Of modest, unassuming manners, of superior intellect, of wide information, especially on medical botany, of deep piety, of boundless charity in deed and word, she tenderly nursed with patience and skill the dying sickness of mother, father, two brothers, and a devoted friend, her girlhood's teacher, Miss Maria Spear, and died the last of her race."[12] The Jones Grove property, to be called the "Francis Jones Smith Bequest" as a means of avoiding the use of Mary's name, was estimated at 1,430 acres after the deduction of one hundred acres each bequeathed separately to three former slaves, the out-of-wedlock daughters of Dr. Francis Smith. Despite the need for immediate cash, Battle initially recommended that the University hold onto Jones Grove, selling off only some timber, because "a hundred years from now [the land] will be worth $100,000." If sold immediately, he thought the property would bring only $15,000 or $18,000. He, W.L. Steele, and J.W. Graham were charged with settling that question. One of the first tasks—to secure a preliminary survey of the Jones Grove lands—was given to Edmund W. Atwater of Chatham County. John Manning, a noted lawyer and trustee of the University, was appointed to help Battle "look after and take care of the interest of the University in said tract of land." The trustees also appointed Battle and Paul C. Cameron to prepare a tablet to be placed in the new Memorial Hall recognizing Mary Smith's "patriotic liberality." Battle said that he personally wrote nearly two hundred tablets, including those for the "four Marys," for placement in Memorial Hall.[13] When finished, the plaque read simply

MARY RUFFIN SMITH
BORN 1814 DIED 1885
FOUNDER OF THE FRANCIS JONES SMITH
FUND FOR THE UNIVERSITY

Before anything could be done with the Jones Grove property, three tracts of 100 acres each were required by Mary's will to be laid off for three of her nieces, Emma Morphis, Annette Kirby, and Laura Toole. Having grown up in a family dominated by men, and wary of reactions to her bequests of land to the daughters of her servant and former slave Harriet, Mary crafted her will deliberately, requiring strict adherence to its provisions. No doubt she remembered how, before his death in 1852, her father might have lost the family's fortune except for the care with which her grandfather Jones had framed *his* will. Consequently, her first instruction was for the tracts to be registered in the women's own names "for their respective lives free from the control or debts of their husbands and after their deaths to their children in fee." To emphasize the point, she added, "If either said Emma, Annette, or Laura shall make conveyance of their estates for life or give a lien on the same by mortgage or otherwise, their estates shall cease and their children respectively shall become immediately entitled to the land of their mothers." Then, as if suspecting that white men might choose unprofitable land for the female former slaves, Mary Smith instructed her executor to assure that each tract consist of "good land of the average of the whole tract with a proper proportion of wood and arable land." Finally, to guarantee adherence to her instructions, she instructed that three men be responsible for selecting the tracts—one chosen by the legatees, one by the University, and a third by the first two. The sisters chose M.S. Hackney of Chatham County, the trustees chose Edmund W. Atwater of Chatham, and those two selected G.W. Foushee.

W.C. Cole, a neighbor born in 1844, had for several years acted as general agent for Mary Smith; he justified the committee's choice of sites on grounds that the best land lay in the middle of the Jones Grove plantation, and to carve out portions of it for "the girls" would jeopardize the sale of the remainder. Consequently—except for thirty acres of Annette's tract—the entire 300 acres assigned to the trio lay on the west side of the Hillsborough-Fayetteville Road. Those tracts, Cole said, would "preserve good shape to the remainder with the public road as a natural boundary nearly the whole line." Whether that was for contiguity, convenience, or segregation, he did not say. It is worth noting, however, that the only remaining portions of the Smith property located west of the road were 18 acres of particularly valuable timber at the northwest corner and twelve acres of virtually worthless swamp near where the Pittsboro road crossed Pokeberry Creek, the latter area described as a "fertile source of malaria" that affected the country for miles around. Once the committee selected the general location of the tracts, each was surveyed by R. James Powell. Interestingly, the property of all three women contained substantial road frontage, usually considered a valuable asset. Annette's tract (the one that included thirty acres east of the Fayetteville Road) skirted around an unnamed public schoolhouse located west of the road.[14]

The carelessness with which earlier land transfers had sometimes been surveyed and registered was suggested in Cole's comment that ownership of one 300-acre Jones Grove tract was in dispute. But, he wrote, since the jury "decided that it was Miss Mary Smith's land," the commissioners should promptly sell the timber "and thereby remove all doubt as to the title."[15]

In June 1886 Battle reported that Powell had produced a plat for the remainder of Jones Grove property "showing not only metes and bounds, but the forests, cleared lands, streams and other features," and that he (Battle) and Walter L. Steele had ridden over the tract and talked with neighbors. The trustees having decided to sell the land, Battle suggested dividing the property (less the tracts already laid off for the three sisters) into five lots, reserving Tract 5, estimating the value of the remaining 1,430 acres (960 acres of which was in woodland) at from $10 to $15 per acre. The estimated annual rental income was $1,000 less $400 in expenses. Powell recommended selling the land in 200-acre lots, rather than renting, expressing the opinion that "the tenant system, and more particularly with white men, is a bad one, for good careful working men with few exceptions have their own land, and where they do not own their own homes, thriftlessness in most cases is the cause." Shortly afterward, the trustees recorded their concern over the financial problems of the University and the "disastrous failure in crops in the State," implying a need to sell the property.[16] Plans to offer lots for sale in the spring of 1889, owing to "the failure of crops for several years in the neighborhood of the land and consequent scarcity of money," were postponed.

Meanwhile, estimates of rental income proved far too high. For the years 1886 through 1888, Cole collected only $526.03 which, with expenses of $364.86, left just $161.17 for the University. In 1890 it was reported that "due to the failure of crops, the rents received have been almost nothing." Inexorably, pressure mounted for the sale of the land, and the trustees finally concluded that they could wait no longer.

Dissatisfied with the existing amateurish surveys and persuaded to divide the property into smaller tracts, Battle commissioned R.B. Clegg, Chatham County Surveyor, to prepare a more professional map, laying out 15 "lots" (exclusive of the 300 acres already granted to the nieces). Clegg was assisted by G.C. Cole and W.J. Riggsbee [sic] as chain bearers and H.R. Ellis as flag bearer.[17]

Cole described Clegg's survey on August 27, 1889: Except for Lots 14 and 15 west of the Fayetteville Road—a wooded 18-acre angle north of lands already surveyed off for the nieces, and the virtually worthless 12-acre swamp southward along Pokeberry Creek—the property was intersected by a line drawn eastward from "the fork of the roads at the Jones Grave Yard to a corner on Bush Creek intersecting with the east and west line between the Grove and Williams lands." Between that line northward to Fearrington Mill Road (then located between the present Fearrington House and Village Way), the first four lots were surveyed. At the eastern side of Lot 4, Cole wrote, "We then ran two north and south lines across the east side and subdivided," still attempting to limit acreage to about 100 each. After Lot 10, Cole described the problem: "Seeing that we could not preserve good form and give a proper proportion of wood and arable lands any further by strictly observing your general instructions of 100 acres as a basis owing to the situation of the remainder, we ran an east and west line beginning at Dr. Ward's corner, making No. 11 which has 115 acres in the southwest corner of the original tract."[18]

A large printed poster, dated September 16, 1889, and circulated over the names of the committee (Battle, Manning, and Merritt), exclaimed, "Jones' Grove Tract For Sale! Fifteen Tracts of Fine Tobacco, Cotton, Grain and Timber Lands For Sale On Easy Terms." The property was further described this way: "Jones' Grove is noted as one of the finest farms in the State. It is in Chatham County, half way between Chapel Hill and Pittsboro, on the main County road. Competent judges say it is admirably adapted to raising Bright Tobacco.

Jones' Grove Tract For Sale!

Fifteen Tracts of Fine Tobacco, Cotton, Grain and Timber Lands For Sale on Easy Terms.

The undersigned will, on WEDNESDAY, THE 13th DAY OF NOVEMBER NEXT, at 12 o'clock, on the premises, offer for sale to the highest bidder, fifteen tracts of very fine cotton, tobacco, grain and timber lands, being the Jones' Grove Plantation, devised to the University of North Carolina by the late Mary R. Smith. The tracts are particularly described as follows:

No. 1. On Chapel Hill road, 101 acres, with an old framed dwelling with three rooms and piazza, a tobacco barn, two cabins, cribs, stables, &c., with a well of good water; about 15 acres of fresh land and 40 in original growth of pine, oak, hickory, &c.

No. 2. On Fearington Mill road, 95 acres, with a framed building (two rooms), tobacco barns, stables, &c.; about one-fourth arable, remainder very fine forest.

No. 3. On same road, 99 acres, with a good log house (two rooms), kitchen, crib and stables; one-fourth arable, balance good woodland, with pine, oak, hickory, dogwood, &c.

No. 4. On same road, 101 acres, with a beautiful building site on a public road; about half arable, remainder forest.

No. 5. 105 acres of woods, heavily timbered and good farming land.

No. 6. Has 101 acres, all woods except two acres; valuable land.

No. 7. 98 acres, with a double cabin, crib and stables; 18 acres of fresh land, good spring, 80 acres of good forest.

No. 8. 103 acres; 8 of cleared land, balance forest.

No. 9. 107 acres, all forest; valuable for timber and good for wheat, &c.

No. 10. 107 acres of forest, rough but fertile; adapted to small grain.

No. 11. 115 acres in the southwest corner of the original tract, with 12 acres of fresh cleared land.

No. 12. 129 acres of very fine land, about half cleared, remainder well timbered, with a good building site on the Long Pond road.

No. 13. 139 acres on the Fayetteville road, with a framed building and kitchen attached, crib and stables, also a log dwelling with crib and stables.

No. 14. 18 acres, situate on the west side of Chapel Hill road; all woods, in the shape of the letter V.

No. 15. 12 acres of swamp land, lying on both sides of the Pittsboro road on Porkberry Creek; fertile soil but subject to overflow.

JONES' GROVE

is noted as one of the finest farms in the State. It is in Chatham County, half way between Chapel Hill and Pittsboro, on the main County road. Competent judges say it is admirably adapted to raising Bright Tobacco. The neighbors are among the best people in the State.

The tracts will be offered by the acre, according to the plots recently surveyed by Mr. Clegg, County Surveyor, at a moderate upset price, and no by-bidders over that price. The terms will be one-third cash, or the equivalent, the residue in two and three years, with eight per cent. interest from day of sale. All the cleared land is rented to good tenants for 1890, and all privileges will go to the purchaser.

Mr. Wm. C. Cole, agent for the University, whose post-office is Chapel Hill, will answer all enquiries and, will be on the land every Wednesday until the sale, for the purpose of showing it.

This is a rare opportunity for those desiring good homes and excellent lands.

Many think that the Seaboard Through Line to Atlanta will soon be straightened by connecting Graham and Sanford, or Graham and Monroe. If so, it will pass through this land.

KEMP P. BATTLE,
JOHN MANNING,
A. H. MERRITT,
Committee.

University of North Carolina,
Chapel Hill, N. C., Sept. 16, 1889.

Money was scarce among farmers toward the end of the nineteenth century, and this poster produced disappointing results. Sales continued for several years (courtesy North Carolina Collection, Wilson Library, UNC-CH).

The neighbors are among the best people in the State." The poster boasted, "This is a rare opportunity for those desiring good homes and excellent lands." Finally, with high hopes, was added, "Many think that the Seaboard Through Line to Atlanta will soon be straightened by connecting Graham and Sanford, or Graham and Monroe. If so, it will pass through this land."[19]

Although information on specific lots was minimal, a careful perusal of the poster's text reveals tantalizing descriptions of the plantation nearly a half century after Francis Jones left it. Lot 1, consisting of 101 acres running from the graveyard along the north/south highway to Fearrington Mill Road included "an old framed dwelling with three rooms and piazza, a tobacco barn, two cabins, cribs, stables, &c., with a well of good water; about 15 acres of fresh land and 40 in original growth of pine, oak, hickory, &c."[20] Lot 2, east of the first lot, consisted of 95 acres "with a framed building (two rooms), tobacco barns, stables, &c.; about one-fourth arable, remainder very fine forest." Lot 3 (99 acres) contained a "good log house (two rooms), kitchen, crib and stables; one-fourth arable, balance good woodland, with pine, oak, hickory, dogwood, &c." Lot 4 (101 acres), the easternmost lot fronting on Fearrington Mill Road, provided "a beautiful building site on a public road, about half arable, remainder forest." Buildings on Lot 7 (98 acres) were described as "a double cabin, crib and stables" with a good water spring. Lot 12 (129 acres) offered "a good building site on the Long Pond road."[21] Lot 13 on the Fayetteville Road contained "a framed building with kitchen attached, crib and stables, also a log dwelling with crib and stables." These surviving buildings attested to substantial tenancy on the Jones Grove lands during the nineteenth century.[22]

These minimal physical descriptions painted a sad picture of the neglect suffered by Delia Jones's ancestral homeplace after she left her father and brother in 1813 for life with James Strudwick Smith in historic Hillsborough (and later in rural Orange County). By the time of the sale three-quarters of a century later, there was nothing left of the Jones "mansion house" in which she was born and her children often visited, and there was no mention of genteel life, thoroughbred horses, race track, and bustling activity of a large plantation once worked by as many as twenty slaves. The site that might have become the location of the state university in 1792, which Francis Jones increased to nearly 4,000 acres, was reduced by the 1880s (after subtracting the Flowers Place and 300 acres for Francis Smith's daughters) to about 1,430 acres. That was the land that the new owner—that same university—was preparing to sell.

The public auction at Jones Grove in November 1889 created widespread public interest but brought disappointing results. Only six of the fifteen tracts were sold, and their prices were below expectations. Lot 1 (101 acres), earlier site of the Francis Jones mansion house, attracted most interest; the final bid was from J.B. Rigsbee for $1,136.25.[23]

Lots 2 (95 acres) and 3 (99 acres), east along Fearrington Mill Road, were purchased by E. M. Fearrington for $1,178 and $1,192.95, respectively.[24] Lot 6 (101 acres) went to James M. Williams for $625, and M.H. Hackney paid $835 for Lot 11 (115 acres).[25] G.W. Foushee acquired 18-acre V-shaped Lot 14, west of the highway, for only $180—the "best buy" of the entire sale. J.J. Hackney paid $114.75 for Lot 15, the 12-acre swamp on Pokeberry Creek, no doubt because it adjoined his home tract.

Sales at the first auction totaled $5,261.95 for 531 acres—about $10 per acre.[26] Putting on the best possible face, the commissioners were assured "by the best men of the neighborhood" that the sale was a good one in view of the nation's distressed farm economy.

Additional sales were slow in coming. By 1892, six years after taking ownership of the plantation, the executor sold only two additional lots, both at very low prices. James M. Williams paid $950 for the 101-acre Lot 4; and E.W. and B.J. Williams purchased Lot 8 (103 acres) for only $500[27] That left Lots 5, 7, 9, 10, 12, and 13, totaling 685 acres, from which the University received only $345.91 in rental income for three years beginning in 1890.[28] Eventual sales included Lot 7 (98 acres) first to Rufus Gardner, who allowed C.J. Bright of Wake County to take it for $625, and Lot 8 (101 acres) in August 1899, 61 acres to E.W. Williams, and the remaining 42 acres to B.J. Williams. Apparently R.J. and Zebulon Johnson were given credit for constructing buildings on Lot 12 (129 acres) when they purchased it in July 1899 for $1,000, for the deed refers to all "appurtenances thereto belonging to the said R.J. Johnson and Zebulon Johnson." Lot 13 (139 acres) was sold in April 1900 to R.L Ward for $850.[29]

Rent on unsold tracts was never impressive, and John Manning's accounts in January 1893 showed income from that source for four years (1886 through 1889) totaled only $1,408.71 minus $488.38 in expenses. For the next three years, the Jones Grove acreage still held by the University produced $345.91 minus $261.91 expenses. Sale prices by that time had reached $7,712.20, but cash receipts amounted to only $3,643.21.[30]

Finally, in March 1904, W. Roscoe Bonsal, a railroad official from Richmond County, offered $2,500 to purchase Lots 5, 9, 10, and 11 (105, 107, 107, and 105 acres, respectively). At least one of these lots had been sold by the University to another buyer who failed to complete the purchase, but within a month Bonsal resold them, along with other property, to Chatham Lumber Company, which in 1919 sold them, together with other property, to J.R. Mason[31]

Purchasers were required to furnish in cash only one-third of the purchase price, and additional payments, including interest up to 8%, were often in arrears from some of the most prominent farmers of Chatham and Orange counties. Of course, the land was mortgaged until the debt was satisfied, and years passed before all collections were made. Because income from rents and sales was invested in a variety of securities, no exact accounting of the Jones Grove bequest has been found. Land sales alone, however, eventually amounted to more than $10,000, and investments were made in state and county bonds, North Carolina Railroad shares, and stock in Raleigh Cotton Mills. As a result, the principal of the Francis Jones Smith Fund grew over the years; by 1902 it amounted to $12,434.95; and by 1904, $14,000.[32]

To their credit, Kemp Battle's successors generally followed his insistence that Mary Ruffin Smith's directives be carried out to the letter. Temptations came close to diverting the fund to other purposes, but upon Battle's retirement from the presidency to a professorship in 1891, the trustees again read out loud Mary Smith's will and recorded in the minutes that they were "unanimously of the opinion that only the interest on the Francis Jones Smith Fund can be used for the educating of students."[33] In other words, the principal from the estate constituted a *permanent* fund, and only its interest was available for expenditure— and that only for Francis Jones Smith Scholarships. The funds, however, did not lie fallow, and in novel ways of lending monies to other university enterprises at competitive interest rates, officials were able to make the Francis Jones Smith Fund serve multiple purposes.

Kemp Battle and his successors spent more than a decade in handling the Jones Grove lands, at the same time seeking buyers for the lots cut out of the Price Creek plantation only six miles northward. Potential purchasers were given the rare opportunity of shopping for more than 3,000 acres in two of the best plantations in the area. Unfortunately for the Episcopalians and the University, the competition occurred during a decade of economic distress leading to a farmer's revolution nationally—the Populist Revolution—that altered political realities in North Carolina and the nation. It is not too much an exaggeration to relate the disposition of Mary Ruffin Smith's eleemosynary contributions to a counter-movement that resulted in the disfranchisement of blacks and the emergence of the white supremacy movement at the turn of the century.

As president of the University, Kemp Battle escaped the onerous university bookkeeping, delegating to Manning, Cole, and others the task of collecting and accounting for tardy rents and installment payments on the Jones Grove lands; even so, as long as he held the presidency, Battle bore the brunt of the task, including competition between the two Episcopal dioceses and the distressingly slow sales of the Jones-Smith lands. Records were kept entirely in handwriting until after the turn of the century, although in 1888 the Remington Typewriter Company offered on a ten-day trial basis a new machine called a "typewriter."[34]

Even after he stepped down from the presidency in 1891, Battle was constantly on call, for as the new chairman of the history department, he remained the spiritual link between Mary Ruffin Smith's legacy, the University of North Carolina, and competing Episcopalians. William L. Saunders, the crippled Secretary of State and editor of *The Colonial Records of North Carolina*, served also as secretary of the UNC Board of Trustees, receiving the accounts until his death in 1891; he was succeeded by Richard H. Battle, younger brother of the executor. The minutes of the Board of Trustees on January 31, 1892, simply read, "K.P. Battle resigned as member of the committee to sell the lands devised by the late Mary R. Smith and President [George T.] Winston was elected in his stead." Not having been close to the late Mary Smith, Winston left the task to his assistants.

A few months later the trustees followed Battle's instructions in directing that "the remains of Dr. James Smith, the father of Miss Mary R. Smith, be removed to the family burying ground at a cost to the University of five dollars."[35] In fact, three bodies—those of Dr. Smith, his wife Delia, and their youngest son Sidney—were moved to the Francis Jones graveyard at Jones Grove, and Kemp Battle could be satisfied that he had kept his promise. Already Dr. Smith's portrait—painted by an unknown artist at the end of his congressional service in 1821—was hanging in the Dialectic Literary Hall.[36] A tablet, costing $125 and memorializing Dr. Smith, joined one for his daughter Mary on a wall in Memorial Hall; it reads:

JAMES S. SMITH, M.D.
BORN 1787 DIED 1852
A TRUSTEE THIRTY-ONE YEARS
MEMBER OF HOUSE OF COMMONS
REPRESENTATIVE IN CONGRESS 1817–1821
MEMBER OF THE STATE CONVENTION
1835

It is not clear just when and to whom the inaugural Francis Jones Smith Scholarship was given. The fund was announced in the 1885–86 catalogue: "Miss Mary Ruffin Smith, of Orange, has left a valuable tract of fourteen hundred and forty acres of land in Chatham County known as the Jones Grove Tract, the income of which, or the proceeds if sold, shall be used for the education of such students as the Faculty may designate. Part of this income will be available during the ensuing session." Only two other funds to assist students then existed—the F.B. Moore Fund of $5,000, interest from which provided tuition scholarships; and the Dr. C.F. Deems Fund (supplemented by William H. Vanderbilt) of $12,800, which provided only loans.

To emphasize the modesty of the benefactor, Kemp Battle added a sentence: "The above name [Francis Jones Smith] is given to the fund at the request of the testatrix." Future observers would regret the benefactor's decision to prevent the use of her own name, for by interesting coincidences, the name "Mary" was associated with the next three specifically designated university scholarship funds: Mary Ann Smith Scholarships (1891, $37,000); Mary Shephard [*sic*] Speight Scholarships (1892, $10,000); and the Mary Sprunt Wood Scholarship (1892, a single scholarship of $75 memorializing Thomas Fanning Wood). The coincidental bequests of all the "Marys" would have been more noteworthy if Mary Ruffin Smith's extreme modesty had not prevented the use of her name for the first scholarships, provided through her generosity. At the centennial alumni banquet in 1889, a toast was drunk to the "four Marys," each of whom left handsome legacies to the University, setting an example for men to follow. Battle later wrote, "The successive swarms of young men benefited [*sic*] by them will keep their memories in perennial freshness."[37]

Interestingly, Mary Smith's request that her name not be associated with the scholarships was forgotten—or deliberately ignored—by some later catalog-writers. For example, in the *Abridged Catalog, Announcement of Courses for 1919–1920*, page 50, is this entry: "The Mary Ruffin Smith Scholarships. (Established in 1885.) Miss Mary Ruffin Smith bequeathed to the University, in memory of her brother, Dr. Francis Jones Smith, a valuable tract of land in Chatham County, of 1460 acres, known as Jones Grove. The will provides that rents on the land, or the interest on the purchase price if sold, shall be used to pay the tuition of such poor students as the faculty may appoint." Those were almost the exact words used in the catalog in 1885–86. The scholarships continued to be called "Mary Ruffin Smith Scholarships" until the 1952–53 catalog renamed them for her brother. By 1959–60, individually named scholarships were no longer listed in the annual catalogs.

When the Francis Jones Smith Scholarships were established, tuition was $60; room rent in one of the 92 "dormitories" (that is, sleeping rooms located in South Building, Old East, Old West, New East, and New West) was $10 per year; and board could be found in private homes at from $8 to $13 per month. Thus annual expenses hardly exceeded $300.[38]

Records of the trustees show that as early as the 1892–93 school year $400 was spent on Francis Jones Smith Scholarships, sufficient to cover tuition for six or seven students. In 1895, the allocation was increased to $450. Two years later the allocation for stipends was 10 students at $60 each. During the next dozen years, the amount allocated ranged from a high of $1,340 in 1903 to a low of $420 in 1909; the average was about $700. For the year 1904, the scholarships carried free tuition in addition to the stipend, but the minutes do not indicate if free tuition generally accompanied a Smith scholarship, thus increasing its dollar value.

Through safe loans to other departments of the University and with good management, the principal of the Francis Jones Smith Fund reached $14,000, and after World War II, it rose to $15,000.[39] At 6% the annual interest of the latter amount would have amounted to $900; so by granting roughly that much for scholarships annually, the University faithfully carried out Mary Ruffin Smith's desire to assist in the education of poor students. Of course, as charges increased and the dollar fell in value, the Smith Scholarships paid smaller and smaller percentages of recipients' total costs.

In addition to aiding indigent students, Mary Smith's money helped accomplish missions that neither she, in writing her will, nor perhaps Kemp Battle, in witnessing it, could have anticipated: The Francis Jones Smith Fund became a significant partner in the modernization of the university campus and, in doing so, contributed substantially to the health and comfort of students and faculty of the university as well as the citizens of the town of Chapel Hill. Remarkably, it did so—with perhaps one exception—without violating either the principal of the fund or the purpose for which it was given. In reality, the Francis Jones Smith Fund helped clean up, wash up, heat up, and light up a campus that, under slightly different circumstances a century earlier, might have been located at Jones Grove.

When Mary Ruffin Smith died in 1885, the living conditions on the campus of the University were little different from those in the humble homes from which most students came. Electricity, running water, and heating and cooling systems were generally known only in a few cities, and only the wealthy could afford them. Dormitory rooms on the campus were still heated by wood-burning fireplaces or stoves, and lighting came from open fireplaces, whale oil or kerosene lamps, or tallow candles. Bathing was done from small wash-pans holding a couple of inches of water brought in buckets from a well or spring. Neither inside the buildings nor conveniently located outside were there adequate sanitary facilities. No wonder, then, that in 1886 the University's Board of Trustees appointed a committee to report on conditions confronted daily by students and faculty. After meeting with the head of the State Board of Health, the committee—composed of Paul C. Cameron, Eugene Grissom, Sr., and John Manning—began its report on a pessimistic note: "The progress of civilization has in some items been slow and simple and many matters remain at the University as they did 80 or 85 years ago—especially in the waste from the human body."[40]

That view was strengthened by the observation of others. Robert W. Winston is quoted as describing unsanitary conditions during his student days at the University in the 1870s, when there were no toilets or privies of any sort: "On the extreme south side of the campus was a rock wall that ran east and west with no entrance, but a stile, which we got over. Every morning after breakfast from 150 to 200 boys would start out with newspapers and corncobs and go over the stile and squat in the woods among the trees and bugs, especially among the tumble bugs."[41]

President Battle fully understood the changing times: "The habits of the students were much influenced by the condition of old times, when the forest stretched for miles from the buildings toward the South. The question of how to introduce the decencies of life was often discussed and proved to be insoluble until the General Assembly gave funds for the construction of water works. At one time water closets of planks, having every appearance of being of a temporary nature, were constructed near the old dormitories, Old East, Old West, and South, but it was not long before they were burned as a public nuisance."[42]

Students themselves complained of squalid conditions but sometimes, throwing caution to the wind, became their own worst enemies. One, Eugene Grissom, Jr., was so nauseated that in 1886 he complained that the health of those living in South Building was being threatened, pleading that "underneath the building should be cleansed—as it has been used a good deal this Winter by the students as a privy."[43]

Cameron's trustee committee further graphically described conditions of the dormitory rooms earlier in the nineteenth century: "[A] pint tin cup tied by a string and hung on a nail just out of the windows was the urinal of all the inmates of the college buildings alike of students, tutors, and professors. This supply of tin cups round the outside walls attracted the attention of the visiting and innocent young ladies who were desirous to know how and for what they were used[; and] besides the unpleasant consequences of those who occupied the rooms, led to the removal of the tin cup as a urinal."

If the report had not been dealing with a deadly serious subject, the additional text might today be read as a parody: "Subsequently and for the last 40 or 50 years a cheap wooden bucket made of soft and porous wood has been substituted for the tin cup. It was a bad exchange. The tin cup was on the outside and often emptied, the bucket is kept inside and used for all purposes and often retained until full, thus corrupting the air of the room and of the entire building, a positive nuisance and no longer to be tolerated."

This condemnation of prevailing unhygienic conditions in 1888 forced the committee to propose a substitute source of relief, one that admitted the intransigence of managing human waste until water could be supplied for sanitary facilities. By the adoption of a solemn resolution, the committee's stop-gap, lesser-of-two-evils solution was to order that henceforth in each room in the college buildings "there shall be kept and owned by the students a chamber pot of *white* [*sic*] stone china of the hardest material, that these urinals shall be emptied at least once in 24 hours by the college servant and removed in iron or tin tubs to the various and remote parts of the campus to induce the growth of grass." The faculty was to inspect all rooms "to insure this ordinance and obtain the highest standard of neatness, cleanliness and purity."[44]

Four years after the adoption of white china chamber pots, President Battle, concluding that the prevailing "system of disposal" was equally hazardous to the health of students and faculty, urged the Board of Trustees to appeal to the General Assembly for an appropriation of $5,000 for the development of a sewerage system. Little action was taken. Two years passed, and again the trustees were told, "The time has come when the University must be supplied with water and with the conveniences that come with a water supply." Various attempts to solve the problem failed; for example, terraces around Old East and Old West were removed, but the results only slightly improved the sanitary condition of those buildings by diminishing dampness on the ground floors.[45] Alarmingly, by that time unsanitary conditions were no longer limited to the campus; three students had died at Robertson's Hotel due to impure water. Since many students boarded off campus, efforts from that time incorporated extension of safe drinking water to the village of Chapel Hill. Professor Francis P. Venable was made sanitation officer to inspect boarding houses. His reports further documented unhygienic conditions threatening human health. Within the year at a cost of $1,500 a well was dug, from which water was forced by steam pumps into large iron storage tanks in the attic of South Building. Funds, however, were not available for the needed apparatus—water closets, shower baths, urinals, wash stands, and slop sinks—that would cost an additional $3,000. Thus the absence of funds for essential installations remained a threat to health on campus and in the village.[46] In 1893, it was estimated that the cost of an adequate water supply would exceed $12,000, and urinals throughout dormitories would require an additional $3,000.

The problem was astronomical: The number of students increased from 198 in 1891 to 316 in 1893 and 462 in 1895. At the same time, the physical dimensions of a 48-acre campus extended to seven brick buildings with tin roofs; one brick building with shingle roof; Memorial Hall with slate roof; a framed building for dissecting corpses; a rented frame building for gymnastic training; five laboratories for practical science; four "museums" for work and illustration in geology, mineralogy, chemistry, biology, and history; twelve recitation and lecture rooms for instruction in fifteen departments; ninety-nine dormitory rooms; a library; a chapel; a YMCA; and two society halls containing over sixty portraits. These physical holdings were worth $500,000, nearly all given by philanthropists. There were also 500 acres of adjoining forest lands. A rare $10,000 appropriation from the General Assembly of 1893 attended to only the most serious needs for repairs to the buildings, with emphasis upon improving indoor health conditions.[47]

The Francis Jones Smith Fund to the rescue! By lending some of the funds to another university function at the going interest rate, the principal could remain inviolate and the interest could pay for scholarships. Mary Ruffin Smith may have had that eventuality in mind when her second codicil specified that "if from any cause such tuition cannot be paid, then I desire such profits or interests to be used exclusively for the maintenance and equipment of the University, not to be liable to any of its debts." (It is difficult for one to take seriously Battle's denial of having suggested that codicil; surely, he was pleased with it.)

For the first time, $1,000 was loaned, and in 1894 President George T. Winston's report boasted that the installation of water supply, showers, urinals, closets, and sewerage had "added greatly to the comfort, decency and healthfulness of the inhabitants."[48] Those facilities, however, were limited to Smith Hall (today's Playmaker's Theater), then serving as the library. Archibald Henderson described the basement of Smith Hall: "The entrance to these conveniences was in the south wall of the building, at the southwest corner; and one descended by a few stone steps to a corridor running the length of the building (east and west), which was divided by a board partition down the center. South of the partition was a series of individual toilets; and to its north were a long slate trough for communal use, half a dozen showers, and several bath tubs." Sewerage ran through a pipe into Chapel Branch, a stream south of the campus. A small cottage was provided as an infirmary. The improvements led to a boast in a report to the trustees: "There has been remarkable healthiness among students and Faculty."[49]

Despite these improvements, water shortages persisted. The need was recognized in the *University Record* for 1896: "For a number of years efforts have been made to get water from wells. But this will not do and the water must be brought from neighboring streams in sufficient quantity to assure the needs of all of our students, from both a sanitary and hygienic point of view. This is an absolute necessity." The appeal continued the following year for "an adequate water supply for health and protection from fire."[50]

Each improvement was inadequate due to the increase in the size of the student body (to 542 in 1897), overly generous use of water, and needs of the newly built electric plant—the latter also assisted by the Smith Fund. In 1899 the trustees made another urgent appeal to the General Assembly for an appropriation for construction of a larger water supply. When the legislature provided only $7,500, President Alderman in 1899 persuaded the trustees to borrow additional amounts from the Smith Fund. Not until 1902 could it be said that "the waterworks furnish an abundance and excellent supply and the sewerage system has been completed."[51] Although the capacity of the waterworks was increased substantially from time to time, demand still outran supply for additional decades—a problem that remained unsolved through much of the twentieth century. Mary Ruffin Smith's money had helped clean up the University at a time when the need was urgent for both comfort and health, and other funds were unavailable.

A second desperately needed utility accessed the Francis Jones Smith Fund for electric power and lighting. In 1895 a visiting committee of the trustees took note of the darkness of rooms and hallways, reporting the near-fatal fall of a student from the third floor of South Building. The committee even found fault with the lighting medium—kerosene: "At present the only light available for this, as well as for the purpose of study, is that derived from oil lamps. Oil lamps are not without danger to students and buildings and are, moreover, if not of good patterns and supplied with first-class oil, as is not by any means the case, to be condemned as light producers.... The day of electricity is here. The broad highway of progress is illuminated by brilliant electric lights and we must march thereon abreast of the foremost. We cannot afford to stumble along dim lanes and by-ways and be left floundering in the rear...."[52] After that condemnation of darkness, the executive committee of the Board of Trustees voted to pay the cost of an electric plant from the Francis Jones Smith Fund and stock in the North Carolina Railroad. Professor J.W. Gore was placed in charge of the plan for extending power to private homes in Chapel Hill, the income to be used to help repay the loans from the endowment fund. An additional $8,000 was borrowed from the Smith Fund, and the Electric Plant, located between Columbia Street and the present Carroll Hall, began operation October 1, 1895, capable of illuminating 800 lights and giving "satisfaction"—more likely, delight—to students and villagers alike. From fuel delivered by the University Railroad, the plant in the first nine months used 6 tons of coal at $4.60, 48 cords of wood at $1.50, 2 barrels of lubricating oil at $29.50, and only $22.50 in salary. The net income was $51.67. Monthly charges to villagers were 75 cents for a single light; $1 for a light on all night; those with 5 lights 62½ cents each and 10 lights 50 cents each—all plus a meter charge of 10 cents for each "Kilo Watt." The purchase price for meters was $15 each. The following June the trustees were told that in five months, electricity had cost the University $75, the students $50.86, and the villagers $56.25—in all, $182.11. Expenses were only $128.70, so the plant had turned a profit of more than $50. The greatest benefit, however, came from the enhanced lighting that brightened the dormitories and classrooms on campus and private homes and businesses in the village. The December 1896 issue of *University Report* happily reported, "The village, grounds, buildings, halls are lighted by electricity generated by the power plant owned by the University. The village is fresher and tidier than in the old days and the walks and campus more sightly." Mary Smith, who never enjoyed such artificial illumination, would have been delighted.

Although his role in bringing electricity to the campus was certainly exaggerated, one of the University's most generous future benefactors claimed major credit. In his biographical sketch in the 1924 edition of the *Alumni History of the University of North Carolina*, William Rand Kenan, Jr., unabashedly proclaimed himself "builder and operator elec. plant and instr. U.N.C. 1895." He justified the claim nearly a half-century later in a letter to newspaper editor Louis Graves, who grew up near the site of the original New Hope Chapel. Although his field was chemistry (he was one of the discoverers of calcium carbide), Kenan wrote,

> It was my good fortune to be associated with this undertaking during the summer and fall of 1895. The power house was composed of five tube boilers of 125 lbs. pressure.... The electric

apparatus was composed of two General Electric multi-polar direct-current machines with a voltage of 110 to 120 volts each.... All the wiring in the building was exposed, that is, held in place by porcelain knobs fastened by means of screws. Where the wires went through a partition or wall porcelain tubes were used as insulators. I remember distinctly standing on a stepladder and driving a screw-driver in the ceiling of the dormitories until my back was broken literally.

Kenan added, "There was, in addition to the above, a storage battery set. This was charged during the early evening and as the plant shut down at midnight, the storage batteries carried the lighting load during the balance of the night. The results were entirely satisfactory and were modern and up-to-date at that time." The future financier and benefactor apparently was unaware that Mary Smith's money was paying his student wage, and he might have been astounded that in 1977 the University's power facilities would be sold to Duke Power Company for $15 million.[53]

Louis Round Wilson, a graduate of the University in 1899 who returned as its librarian two years later, testified about the enhancements that electricity brought to the campus: "No money spent by the University has contributed more to the comfort and efficiency of the faculty and students than the amounts utilized in dispersing the stygian blackness of the hallways of the University buildings and in eliminating the open fireplaces and inefficient stoves, before and around which students and faculty had shivered for more than a full century."[54]

Loans from the Francis Jones Smith Fund not only lit up the campus; they also earned interest for the fund established by Mary Ruffin Smith, who at her home outside Chapel Hill had read and knitted in the dim light from oil lamps. Her money not only was earning interest that provided scholarships to poor students; it was also making a profit while lighting up an entire community. The trustees were told in lyrical terms about the brightening of the University, which presumably increased learning and morality: "The broad avenues of the campus are made brilliant by the rays of the arc lamp... If men love darkness more than light because their deeds are evil, then the more light we have the less evil we may expect." And one trustee suggested that if there had been electric lights in Rome in 44 B.C., the fatal meeting at the house of Brutus at the "dead hour of midnight" might never have been assembled.[55]

The extension of electricity to homes and businesses in Chapel Hill necessitated the collection of monthly power bills. The trustees were told in 1895 that the Smith Fund was entitled to "the whole income to be derived from the plant and its extension." However, at least one trustee must have expressed some concern for the continual lending of the endowment fund principal, because the minutes recorded the opinion that "the loan from the Francis Jones Smith Fund for the purpose of erecting the Electric Plant should not be a precedent for the loan of other endowment funds to the University."

Among academicians, few opinions are unanimous. It may not be surprising, therefore, that not all trustees agreed that, while the heating of buildings by firewood was antiquated, expensive, inconvenient, and inadequate, it was also unhealthy. A committee in 1900 expressed the opinion that from a hygienic point of view, heating and ventilating dormitory rooms by open fireplaces had never been surpassed. A large room, with sufficient air for its inhabitants and adequate ventilation via chimney draft, featuring "Spartan simplicity," was preferable to one heated by steam (dampness), furnished with carpets ("those great germ collectors"), and hung with heavy window curtains (keeping out fresh air and sunlight). The new president, Francis P. Venable, however, was unmoved, and he recommended that additional endowment funds be borrowed for the building of an adequate heating plant. The trustees sided with the president, and an additional $2,600 was borrowed from the Francis Jones Smith Fund and various amounts from other endowment funds. *The Record* in 1902 boasted, "The central heating system has been in operation since the early fall, and has given general satisfaction. The halls and lecture rooms were never before properly heated. It is, besides, an added safeguard against fire." Soon the plant was heating fourteen buildings on campus, and Mary Ruffin Smith's money continued to serve multiple purposes.[56]

Two more functions of the University of North Carolina benefitted from the Francis Jones Smith Fund, and evidence has not been found of repayment of one of those expenditures. The wiring for the Carr Building, dedicated in 1900, was paid for from electric plant income. Then, in 1904, when railroad magnate W. Roscoe Bonsal bought the remaining Jones Grove lots (numbers 5, 9, 10, and 11) for $2,500, the trustees resolved "that on receipt of said $2,500, the sum of $1,500 be appropriated for the Summer School to be held in June next."[57] As a result of the latter action, 238 students from many North Carolina counties, four states, and Germany attended a four-week tuition-free summer session in 1904. The only charges for the entire term were $5 for use of the library, gymnasium, and laboratories; $2 for a dormitory room (proudly noted as being furnished "with electric light and baths"); and $8 for table board at the recently remodeled Commons Hall. A further incentive was reduced rates on railroads (the 10-mile University Railroad had begun operation in 1879). Students chose from 42 courses categorized in three areas: common school subjects and methods; psychology and pedagogy; and high school and college subjects. The catalog opined that "a glance through the courses here offered will convince the progressive teachers of North Carolina that it is the part neither of wisdom nor economy for them to leave the State in order to secure the best instruction in both text-books and methods." Among the visiting lecturers were prominent men—no women—such as Charles B. Aycock, Charles D. McIver, William L. Poteat, Josephus Daniels, Josiah W. Bailey, and—of course—"old Pres," Kemp P. Battle, who probably somehow worked into his lectures the names of Mary Ruffin Smith and the other "Marys."[58]

When the principal of the Smith scholarship fund was loaned for these and additional purposes, few except officers directly involved in the implementation understood the significance of what was then a novel approach. The experiment, soon extended to additional funds and operations of the University, validated the wisdom of Mary Ruffin Smith's codicil authorizing the use of the fund's principal for investment in "the maintenance and equipment of the University, not to be liable for any of its debts." Her money, then, performed multiple duty—by lending funds to meet pressing institutional needs and by earning interest to perpetuate scholarships in the name of Francis Jones Smith. As practical business persons, Kemp Battle and Mary Ruffin Smith were two of a kind.

During those turn-of-the-century years when Smith monies were being used to clean up, warm up, and light up the university campus and village of Chapel Hill, few could have predicted the day when those services would be performed by private enterprise. It is not too much of a stretch, therefore, to envision a role of Mary Smith's money in decisions made three-quarters of a century later when the University sold its utilities to profit-making enterprises. The old plant of the Chapel Hill Telephone Company was acquired in 1925, but in

1977 it, along with water, sewer, and power services, was sold for cash. Southern Bell paid $25 million for the telephone franchise, Duke Power Company $15 million for the electrical facilities, and the Orange Water and Sewer Authority $1.5 million for the water and sanitation services. From the income, the General Assembly reserved for its own use $10 million, and Nelson Ferebee Taylor, chancellor from 1972 to 1980, succeeded—against fierce opposition from other campus constituencies—in applying the remaining $31.5 million to the construction of a new central library, the renovation of Louis Round Wilson Library, and improvements in other campus libraries. Appropriately, the papers found at Oakland following Mary Smith's death are now preserved in the venerated Wilson Library. The pity is that more had not been saved—including some of Mary's own writings—to provide a more comprehensive biography of the remarkable woman who willed her earthly wealth to her church and state. As if she planned it, neither photographic likeness nor physical description of her has yet been positively identified. But hope remains.

Chapter 11

End of the Trail

One hundred years after the fathers respectively of Francis Jones and Mary Parke bestowed upon them each 700 acres of prime land and the industrious Revolutionary War veteran began amassing one of the largest acreages in Orange and Chatham counties, not a single "white" member of the Jones-Smith family was alive.

Francis, Mary, and Ruffin Jones were dead before midcentury, and James and Delia Jones Smith died shortly afterward. Of the younger Smiths, Sidney was the first to go, a victim of his loose living and alcoholism. Frank succumbed to his own debauchery and guilt. Mary put them all in their grave and used much of their money as loans, helping neighboring farmers through the agricultural crises of the 1870s and 1880s.

True, four daughters of maid Harriet, fathered by the Jones's grandsons Francis and Sidney Smith, were alive, each having been given a hundred acres from the last surviving child of James Strudwick and Delia Jones Smith. So, too, went 25 acres to Harriet's son Julius, fathered by a freedman.

Upon the death in 1881 of Maria Louisa Spear, lone survivor Mary Ruffin Smith turned to her trusted advisor, University President Kemp Plummer Battle, who, with the assistance of neighbor William C. Cole, guided her affairs both during and after her lifetime. Mary Smith and Kemp Battle, a pair of hearts that beat as one when determining the disposition of what in the last quarter of the nineteenth century in central North Carolina was a substantial fortune. It was all to go to church and state.

The dollar figures quoted in the settlement with the chief beneficiaries of Mary Ruffin Smith's will—the North Carolina and East Carolina Episcopal dioceses, the University of North Carolina, the Chapel of the Cross, and St. Mary's School—may appear modest in terms of a twenty-first century economy, but their relative value needs to be interpreted in current economic realities. For example, internal improvements—electricity, heat, water, sewage disposal—accomplished with the aid of the Francis Jones Smith endowment at the University would, in twenty-first-century dollars, dwarf the figures spent on those advancements in the 1890s. Even the scholarship stipends would appear much more impressive in today's dollars.

Except for the Jones Grove cemetery, which holds the body of every "legitimate" member of the Jones-Smith family (plus that of Maria Spear), few landmarks survive as reminders of the three great plantations once owned by Francis Jones and inherited by the Smiths. Even before the Civil War, young Sidney Smith sold his Flowers Place, which reached from the Jones Grove tract to New Hope Creek.

After the death of Mary Ruffin Smith, the Price Creek plantation was divided and sold in parcels for the benefit of the Episcopal dioceses, but fortunately the home occupied by the Smiths in 1847 was preserved and, recently restored, continues to serve as a landmark along Smith Level Road.

The Jones Grove property was also divided and sold by the University. Tract No. 1, which ran along the east side of the Hillsborough-Fayetteville Road, was purchased by J.B. Riggsbee, who later divided it between his two daughters. The northern half is now occupied by the Fearrington House, and the southern half—the original location of the Jones home—is now the site of Galloway Ridge Retirement Community. Much of the remainder of the Jones Grove lands was eventually incorporated into Fearrington Village.

By the end of the Great Depression, the three hundred acres bequeathed to Emma Morphis, Annette Kirby, and Laura Tool had passed into the hands of local white families. The sole surviving remembrance of the trio in the Jones Grove community is Emma Morphis's grave, scarcely identifiable across the busy highway from the burial site of her father. Farther up the road, Cornelia's tract on the northern edge of the Price Creek plantation remained in her family's hands only until shortly after her death.

Sic transit gloria.

Opposite: **The memory wing of The Arbor, Galloway Ridge Retirement Community's health center, now occupies the site of Francis Jones's manor house. The Jones Grove cemetery lies in the woods at left (H.G. Jones collection). The five-star Fearrington House and surrounding complex now occupy the northern half of Lot 1, originally sold by the University to J.B. Riggsbee (H.G. Jones collection).**

Chapter Notes

Chapter 1

1. With the Revolution, of course, the victorious government seized the remaining Granville land, and henceforth some grants were made in the name of the State of North Carolina.

2. Granville Grant No. 2070, North Carolina State Archives; Chatham County Deed Book C, p. 422. Hereinafter, reference to Chatham County deed books will be cited as county (CC) plus the letter or number of the deed book, followed by a slant and page number (in this case CC C/422.)

3. John L. Cheney Jr. (ed.), *North Carolina Government 1585–1979: A Narrative and Statistical History* (Raleigh: Secretary of State, 1981), pp. 154, 156–7, 159, 202, 215, 236. Jones's given name was spelled variously in records—Tignal, Tignall, Tingall, Tyngal, etc.

4. CC C/422; CC S/12.

5. *Statutes at Large of the United States of America, 1789–1873,* p. 529.

6. Pension application based on service of Francis Jones, No. S8768, National Archives, Washington, D.C. Delia Jones married James Smith on October 18, 1813, with her brother Ruffin Jones as bondsman. Chatham County Marriage Bonds, State Archives.

7. For Dr. Smith's financial woes, see Chapter 2.

8. Official records reveal the involvement of General John Butler of Orange County, Colonel Archibald Lytle of Orange County, and Colonel Holt Richardson of Virginia in battles in North and South Carolina. David Southern points out that General Butler lived at Mount Repose on Haw River and would have been known to Dr. Smith, who prepared the application for his father-in-law's pension.

9. www.carolana.com/sc/revolution_battle_of_hobkirks_hill.html; Pauli Murray, *Proud Shoes: The Story of an American Family* (Boston: Beacon Press, 1999), p. 34.

10. Kemp P. Battle, *History of the University of North Carolina* (Raleigh: Edwards & Broughton, 1907, 1912; reprint, Spartanburg: The Reprint Company, 1974; 2 vols.), 1: 22–3. For the story of the bequest of Jones Grove to the University of North Carolina nearly a century later, see Chapter 10.

11. CC C/422, S/12. The tract was originally a grant from Lord Granville to Parker in 1763. See Granville Grant No. 2070, North Carolina State Archives. It should be noted that frequently farmers did not bother to have their deeds promptly recorded in the county register's office; for example, the 1803 gift from Francis's father was not recorded until 1811, eight years after it was written.

12. Original deed dated May 6, 1789, signed "Saml Parke" and witnessed by Gideon Goodwin and Mark Morgan, in Mary Ruffin Smith Papers, Folder 9, Southern Historical Collection, University of North Carolina at Chapel Hill (hereinafter cited as Mary Ruffin Smith Papers, SHC); Orange County Deed Book 4, page 450, Office of Register of Deeds, Hillsborough, North Carolina. Parke had received this land as a grant from Lord Granville, August 2, 1760; he sold it to William Merritt, who defaulted, and at a sheriff's sale May 6, 1787, Parke bid it in for £169 current money; that deed was dated October 4, 1787. Hereinafter Orange County deed books will be cited as "OC" followed by book number/page number. A further note: Although the Orange County books originally bore letter designations (for example, "A"), the letters were later converted to numerals, which are used herein. A conversion table has been prepared by Orange County Register of Deeds Joyce Pearson. David Southern copied most of the Orange County land records cited herein. The "Price Creek" plantation, which became the home of the James Smith family in 1847, was eventually bequeathed to the Protestant Episcopal Diocese of North Carolina.

13. CC E/247; E/234; J/7; S/11, 12; V/369; G/325; G/411; H/336; J/55.

14. To trace Lot 9 beginning with its sale by the university trustees in 1793 through Jones's complicated involvement, see OC 6/8, 7/213, 7/215, 11/240, 11/242, 13/31, 13/440, 13/441, 13/478, 14/722. Whether or not Francis Jones was otherwise associated with the institution during his lifetime, his Jones Grove plantation eventually became the property of the university; see Chapter 10 for details of the latter transaction.

15. CC 0/42; OC 13/106–7; CC R/60; CC S/113; OC 14/727.

16. CC P/375; R/61; U/301.

17. CC X/123; AD/217; AF/165.

18. Image of petition is reproduced in Stewart E.

Dunaway, *Orange County North Carolina Mill Records (1782–1859)* (Raleigh: Author, 2010), p. 70; for the court case, see Chapter 2.

19. North Carolina State Grant 1609; CC V/169. Ruffin's surname is incorrectly spelled in the deed index as "Johens." CC AC/430.

20. See Chapters 6–10.

21. The race paths, identified in the deeds as the dividing line between the plantations received by Francis Jones from Tignal Jones and Robert Cobb (CC S/12 and J/7), ran northwesterly along a ridge southwest of present Camden Park (the beginning of Ewens Branch, which runs into Bush Creek). That places the race paths roughly along what in 2014 is West Camden, extending to approximately the Fearrington House.

22. Original notice in Mary Ruffin Smith Papers, SHC.

23. OC 18/92.

24. For Smith's spotted career, see Chapter 2.

25. Will of Francis Jones, Orange County Will Book F, pp. 198–200.

Chapter 2

1. Jean B. Anderson, "Smith, James Strudwick," in William S. Powell (ed.), *Dictionary of North Carolina Biography* (Chapel Hill: University of North Carolina Press, 1979–96; 6 vols.), 5: 380; Minutes of the Orange County Court of Pleas and Quarter Sessions, August 1788. The ubiquity of the name James Smith in records of Orange and Chatham counties offers other possibilities of identification, but none appears sufficient to challenge Anderson's opinion. For example, one James Smith sold tracts in 1805 and 1808 near the Chatham County residence of Francis Jones, whose daughter Delia would become the wife of James Strudwick Smith. See CC O/77 and O/414. Governor Burrington managed to amalgamate many royal grants in the Hawfields, all originally issued ca. 1730 in Bath County; the colony of North Carolina was still issuing royal grants within the later Granville boundaries as late as 1744.

2. *Hillsborough Recorder*, April 1, 1841.

3. Eva Burbank Murphy, "Strudwick, William Francis," in Powell, *DNCB* 5: 473; Jean B. Anderson, "Strudwick, Edmund Charles Fox," in Powell, *DNCB* 5: 471; Mary Claire Engstrom, "Webb, James," in Powell, *DNCB* 5: 144; Jean B. Anderson to H.G. Jones, email, November 9, 2012.

4. See later in this chapter for the story of how Dr. Smith acquired the honorary degree.

5. J.S. Smith, 308 High Street, Philadelphia, to Duncan Cameron, Stagville, December 19, 1811, in Cameron Family Papers (00133), Southern Historical Collection. See below for Smith's eventual receipt of an honorary M.D. degree, through political influence, from the University of Pennsylvania.

6. See below.

7. James S. Smith Account Books (02930), Southern Historical Collection. Ledger A, covering years prior to 1823, appears not to have survived, but Volume 1 (labeled inside as Ledger B) and Volume 2 (presumably Ledger C) cover the periods 1823–28 and 1828–32, respectively. Volume 3 (Day Book for 1828–1832) contains daily entries which were later transferred to ledgers, but Volume 4 (a Day Book for an indeterminate period) is too burned and brittle to be handled. No ledger has been found for the period after 1832. James Smith's son Francis Jones Smith joined him in practice about 1838. Account books of Dr. Francis Smith are preserved separately in the Mary Ruffin Smith Papers, SHC.

8. Tellingly, however, two of Smith's benefactors lost confidence in the doctor. Historian Jean Anderson wrote, "Though Duncan Cameron subsidized Smith's medical education, the Camerons never felt much affection or respect for him; he made enemies not only because of his political involvement ... but because of a self-serving ambition that dominated his character. Dr. Webb once gave a deposition under oath that he would not trust Smith's word when Smith's interests were concerned." Anderson, "Planter's Choice," unpublished manuscript, p. 8.

9. Historian David Southern suspects that the sponge and acid may have been used by Day in applying faux marbling to furniture in his cabinet shop.

10. Turner to Mary Ruffin Smith, September 9, 1880, in Mary Ruffin Smith Papers, SHC, Folder 1. Turner, a controversial newspaper editor in Raleigh, was the son of the Orange County sheriff whose name will be mentioned later in this chapter.

11. For more on relations between Smith and Murphey, see later in this chapter. Murphey suffered the ultimate indignity in 1829 when, despite the fact that as a legislator he had sought to abolish imprisonment for debt, he himself was incarcerated in Greensboro for twenty days because he could not pay off a note. It is not clear whether his note to Dr. Smith was ever paid, for he died February 1, 1832, a broken man at age 55. See H.G. Jones, "Murphey, Archibald DeBow," in Powell, *DNCB*, 4: 345. Dr. Smith and Judge Murphey are mentioned by name among prominent Hillsborough citizens who assembled at a King Street tavern in late February 1830 to pay their respects to the celebrated travel writer Anne Royall, who was visiting and collecting material for her three-volume *Mrs. Royall's Southern Tour* (1830–31): "We dined at Hillsboro['], a most delightful town. It is on a stream called Eno, ... as you approach it from the stream; every house is seen at once.... The citizens all flocked in from the other taverns to see me, and as many as could find a seat at the table, it being court time, sat down; Judge Murphey in front, and Dr. Smith on my right, while a crowd occupied the floor, as dense as they could stand.... (131) Judge Murphey is the same mentioned to have been absent, at Greensboro; he was attending court at this place, and came in, immediately and took dinner with me, as a mark of respect, his lodgings being at another house. I had heard much of Judge Murphy (*sic*), and was much gratified to see him. He is a tall, spare man, with a keen, thin Ciceronian face, and a very mild countenance; but nothing can equal the sweetness of his manners. He is one of the most interesting men in North Carolina. [/]

Dr. Smith, I believe, is a citizen a tall, fine figure, and a man of easy, gentleman-like manners (132)." Mrs. Anne [Newport] Royall, *Mrs. Royall's Southern Tour, or Second Series of the Black Book* (Washington, D.C., n.p., 1930–31; 3 vols.), 1:131–32.

12. Hawks then represented the borough of New Bern; Smith represented Hillsborough.

13. See Chapter 5 for more on the Spear family.

14. Mrs. Maria Spear died December 13, 1835; her tombstone stands beside that of her sister, Susan Esther Baker, in St. Matthew's Episcopal Church cemetery in Hillsborough.

15. Murphey to Ruffin, June 9, 1814, in William Henry Hoyt (ed.), *The Papers of Archibald Debow Murphey* (Raleigh: North Carolina Historical Commission, 1914; 2 vols.), 1: 69–70. The circular to which Murphey was responding has not been found.

16. Undated [1814] circular letter in Hoyt, *Murphey Papers*, 2: 14–18.

17. Mangum to Cameron, June 18, 1816, in Henry T. Shanks (ed.), *The Papers of Willie Person Mangum* (Raleigh: State Department of Archives and History, 1950–56, 5 vols.), 1: 9.

18. Henderson to Bennehan, August 9, 1817, in J.G. deRoulhac Hamilton (ed.), *The Papers of Thomas Ruffin* (Raleigh: North Carolina Historical Commission, 1918–20; 4 vols.), 1: 192. Dickens's surname is spelled Dickins in Powell, *DNCB*, 2: 64.

19. Hinton to Henderson, August 8, 1817, in Hamilton, *Ruffin Papers*, 1: 192.

20. "To the Electors of Orange, Person, and Wake," two-page circular dated July 4, 1817, in *Early American Imprints*, Series 2, no. 42138, North Carolina Collection, University of North Carolina Library.

21. See, for example, *Annals of Congress*, 15th Cong., 1st Sess., p. 1664.

22. Smith to Ruffin, January 27, 1819, in *Ruffin Papers*, 1: 213. If Smith developed a continuing relationship with many other congressional leaders, he failed to document it in his few surviving manuscripts.

23. *Annals*, 15th Cong., 1st Sess., 442–43.

24. Smith later purchased several of these grants.

25. "To the Freemen of Orange, Wake and Person Counties," July 3, 1819 (NCC Cp329.1/S651t2).

26. *Annals*, 16th Cong., 1st Sess., p. 2241.

27. *Annals*, 16th Cong., 1st Sess., pp. 921–22. The debate revealed that the Census of 1810 for the entire country had cost only $69,000. The population census continued to record the name of only the head of each household until 1850.

28. *Annals*, 16th Cong., 1st Sess., p. 1587, 1632.

29. *Annals*, 16th Cong., 1st Sess., pp. 1803–04.

30. *Annals*, 16th Cong., 1st Sess., p. 1904.

31. *Annals*, 16th Cong., 1st Sess., pp. 1906–07.

32. *Annals*, 16th Cong., 1st Sess., p. 1908.

33. *Annals*, 16th Cong., 1st Sess., p. 966–67.

34. "Speech on the Districting Clause of the Apportionment Bill" in J.G. deRoulhac Hamilton (ed.), *The Papers of William A. Graham* (Raleigh: State Department of Archives and History, 8 vols., 1957–92), 2: 326–27.

35. This and similar original deeds are preserved in the Mary Ruffin Smith Papers, Southern Historical Collection, Folders 7–11. Following Smith's death, his children sold all remaining grants to Joseph B. Cofield of Adams County, Illinois, for $1,500.

36. Nat. Cutting to James S. Smith, March 23, 1820, in *Ruffin Papers*, 1: 233. It is not clear whether it was Smith who enabled the War Department to obtain a copy of this important document that later allowed many Revolutionary veterans and widows in North Carolina to qualify for federal pensions. James Smith did not know at the time that two decades later he would seek to prove his father-in-law's service through similar records.

37. *Hillsborough Recorder*, June 21, 1820.

38. Trustee Minutes, Medical Department, University of Pennsylvania, August 27, 1821, p. 238; email from Nancy R. Miller to H.G. Jones, February 16, 2012. The oversize diploma granting "Jacobum S. Smith" an honorary doctor of medicine degree is in the Mary Ruffin Smith Papers, but the parchment is so badly crinkled that a good image is impossible without damage to the document.

39. See Christopher Benedetto, "A Most Daring and Sacrilegious Robbery," *New England Ancestors* 6(2), (Spring 2005).

40. Kemp Battle wrote that the granting of such honorary degrees was not unusual early in the nineteenth century. He cited "a curious University law" that permitted diplomas to be issued "to the so-called 'professions,' law, medicine, teaching and ... preaching ... for the asking by any alumnus who, after graduation, pursued for three years either of these 'learned' professions." Battle, 1: 781.

41. *Catalog of the Trustees, Officers & Medical Class*, University of Pennsylvania, Session 1837–38.

42. Battle, 1: 297–98, 301.

43. *Hillsborough Recorder*, March 21, 1821. Missing issues of the newspaper make assumptions in politics precarious.

44. *Hillsborough Recorder*, August 22, 1821; Saunders to Ruffin, December 15, 1821, in *Ruffin Papers*, 1: 255.

45. William R. Smith, "Brief Sketch of ... J. Strudwick Smith," in *Orphan's Friend and Masonic Journal* (Oxford, N.C.), June 15, 1934; *Hillsborough Recorder*, January 2, 1835, February 29, 1836. See also R.B. Studebaker and J. Frank Ray, *The History of Eagle Lodge No. 19, A.F. & A.M.* (Hillsborough: The Lodge, 1993), pp. 16–33. Historian Jean Anderson remembers that in the 1970s a poorly framed portrait of Smith was hanging in the Masonic Lodge; it was a copy of a larger portrait that once hung in the Grand Lodge in Raleigh.

46. *Hillsborough Recorder*, July 10, 1822; June 1, July 9, 1823.

47. A.D. Murphey, *Report of the Convention Committee to the Legislature of North-Carolina, 1816* (Raleigh: Printed by Tho. Henderson, Jun., State Printer, 1816),. NCC VCC342/N87g. For secondary studies on the sectional controversies, see, for example, Thomas E. Jeffrey, *State Parties and National Politics:*

North Carolina, 1815–1861 (Athens: University of Georgia Press, 1989).

48. *Hillsborough Recorder*, August 22, 1821.

49. *Graham Papers*, 3:47–8. Unknown at the time, the antagonists would become neighbors the next year when Hawks moved to Hillsborough to work as a lawyer before turning to the ministry.

50. *Debate on the Convention Question, in the House of Commons of the Legislature of North-Carolina, Dec. 18 & 19, 1821* (Raleigh: Printed by J. Gales & Son, 1822).

51. *Proceedings of the Friends of Convention, at Meeting Held in Raleigh, December 1822* (Salisbury: Printed by Philo White, 1823), NCC VC353/N87p, bound in volume titled *N. Carolina State Papers*. Another version of the proceedings was published by Thomas Henderson, State Printer, Raleigh, 1822.

52. *Hillsborough Recorder*, September 10, 1823; *The Journal of a Convention Assembled at the City of Raleigh, on the 10th of November, 1823; To adopt such measures as were deemed necessary to procure an Amendment to the Constitution of North-Carolina* (Raleigh: J. Gales & Son, State Printers, 1823).

53. *Hillsborough Recorder*, November 17, 1824.

54. Smith to Mangum, January 23, 1825, in Shanks, *Mangum Papers*, 1: 182–83.

55. Smith to Willie P. Mangum, February 9, 1825, in Shanks, *Mangum Papers*, 1: 188–90.

56. *Raleigh Register*, November 10, 1801; *Raleigh Star*, March 6, 1812; *Raleigh Register*, January 9, 1818; June 21, July 12, 1825; November 10, December 12, 1826; Charles L. Coon, *North Carolina Schools and Academies: A Documentary History, 1790–1840* (Raleigh: Edwards & Broughton for North Carolina Historical Commission, 1915), pp. 280–320 *passim*.

57. *Private Laws of North Carolina, 1824*, c. 69, p. 83. The chartered name of the female institution was "Hillsborough Female Academy," but Green usually called it "Hillsborough Female Seminary." See, for example, *Hillsborough Recorder*, July 13, 1825, June 11, 1828.

58. Jean B. Anderson to H.G. Jones, email attachment concerning *Susannah Brooks vs. Town Commissioners: Ejectment*, Superior Court Minutes, Orange County, March Term 1834. Mary Claire Engstrom, after extensive research in town records, entered certain changes, including lot numbers, on a copy of Claude Joseph Sauthier's 1768 *Plan of … Hillsborough*, the earliest known map of the town. See Engstrom, "Early Quakers in the Eno River Valley ca. 1750–1847," Appendix III, in *Eno* 7(2), (1989). The site in the twenty-first century is occupied by Orange County government facilities.

59. Smith to Mangum, February 3, 1825, in Henry T. Shanks (ed.), *The Papers of Willie P. Mangum* (Raleigh: State Department of Archives and History, 1850–56; 5 vols.), 1: 189.

60. *Raleigh Register*, July 15, 1825; *Hillsborough Recorder*, July 13, 1825. The trustees of the Hillsborough Female Academy in 1839, in addition to the original incorporators Smith and Cain, were Cadwallader Jones,

Sr., Priestly H. Mangum, Hugh Waddell, Nathan Hooker, and Stephen Moore. *Raleigh Register*, February 25, 1839. A year-by-year tracing of the school's history between 1826 and 1838 is difficult because of the gaps in newspaper holdings.

61. The copy of the circular preserved in the North Carolina Collection in the University of North Carolina Library (Cb378/H651) was originally folded and mailed to General William Lenoir at Fort Defiance, Caldwell County; the postage was 18¾ cents in 1826. For a brief sketch of Green, see Rachel Brown De Rosset in Powell, *DNCB* 2: 362, and for Hawks, Gertrude S. Carraway, 3: 76. Green's association with Hawks is reported in N.S. Richardson, "A Sketch of the Life and Character of Rev. Francis L. Hawks," in *American Quarterly Church Review*, April 1867, p. 15.

62. Charles L. Coon, *North Carolina Schools and Academies 1790–1840* (Raleigh: Edwards & Broughton, 1915), pp. 620–27; *Warrenton Reporter*, May 4, October 27, 1826; *Raleigh Register*, May 30, 1828; John Goff Rand Papers, Smithsonian Institution, Washington, D.C. Of Rand's invention, Pierre-Auguste Renoir said, "Without colors in tubes, there would be no Cézanne, no Pissarro, and no Impressionism." Perry Hurt, *Smithsonian* 44(2), May 2013, p. 20. The Rev. C.C. Brainerd succeeded William Mercer Green briefly as rector of St. John's Episcopal Church at Williamsborough.

63. The influence of the Spears on Mary Smith, and on education in North Carolina generally, will be discussed more fully in Chapter 5.

64. *Journal of the Proceedings of the Ninth Annual Convention of the Protestant Episcopal Church in the State of North Carolina Holden in St. Peter's Church, Washington, North Carolina … 1825*, p. 15, hereinafter cited as *Journal … North Carolina*, 1825.

65. *Journal … North Carolina*, 1826, pp. 3, 22, 29; Parish Register, St. Matthew's Episcopal Church, 1824–1881; Rev. N. Brooks Graebner, conversation, November 8, 2012.

66. Joseph Blount Cheshire, *An Historical Address Delivered in Saint Matthew's Church, Hillsboro, N.C., on Sunday, August 24, 1924, Being the One Hundredth Anniversary of the Parish* (Hillsborough: The Vestry [printed by Christian & King Printing Company, Durham, NC], 1925), p. 33.

67. See Chapters 6 through 9 for Mary Smith's subsequent support of Episcopalian causes.

68. *Journal … North Carolina*, 1831, p. 7.

69. Mangum to Mangum, September 7, 1826, in Shanks, *Mangum Papers*, 1: 300–01.

70. *Hillsborough Recorder*, September 17, 1828. To Smith's chagrin, Orange voted 1,057 for Jackson to Adams's 440. Caswell County, originally the northern part of Orange, went for Jackson 941 to 26 and Jackson swept the state 37,867 to only 13,918 for Adams. John L. Cheney, Jr. (ed.), *North Carolina Government 1585–1979* (Raleigh: Secretary of State, 1981), p. 1329.

71. Smith to Ruffin, March 22, 1829, in *Ruffin Papers*, 1: 487.

72. Single-sided circular, "To the Electors of Orange County," Hillsborough, July 1, 1829, NCC Cb329.1/

S651t1. The text of the circular was also published in the *Hillsborough Recorder* on July 8, 1829.

73. William Montgomery to Willie P. Mangum, June 6, 1832, in Shanks, *Mangum Papers*, 1: 550. The published papers of Mangum and other nineteenth-century officials reveal the role of personal service to voters. Pleas for jobs were common. A young Calvin H. Wiley asked Mangum's intervention with a New York publisher in his efforts to get his manuscript, *Alamance, or the Great and Final Experiment*, in print. Wiley to Mangum, June 29, 1847, in *Mangum Papers*, 5: 68.

74. *The Harbinger* (Chapel Hill), September 3, 10, 17, 1833.

75. Graham to Graham, August 12, 1833, in *Graham Papers*, 1: 261.

76. Smith to Mangum, February 16, 1834, in Shanks, *Mangum Papers*, 2: 84. By 1834 Mangum had gravitated to the Whigs.

77. *Hillsborough Recorder*, July 9, 1834; January 2, 1835.

78. *Hillsborough Recorder*, February 13, April 12, 1835.

79. *Hillsborough Recorder*, May 15, 29, 1835.

80. *Proceedings and Debates of the Convention of North-Carolina, Called to Amend the Constitution of the State, Which Assembled in Raleigh, June 4, 1835. To Which Are Subjoined the Convention Act and the Amendments to the Constitution, Together with the Vote of the People* (Raleigh: Printed by Joseph Gales and Son, 1836), NCC C342/1835p. For a secondary account of the convention, see also Harold J. Counihan, "The North Carolina Constitutional Convention of 1835: A Study in Jackson Democracy," *North Carolina Historical Review* 46 (December 1969): 335–64.

81. *Proceedings*, pp. 32–40. For Smith's role in the debate on the issue, see Joseph W. Pearson, "William Gaston, the Borough Controversy, and North Carolina's Changing Political Culture in the 1835 Constitutional Convention," *North Carolina Historical Review* 88 (October 2011): 408–09.

82. *Proceedings*, pp. 164, 178.

83. *Proceedings*, p. 80; *Charlotte Journal*, July 3, 1835.

84. *Proceedings*, pp. 244, 307, 331.

85. *Hillsborough Recorder*, November 13, 1835.

86. Smith to Graham, December 2, 1835, in *Graham Papers*, 1: 401–02.

87. *Hillsborough Recorder*, February 29, October 21, November 11, 1836.

88. John Scott to Willie P. Mangum, March 25, 1836, in Shanks, *Mangum Papers*, 2: 411. Mangum had broken with the Jackson administration over the national bank issue and was now firmly in the Whig column.

89. *Hillsborough Recorder*, July 11, 1839; June 4, 1840. Tyler had run for vice-president in 1836 as a Democrat; his selection as a running mate for Harrison would soon lead to the presidency and political suicide.

90. *Hillsborough Recorder*, September 3, 17, 24; October 15, 1840. A reader has a right to wonder if politicians of that era might have been equipped with larger bladders than their successors in the twenty-first

century, or if there might have been a difference between the holding capacities of members of the opposing political factions. In the days before indoor plumbing, the newspapers have little to say about how bodily relief was afforded at vast gatherings, particularly during hours-long speeches in towns like Hillsborough. The question is pertinent here because Dr. James Smith's home was located next door to the Masonic Lodge, where many of those marathon speeches were made.

91. *Hillsborough Recorder*, April 30, May 28, September 3, October 2, 22, November 12, 1840.

92. Hugh T. Lefler and Paul Wager (eds.), *Orange County—1752–1952* (Chapel Hill: Orange Printshop, 1953), pp. 89–90.

93. *Hillsborough Recorder*, December 17, 1840.

94. *Hillsborough Recorder*, April 1, 1841.

95. Single-sided handbill titled "To the voters of Wake, Person and Orange," Hillsborough, March 29, 1841, NCC Cb329.1/S651t.

96. *Hillsborough Recorder*, April 15, April 29, May 20, 1841.

97. *Hillsborough Recorder*, November 25, 1841.

98. *Hillsborough Recorder*, May 5, June 4, 1840.

99. *Hillsborough Recorder*, July 28, August 11, 1842

100. *Hillsborough Recorder*, March 20, 1843, quoting *Milton Chronicle*.

101. *Hillsborough Recorder*, October 28, 1841; January 27, September 1, 1842; June 29, 1843.

102. *Hillsborough Recorder*, July 13, 1843.

103. *Hillsborough Recorder*, September 7, 1843; March 19, April 4, May 9, 23, 30, June 6, July 18, August 8, 1844.

104. *Hillsborough Recorder*, September 12, 1844.

105. *Hillsborough Recorder*, October 17, November 7, 12, 1844.

106. *Hillsborough Recorder*, August 20, 1843; August 28, 1845; August 12, 1847.

107. *Hillsborough Recorder*, December 17, 1846.

108. OC 13/46, 14/147.

109. Murphey was actually imprisoned once briefly for debt.

110. OC 14/147, 375; 18/91. The deed from Yarbrough does not say that Smith *owned* the house that he occupied. Historian Mary Claire Engstrom wrote that Lot 22, which became Smith's home, was owned earlier by Quakers John Slater and John Stubbs, who in 1757 built a house that later came into possession of Edmund Fanning, a loyalist official and land speculator, who lived on adjoining Lot 23. When Fanning's holdings were confiscated by the new state during the American Revolution, Lot 22 was acquired by Memucan Hunt. Engstrom, "Early Quakers in the Eno River Valley ca. 1750–1847," in *Eno* 7(2) (1989): 23, 66. General Samuel Benton, grandfather of U.S. Senator Thomas Hart Benton, was said to have been buried in Lot 22. *Hillsborough Recorder*, June 30, 1875.

111. OC 20/112, 114, 411, 116; 34/278. The deed was so old that both the seller and witness, Francis and Ruffin Jones, had died, and their signatures were attested to before Judge William H. Battle by Austin Kirby. See *Mary R. Smith vs. Josiah Turner et al*, pp. 433–42, in

Equity Cases Argued and Determined in the Supreme Court of North Carolina, June Term, 1847, which relates to this deed.

112. Jean B. Anderson, "Smith, James Strudwick," in Powell, *DNCB,* 5: 380.

113. *Hillsborough Recorder,* May 10, June 21, November 8, 29, 1820. Smith's office may have been in the old Slater Tavern on Lot 22, in which case the newspaper office would have been located on the site of the later structure erroneously named "Colonial Inn." Josiah Turner, Sr. was sheriff of Orange County, 1812–20.

114. *Hillsborough Recorder,* August 22, 1821.

115. *Hillsborough Recorder,* March 10, 1824.

116. OC 22/62, 100; 21/496.

117. CC Z/393–94.

118. OC 25/511; 28/434, 439; 25/504.

119. *Hillsborough Recorder,* November 3, 1834; March 27, April 10, 1835.

120. *Hillsborough Recorder,* February 29, October 21, 1836.

121. *Hillsborough Recorder,* November 26, June 25, 1840; August 5, September 9, 1841.

122. OC 28/441; 31/275. The deed from Smith to Campbell and Jones was not registered until 1845.

123. CC AF/51; OC 25/511.

124. OC 28/436, 26/146, 31/393. The name Crain/Crane is spelled both ways in the same document; he signed as "Crain." In 1843, for "natural love and affection," Smith had given his son Sidney the 120 acres acquired previously from David Strayhorn on the Eno; and although his deed conveying the mill site to son Francis in 1845 mentions a price of $3,000, both of these actions appear to have been associated with his efforts to protect the properties from creditors. OC 32/200, 31/393.

125. *Hillsborough Recorder,* July 10, August 19, 1845.

126. OC 32/56, 32/95, 32/104, 32/105, 32/99, 31/125; 32/50, 32/51; 31/404, 352. At least some of these transactions with Turrentine may have been sheriff's sales. Smith's sale of the lot on which he lived (Number 22) suggested that he was preparing to move to the Price Creek plantation.

127. OC/396–401.

128. OC 31/398. The reference to building materials suggests that the house on Price Creek plantation was under construction in 1845, and it, together with Dr. Smith's poor management, had added to the debts that led to his bankruptcy.

129. Undated fragmentary document found in uncataloged papers given by Jacqueline Key to be added to the Mary Ruffin Smith Papers in the SHC.

130. *Hillsborough Recorder,* March 11, September 17, 1846.; OC 31/393; manuscripts dated August 19 and October 1, 1846, in Mary Ruffin Smith Papers, SHC.

131. *Hillsborough Recorder,* December 17, 1846.

132. OC 32/155.

133. OC 31/441. The indenture included three notes owed Smith by an Illinois citizen, as well as one on his son Francis J. Smith for $395.46 and half of a Mississippi judgment on the estate of Dr. Thomas J. Faddis.

134. Draft notes in handwriting of James S. Smith

in *Joseph Wood & Others vs. J.S. Smith & Others* in untitled papers given by Jacqueline Key to the Southern Historical Collection. These five folders of tattered papers, originally found in the Price Creek house, are not yet cataloged, and I am grateful to Archivist Jay Gaidmore for allowing me access to them.

135. Smith and Turner had an on-and-off friendship.

136. Mary R. Smith vs. Josiah Turner & Al, in *Equity Cases Argued and Determined in the Supreme Court of North Carolina,* June Term, 1847, Vol. 4, NBSP Vol. 39, pp. 433–42. Orange County Deed Book D, referred to in the decision, has been renumbered as Deed Book 31.

137. OC 34/278.

138. OC 33/240. The document was not registered until two years later, February 1849.

139. CC AH/499, 500.

140. CC AH/369.

141. OC 33/239. Registered February 1849.

142. OC 33/354.

143. OC 33/374.

144. Fragments of documents in Folder 1 of uncataloged Smith family papers, given by Jacqueline Key to the SHC.

145. See Mary Clare Engstrom, "John Berry," in Powell, *DNCB,* 1: 146, and "John A. Faucett" in *North Carolina Architects and Builders,* http://ncarchitects.lib.ncsu.edu/people/P000335.

146. John G. Zehmer Jr., "Architectural Descriptions of Buildings in Chapel Hill, North Carolina, November 18, 1970." Typescript in North Carolina Collection, University of North Carolina at Chapel Hill. Zehmer failed to report that the windows on the second floor were six over four and on the first floor six over six. An alteration to the house was revealed in 1872 when Maria Spear wrote that Mary Smith was "so busy building a cotton house, moving and rebuilding a crib ... changing some old tenants for new, moving others, having the front Piazza new roofed & floored that she hardly has time to breathe."

The part of the Price Creek plantation containing the house was purchased in 1904 from the two Episcopal dioceses by a consortium of O.B. Barnes, J.F. Pickett, and A.E. Lewis, but shortly afterward the house with a smaller acreage was acquired by William Compton Cole (1844–1924), Mary Smith's former farm manager. The property passed to Cole's son George, then to the latter's three daughters, before being purchased by Diane Eckland, who renovated the house in 2003. Eckland, a restorer of old homes, reported that she found in the attic "bills of sale for the lumber that had come from Virginia by horse and buggy, and for the 17 chimneys that cost a total of $350." Jeffrey and Jacqueline Key purchased "Oakland" and made further changes. See "This Other House," *Chapel Hill News,* June 15, 2007. Additional information on the house may be found in the files of the Historic Preservation Section of the North Carolina Office of Archives and History.

147. OC 31/396.

148. OC 31/401. Kell died before the bill of sale was recorded in November 1845, but his signature was

proved by Joseph Allison, county clerk. The original bill of sale is found in the Mary Ruffin Smith Papers, SHC.

149. OC 31/400.

150. Original bill of sale in Mary Ruffin Smith Papers, SHC. See also OC 31/329. See above for Dr. Smith's threat to sell his granddaughter Cornelia and her mother, Harriet.

151. See above.

152. *Hillsborough Recorder*, December 15, 1852; *Fayetteville Observer*, December 21, 1852. In a letter dated September 9, 1880, Josiah Turner, Jr., a controversial editor in Raleigh and son of former sheriff Josiah Turner who figures heavily in the Smith story, asked Mary Smith for first-hand information on her father. Turner had originally planned to write a history of the "Holden-Kirk War" but had concluded instead to write a history of Orange County "and her great men," adding, "Your father's life and acts make a considerable chapter in the history of the county and state." Turner said he already knew much about James S. Smith but wanted to learn more because John W. Wheeler's writings slighted the Whigs. Wheeler, he said, was "more for his party than his country." Turner was correct; in *Historical Sketches of North Carolina* (Philadelphia: Lippincott, Grambo and Company, 1851, 2 vols. in 1, 2: 336), Wheeler gave Smith a single sentence: "Dr. James S. Smith represented the town of Hillsboro' in the House of Commons in 1821, and the District, in Congress, in 1817, in which he served until 1821." Whigs dismissed the book as a "Democratic Stud Book." In a later book, Wheeler did not even deign to mention Smith. Would that Mary Smith had furnished the information requested. Even if Turner had produced a book as faulty as Wheeler's, the documentary sources collected might have provided later scholars with grist from which a badly-needed history of Orange County—including the role of the dysfunctional Smith family—could be written. Turner's letter is in the Mary Ruffin Smith Papers, SHC.

153. Prior to this study, the original burial site of James Smith was forgotten by younger generations. In fact, the family chose a knoll within sight of the residence in what is described by the Cemetery Census of Orange County as "206 Unidentified Cemetery—Carrboro Area [Smith Level Road]." (The coordinates are 35d 52m 27.7s N; 79d 04m 47.1s W.) The survey reported, "No one seems able to provide a clue to the graves inside the wall." The current owners of the property, Paul and Bruce Long, were quoted as saying that "two people (a man and woman) were buried in the cemetery in the mid–1800s but the names are unknown." They were nearly correct. In fact, *three* Smiths were buried in the graveyard now bordered by dry stone walls—James (in 1852), Delia (in 1854), and Sidney Smith (in 1867). In 1897, all three bodies were disinterred and moved to the Jones Grove Cemetery upon instructions of Mary Ruffin Smith's executor, Kemp P. Battle. See Chapter 5.

154. Pauli Murray wrote that the move was made after the birth of Emma, which appears to have been during the winter of 1846–47. Mary testified in court that the house was occupied in November 1847.

155. Original affidavit, dated September 27, 1847, in *John A. Faucette & Others vs. James S. Smith*, Superior Court of Orange County, September Term, 1847, in Mary R. Smith Estate Papers, Orange County Estates Papers, State Archives.

156. Presumably several slaves had died or been sold after the 1850 census, when the count was 30. On the other hand, the discrepancy may be accounted for partially by Mary Smith's purchase in 1845 of Harriet, Julius, and Cornelia, and the subsequent births of Emma, Annette, and Laura, who otherwise were not accounted for in Delia Smith's estate.

157. Delia Smith Estate Papers, Orange County Records, State Archives. The holder of one of the notes was probably Edward Mallett, son of Charles Peter Mallett, indicating an early connection between Mary Ruffin Smith and the Mallett family, a relationship that grew in later years.

158. Sidney had sold his Flowers Place five years earlier, so his wealth consisted mostly in personal loans or mortgages.

Chapter 3

1. For names of these academies, see Chapter 2.

2. Battle, 1: 796; *Catalogue of the Trustees, Faculty and Students of the University of North Carolina* for 1833 through 1836; *Catalogue of the Members of the Dialectic Society Instituted in the University of North Carolina, June 3, 1795, Together with Historical Sketches* (published for the Society 1896, electronic edition).

3. For Graham's indebtedness to the Smiths, see chapters 4 and 5.

4. *Hillsborough Recorder*, July 11, 1839; "May it please the Court," testimony in an unidentified court case involving the Smith family in 1847; partial document in Sidney Smith's handwriting in folder of papers given by Jacqueline Key to the Southern Historical Collection but not yet cataloged in 2012.

5. Battle, 1: 427; Edward H. Armstrong to Thomas G. Armstrong, April 21, 1861, in Julien Dwight Martin Papers, Southern Historical Collection.

6. Murray, *Proud Shoes: The Story of an American Family* (New York: Harper, 1956; Beacon Press edition, 1999), p. 36.

7. No books that are known to have been owned by Sidney Smith have been found, so it is not difficult to suspect that Cornelia remembered the shelves of medical books owned by Sidney's father and brother; for reference to these books given to the University of North Carolina Library, see Chapter 4.

8. Mary Ruffin Smith Papers, SHC. Goldston's daily boarding charge was generally 75 cents for Sidney and 25 cents for his horse.

9. Murray, *Proud Shoes*, pp. 35, 40, 43.

10. Murray, *Proud Shoes*, pp. 42–3. Reuben Day presumably was the father of Julius, Harriet's son, who did not share the privileged attention given by the Smith family to Harriet's daughters sired by the white brothers.

11. Murray, *Proud Shoes*, p. 50.

12. Murray, *Proud Shoes*, pp. 52, 16. An examination of voluminous court records would be required to ascertain the correctness of such assertions.

13. Murray, *Proud Shoes*, p. 5. On page 90 Murray repeated the oft-accepted nineteenth-century definition of racial categories: octoroon, seven-eights or more white blood; quadroon, three-fourths white blood; and mulatto, five-eighths to three-eighths white blood. After the overthrow of Republican political power in the 1890s and the imposition of racial segregation by the Democrats, official records generally classified every nonwhite as "n" (for Negro).

14. For additional references to Sidney's political activities, see Chapter 2.

15. *Hillsborough Recorder*, June 4, August 13, 1846. No doubt some of his detractors sneeringly called the new commoner "Landslide Sidney."

16. *Journal of the Senate and House of Commons of the General Assembly of North Carolina at Its Session 1846–47* (Raleigh: Printed by Thos. J. Lemay, Office of the Raleigh Star, 1847), pp. 290, 300, 470. NCC C328.1/N87.

17. Powell, *DNCB* 8: 182.

18. *Hillsborough Recorder*, December 10, 1846; January 21, 28, February 4, 1847.

19. *Journal ... 1846–47*, pp. 467–528 *passim*.

20. Graham to Graham, January 10, February 28, 1847, in *Graham Papers* 3: 171, 182. For more on the Mecklenburg regiment's "revolt," see Sion H. Harrington III, "Heel Volunteers in the Mexican-American War," *Tar Heel Junior Historian*, 52(1), (Fall 2012), pp. 22–3.

21. *Hillsborough Recorder*, January 28, 1847.

22. *Journal of the Senate and House of Commons ... 1847*, pp. 401, 465.

23. Battle, 1: 506–09.

24. This undated document is among a badly deteriorated group of papers found in the former Mary Smith house a few years ago and given by Jacqueline Key to the Southern Historical Collection. The papers have not yet been analyzed and cataloged, and I am grateful to Jay Gaidmore, then university archivist, for allowing me access to them. See Chapter 2 for more on the court cases.

25. *Mangum Papers*, 5: 110n; *North Carolina Reports* 40 N.C., Appendix, pp. 421–31; "Reports from the Committee on Privileges and Elections in the Case of the Contested Election in the District of Orange," *Senate Documents*, 1848–49, Doc. No. 16; *Hillsborough Recorder*, August 9, 16, September 27, November 8, 1848; January 24, April 25, 1849.

26. Smith to Graham, September 6, 1851, *Graham Papers*, 6: 201.

27. Bryan to Graham, January 25, 1852, in *Graham Papers*, 6: 239. The senior Haywood, a strong Democrat, served in the United States Senate from 1843 to 1846. He died nine months after the mentioned affair. Bryan, a Whig, was the brother-in-law of Governor Graham.

28. *Hillsborough Recorder*, June 9, 1852.

29. *Hillsborough Recorder*, December 15, 1852.

30. *Hillsborough Recorder*, June 6, August 1, 29, 1855. Miller was correct; Dr. Smith indeed had voted against the amendment that extended suffrage to all Christians, a vote that pleased the American Party.

31. *Hillsborough Recorder*, February 6, June 18, November 12, 1856.

32. Battle, 1: 698–706.

33. *Hillsborough Recorder*, March 23, 1859.

34. *Hillsborough Recorder*, May 7, 1860.

35. *Hillsborough Recorder*, December 19, 1860; January 2, 1861.

36. Enclosure with Sidney Smith, John W. Carr, and Jones Watson to William A. Graham, February 7, 1861, in *Graham Papers*, 5: 225; *Hillsborough Recorder*, February 13, 1861; Smith to Graham, February 16, 19, 1861, in *Graham Papers*, 5: 237–38.

37. Edward H. Armstrong to Thomas G. Armstrong, April 20, 1861, in Julien Dwight Martin Papers, SHC. The archivist who annotated this source on the Web misidentified Sidney Smith. Another student with the same name (from Dayton, Alabama) had left Chapel Hill by 1859.

The speaker in 1861 was certainly the local Sidney Smith, noted for his fiery oratory.

38. *Hillsborough Recorder*, March 6, April 24, May 22, 1861.

39. Phillips to Graham, February 6, 1864, in *Graham Papers*, 6: 35.

40. OC 35/180. The acreage was not recorded.

41. CC AK/111. According to the slave census of 1860, Jehial Atwater owned 24 slaves, Jahaza owned 34.

42. Untitled manuscript booklet in Mary Ruffin Smith Papers, SHC, folder 17.

43. Orange County Will Book G, p. 517.

44. Murray, on page 51 of *Proud Shoes*, was badly mistaken about Cornelia's age when her father died; she was 23, not 16; and Dr. James Smith had been dead 15 years, not "a year or so."

45. Certificate dated December 6, 1864, in Mary Ruffin Smith Papers, SHC. Camp Holmes was located a mile or so north of Peace College in Raleigh.

46. Mallett to his son Charles B. Mallett, April 25, 1865, in Charles Beatty Mallett Papers, SHC; Iona and Peter Opie, *The Lore and Language of Schoolchildren* (Oxford: Oxford University Press, 1959), p. 47. Note that the word is written as "Dout" rather than "Doubt."

47. Nearly three decades later his body, along with those of his parents, was disinterred and moved to Jones Grove.

48. Murray, *Proud Shoes*, p. 43.

49. Sidney Smith Estates Papers, Orange County Estates Records, State Archives. For more on Sidney Smith's death, see Chapter 5.

50. The text of Graham's will is printed in Hamilton (ed.), *Graham Papers*, 8: 506. He died in 1875.

51. Estate records of Sidney Smith in Orange County Records, State Archives. The $650 owed Sidney Smith's estate by Ashe and Mitchell was satisfied when on June 1, 1868, they transferred to Francis and Mary Smith two lots at College (Cameron) Avenue and Mallett and Kenan Streets in Chapel Hill (OC 47/595).

Ashe moved to Bakersfield, California, and served in that state's legislature.

52. Judge Tourgee, a "Carpetbagger" from Ohio, moved to North Carolina after the Civil War and was influential in the convention of 1868 that adopted a new state constitution extending civil rights to freedmen. After leaving the state, he wrote about his experiences in an autobiographical novel titled *A Fool's Errand by One of the Fools.*

Chapter 4

1. Battle, 1: 796; *University of Pennsylvania Catalogue of the Trustees, Officers, & Medical Class, Session 1837–38,* p. 15; email, Nancy R. Miller to H.G. Jones, February 16, 2012.

2. See Chapter 3.

3. Murray, *Proud Shoes,* p. 47.

4. Augustus White Long, *Son of Carolina* (Durham: Duke University Press, 1939), p. 33.

5. Murray, *Proud Shoes,* p. 40.

6. Respective death certificates show that Cornelia Fitzgerald died July 9, 1924, and was buried in the Fitzgerald Cemetery, which has since been incorporated into Maplewood, Durham's old cemetery originally reserved for whites (http://cemeterycensus.com/nc/durh/cem048.htm); Annette Kirby died July 22, 1926, and was buried in Zion Church cemetery in Chapel Hill; and Emma Morphis died April 1941 and was buried on her own farm across the road from Galloway Ridge in Chatham County. The death of Laura Toole, from whom Gray (Grey) Toole was divorced in a nasty State Supreme Court case in 1893, occurred after 1920, at which time she was living with a daughter in Connecticut. *Mecklenburg County Divorces, 1846–1969,* p. 356; Gray J. Toole v. Laura Toole, *North Carolina Reports* 112: 125–130, February term 1893. Gray Toole, who claimed once to have been President Grover Cleveland's personal barber, served as a lieutenant in Company D of North Carolina's 3rd Regiment in the Spanish-American War.

7. Murray, *Proud Shoes,* pp. 42–9.

8. *Hillsborough Recorder,* November 26, 1840; receipt dated March 3, 1839, in Mary Ruffin Smith Papers, SHC.

9. *Hillsborough Recorder,* December 17, 1846.

10. Francis J. Smith Account Book, "Vol. 6," identified as Folder 18 in Mary Ruffin Smith Papers, SHC. Some of the books were mutilated by over-writing, apparently by employees at the Price Creek farm. See Chapter 4, for details of the September 1872 tragedy in which lightening struck Harriet, leaving her an invalid.

11. Long, *Son of Carolina,* pp. 31–4.

12. Long, *Son of Carolina,* p. 33. It should be remembered that Oakland on the Price Creek plantation was not occupied until after Emma's birth in 1847. Consequently, only Annette and Laura could have been conceived in the "office" described by Professor Long.

13. Frank's return has not been found in the 1870 agriculture schedule for Chatham County.

14. Murray, *Proud Shoes,* pp. 232–3; Holt to Mary Smith, November 5, 1875, in Mary Ruffin Smith Papers, SHC.

15. "Report of the Hon. Kemp P. Battle, LL.D., Executor of the Will of the Late Mary R. Smith" in *Journal of the ____ Annual Convention of the Protestant Episcopal Church in the Diocese of North Carolina ... 1886,* Appendix A, p. 7; Long, *Son of Carolina,* p. 33. For Maria Spear's first-hand account of Frank Smith's last several years see p. 127.

16. The *Charlotte Journal* on December 18, 1835, announced, "Died in Hillsborough, on the 13th ultimo, Mrs. Maria Spear, in the 60th year of her age." Although a tombstone in St. Matthew's Church cemetery is engraved with her name, no date is legible.

17. See Chapter 2.

18. Maria Spear's affidavit in *Faucett vs. James S. Smith,* Sepember 27, 1847, in Mary Ruffin Smith Estate Papers, State Archives.

19. CC AV/368.

20. Estate papers of Francis J. Smith and Mary R. Smith, Orange County Records, State Archives.

21. Battle, 2: 504, 797. A complete list of titles was published in "The Francis J. Smith Donation," *University of North Carolina Catalogue, 1877–78,* pp. 48–9. In addition, one book bearing the bookplate of "James S. Smith, Hillsborough, N.C." is preserved in the North Carolina Collection: John Redman Coxe, *Practical Observations of Vaccination; or Inoculation for the Cow-Pock* (Philadelphia: James Humphreys, 1802). It is cataloged as VC097/S651c.

Chapter 5

1. See Chapter 2.

2. For brief sketches of Hawks and Green, respectively, see Powell, DNCB 3: 76; 2: 362.

3. Green's "Summer Examination of Hillsboro' Female Seminary, June 24, 1828"; Green to Mary Smith, August 24, 1833, both in Mary Ruffin Smith Papers, SHC, Folder 3. The official name of the institution was "Hillsborough Female Academy," although Green called it "Seminary." The name "Hillsborough" was often written as "Hillsboro" (with or without an apostrophe).

4. Original document dated February 25, 1824, in Mary Ruffin Smith Papers, SHC, Folder 9.

5. The latter transaction was witnessed by Mary's youngest brother, who spelled his middle name "Sydney" in this single instance.

6. Murray, *PS,* p. 38.

7. Murray, *PS,* pp. 42–3.

8. The original bills of sale for the slaves mentioned herein are preserved in the Mary Ruffin Smith Papers, SHC. Pauli Murray, in *Proud Shoes,* page 37, was mistaken in asserting that the original purchase of Harriet was a gift to Mary on her eighteenth birthday (she would have been twenty in 1834). Instead, Harriet became Mary's property eleven years later, following the birth of Cornelia—and then only by paying her father a one-hundred-dollar profit. The author was misled

because Kell's original sale receipt, dated 1834, was not officially recorded in the courthouse until 1845. Dr. Smith failed to legally record several important transactions until years afterward, not an unusual practice at the time. For more on the purchase of Harriet, see Chapter 2.

9. Murray, *PS*, p. 46.

10. Based on inconsistent census records, Emma was born 1846 or early 1847, Annette in 1848 or 1849, and Laura about 1851.

11. Murray, *PS*, p. 36. Murray's claim that the new house called "Oakland" became "a center of political and cultural activity" is unrealistic, because by that time Dr. Smith's financial misadventures had sullied his reputation.

12. Murray, *PS*, p. 48.

13. Murray, *PS*, p. 38.

14. The book, with a transmittal letter from Murray to the Librarian of UNC, December 17, 1959, is cataloged in the North Carolina Collection as FVC097/S655. The book deserves careful study by a scholar knowledgeable in nineteenth-century music.

15. Murray, *PS*, pp. 36, 161. Murray was mistaken about Maria's birthplace; she was born in Paddington, England.

16. Murray, *PS*, pp. 231–32.

17. Battle, *History of the University of North Carolina*, 2: 344.

18. James Boswell was author of the *Life of Samuel Johnson* (1791), considered a masterpiece of biography.

19. Handwritten invitation to Jones's funeral dated February 24, 1844, at the residence of James S. Smith, Hillsborough; original document in Mary Ruffin Smith Papers, SHC, Folder 3; *Hillsborough Recorder*, December 15, 1852, and November 22, 1854.

20. See below, for the baptism of Julius's daughter.

21. Murray, *PS*, p. 21. It is not clear whether the Bible was given at baptism or at confirmation. Glenda Gilmore in *Defying Dixie: The Radical Roots of Civil Rights 1919–1950* (New York: W.W. Norton, 2008), p. 443, wrote, "Six weeks later [after her ordination in Washington Cathedral, January 8, 1977], Murray held her grandmother Cornelia Smith Fitzgerald's Bible as she stepped up to the front of the chapel.... Murray took a long look at the balcony where her great-grandmother Harriet and her grandmother Cornelia had sat as slaves. As she began her sermon, she gripped a lectern engraved with her great-aunt Mary Smith's name."

22. The foregoing references are from the records of the Chapel of the Cross, Chapel Hill. I am indebted to Ernest Dollar for furnishing a compact disc containing images of these church records. Emma was the first of the four sisters to marry; Cornelia married Robert Fitzgerald on August 8, 1869. See also Murray, *PS*, p. 218. *Journal of the Fortieth Annual Convention of the Protestant Episcopal Church in the State of North Carolina*, 1855, p. 34, shows eleven "colored" baptisms in 1854 at the Chapel of the Cross. Cornelia Smith had her first child, Mary Pauline Fitzgerald, christened at St. Matthew's Episcopal Church in Hillsborough by Dr. Curtis, its rector. Murray, *PS*, 229.

23. Murray, *PS*, pp. 53–4. The Swains were Presbyterians, but my initial doubt about the accuracy of Cornelia's claim of simultaneous confirmations was allayed by the university president's biographer, who wrote, "Swain was right ecumenical, and I have seen other instances of his involvement with the Chapel of the Cross. So I would guess that this account [by Cornelia] is accurate." Willis P. Whichard to H.G. Jones, email, May 21, 2012.

24. http://thechapelofthecross.org/about-us/history/163.html ; Spencer, quoted in Hope Summerell Chamberlain, *Old Days in Chapel Hill, Being the Life and Letters of Cornelia Phillips Spencer* (Chapel Hill: University of North Carolina Press, 1922), p. 289.

25. Cole to Spencer, February 3, 1886, original letter in University Papers (40005), SHC, Letters show that Mary Smith made contributions to additional congregations such as Christ Church in Raleigh and an Episcopal church in Ansonville. For additional bequests to the Chapel of the Cross, see Chapter 9.

26. Spencer, "A Notable Woman North Carolina Has Produced," *State Chronicle* (Raleigh), February 25, 1886.

27. Chamberlain, *Old Days in Chapel Hill*, p. 258. Although it is not exhaustive, Spencer's obituary notice in the *Church Messenger* (mentioned above) may have redeemed her promise. Among few references to Mary and Maria in extant private correspondence (other than Maria's letters to the Mallett girls mentioned later) is this sentence in a letter from Lucy Battle to William H. Battle, August 15 1856: "Miss M[aria] Spear & Miss M[ary] S[mith] came in on Wednesday & stayed until last evening." William H. Battle Papers, SHC. There is evidence elsewhere that Mary Smith was frequently welcomed in the homes of the Battles, father and son.

28. Murray, *PS*, pp. 52–3.

29. Murray, *PS*, p. 159.

30. Murray, *PS*, p. 160.

31. Murray, *PS*, p. 160.

32. Battle, *History of the University*, 1: 743.

33. Charles Peter Mallett to Charles Beatty Mallett, April 18–29, May 1–10, 1865, in Charles B. Mallett Papers, SHC. This important letter-journal, beginning April 18 and continuing for many days, contains an important chronicle of those historic weeks in Chapel Hill. See also Charles P. Mallett to Henry A. London, April 30, 1865.

34. See Chapter 3.

35. *Journal ... East Carolina*, 1896, p. 20.

36. Murray, *PS*, p. 163. If the story is true, perhaps the flag was one owned by Dr. Smith when he was in the Congress.

37. Murray, *PS*, p. 164. Later correspondence of Maria Spear does not support Murray's assumption that the "girls" were living in the "Big House." If so, it is strange that they escaped attention in Maria's letters. Harriet was living in her own cabin at the time of her injury from lightning and her subsequent death.

38. Murray, *PS*, pp. 164–65, 217; Records of Chapel of the Cross for 1864; Orange County Marriage Records, 1868; Maria Spear to Carrie Mallett, March

19, 1868, in Charles B. Mallett Papers, SHC. Except for Laura, who moved to Charlotte after her marriage, all of the "girls" remained in close touch with Mary Smith both in distance and communication.

39. Murray, *PS*, p. 208.

40. Murray, *PS*, p. 218. Hunter also served as postmaster at University Station 1856–58 and 1861–65.

41. Smith to Mangum, February 9, 1825, in Henry T. Shanks (ed.), *The Papers of Willie P. Mangum* (Raleigh: State Department of Archives and History, 1950–56; 5 vols.), 1: 188–89; *Private Laws of North Carolina*, 1824, chapter 69. See also Chapter 2.

42. James S. Smith Account Books (02930), Ledger 1, p. 159, and Ledger 2, June 11, 1830, in SHC; *Charlotte Journal*, December 18, 1835. On November 9, 1835, Phebe Kirkland wrote to Eliza Johnston, Marion, Alabama, "Old Mrs. Spear is very low from which surely she has been lingering for a long time with a disease which is incurable. Miss M[aria] has a very flourishing school. Elizabeth Smith assists her." Eliza Mary Bond Weisinger Papers (04443), SHC. Interestingly, no entry has been found in Dr. Smith's accounts for the younger daughter, Elizabeth Spear, who married Samuel Bryan Smith in 1831 and was teaching in the seminary in 1839, or for the father, if he accompanied the family to Hillsborough. Susan Baker's tombstone provides information that she and her sister were daughters of Thomas and Mary Baker of England. The house in Hillsborough owned by Susan Baker was sold after the Civil War "to Mr. Mickle, he to Mr. Morris, Mr. Morris to the church, & it is now the parsonage." Maria Spear on an undated (but probably 1867) document in Charles B. Mallet Papers, SHC, Folder 19. For more on the "Triangle Lot" on which Susan Baker lived and boarded some of the students of the Hillsborough Female Seminary, see Stewart E. Dunaway, *Hillsborough North Carolina— History of Town Lots, The Complete Reference Guide* (Hillsborough: Stewart E. Dunaway, November 19, 2012), pp. 36–7. Baker's 1846 will is found in Orange County Will Book F/330.

43. *Alumni Directory, 2007* (Chapel Hill: University of North Carolina Alumni Association, 2007; 2 vols.), vol. 2, p. 2139. That the young man was exceptional in other ways is suggested by his prompt repayment of the assistance given him by the diocese for his seminary training; this entry appeared in the diocesan minutes: "Resolved, that the sum of $200, returned by the Rev. W.W. Spear, through the Rev. W.M. Green, together with all other sums that may be returned from the same source, be placed in the hands of the President of the Standing Committee, to be appropriated ... to assisting pious and indigent young men in preparing for the ministry." *Journal ... North Carolina*, 1836, p. 43.

44. http://www.gracechurchcharleston.org/page_ to_print.cfm?id=161&co.... A contributor to *A Critical Dictionary of English Literature, and British and American Authors...,* Spear also published some obscure items, a couple of which are preserved in the University of North Carolina library. In 1888, the minister was living in Ephrata, Pennsylvania, from where he wrote an article for the *New York Observer* about an experience at the University of North Carolina. Titled "A Noted Revival," the story was submitted by Cornelia Phillips Spencer to the *North Carolina Presbyterian* on July 11, 1888. At least one other brother is mentioned in Maria's correspondence.

45. John S. Henderson, "Episcopacy in Rowan," in Jethro Rumple, *A History of Rowan County, North Carolina, Containing Sketches of Permanent Families and Distinguished Men* (Salisbury: J.J. Bruner, 1881), pp. 418–21. John Stark Ravenscroft was consecrated first Bishop of North Carolina in 1823 in Philadelphia. If Marie was one of the first persons confirmed by the new bishop, would the ceremony have been held in Hillsborough or in Salisbury? The bishop served simultaneously as rector of Christ Church, Raleigh, but he traveled over the state before dying in 1830.

46. No copy of the *Church Messenger* for January 27, 1881, to which the tribute was credited, has yet been seen by the author.

47. http://www.burwellschool.org/research/ pPerson.php?id+297; Mangum Papers, 3: 45, 271, 365.

48. Deposition of M.L. Spear in [court case of] *Thomas Faucette, administrator for John Merritt dec'd & others vs. James S. Smith*, September 27, 1847, in Mary Ruffin Smith Estate Papers, Orange County Records, State Archives.

49. Further research may reveal that the house, in which Maria was living with the freedwomen, was owned by Mary Ruffin Smith. It is probable that Maria was teaching in Chapel Hill in the late 1850s, for in a letter to Cornelia Spencer in 1856, Sarah Fetter wrote, "We hope to have Miss Maria Spear here this winter. I shall feel so relieved when Sue & Kate go to school." November 20, 1856, in Cornelia Phillips Spencer Papers, SHC, Folder 1. The author suspects that in some of the "lost years" before she went to Fayetteville, Maria Spear was living with the Smiths.

50. C.P. Mallett to Maggie Mallett, October 17, 1866, and December 5, 1867, in Charles B. Mallett Papers, SHC, Series 1, Folder 20.

51. Tom Vincent, "'Evidence of Womans [*sic*] Loyalty, Perseverance, and Fidelity': Confederate Soldiers' Monuments in North Carolina, 1865–1914," *North Carolina Historical Review* 83(1) (January 2008): 64–72; Alice Campbell, "Confederate Monument of 1868," n.d., unpublished manuscript in Charles B. Mallett Papers, SHC; Carrie Mallett Hale, "The Monument at Cross Creek, 1868," in J.E.B. Stuart Chapter, UDC, comp., *War Days in Fayetteville, North Carolina: Reminiscences of 1862 to 1865* (Fayetteville: The Chapter, 1910), pp. 57–8.

52. "Fayetteville" in Mrs. S.L. Smith (comp.), *North Carolina's Confederate Monuments and Memorials* (N.p.: North Carolina Division, United Daughters of the Confederacy, 1941), p. 62.

53. Maria Louisa Spear [hereafter MLS] to Maggie Mallett [hereafter MM], n.d., but probably June 1867, in Charles B. Mallett Papers [Hereafter Mallett Papers], SHC, Series 1, Folder 19.

54. MLS to MM, August 27, 1867; MLS to MM, November 18, 1867; MLS to MM[?], n.d. [late 1867], Mallett Papers.

55. MLS to Carrie Mallett [hereafter CM], March 19, 1868, in Mallett Papers. Of Mrs. Britton, Maria wrote, "You know she took six or seven shares," an act of considerable generosity after the fall of the Confederacy.

56. MLS to Alice Mallett, December 20, 1870, Mallett Papers.

57. The quilt also had been lent for exhibition in the state in 1934. India W. Thomas, House Regent, Confederate Museum, Richmond, VA, to Mrs. Edwin Robeson MacKethan, Fayetteville, April 29, 1934, in Mallett Papers. Note: This letter acknowledges receipt of "Miss Maria Spear's picture." The national headquarters of the United Daughters of the Confederacy finds no picture of Miss Spear, so the reference may be to a picture of the quilt.

58. C.B. Mallett Papers (03165), SHC. Unless otherwise noted, Maria's letters referred to hereafter are preserved in the Mallett Papers.

59. Unfortunately, Maria commented more on the passengers than on the railroad train, which may have been pulled by the locomotive "George McNeil," named for one of the company's directors, a business partner and son-in-law of William Kirkland of Hillsborough. Prior to Maria's trip, the earliest postwar mention of the rehabilitation of the railroad all the way to Egypt (near the present village of Cumnock) appeared in 1867. See S. David Carriker, *Railroading in the Carolina Sandhills: Volume 1: The 19th Century (1825–1900)* (Matthews, NC: Heritage Publishing Company, 1985), pp. 37–40.

60. Sam's son Henry soon married Emma, Harriet's second daughter and Mary Smith's niece.

61. "Mr. Guthrey" was Colonel Hugh B. Guthrie, a former legislator and sometime postmaster, who had purchased from Nancy S. Hilliard the Eagle Hotel for $10,000 and changed its name to Union Hotel. Jane Cave was, according to Battle, "a descendant of a 'land giver.'" More specifically, she was the daughter of Dr. Hudson Cave and great-granddaughter of "land giver" Christopher Barbee. Battle, *History of the University*, 1: 612, 673; 2: 261.

62. General Smith D. Atkins, commander of Federal troops occupying Chapel Hill, had married President David L. Swain's daughter Eleanor in 1865, much to the consternation of some local residents.

63. Maria added a puzzling comment: "Sidney left a will, in which he gave her [Mary] every thing he possessed, but I know what will be the result: Say nothing of all this, in your reply & not a word that could give offense." Could Maria have been implying disappointment that Sidney's daughter had been ignored in the will? After all, Cornelia was, at her father's death, 23 years old and had been a free woman for two years; yet her name was absent from the will. For more on Sidney Smith's death, see Chapter 3.

64. The housekeeper apparently was something of a character, described unflatteringly as "florid, fat, and fully forty." Augustus White Long, *Son of Carolina* (Durham: Duke University Press, 1939), p. 6.

65. "Theney" was probably Mary's former slave named Parthenia.

66. If Maria meant exactly 40 years ago, she would have begun teaching only in 1828. Unfortunately, she failed to mention any of the schools at which she taught.

67. No indication has been found to indicate that Maria sought to teach Harriet's daughters, in 1866 ranging in age from 15 to 22 years, or their children. Pauli Murray justifiably criticized Mary Smith for neglecting the education of her nieces.

68. One of Maria's rare references to painting is found in a letter to Carrie, March 19, 1868, in which she expressed delight in receiving an order from Wilmington friends for a painting: "It will be a relief." There are also few mentions of music or musical instruments associated with either spinster. See above, for Murray's delivery of a "handwritten music book which belonged to Mary Ruffin Smith" and was "passed to my grandmother, Mrs. Cornelia Smith Fitzgerald, along with other personal effects."

69. Murray, *PS*, p 11.

70. See Chapter 6.

71. See above.

72. Was the cap a part of the shroud? If so, how was the maker of he cap chosen among the neighbors?

73. To Carrie, December 13, 1873. The sewing machine would outlive her friend, after which Mary gave it to Maria's sister, Elizabeth Spear Smith.

74. Murray, *PS*, p. 169.

75. It is not clear if this "Mr. Cole" is Edward Cole, a mulatto freedman preacher to whom Mary left a small bequest, or William C. Cole, a white neighbor, who became Mary Smith's trusted farm manager and whom Kemp Battle deputized to handle many transactions during the settlement of her estate.

76. See above.

77. Maria to "My dear Girls, February 3, 1875.

78. Kemp Battle made it clear that Frank's mind had failed.

79. Long, *Son of Carolina*, p. 32.

80. For correction of errors in the obituary, see Chapter 4.

81. For more on Frank's estate, see Chapter 4.

82. CC BH/342; CC DV/85.

83. OC 47/595; OC 48/33; OC 48/71. "Mariah" was Maria Sybil North Mitchell, widow of Elisha Mitchell.

84. OC 47/390.

85. The "very gentlemanly & kind young man" may have been Reuben Durham, mulatto, 22 years old when the 1880 census was taken, or he may have been either Ed Cole, mulatto, or William C. Cole, white.

86. It is not clear where Dr. William Peter Mallett lived at that time of the home stay. In the 1870 census, he and his family were living near Cary in White Oak Township, Wake County, his nearest neighbor being Rufus H. Jones. However, the doctor may have still owned the house on Cameron and Mallett streets in Chapel Hill where his brother, Charles Peter Mallett, lived from 1858 to 1868. The names of both Mallett and Jones are of special interest. The doctor performed one of the first cesarean sections in the South in which the mother survived; and in the settling of Mary Smith's

estate, Rufus H. Jones was given her gold spectacles and watch. It is tempting to suspect a family connection between Mary Smith and Rufus Jones.

87. See Chapter 8.

88. January 7, 9, and undated, 1881, Papers of Cornelia Phillips Spencer, SHC, Folder 12; http://biography.yourdictionary.com/claude-nicolas-ledoux.

89. The date of Maria's death (January 6) is from her tombstone. Mrs. Birdsall was a governess or housekeeper with the Mallett family in Fayetteville. The flowers referred to had been received by Maria a short time before she died. Flowers and gifts were exchanged frequently between the Mallett family and the two spinsters.

90. December 18, 1881; copy of note from the archives of the Chapel of the Cross, courtesy of Ernest Dollar. The grave marker at Jones Grove reads, "Maria Louisa Spear/born/April 12, 1804/died/Jan. 6, 1881."

91. Spencer, "A Notable Woman North Carolina Has Produced," *State Chronicle* (Raleigh), February 25, 1886.

92. Battle to Mary Smith, March 26, 1883, in Mary Ruffin Smith Papers, SHC.

93. Elizabeth Smith to Mary Smith, undated, in Mary Ruffin Smith Papers, SHC.

94. W.W. Spear to Cornelia Spencer, January 3, 1886, in University Papers (60005), SHC. The "pictures" have not been identified in the library.

95. *News & Observer* (Raleigh), November 15, 19, 1885.

96. Dick Mottsman, "'Pop' Morphis, Janitor at U.N.C., Remembers University Life in 1880s," *Durham Morning Herald*, May 25, 1947.

97. *News & Observer* (Raleigh), November 19, 1885.

98. Spencer, *State Chronicle* (Raleigh), February 25, 1886.

99. For her bequests, see Chapters 6 through 9.

Chapter 6

1. Demonstrating that errors are easily perpetuated in censuses, Mary—instead of Maria—was identified as having been born in England. The census-taker simply mismatched the two lines of the page.

2. Codicil 1 affecting this bequest.

3. Codicil 4 affecting this bequest.

4. Codicil 4 affecting this bequest.

5. Codicil 1 affecting this bequest.

6. Codicil 2 affecting this bequest.

7. Mary R. Smith's will is recorded in Office of Clerk of Superior Court, Orange County, H/394, and in the Office of Clerk of Superior Court, Chatham County, F/309. Thornton Mitchell's *North Carolina Wills* gives two other registrations—E/377 (1885) and H/394 (1888). A copy of the handwritten will is also filed in the Mary Ruffin Smith Papers in the Southern Historical Collection.

8. A rockaway was a four-wheeled horse-drawn coupé-type carriage first introduced in Rockaway, New Jersey, in 1830. Its top projected forward to protect the driver in inclement weather.

9. Dr. Mallett may have been living near Cary at that time

10. Mary could not have imagined the import of this last authorization in subsequent years.

11. Although Sallie McGuire, the black servant who lived with Mary for more than ten years, died before the estate was settled, a subsequent legal opinion held that each of the five surviving beneficiaries was eligible for only one-sixth ($133.33) of the total.

12. The latter codicil effectively repealed the portion of the will favorable to "Little Sam" Morphis. Was Mary's gift to Emma (for Sam) of the 52-acre McCauley tract in 1882 in lieu thereof?

13. *Orange County Observer* (Hillsborough), November 28, 1885.

14. R.H. Battle to Kemp P. Battle, November 18, 1885, in University Papers (40005), SHC, Folder 519.

15. Mary R. Smith Estate Papers, Orange County Records, State Archives. These materials, with many other sources used in this book, were copied by David Southern of Durham.

16. Cole to Spencer, February 3, 1886, in University Papers (40005), SHC, Folder 525.

17. See Chapters 7 and 10.

18. Affidavit dated December 5, 1885, in University Papers (40005), SHC, Folder 520.

19. Louisa Allen Holt, daughter of William and Elizabeth Allen Hogan, was the second wife of William Raney Holt, physician and early breeder of Devon cattle, whose imposing residence, "The Homestead," still stands at Lexington. Battle described Mrs. Holt as Mary Smith's closest living relation. Powell, DNCB, 3: 191; Battle, 1: 27. For the association of William R. Holt's name with the Chapel of the Cross, see Chapter 9.

20. Mary R. Smith Estate Papers, Orange County Records, State Archives. Did the piano go to the Chapel of the Cross? Archibald Henderson mentioned a piano or organ in his history of the church, and Pauli Murray mentioned that her grandmother Cornelia owned a piano.

21. *Chatham Record* (Pittsboro), September 26, 1895.

22. Battle, 2: 766, 772.

23. See Chapter 7.

24. Was this "memorial" the eagle lectern?

25. Recorded in Battle's final report of lands sold in *Journal of the Twenty-sixth Annual Council of the Protestant Episcopal Church in the Diocese of East Carolina, 1909*, pp. 96–9. This journal is hereinafter cited as *Journal ... East Carolina*, year, page. Dr. Harris, a former captain in the Confederate Army, was dean of the Medical School at the University.

26. Is this the portrait that in 1912 hung in the Dialectic Society (Battle, 2: 822)? Or the image in the State Archives and reproduced on the UNC Virtual Museum webside?

27. Both entries are dated November 1, 1897. See *Journal ... East Carolina*, 1909, p. 99.

28. The cemetery, No. 133 in *Chatham County Cemetery Survey*, enclosed within a three-foot-high rock wall, is owned by the University of North Carolina and

lies in woods touching the southern edge of Galloway Ridge, Inc., in Williams Township, Chatham County, near the junction of U.S. 15/501 and SR 1700 (Mt. Gilead Road). The iron gate, remembered by historian Jean Anderson prior to the purchase of the adjoining land by Galloway Ridge, is missing. Email, Anderson to H.G. Jones, September 6, 2012.

29. The coordinates are 35d 47m 32.0s N 79d 05m 51.0s W. For a plat of the one-tenth-acre cemetery and its surrounding .225-acre setting as of 1979, see Chatham County Plat Book 30/36. For additional information, see http://cemeterycensus.com/nc/chat/cem133.htm.

Chapter 7

1. "Report of the Hon. Kemp P. Battle, LL.D., Executor of the Will of the Late Mary R. Smith," in *Journal of the Seventieth Annual Convention of the Protestant Episcopal Church in the Diocese of North Carolina ... 1886*, p. 24; Appendix A-III, pp. 3–9. This journal hereinafter will be cited as *Journal ... North Carolina*, year, page number.

2. *Journal ... North Carolina*, 1886, pp. 25, 27, 30–1, 43.

3. These two "lots" are not to be confused with Lots 1 and 2 in the plat of 15 tracts later laid out by George W. Tate, county surveyor, during the sale of the remainder of the plantation.

4. Julius Smith and his wife Fannie sold his 25 acres on January 28, 1886, to Wesley Cole for $300 (OC 51/24). That sale was made before the court ruling requiring the two dioceses to share the estate; consequently a new deed dated May 1890 was issued. On the other hand, although she did not live long on it. Cornelia cherished her farm throughout her life, raising vegetables, fruit, and other crops. Her land was eventually sold by her descendants to W.G. Fields and wife in 1947 (OC 128/290).

5. Will of Mary R. Smith, paragraph 3; OC 32/328; OC 51/150.

6. Burgwyn to Spencer, March 4, 1886, in University Papers (40005), SHC, Folder 527.

7. *Journal of the Proceedings of the Primary Convention [of the] Protestant Episcopal Church in the Diocese of East Carolina ... 1883*, pp. 8, 16, 22. The "Primary Convention" was the initial meeting of the new diocese. For the next three years, the diocese named its annual meeting "Convention," but beginning in 1887, the meeting was called "Council." As a result, the title of the 1887 publication was *Journal of the Fourth Annual Council of the Protestant Episcopal Church in the Diocese of East Carolina*, hereinafter shortened to *Journal ... East Carolina*, followed by year and page number.

8. *Journal ... East Carolina*, 1886, p. 24.

9. *Journal ... North Carolina*, 1887, pp. 27–9, 31, 46–7, 66.

10. *Journal ... East Carolina*, 1887, pp. 22–3.

11. *Journal ... North Carolina*, 1887, pp. 46–7.

12. *Journal ... North Carolina*, 1888, p. 72. The pro-posed school was to have been named for Thomas Atkinson, former Bishop of North Carolina and a founder of St. Augustine's School in Raleigh and Ravenscroft School in Asheville.

13. *Journal ... North Carolina*, 1888, pp. 64, 39.

14. *Journal ... East Carolina*, 1889, p. 23.

15. *Journal ... East Carolina*, 1889, p. 23; "Trustees of the Diocese of East Carolina v. Trustees of the Diocese of North Carolina, *North Carolina Reports*, Vol. 102 (February-March 1889), pp. 299–304; Mary R. Smith Estate Papers, Orange County Records, State Archives.

16. "Miss Mary Smith; Bequest," in *University Magazine*, New Series 5 (January 1886), p. 89.

17. *Journal ... East Carolina*, 1889, pp. 23–6.

18. *Journal ... East Carolina*, 1889, pp. 23–6.

19. See Chapter 5.

20. *Journal ... North Carolina*, 1887, pp. 46–7; *Ibid.*, 1888, pp. 33, 46. What was the chancel furniture? Perhaps the Mary Ruffin Smith lectern? The full relationship between the estate and the Chapel of the Cross is beyond the scope of this chapter.

21. *Journal ... North Carolina*, 1889, pp. 25, 48.

22. *Journal ... North Carolina*, 1890, pp. 46–7.

23. *Journal ... North Carolina*, 1890, p. 51; 1891, p. 27.

24. *Journal ... East Carolna*, 1890, p. 23.

25. *Journal ... East Carolina*, 1889, p. 24.

26. *Journal ... North Carolina*, 1890, pp. 58–9; *Journal ... East Carolina*, 1890, p. 22.

27. *Journal ... North Carolina*, 1890, p. 58.

28. *Journal ... East Carolina*, 1893, Appendix B, p. 9; 1894, Appendix B, p. 11. The East Carolina Diocese was more meticulous in publishing comprehensible reports, including—happily for researchers—the final account of land sales.

29. *Journal ... North Carolina*, 1902, p. 23; *Journal ... East Carolina*, 1902, p. 25. Apparently small amounts of back rent were collected years later; for example, as late as 1910 the eastern diocese received "from Miss Mary Ruffin Smith Fund, old claims for rent on land $24.75." *Journal ... East Carolina*, 1910, p. 139.

30. The normal school is now St. Augustine's University in Raleigh; Mrs. Mallett was Caroline De Berniere Mallett, wife of Dr. William P. Mallett, in whose home Mary Smith often visited.

31. *Journal ... North Carolina*, 1893, p. 35. Henry A. London was appointed to the land sales committee with Battle and Manning. This committee also sought to sell the Jones Grove lands that had been willed to the University.

32. *Journal ... East Carolina*, 1897, p. 28.

33. *Journal ... North Carolina*, 1890, pp. 58–9.

34. OC 57/194.

35. This deed has not been seen by author.

36. OC 55/256.

37. OC 55/256.

38. *Chatham Record* (Pittsboro), November 4, 1897; *Journal ... North Carolina*, 1898, p. 25. London, publisher of the *Chatham Record*, was a rabid Democrat, and his paper was filled with venomous attacks on

"Black Republicans" and "Fusion" officeholders of the decade. For him, the white supremacy campaign, including the "Wilmington Race Riot" and the expulsion of Alex Manly and other blacks from that city, were victories of democracy. Battle, while also a Democrat, was more moderate on the race issue; he must have been an uncomfortable companion during conversations on race and politics.

39. *Journal ... North Carolina*, 1899, p. 27. J.G. Daniel was the purchaser of those Lots 14 and 15, both across the line in Chatham County. CC DV/783.

40. *Journal ... East Carolina*, 1901, p. 40.

41. *Journal ... North Carolina*, 1902, p. 24; *Journal ... East Carolina*, 1902, p. 26.

42. *Journal ... North Carolina*, 1904, p. 25.

43. OC 58/53.

44. OC 59/359.

45. OC 57/416.

46. OC 56/193.

47. OC 55/256, 258.

48. OC 59/494.

49. OC 56/226.

50. CC EH/391.

51. CC DK/143 and DV/84.

52. *Journal ... North Carolina*, 1909, p. 33.

53. *Journal ... East Carolina*, 1909, p. 99. This figure is only for land; see above, for accounting of the personal estate. The figures published by the two dioceses contain inexplicable anomalies; even so, lacking modern bookkeeping practices and automated equipment, Battle and his colleagues performed their thankless task admirably.

54. *Journal ... East Carolina*, 1909, pp. 96–99.

Chapter 8

1. See Chapter 7.

2. *Journal ... North Carolina*, 1924, pp. 172–3

3. *Journal ... North Carolina*, 1896, p. 21, 65, 33.

4. *Private Laws of the State of North Carolina, 1897*, Chapter 86; Martha Stoop, *The Heritage: The Education of Women at St. Mary's College, Raleigh, North Carolina, 1842–1982* (Raleigh: The College, 1984), passim.

5. *Journal ... North Carolina*, 1898, pp. C-xi, C-xviii. It is worth remembering that the late Duncan Cameron had helped Mary's father, James S. Smith, to attend medical school at the University of Pennsylvania. See Chapter 2.

6. *Journal ... North Carolina*, 1897, p. 34. Another early payment of $972.63 was made to St. Mary's in 1899. *Journal ... North Carolina*, 1900, p. C-xvi. See also "St. Mary's School," *News and Observer* (Raleigh), May 14, 1897. Mary E. Chapeau, also known as Mrs. P.T. Chapeau, was the sister of the Rev. John Singletary, who served as rector of St. Peter's in "Little Washington" in 1837–43. She had left a modest fund to the Diocese of North Carolina about 1868, the principal and interest designated as a "Fund for the Education of Children of Deceased Clergymen." By establishing this scholarship, the diocese atoned for its tardiness in carrying out the agreement. Part of the scholarship in the Chapeau name

was paid from the Mary Ruffin Smith bequest. *Journal ... East Carolina*, 1898, p. 37; 1900, p. 50; 1901, pp. 34–5; Edmund Hoyt Harding, *St Peter's Parish, Washington, N.C.: A Record of a Century, 1822–1922* (Charlotte: Queen City Printing Company, 1922).

7. Quoted in *Journal ... North Carolina*, 1901, pp. 24–5; *Journal ... East Carolina*, 1900, p. 50. The eastern diocese's amount was amended to $3,000 the next year. *Ibid*, 1901, p. 28 note.

8. *Journal ... North Carolina*, p. 1906, pp. 23, C-xi-xii; 1905, pp. 33; *Journal ... East Carolina*, 1906, p. 52. Interestingly, the East Carolina diocese insisted that its contribution be considered a lien on St. Mary's property rather than an outright gift.

9. *Journal ... East Carolina*, 1905, pp. 54–5; *Journal ... North Carolina*, 1910, pp. 138–9.

10. Interestingly, this report by Bishop Cheshire to the Diocese of North Carolina was published in *Journal ... East Carolina*, 1906, p. 54. When studying either diocese, reference to both journals is required. During the intervening years, the Diocese of South Carolina had joined in supporting St. Mary's School.

11. Very likely the value should have read "$250" since the tuition alone was about $200. *Sixty-third Annual Catalogue, St. Mary's, Raleigh, N.C.*, 1905–6, p. 49.

12. *St. Mary's School Bulletin, Catalogue Session of 1923–1924*, p. 91.

13. It is not clear whether the single scholarship contained all the funds previously divided into three scholarships, or whether some of the original funds had been sequestered. The Mary E. Chapeau Endowed Memorial scholarship in 1902 was primarily for daughters of Episcopal clergy; candidates were nominated by the "Bishops of the Dioceses of North Carolina and East Carolina." *St. Mary's College [Catalogue]*, 1992–3, p. 51. The Mary Ruffin Smith Scholarship was offered as late as 1998, the last year that Saint Mary's was both a high school and junior college. Lois Jean Ott to H.G. Jones, email, March 27, 2014.

14. See Chapter 9. In addition, Erwin had a family connection with St. Mary's; his wife was a daughter of the school's founder, Dr. Aldert Smedes.

15. For some years in the twentieth century the school operated as St. Mary's College, but its name was returned to "St. Mary's School" in 1998.

Chapter 9

1. Coincidentally, Mary and Rector Curtis left Hillsborough at about the same time. After several years in South Carolina, Curtis returned to St. Matthew's in 1856 for another stint. By then, Mary was worshiping in Chapel Hill. For further information on Curtis, see "Curtis, Moses Ashley," in William S. Powell (ed.), *Dictionary of North Carolina Biography*, Vol. 1, pp. 475–6.

2. See, for example, Murray, *Proud Shoes*, p. 53.

3. The fact that the parish could afford no more than a deacon brings to mind a story told by Kemp Battle: Sally Williams, the former devoted nurse and house-

keeper for the Rev. William Green, was so distressed that she asked plaintively, "Can't we raise enough to hire a little deac?" Her plea was answered; a "little deac" was hired. Battle, 1: 609.

4. See Chapter 5.

5. See Chapter 5.

6. See Chapter 5.

7. The reports appeared annually in the minutes of the diocese. *Journal ... North Carolina*, 1885, p. 94; 1886, pp. 43, 38, 64; 1887, pp. 23, 46–7, 83; 1888, pp. 33, 46; 1889, p. 10; 1890, p. 17; 1891, p. 93.

8. *Journal ... North Carolina*, 1889, pp. 25, 48; 1890, pp. 40, 46–7.

9. *Journal ... North Carolina*, 1890, pp. 51, B-10.

10. *Journal ... North Carolina*, 1891, p. 26.

11. *Journal ... North Carolina*, 1892, pp. 88–9; 1893, pp. 79, 95, 99; 1895, p. 79.

12. For biographical sketches of Cheshire, Lyman, and Watson, see, respectively, Powell, *DNCB* 1: 363–5; 4: 110–11; and 6: 130–31.

13. *Journal ... North Carolina*, 1905, p. 37.

14. *Journal ... North Carolina*, 1906, pp. 79, 51; *Journal ... East Carolina*, 1905, p. 51.

15. Battle, 2: 684; *Journal ... North Carolina*, 1905, p. 37; 1906, pp. 28–9.

16. *Journal ... East Carolina*, 1910, pp. 16, 28.

17. *Journal ... North Carolina*, 1910, p. 34. Archibald Henderson, in *The Chapel of the Atonement and The Chapel of the Cross at Chapel Hill, North Carolina* (Hartford, CT: Church Missions Publishing Company, 1938), p. 53, erred in giving the minister's salary as $2,000. A new history of the parish is sorely needed.

18. *Journal ... North Carolina*, 1925, pp. 134–35.

19. *Journal ... North Carolina*, 1925, p. 59.

20. For brief biographies of Erwin and Holt, see, respectively, Powell, *DNCB*, 2: 65 and 3: 191.

Chapter 10

1. See Chapter 1. In defense of the elder Tignal's other son, Francis Jones was then only beginning the vast accumulation of acreage that would eventually make him land-rich.

2. No evidence has been found to suggest a close relationship between these Joneses and Smiths and other families bearing the same surnames who lived in or near Chapel Hill or were otherwise associated with the University. However, it is interesting that Lot 9 on Franklin Street, now the site of the University Methodist Church, was for some time the site of the dwelling house of Augustus White Long, whose memory of Dr. Frank Smith is recorded in Chapter 4.

3. The race track appears to have extended northwesterly-southeasterly on the ridge between the present West Camden and the Fearrington Village lake.

4. See Chapter 5.

5. Will of Francis Jones, Orange County Will Book F/198.

6. For the origin of the Price Creek plantation, see

Chapter 1, and for the controversy that it caused between two Episcopal dioceses, see Chapters 6 and 7.

7. CC AK/111.

8. Orange County Will Book H/394. For disposition of the Price Creek property to the Episcopal dioceses, see Chapter 7.

9. R.H. Battle to Kemp P. Battle, November 18, 1885, in University Papers (40005), folder 519, SHC.

10. See Chapter 6.

11. See Chapter 6.

12. Battle, 2: 344.

13. University of North Carolina, Board of Trustees, Minutes, Volume S-8, 1883–91, December 2, 1885, pp. 187, 189–90, 213–14, 216; Minutes ... February 27, 1889, pp. 409, 395. There is a notation on Page 404 that "March 31, 1884 [*sic*]," Mary Smith gave $125 for a tablet for her father. Was the portrait of James S. Smith that was framed at Price Creek after Mary's death the one that later hung in the Dialectic Society Hall before becoming lost? Battle, 2: 316; see above, Chapter 6.

14. CC BP/580–82. The three lots as laid off are described in CC BP/582–90, but in the actual deeds, the tracts allotted to Laura and Annette were reversed. Laura ended up with the northernmost tract and Emma the southernmost tract west of the Chapel Hill-Pittsboro Road, while Annette received the tract in the fork of the Pittsboro and Fayetteville roads plus 30 acres on the east side of the Fayetteville road. The individual deeds are recorded in CC BP/585–90. The name of the school house around which Annette's land skirted is not recorded.

15. Minutes of the Board of Trustees, March 19, 1886, pp. 224–25.

16. Minutes of the Board of Trustees, June-August 1886, pp. 223–67.

17. The Clegg survey has not been found among the records of the University.

18. W.C. Cole to "Hon. K.P. Battle, John Manning and A.H. Merritt," August 27, 1889, in University Papers (40005), SHC, Box 17, Folder 597.

19. Poster, "Jones' Grove Tract for Sale!" in North Carolina Collection, Cb378/UD14. The railroad, of course, never materialized.

20. This Lot 1, the future location for both Galloway Ridge and the Fearrington House, contained the original "Jones Grove" home site of Francis Jones, the foundation of which now is covered by portions of the continuing care community of Galloway Ridge. For the descent of the lot, see Chapter 1

21. Some years later, the Pulitzer prize-winning playwright Paul Green and his wife Elizabeth owned this tract with a plan to build there; instead, they sold it in favor of a site named "Windy Hill" on Old Lystra Road. Interestingly, Elizabeth Lay Green grew up at St. Mary's School—another beneficiary of Mary Ruffin Smith's money—where her father, the Rev. George William Lay, was rector from 1907 until 1918.

22. Unfortunately, no similar descriptions have been found of the nearly 2,000-acre Flowers Place that Francis Jones willed to his grandson Sidney Smith, who sold it to the Atwater brothers in 1855.

23. CC HH/598. The surnames Rigsbee and Fearrington are spelled variously in the community. The descent of this to its present-day ownership is the following: J.B. Rigsbee divided the lot in 1916, giving the northern half to his daughter Betty Hackney, the southern half (now the location of Galloway Ridge) to another daughter Runa Rigsbee (CC FJ/670); in 1921 Runa Rigsbee sold her half to J.B. Fearrington (CC GO/90); J.B. Fearrington deeded the southern half in 1960 to Jesse O. Fearrington (CC 314/65); Jesse Fearrington and wife Willa and Edwin M. Fearrington sold 926.826 acres (including the southern half-lot) to Fitch Creations, Inc. (CC 386/112); and in 2003 Fitch Creations sold the southern half of Lot 1 to Galloway Ridge, Inc. (CC 1066/357).

24. CC DN/276.

25. CC DV/333; EN/452. Apparently Hackney defaulted or otherwise returned his tract, for Lot 11 (105 acres) was sold in 1904 by the University to W. Roscoe Bonsal (CC DV/333); see also CC EN/452.

26. John Manning reported slightly different results: 555 acres sold for $5,751.90. Minutes of the Trustees, February 20, 1890, Vol. S-8, p. 460.

27. CC HR/61.

28. Minutes ... Trustees, January 28, 1893, p. 190.

29. CC DK/155; HR/61; DN/346; Minutes ... Trustees, February 20, 1890, p. 460; CC DG/574.

30. Minutes ... Trustees, Volume S-9, February 1893, pp. 190–95.

31. CC DV/333; Minutes ... Trustees, Vol. S-10, p. 495; CC DY/182; FP/287.

32. Minutes ... Trustees, Volume S-10, pp. 306–07; S-11, p. 25.

33. Minutes ... Trustees, Volume S-9, p. 41.

34. University Papers, March 12, 1888, SHC, Folder 563. Not until 1909 was an "adding machine" authorized for the bursar. Minutes ... Trustees, Vol. S-11, 1909, p. 250. President Venable was finally persuaded in 1904 to hire a "stenographer" because his time was too valuable for him to "spend a considerable portion of it in conducing his correspondence." Minutes ... Trustees, Vol. S-11, 1904–16, p. 8. The minutes of the trustees were recorded in handwriting until 1914, when they gradually yielded to pasted-in typewritten copies.

35. Minutes ... Trustees, Vol. S-9, p. 155, 166; S-8 , pp. 404, 409.

36. Battle, 2: 822. At the time of this writing, the location of the original portrait—if it still exists—has not been determined. Fortunately, Raleigh photographer Albert Barden, who had access to this or another portrait about 1961, made a black-and-white negative, which is now in the North Carolina State Archives.

37. Battle, 2: 425. Puzzlingly, Battle also wrote that "it is a coincidence that she [Mary Ruffin Smith] was akin to the two other female benefactors of the University, Mary Ann Smith and Mary Elizabeth (Morgan) Mason, but these latter were not akin to another." That relationship has not yet been established by the author. Battle, 2: 345.

38. *The University of North Carolina at Chapel Hill: The Catalogue,* 1886–87, p. 14. Catalogue references to the scholarships varied only slightly. Names of scholarship recipients were not printed.

39. *Endowment, Trust and Special Funds Annual Report, 1941–1942* (UNC Accounting Department, typed report), p. 87; *Report of Audit, Year Ending June 30, 1970.*

40. Minutes ... Trustees, Vol. S-8, 1883–91, August 26, 1886, p. 259.

41. Quoted in Arthur Stanley Link, "A History of the Buildings at the University of North Carolina" (senior honors thesis, Department of History, University of North Carolina, 1941), p. 130. Link, who later became one of the nation's most notable historians, failed to cite the source of the preceding statement. Nor did he reveal the source of a citation to an off-color exchange allegedly made between Professors Walter Toy and George Winston during a faculty meeting. According to Link, Professor Toy rose and, "in his charming manner, he [Toy] said, 'Mr. President, it seems to me that our private arrangements for students are quite raw and crude[,] and I move you, sir, that we forthwith erect in the rear of the campus an appropriate pissoir.' Whereupon Professor George T. Winston arose and, remarking on the absence of any funds in the Treasury, suggested that he thought the boys should be permitted to 'piss-whar they please!'" Link, *Ibid,* pp. 1–2. Oddly, Link provided a note number in the text but did not supply the corresponding citation in his footnotes. Interestingly, when Professor Link, eventual president of the American Historical Association, visited the campus many years later and was pleased to learn that his senior thesis was one of the most frequently used cataloged items in the library, he did not offer to furnish the original source of the citation. The rock wall, just north of present-day Wilson Library, probably marked the route of the original Raleigh-Salisbury road.

42. Battle, 2: 181. There were other descriptions of efforts to relieve conditions attending human waste by the construction of a "Comfort House" near the rock wall just north of the eventual location of the Louis Round Wilson Library. Though accompanied by foul smell and indescribable threats to health, several more of these "relief stations" were built in the same area. Archibald Henderson remembered, "After a time, the students, for sanitary reasons, burned the largest of these structures, and not long afterward the University authorities condemned the remainder." Even several small connected brick structures offered little improvement without a proper water supply. Henderson, *The Campus of the First State University* (Chapel Hill: University of North Carolina Press, 1949), p. 296. See also James E. Wadsworth, "UNC Became Involved In the Utilities Business Around 1880," *Chapel Hill Newspaper,* February 18, 1973.

43. Letter, February 10, 1886, in University Papers (40005), SHC, Folder 525.

44. Minutes ... Trustees, Vol. S-8, 1883–91, p. 259.

45. Minutes ... Trustees, Vol. S-9, 1891–98, February 18, 1892, p. 73.

46. Minutes ... Trustees, Vol. S-9, 1891–98, pp. 157,

171, 173; Henderson, *Campus of the First State University*, p. 297.

47. Battle, 2: 493, 480.

48. Minutes ... Trustees, Vol. S-9, 1891–98, February 23, 1894, p. 293.

49. Henderson, *Ibid*, p. 296; Battle, 2: 511. See also John V. Allcott, *The Campus at Chapel Hill: Two Hundred Years of Architecture* (Chapel Hill: Chapel Hill Historical Society, 1986) and Rachel Long, "Building Notes: University of North Carolina at Chapel Hill" (typescript, 1984, in North Carolina Collection, University of North Carolina Library).

50. *University Record*, 1(1) (December 1896), pp. 3–4; *Ibid*, 1(2) (February 1897), p. 18.

51. *The Record*, 1(3) (1901–02), p. 13.

52. Minutes ... Trustees, 1891–98, p. 456.

53. Daniel Lindsey Grant (ed.), *Alumni History of the University of North Carolina* (Chapel Hill: Alumni Association, 1924, p. 338; Kenan to Graves, *Chapel Hill Weekly*, August 20, 1943. James E. Wadsworth, in the *Chapel Hill Newspaper*, February 18, 1973, wrote that by 1901 the heat and electrical plant was providing service to fourteen buildings and that the electricity was turned on just before dark and all power was turned off at 10 p.m.

54. Wilson, *The University of North Carolina 1900–1930* (Chapel Hill: University of North Carolina Press, 1957, p. 122.

55. Minutes ... Trustees, Vol. S-9, 1891–98, *passim*. See also John V. Allcott, *The Campus at Chapel Hill: Two Hundred Years of Architecture* (Chapel Hill: Chapel Hill Historical Society, 1986), pp. 54–5.

56. Minutes ... Trustees, 1898–1904, pp. 171, 229, 305–07; *The Record*, new series vol. 1(3) (1901–02), p. 13. In addition to purchasing wood and hiring local workers to cut wood for the campus, five students paid much of their expenses in 1897 by cutting and sawing wood. *University Record*, 1(2) (1897), p. 19.

57. Minutes ... Trustees, Vol. S-10, 1899, p. 204; 1904, p. 495.

58. *The University of North Carolina: The Catalogue*, 1903–04, pp. 129–137; 1904–05, pp. 139–145.

Bibliography

Manuscript Collections

Cameron Family Papers, Southern Historical Collection, University of North Carolina at Chapel Hill.

Chapel of the Cross, Chapel Hill, North Carolina. Vestry Records.

Chatham County Register of Deeds, Pittsboro, North Carolina. Deeds and land records.

Mallett, Charles Beatty, Papers, 1840–1954, Southern Historical Collection.

Martin, Julien Dwight, Papers, Southern Historical Collection.

National Archives, College Park, Maryland. Original applications for participation in the American Revolution.

North Carolina State Archives, Raleigh. Early estates and land records.

Orange County Clerk of Superior Court, Hillsborough, North Carolina. Original court records.

Orange County Register of Deeds, Hillsborough, North Carolina. Deeds and land records.

Rand, John Goff, Papers. Smithsonian Institution, Washington, D.C.

Smith, Delia Jones. Orange County Estates Papers, North Carolina State Archives.

Smith, Francis Jones. Orange County Estates Papers, North Carolina State Archives.

Smith, James Sidney. Orange County Estates Papers, North Carolina State Archives.

Smith, James Strudwick, Papers, 1787–1852, Southern Historical Collection.

Smith, Mary Ruffin. Orange County Estates Papers, North Carolina State Archives.

Smith, Mary Ruffin, Papers, 1750–1904. Southern Historical Collectionn

Spencer, Cornelia Phillips, Papers, Southern Historical Collection.

University of North Carolina. Minutes of the Board of Trustees. Southern Historical Collection.

University of North Carolina Papers (40005), Southern Historical Collection.

Books

Allcott, John V. *The Campus at Chapel Hill: Two Hundred Years of Architecture.* Chapel Hill: Chapel Hill Historical Society, 1986.

Alumni Directory, 2007. 2 vols. Chapel Hill: The University of North Carolina Association, 2007.

Battle, Kemp Plummer. *History of the University of North Carolina.* 2 vols. Raleigh: Edwards & Broughton, 1907, 1912; reprint, Spartanburg: The Reprint Company, 1974.

Boswell, James. *The Life of Samuel Johnson ....* London: Henry Baldwin for Charles Dilly, 1791.

Carriker, S. David. *Railroading in the Carolina Sand Hills: Volume 1: The 19th Century (1825–1900).* Matthews, NC: Heritage Publishing Company, 1985.

Catalogue of the Members of the Dialectic Society Instituted in the University of North Carolina, June 3, 1795. Together with Historical Sketches. Published for the Dialectic Society of the University of North Carolina, 1896, electronic edition.

Catalogue of the Trustees, Faculty and Students of the University of North Carolina [1833–1836].

Chamberlain, Hope Summerell. *Old Days in Chapel Hill: Being the Life and Letters of Cornelia Phillips Spencer.* Chapel Hill: University of North Carolina Press, 1926.

Cheney, John L., Jr., ed. *North Carolina Government 1585–1979: A Narrative and Statistical History.* Raleigh: Secretary of State, 1981.

Cheshire, Joseph Blount. *An Historical Address Delivered in Saint Matthew's Church, Hillsboro, N.C., on Sunday, August 24, 1924, Being the One-Hundredth Anniversary of the Parish.* Hillsborough: The Vestry of Saint Matthew's Episcopal Church [printed by Christian & King Printing Company, Durham], 1925.

Coon, Charles L., ed. *North Carolina Schools and Academies: A Documentary History, 1789–1840.* Raleigh: Edwards & Broughton for North Carolina Historical Commission, 1915.

Coxe, John Redman. *Practical Observations of Vacci-*

nation, or Inoculation for the Cow-Pock. Philadelphia: James Humphreys, 1802.

Debate on the Convention Question, in the House of Commons of the Legislature of North-Carolina, Dec. 18 & 19, 1821. Raleigh: J. Gales & Son, 1822.

Dunaway, Stewart E. *Hillsborough, North Carolina—History of Town Lots, the Complete Reference Guide.* Hillsborough: Stewart E. Dunaway, 2012.

Dunaway, Stewart E. *Orange County North Carolina Mill Records (1782–1859).* Raleigh: Stewart E. Dunaway, 2010.

Equity Cases Argued and Determined in the Supreme Court of North Carolina, June Term, 1847, Vol. 4, NBSP Vol. 39, pp. 433–42.

Gilmore, Glenda. *Defying Dixie: The Radical Roots of Civil Rights 1919–1950.* New York: W.W. Norton, 2008.

Grant, Daniel Lindsey, ed. *Alumni History of the University of North Carolina.* Chapel Hill: University of North Carolina Alumni Association, 1924.

Hamilton, Joseph Gregoire de Roulhac, ed. *The Papers of William A. Graham.* 8 vols. Raleigh: State Department of Archives and History, 1957–92.

Hamilton, Joseph Gregoire de Roulhac, ed. *The Papers of Thomas Ruffin.* 4 vols. Raleigh: North Carolina Historical Commission, 1918–20.

Harding, Edmund Hoyt. *St. Peter's Parish, Washington, N.C.: A Record of a Century, 1822–1922.* Charlotte: Queen City Printing Company, 1922.

Henderson, Archibald. *The Campus of the First State University.* Chapel Hill: University of North Carolina Press, 1949.

Henderson, Archibald. *The Chapel of the Atonement and The Chapel of the Cross at Chapel Hill, North Carolina.* Hartford, CT: Church Missions Publishing Company, 1938.

Hoyt, William Henry, ed. *The Papers of Archibald Debow Murphey.* 2 vols. Raleigh: North Carolina Historical Commission, 1914.

Journal of the ... Annual Convention of the Protestant Episcopal Church in the Diocese of East Carolina [1885–1924].

Journal of the ... Annual Convention of the Protestant Episcopal Church in the State of North Carolina [1885–1924].

Journal of a Convention Assembled at the City of Raleigh, on the 10th of November, 1823; To adopt such measures as were deemed necessary to procure an Amendment to the Constitution of North-Carolina. Raleigh: J. Gales & Son, 1823.

Journal of the Senate and House of Commons of the General Assembly of North Carolina at Its Session 1846–47. Raleigh: Printed by Thos. J. Lemay, 1847.

Lefler, Hugh T., and Paul Wager, eds. *Orange County—1752–1952.* Chapel Hill: Orange Printshop, 1953.

Long, Augustus White. *Son of Carolina.* Durham: Duke University Press, 1939.

Mecklenburg County Divorces, 1846–1969.

Report of the Convention Committee to the Legislature of North-Carolina, 1816. Raleigh: Tho. Henderson, Jun., 1816.

Murray, Pauli [Anna Pauline]. *Proud Shoes: The Story of an American Family.* Boston: Beacon Press, 1999. Originally published 1956 by Harper.

North Carolina Reports 112: 125–130. February term, 1893.

Opie, Ione, and Peter. *The Lore and Language of Schoolchildren.* Oxford: Oxford University Press, 1959.

Powell, William S., ed. *Dictionary of North Carolina Biography.* Chapel Hill: University of North Carolina Press, 1979–1996, 6 vols.

Private Laws of North Carolina, 1824.

Proceedings and Debates of the Convention of North-Carolina, Called to Amend the Constitution of the State, Which Assembled in Raleigh, June 4, 1835. To Which Are Subjoined the Convention Act and the Amendments to the Constitution. Together with the Vote of the People. Raleigh: Joseph Gales and Son, 1836.

Proceedings of the Friends of Convention, at Meeting Held in Raleigh, December 1822. Salisbury: Philo White, 1823.

Royall, Anne. *Mrs. Royall's Southern Tour, or Second Series of the Black Book by Mrs. Anne Royall ... in Three or More Volumes.* Vol. 1, Washington, D.C., 1830.

Rumple, Jethro. *A History of Rowan County, North Carolina, Containing Sketches of Prominent Families and Distinguished Men.* Salisbury: J.J. Bruner, 1881.

Shanks, Henry T., ed. *The Papers of Willie Person Mangum.* 5 vols. Raleigh: State Department of Archives and History, 1950–56.

Smith, Mrs. S.L. *North Carolina's Confederate Monuments and Memorials.* N.p.: North Carolina Division, United Daughters of the Confederacy, 1941.

Spencer, Cornelia Phillips. *The Last Ninety Days of the War in North Carolina.* New York: Watchman Publishing Company, 1866.

Statutes at Large of the Congress of the United States, 1789–1873.

Stoops, Martha. *The Heritage: The Education of Women at St. Mary's College, Raleigh, North Carolina, 1842–1982.* Raleigh: St. Mary's College, 1984.

Studebaker, R.B., and J. Frank Ray. *The History of Eagle Lodge No. 19, A.F. & M.* Hillsborough: Eagle Lodge, 1993.

U.S. Congress. *Annals of the Congress of the United States, 1787–1824.* 42 vols., Washington, D.C.: United States Congress, 1834–56. *Citation in footnote: Annals of Congress, 18th Cong., 1st sess., 358, 361.*

United Daughters of the Confederacy, J.E.B. Stuart Chapter, comp. *War Days in Fayetteville, North Carolina: Reminiscences of 1862 to 1865.* Fayetteville: J.E.B. Stuart Chapter, 1910.

University of North Carolina. Accounting Department. *Endowment, Trust and Special Funds Annual Report, 1941–1942.* Typed report.

University of Pennsylvania. Catalogue of the Trustees, Officers, & Medical Class, Session 1837–38.

Wheeler, John W. *Historical Sketches of North Carolina.* 2 vols. in 1. Philadelphia: Lippincott, Grambo and Company, 1851.

Wilson, Louis Round. *The University of North Carolina 1900–1930.* Chapel Hill: University of North Carolina Press, 1957.

Articles

Anderson, Jean Bradley. "Planter's Choice." Unpublished manuscript furnished by author.

Benedetto, Christopher. "A Most Daring and Sacrilegious Robbery." *New England Ancestors* 6(2), Spring 2005.

Engstrom, Mary Claire. "Early Quakers in the Eno River Valley ca. 1750–1847." *Eno* 7(2), 1984 (1989)

Harrington, Sion H., III. "Heel Volunteers in the Mexican-American War." *Tar Heel Junior Historian* 52(1), Fall 2012.

http://biography.yourdictionary.com/claude-nicolas-ledoux

"Miss Mary Smith Bequest." *University Magazine*, New Series 5 (January 1886).

Mottsman, Dick. "'Pop' Morphis, Janitor at U.N.C. Remembers University Life in 1880s." *Durham Morning Herald*, May 25, 1947.

Richardson, N.S. "A Sketch of the Life and Character of Rev. Francis L. Hawks." *American Quarterly Church Review*, April 1867.

Smith, William R. "Brief Sketch ... of J. Strudwick Smith." *Orphan's Friend and Masonic Journal*, June 15, 1934.

Spencer, Cornelia Phillips. "A Notable Woman North Carolina Has Produced." *State Chronicle* (Raleigh), February 25, 1886.

Vincent, Tom. "'Evidence of Womans [*sic*], Perseverance, and Fidelity': Confederate Soldiers' Monuments in North Carolina, 1865–1914." *North Carolina Historical Review* 83(1) (January 2008): 64–72.

Wadsworth, James E. "UNC Becomes Involved In the Utilities Business Around 1880." *Chapel Hill Newspaper*, February 1973.

Newspapers

Chapel Hill Newspaper
Charlotte Journal
Chatham Record (Pittsboro)
Church Messenger
Durham Morning Herald
The Harbinger (Chapel Hill)
Hillsborough Recorder
Orange County Observer (Hillsborough)
News & Observer (Raleigh)
Raleigh Register
St. Mary's School Bulletin (Raleigh)
State Chronicle (Raleigh)
University Magazine (Chapel Hill)

Index

Numbers in **_bold italics_** indicate pages with photographs. Because the story overlaps slavery at its end, slaves are identified by a parenthetical descriptor. Former slaves have been given the names of their owner, and, if they married after freedom, both their original master's surname and their original name have been provided.